WHAT MIGHT BE

OUR COMPELLING INTERESTS

AN INITIATIVE OF THE
UNIVERSITY OF MICHIGAN
WITH SUPPORT FROM THE
ANDREW W. MELLON FOUNDATION

Earl Lewis and Nancy Cantor, Series Editors

What Might Be

CONFRONTING RACISM TO
TRANSFORM OUR INSTITUTIONS

SUSAN STURM

PRINCETON UNIVERSITY PRESS

PRINCETON & OXFORD

Published by Princeton University Press
41 William Street, Princeton, New Jersey 08540
99 Banbury Road, Oxford OX2 6JX

press.princeton.edu

ISBN 978-0-691-24674-1
ISBN (e-book) 978-0-691-24675-8

British Library Cataloging-in-Publication Data is available

Editorial: Eric Crahan and Rebecca Binnie
Production Editorial: Jill Harris
Jacket Design: Karl Spurzem
Production: Danielle Amatucci
Publicity: Alyssa Sanford and Carmen Jimenez

Jacket image: mogilami / Shutterstock

This book has been composed in Arno

Printed in the United States of America

10 9 8 7 6 5 4 3 2 1

To Lani Guinier, whose indomitable spirit, powerful vision, and unwavering belief in cross-racial collaboration continue to inspire change agents across the generations.

CONTENTS

AUTHOR'S NOTE

AROUND THE TIME I began working on this book, I told the dean of a prominent law school that I was writing about how people who work in predominantly white institutions navigate the inevitable tensions involved in confronting racism. My topic must have struck a nerve. A white man who had drawn harsh criticism both for failing to do enough and for doing too much to address racism in his institution, he responded vehemently: "Do not write this book. Writing about race as a white person can only get you in trouble."

My current and former students recounted the same risks but drew the opposite conclusion. "You have to write this book," one of them insisted. "Your students have had the chance to learn with and from you about the ups and downs of pursuing change in institutions where racism is entrenched— the failures along with the successes. We have been transformed by exploring together how we could serve as catalysts for change. You have given us the chance to observe up close how a white person can use her power to push for transformative change. We want you to bring this wisdom to a larger audience—particularly white people—so they too can be inspired by the stories and insights from your cross-racial collaborations and struggles." Taking these words to heart, I wrote this book for people who want to tackle the complexities of racism and are willing to work in and with predominantly white institutions to make fundamental change happen, notwithstanding the inevitable setbacks and failures.

The question of how to tackle racism has been at the heart of my life's work with aspiring change agents in a spectrum of social positions—students, community advocates, college presidents, professors, teachers, diversity officers, researchers, theater artists, judges, lawyers, and activists who are willing to engage in reflection, collaboration, and action. I have had the opportunity to learn how change toward more equitable institutions happens, what gets in the way, and how that work for change can become more effective, transformative, and enduring.

What Might Be offers stories and strategies to buttress hope and support people trying to address racism as part of broader efforts to make institutions more humane and effective in responding to the challenges of a troubled world. The book is intended for people looking for ideas and examples of what it looks like when white people build effective, trustworthy collaborations with people of color to address racism and transform predominantly white institutions. Building on the insights of change agents and scholars who are documenting and advancing anti-racism efforts, the book is intended to inform and support those willing to try, fail, learn, and continue pursuing change over the long haul.

As a law professor, I have developed and taught courses that equip students to use the law as a vehicle for positive social change, rekindling in them the sense of hope and urgency for change that first called them into the profession. As an action researcher, I have worked with organizations—court systems, law schools, higher education institutions, legal organizations, police departments, community-based organizations, advocacy groups, the theater industry—to better understand and address the cultural dynamics that produce what I have called "second generation employment discrimination"—social practices and patterns of interaction within institutions that tend to exclude nondominant groups.[1] I have been primarily drawn to educational, cultural, and legal institutions because they shape how our society understands and addresses race. These institutions are petri dishes, a rich medium in which the process of reimagination, collaboration, and transformation can develop. As sites where people can and at times do interact constructively across racial lines, they serve as important laboratories for advancing the goals of anti-racism and full participation.

In all of these situations, I have had the chance to study and support the development of multiracial collaborations using an architectural approach to problems involving race and bias. That approach entails understanding the structures and systems that shape how people interact and that normalize racial hierarchy, and then reconfiguring that architecture to enable what I have called full participation—contexts that enable people, whatever their race or identity, to participate, belong, succeed, thrive, and contribute to the thriving of others.[2]

As a teacher, scholar, and change agent, I focus on racism because in America, it is a fundamental source of inequality built into the structure of our political, legal, social, and economic institutions. For that reason, the book embraces an understanding of racism that I learned from Lani Guinier, my dear friend and collaborator who died before her time. For Lani, racism was

about power, not only in the way individuals exercise their power to exclude
or denigrate others because of their race but also as the foundation for the
unequal distribution of social goods. As Lani put it, "Racism treats the inequitable distribution, generation, and transfer of resources as normal, natural,
and fair."[3] Race is constitutional in our democracy, both in the sense of being
built into the structure and content of the U.S. Constitution itself and in the
sense of constituting the arrangements shaping how people in institutions
interact, how resources are allocated, and how decisions are made affecting
everyone's lives. Race and racism infuse the systems governing our lives and
the public narratives about who belongs and who doesn't; they must be recognized as an organizing category in any effort seeking to advance more equitable, just, and legitimate institutions.

My own orientation to race first developed through the lens of the Black/
white paradigm. I sensed early on what Clint Smith later noted in his recent
book *How the Word Is Passed*: "Blackness is not peripheral to the American
project; it is the foundation upon which the country was built."[4] I learned
about the historical roots of racism largely through the history of the enslavement of Black people in the United States. That is the paradigm I was introduced to growing up in the aftermath of the civil rights movement of the 1960s.
It was the form of discrimination my family connected to my father's experience growing up in Germany when Hitler came to power. And as Richard
Rothstein and Leah Rothstein demonstrate in *Just Action: How to Challenge
Segregation Enacted under the Color of Law*, the legacy of slavery and Jim Crow
continues to shape the experience of Black people in the United States, with
segregation remaining at its most severe and the economic and social impacts
particularly pronounced for Black communities.[5]

At the same time, I have learned that the Black/white paradigm does not
adequately describe or frame the meaning of race and racism in the United
States. Treating race as a binary defined in terms of Blackness and whiteness
risks glossing over the varied histories, circumstances, and challenges experienced by people in different racial groups, as well as within racial groups.
Other identities interact with race to shape people's experience of inclusion
and exclusion. This is true for people grouped together under the category of
"Black," which encompasses people whose ancestors were enslaved in the
United States as well as people whose families emigrated more recently to the
states from other countries. Indigenous and native people, Latino/a/e and
Hispanic people, and people often grouped together under the umbrella of
"Asian American" are racialized in different ways.

In writing a book with anti-racism as its focus, I found myself in the throes of a contradiction: How do I address race and racism as a foundational category without ignoring the ways that they operate differently within and across different racial groups and intersect with other forms of identity and experience? Other aspects of inequality—sex, gender, class, religion, age, disability, and sexual orientation, to name a few—also operate to prevent people from experiencing full participation in the institutions that affect them. Recognizing existing racial categories is necessary to engage with a world organized to reinforce that categorization but insufficient to convey the evolving meaning of those categories.

To confront racism without treating race as fixed in its characteristics and meaning, I embrace the practice of treating race as a "doing" rather than a "being."[6] As social theorist Stuart Hall has taught me, "race works like a language." Its meaning "can never be finally fixed, but is subject to the constant process of redefinition and appropriation," of being "made to mean something different in different cultures, in different historical formations at different moments of time." It emerges through social interactions, through relationships that are structured by institutions that organize those interactions and assign social status to people based on group membership.[7]

This makes it important to ask in any situation, including in writing this book, "What does race mean here and from whose perspective?" My own racial identity as a white person is no exception. Whiteness too takes different forms depending upon people's power, perspective, position, and practice in a specific context. The significance of being white will depend upon on how we "do" race as white people. I navigate these complexities by grounding the ideas and concepts offered here in specific narratives and contexts, inviting the reader to recognize how stories involving particular racial dynamics might be relevant in other contexts.

This book shares what I have learned about becoming a white person who can operate with integrity and impact in institutions previously set up by and for white people. It explores how to collaborate across racial lines, take account of power, and situate race and racism in the broader context of meaning making. I try to deal head-on with the contradictions built into framing a project around race by inviting readers to explore how strategies for addressing racism can be applied to other categories of exclusion. Recognizing the necessity and the limits of race as a category for addressing problems can inform and guide how we address those other categories in transforming the structure of institutions.

Those of us who have tried to confront racism in institutions know that these issues are complex and intertwined with dynamics that extend beyond race and identity. That realization informs my approach to generating the stories and insights shared in this book: using practice to inform theory, drawing on theory to improve practice, and learning from stories and examples about how change does and doesn't happen. Reflection has served both to learn about and make change. *What Might Be* shares what I have learned from this systematic reflection about practice in multiracial collaborations. I have combined an improvisational mindset—trying different things to see what works and what doesn't—with the rigor of systematic reflection, informed by interdisciplinary knowledge about dynamics and causal relationships operating at different levels. This method reflects my own experiences, conversations, and concerns in each situation, recognizing that my identity and involvement necessarily shaped the dialogue and the dynamics of change. It is intended to spark inquiry and support future engagement, rather than to provide a definitive account of anti-racism efforts.

The book distills the lessons from my research and experience, shared through the vehicle of stories. Some of these stories involve composite characters representing amalgams of different people's backgrounds and experiences with anti-racism's paradoxes. These stories are based on real people I have worked with but I use fictionalized characters both to protect confidentiality and to help illustrate common dynamics, barriers, challenges, and possibilities for learning from struggle and failure. The book also includes stories of people and institutions that are clearly identified and whose work is publicly available or, in some cases, people I have interviewed and from whom I have received permission to name them and use their story. These real-life stories illustrate important concepts and strategies that enable people to stay engaged in the face of inevitable contradictions and sustain change over the long haul. I also include my own narratives of success and failure in navigating anti-racism paradoxes, which have helped me develop frameworks and tools that can support others in getting unstuck. I have learned that transforming the policies and practices of racism has to start with one's self.

Finally, a word about language and capitalization. Language itself cannot escape the paradoxes and conflicts built into anti-racism efforts. It is not surprising, then, that there is no clear consensus about what language or capitalization to use regarding race and racism. In keeping with the value of self-determination embedded in the idea of full participation, I try to use the language and capitalization practices preferred by members of nondominant groups. I capitalize "Black" and "Brown" and not "white." And although the category "Asian American" originated in predominantly white institutions, it has also become a useful frame used by groups organizing across different nationalities who have experienced a similar kind of exclusion. There does not seem to be a consensus at this point about how to refer to people who have previously been called "Latino," "Hispanic," or more recently "Latinx." For now, I will try "Latino/a/e." I also use the abbreviation BIPOC (Black, Indigenous, People of Color) when that is the term used by the people I quote to refer to people of color with different races and ethnicities.

Writing a book about anti-racism as a white woman in a position of power places me in the middle of the paradoxes I explore in this book, and may well get me in trouble, as my conversation with the dean predicted. I am actually hoping that the book might get me into what Georgia congressperson and civil rights activist John Lewis called "good trouble." He advised: "Do not get lost in a sea of despair. Be hopeful, be optimistic. Our struggle is not the struggle of a day, a week, a month, or a year, it is the struggle of a lifetime. Never, ever be afraid to make some noise and get in good trouble, necessary trouble."[8]

Many of the people and practices I recount in this book have been willing to get into good trouble. In my experience, learning to navigate the contradictions built into engaging with racism is what enables us to stick with the struggle to transform our institutions and ourselves over the long haul. I am excited to share what I have learned.

WHAT MIGHT BE

Introduction

Earl Lewis and Nancy Cantor

The only way not to discriminate is not to discriminate.

—JUSTICE JOHN ROBERTS

In order to get beyond racism, we must first take account of race. There is no other way.

—JUSTICE HARRY BLACKMUN

EVERYWHERE WE TURN TODAY, we are reminded of the essential paradox of our nation, one literally built on distinctions of race and yet insistent on framing all as one.[1] As legal scholar Jeannie Suk Gersen noted in her analysis of the intellectual tug-of-war between Roberts's colorblind and Blackmun's reparative justice approaches to affirmative action,[2] we seem stuck between competing, seemingly contradictory options. We are a nation founded on the principle of *e pluribus unum*, yet, at the same time, one unwilling to face its history of discriminatory exclusion, whether of those whose native lands were stolen, those enslaved to build our wealth, or those whose diasporic energy drives innovation going forward. Yes, paradox is what we live with every day, whether in our history or in the current moment, and it is at the heart of this volume that tackles the contradictions inherent in moving anti-racism forward without losing the will of the very people and institutions needed to equalize power and opportunity. This important new volume reminds us that we live the stories of the paradoxes in our daily lives and daily experiences. And as central as the theme of paradoxical possibility is to the overarching purpose of our book series, Our Compelling Interests, and our focus on the value of diversity for democracy and a prosperous society, we cannot escape how the paradoxes inform our personal and scholarly stories—as we suspect they will for so many of our readers.

One of us is an African American historian who has lived the ups and downs of the opportunity struggles in this nation firsthand, as a boy growing up in the segregated South, who later attended integrated schools in the short period of progress post–*Brown v. Board*; who then became a leading national figure in the humanities, including recently as an awardee of the National Humanities Medal; and who currently spearheads a national network of universities working with their communities on reparative justice. The other is a white social psychologist whose colleagues pioneered the practice of intergroup dialogue[3] and has now lived in a majority Black and Brown city where the very anchor institutions, including the one she has led, have excluded its citizens historically but are now being galvanized to win the trust of the community in pursuit of equitable growth. We know firsthand both the paradoxes of mixing reparative justice with *e pluribus unum*, and yet the possibilities to be reaped if we keep plugging away, even as we have witnessed the path forward as anything other than a straight line. And, together, having played central roles at the University of Michigan in defending affirmative action in the *Gratz* and *Grutter* cases,[4] the nonlinear path of racial equity is all too real, even as once again we hope that enough people in our nation will see how we all benefit by taking down what Gary Orfield called "the walls around opportunity,"[5] in his volume in this series, in order to move toward the full participation that underlies the many examples of anti-racism work that Susan Sturm documents in this volume.

The Value and the Paradox of Pursuing Full Participation

If we begin, as we have in this series, with the premise that diversity is a compelling interest for this ever-more diversifying nation, then we must confront, as this current volume does straight on, the opposing gravitational pulls that push us to find avenues for full participation of groups consistently sidelined from opportunity and yet pull us back to protecting individual and institutional rights and privileges accrued over centuries and perpetuated across our often divided and divisive social landscape today. Stated simply, as Sturm does throughout this volume, we need to question and learn how to do anti-racism work and make progress on full participation by enlisting those with place, power, and position in collaboration with those without it. Yet, as straightforward as that goal may be, how to do so when we have few lasting precedents in our history is not obvious. On the one hand, we certainly know that the country as a whole will benefit, economically and in terms of a well-functioning democracy, if fewer members of our population are sidelined from opportunity, as Anthony Carnevale and Nicole Smith argued in our first volume,[6] especially in the midst of the growing "diversity explosion" that William Frey has documented.[7] On the other hand, we live now and have across our history with the paradoxical reality that the pervasiveness of intergroup hostility and a zero-sum mindset fanned in the public rhetoric have systematically worked against the best of our national interests, ensuring, as Eduardo Porter unpacks in his trenchant analysis in *American Poison: How Racial Hostility Destroyed Our Promise*,[8] that policies and practices that would benefit all Americans become political third rails, especially when race is a defining obstacle to full participation. One only has to think of the shared interests, clouded by divisive rhetoric, that connect beleaguered majority minority urban communities with the need for jobs, education, environmental protection, health care, digital connectivity, nutritious food, and more in rural, largely white communities. And returning to the contradictory rhetoric of colorblind versus race-conscious college admissions, one only has to examine the latest data from Anthony Carnevale and colleagues at the Georgetown University Center on Education and the Workforce: "Our models make one thing very clear: the most effective way of increasing socioeconomic diversity at selective colleges is to consider race in the admissions process, not to ignore it."[9] When will we learn as a society that zero-sum benefits only those already with privileged access to opportunity? The paradox of our interconnected yet discriminatory history frequently results in the possibility of benefiting many with practices focused on one group or community, as Sturm argues throughout this volume.

Confronting Our Legacy of Racial Injustice in the Midst of Backlash

Surfacing the possibility of actually benefiting many, even as we focus on particular minoritized groups, brings us always to the question of the elephant in the room in any context of anti-racism work: can we reconcile the seemingly genuinely increasing recognition that our legacy of racial injustice has structured power and privilege, access and success, inequitably, with the ever-present backlash against anything that speaks of reparative justice? As Sturm documents with richly described case studies, there is no shortage of contexts in which people, from organizational, corporate, and political leaders to community residents, from the courts to arts and cultural and educational institutions to community groups addressing policing, are speaking out about the legacy of structural racism in their institutions that so impedes full participation and justice from working. Any number of major corporations have made explicit their recognition of inequitable avenues of access and success, especially linking commitments going forward to the injustices revealed in the horror surrounding the murder of George Floyd. And while many states may not go as far as California in its reparations task force recommendations, local communities across the map are mobilizing to consider the racist legacies of redlining that have left many communities of color burdened by underresourced schools, environmental toxicity, inadequate health care, and unaffordable housing, combining to undermine any hope of intergenerational wealth building.[10]

Yet, as promising as all of these efforts are, and as Sturm documents in her case studies, the paradoxes of any anti-racist efforts—including the contradictory push to protect those in and with power from losing out in the process of redressing past and present wrongs—are never far behind even these genuine appeals to action. For example, consider the risk aversion expressed now in the face of Justice Roberts's endorsement of colorblind college admissions and the specter of retreat well beyond the university setting, not to mention the evidence of a backlash already mounting across state legislatures. For behind that colorblind comfort, as argued not only by Roberts but even forty-five years earlier when Justice Powell established the compelling interest of race-conscious admissions, is the fear of intergroup resentment. As noted civil rights attorney Elise Boddie observed: "Justice Powell argued fairly explicitly in *Bakke* that broadening affirmative action would be racially divisive because it would cost whites, as a group, access and power."[11] And no matter how much one can argue that practices of sidelining and opportunity hoarding have harmed many white communities as well, and that there is shared benefit to be gained in a reparative justice approach, not to mention the overall societal benefits of including the fastest-growing demographics, the divisive backlash (that Powell and later Roberts feared in the admissions cases) repeatedly emerges, sometimes explicitly and at other times obliquely, across many contexts, from local to statewide to national, including robust anti-DEI campaigns playing out from school boards to universities. Consequently, to reap the benefits of what Sturm outlines as the paradoxical possibilities undergirding anti-racism efforts, there is the overarching need to learn how to create some sense of common ground. In his commentary Justice Goodwin Liu invites readers into his law class and his attempts to remind students they are multipositional and not just intersectional. By altering positionality through a range of classroom exercises, Liu hopes to enable each to see the other as more than a single social category. For him this is a pathway to confronting the paradoxes. As John Inazu commented in Eboo Patel's volume in our series, *Out of Many Faiths: Religious Diversity and the American Promise*,[12] while it may be hard to come to some agreement about what constitutes the common good, we can sometimes bridge the gaps across groups enough to meet on common ground.

This volume raises important questions about leadership and change. Commentator Anurima Bhargava notes that institutional leadership is often required to produce the change that can break through the paradoxical conundrum. She writes, change is work; it "is psychological and sociological and institutional and cultural." Freeman Hrabowski, a featured subject of one of Sturm's case studies, and a commentator in this volume, reminds us that change often follows a concerted effort to diagnose the culture of the institution. Drawing on lessons from his childhood, including when he and other Black children took to the streets of Birmingham in 1963 to overthrow segregation, he situates the importance of being invited to lead. Once invited, would-be leaders need to be mindful of structural barriers to change and aware that one must then address altering the culture. It is not enough to focus on merely altering the individuals, he concludes. Toward this end, Bhargava uses the case of DEI work to tell a story and underscore a point: using the metaphor of sitting at the table she observes, *diversity* may mean a seat at the table, *inclusion* may suggest you sit at the table and select off the menu, and *belonging* may have you choosing the menu. Ultimately, she questions, you may want to go beyond DEI and build and curate your own table and menu. This may prove to be the last stage of change.

Finding common ground in the ever-fraught territory of racial justice work is never going to be easy, especially as it requires crossing the boundaries of the highly segregated lives that we all inherited—overcoming the disparate ways in which we have learned to view the world grounded in such different positionalities in organizations and lived experiences in communities. Like everything else in this work, any movement forward requires grappling with the sequelae of de jure and de facto practices, not the least of which are the redlining and housing policies that literally rooted us all in separate universes, as Richard Rothstein exhaustively documented in *The Color of Law*,[13] with schools now highly segregated by race and class, even in progressive northern states with increasingly diverse school-age populations,[14] dooming us all at very young ages to "learn" apart and to see each other and our daily world from fundamentally different views that carry over to our workplaces, our community and cultural engagements, and all the institutions that Sturm studies as ground zero for anti-racism work. This grounding in different worlds from the start handicaps but cannot doom the search for that common ground and purpose, even if it means juggling back and forth between surfacing race as a divider and pushing forth to find our all too often hidden commonalities, as theorists of intergroup dialogue have shown can happen.[15]

Finding Common Ground in Anti-Racism Work

Consideration of the challenges of finding that common ground in anti-racism work, across groups and communities and people in and outside of power in institutions, brings us back to our national founding principle of *e pluribus unum* explored beautifully in this volume and underlying all of the volumes in this series. Indeed, we are witnessing a time now of such divisiveness that the need for strategies to rekindle a quest for common ground is never more front of mind—a time reminiscent of the sad days fifty-five years past that led the Kerner Commission to question whether we were headed toward "two societies, one Black, one white, separate and unequal,"[16] a conclusion reinforced in Gary Orfield's volume documenting the demise of school integration in the decades following the brief period of successful efforts to build on *Brown v. Board*.[17]

Hence, as we asked in launching Our Compelling Interests, we ask again at this moment of resurgent backlash: "What happened to our aspirations for finding common cause, despite observable difference, for *e pluribus unum*?"[18] We all claim to yearn for that springboard to jump over those long-entrenched, centuries-old, currently reinforced racial barriers—to learn, as Katherine Phillips noted, to value diversity as much as we sit comfortably with homogeneity[19] so as to benefit from our collective intelligence, our "diversity bonus," as Scott Page urged us to consider in his volume.[20] Perhaps surprisingly, and reassuringly in today's context of the promotion of a colorblind ethos that urges us to turn away from rather than plunge into these divisive waters, we believe that readers will find in this volume some considerable cause for hope. Sturm moves us closer to affirmatively answering that question, as she unpacks the paradoxical possibility of finding common purpose among competing perspectives on race and racial justice, and sticking with the work it takes over the long haul to bring to life the ever-present but deeply covered-over benefits of coming together across racial lines.

Indeed, how can we not find at least a sliver of optimism in the local, place-based, institution-focused work covered here by collectives of change agents, putting up with the nonlinearity of progress met with repeated obstacles on the ground that so often overshadow that very movement forward, and remind everyone involved of the backdrop of resistance, whether legal or legislative or within the institutions that must become open to change for change to happen. Yes, the work is inevitably caught in the back-and-forth of trying to face racism and move step-by-step forward but also operate within the very systems and often within our own positions of privilege in them, which creates a countervailing force—surfacing the question of the moment that this volume addresses head-on: Can we all make it through the contradictions over the long haul? Can local and institutional work maintain momentum so as to accumulate successful examples that advance systemic change? While the jury is out on that fundamental question of our time, Sturm's ability to interweave stories of anti-racism work on the ground with both broader ideas for change and practical strategies to pursue them sets a course to navigate those inevitable paradoxes inherent to this work. As such, reading the stories here surely will remind us of the need, to quote Sturm, to "link small steps to big goals," as the warrior of justice Lani Guinier (to whom this volume is dedicated) urged us all,[21] and to recognize the power of diverse communities cocreating change when power itself is shared with rather than lorded over, in the service of our compelling interests, together.

1

The Paradoxes of Anti-Racism

THE PACKED CROWD of Black, Brown, and white faces cheered wildly as Britton Smith stepped forward to be honored at the Inaugural Gala of the Broadway Advocacy Coalition (BAC) for his role in launching BAC. As I turned my gaze first to Britton and then to the excitement-filled room, I couldn't help noticing both the commonalities that had drawn this divergent group together and the differences that we had to navigate to make our collaboration work. Britton—an actor, songwriter, and lead singer of the funk liberation band Britton and the Sting—was one of six Black Broadway artists who founded BAC in 2016 as a direct response to the nation's pandemic of racism and police brutality. I am a white law professor who plays classical piano and became part of BAC's leadership team, invited to help advance its mission of dismantling the systems that perpetuate racism by connecting artists and community advocates of color with legal and policy knowledge and resources. Together we had built a bridge of mutual appreciation where we could navigate our differences and take effective action to change the public narrative about race. Britton turned to me, put his hand on his heart, and mouthed the words, "Can you believe this?"

There we were, a collection of mostly Black and Brown artists, lawyers, law students, advocates, and people affected by mass incarceration who usually occupied very different worlds. We had very different backgrounds. We spoke different languages. We had very different relationships to power. But we had joined forces out of a shared thirst for fundamental change needed to tackle systemic racism.

Our collaboration began in July 2016 with an email I received from Britton forwarded by Jeanine Tesori, a Tony Award–winning composer with a track record of social justice activism.[1] Britton wrote: "The senseless deaths of Alton Sterling and Philando Castile, along with countless others, have opened the eyes and ears of the community and the nation to the problem that is plaguing this country. An overwhelming number of friends and colleagues in the Broadway community have expressed a deep desire and need to participate in creating a solution." Britton and his colleagues were searching for an organizational partner with resources and access to legal and policy power so that Black Broadway artists could, as he put it, "understand how to actively participate in the movement toward radical change in our system, our neighborhoods, and our way of thinking." Excited about the possibilities for genuine impact, I jumped at the opportunity presented by Britton's request and enlisted Columbia Law School and the Center for Institutional and Social Change in hosting Broadway for Black Lives Matter—the event that would launch BAC.

Our first meeting took place on a Sunday afternoon in a classroom at Columbia Law School. Broadway artists squeezed into a space also filled with law professors, advocates, Black police officers, and people with firsthand experience of the criminal legal system. Sharing a passionate commitment to change the public narrative about race, each group had realized the need to step beyond the limits of their own way of working.

Over the next six years, we developed a collaboration that would grapple with the collision of worlds that this work necessarily entailed. Drawing on our different racial and professional vantage points, we developed the Theater of Change, a course and methodology bringing together law students, performing artists, and advocates directly affected by mass incarceration to learn how to blend artistry and activism as a vehicle for promoting transformative change.

Looking around the room at the gala, I reveled in what BAC had become: a vibrant, multiracial, interdisciplinary organization that uses storytelling to create lasting impact and collaborations on policy issues ranging from reducing mass incarceration to education equity to immigration. We had demonstrated to each other that we could change the meaning of race in our interactions so that trust could be built across the chasm of historical racial divides, and then use these reimagined relationships to understand what change was needed and how to inspire and motivate people in positions of influence to make those changes. BAC had even been awarded a special Tony for creating "an unparalleled platform for marginalized members of our theatre community and tools to help us all do better as we strive for equity."[2]

As a white law professor who spent her days in a predominantly white law school, it wasn't every day that I got to be in a banquet room in New York's theater district surrounded by people of color who were setting the agenda, celebrating each other, and including me as part of that community. Decked out in the red dress I had worn to the Tony Awards, I had just had my turn onstage as co-honoree that evening. It was one of the highlights of my life to be celebrating with (and celebrated by) a community led by Black people to advance anti-racism. The shared pride and infectious joy in the room made it clear that this was really a celebration of the community that BAC had given birth to. "This room is a labor of love," I had said, giving words to the feeling I sensed in the room.

True as it was, BAC's celebratory history and my valued place in it were only part of the story. That journey also placed me in the middle of the inevitable conflict and contradictions built into doing anti-racism work. What was my role as a white woman in an organization set up to center the voices and leadership of Black and Brown people? How could I offer legal expertise and access to policy power without hogging the limelight and displacing the know-how of those closest to the problem of racism and mass incarceration? How could I enlist the support of a predominantly white institution like Columbia Law School, when that institution itself perpetuated the racist institutions and practices we sought to dismantle?

Over the years, I have heard from some of my Black and Brown collaborators about the tensions they felt in working with me and other white people involved in BAC's work. Was it up to them to raise the racial awareness of their white colleagues when taking that on would in itself be transferring the burden to their shoulders, yet another legacy of racism? And how would they develop relationships of trust with white people when, even though unintentionally, those people would sometimes use their power and privilege in ways that undermined their Black and Brown coworkers? How would they center issues of racism without sidelining other forms of oppression, such as gender, disability, and sexual orientation? How could they access and benefit from the resources, policy knowledge, and power held by white-led institutions without becoming co-opted or dominated by them?

These questions illustrate an inescapable feature of anti-racism work: it is paradoxical. It requires the capacity to straddle contradictory yet interdependent realities that seem irreconcilable but must and can both be navigated. That racism is paradoxical is well-documented, particularly by critical race scholars. Race is both a category that fails to capture anyone's full identity and a foundational feature of current social realities; a practice that both reproduces inequality and forges community among marginalized people.[3] In *Seeing a Color-Blind Future: The Paradox of Race*, Patricia Williams writes: "If racial and ethnic experience constitutes a divide that cannot be spoken, an even greater paradox is the degree to which commonality may be simultaneously created as well as threatened by notions of ethnicity and race."[4] Cornel West observes that "the paradox of race in America is that our common destiny is more pronounced and imperiled precisely when our divisions are deeper."[5] Failing to take race into account perpetuates the conditions reproducing racial hierarchy, while acknowledging racial difference can also reinforce those hierarchies.

Learning to navigate these polarities is pivotal to approaching anti-racism work in a transformative way. The contradictions stem not only from racism's paradoxical nature but also from paradoxes built into any effort to bridge the gap between a desired future and an unacceptable status quo. As Deepak Bhargava and Stephanie Luce point out in *Practical Radicals: Seven Strategies to Change the World*, systemic change requires strategies that are both top-down and bottom-up, forced and guided, scripted and improvisational.[6] Anti-racism work necessitates confronting paradoxes at the intersection of racism and change.

Rather than hiding or running from these tensions, we have to learn how to treat them as triggers for learning and growth. By reorienting our relationship to paradox, it becomes possible to develop the connective tissue enabling us to bridge polarities and stay invested in the work over the long haul. When this happens, the hard work it entails can yield the kind of community, creativity, and change I was experiencing with BAC.

For me to build the trust so crucial to this cross-racial collaboration, I had to go through my own learning and transformation. During brainstorming sessions with my Black colleagues, I would jump in to assert my ideas about the direction we should take, often using a tone of voice that, I would later learn, conveyed to people of color in the room that I thought I—and not they—had the answers to how best to develop BAC's methodology. I would speak authoritatively (and at length) about law, policy, and theories of change without attending to the reality that, for many people of color, law and policy themselves evoked trauma. While it was true that I had information and insight that could help the group achieve its goal, definitively asserting my form of expertise had a way of pushing out theirs. It didn't matter whether I was right if the way I was speaking triggered and displaced my colleagues of color. I was caught on one side of what I call the paradox of racialized power.

For me, these struggles began long before my work with BAC. My family nourished in me a thirst for justice, fueled by my father's experience of persecution in Nazi Germany, recounted every year at Passover with a message that we could never let that happen again. My parents made explicit the connection between anti-semitism and the civil rights movement, encouraging my growing interest in racial justice. Yet I had witnessed racism in my own family and in so many of my day-to-day interactions living in a racially stratified community.

Growing up, my relationships with people of color were limited, which was not surprising given the predominant whiteness of my family, neighborhood, classrooms, and workplaces. All of my friends and close colleagues were white. Until my thirties, when I started working with Lani Guinier, my work involving race had been done *with* white people *for* people of color. In high school, I volunteered for Head Start, floundering as I tried to figure out what I could do to help mostly Black and Brown preschoolers get ready for kindergarten. In college at Brown University, I started Volunteers in Probation, matching mostly white college students as mentors for young Black people, somehow believing that we were equipped to guide them through situations beyond our experience and knowledge, and hoping to help them avoid further contact with the criminal legal system. In law school, I worked for a white court official charged with implementing the order to improve conditions in the Rhode Island prison system, where those incarcerated were disproportionately Black and Brown. In my early legal practice, I was part of an all-white team challenging racial discrimination in rental and employment practices. I had been primed not even to notice that white people like me were perpetuating the power dynamics that kept racial hierarchy intact.

I also grew up learning that my father's experience of injustice did not mean that he would intervene when my mother, herself a survivor of abuse, used violence to enforce her will over her children. The role of heading off its most destructive expression fell to me as I tried to heal the divisions within my family. I have come to see my experience growing up as a major source of my passion for bridging the painful and destructive cultural divide of racism.

Underlying the necessity I felt to confront systemic racism—the racially hierarchical arrangement of power and privilege that has naturalized the unequal distribution of social goods[7]—was a value I would eventually call "full participation." It was very important to me that I work to build environments that enabled everyone, whatever their race and background, to speak openly, feel like they belonged, offer their perspective, be heard, find people they connected with, participate in decisions affecting them, have their concerns addressed, and make contributions to the community.[8] These values are what racism violates and what anti-racism advances. Full participation would become my bellwether for assessing the adequacy of any of my actions and responses.

I had chosen to go to law school to learn how to use the law to tackle the racism and structural inequality I had encountered growing up, and from day 1, I found myself smacked in the face by the fact that the very instrument I hoped to rely on to push for justice was a source of injustice. As a law professor in an elite law school that purports to be about advancing justice and yet remains racially stratified, I am reminded every day that I am straddling a set of apparently inescapable contradictions.

I would begin each semester of teaching law students resolved that *this* semester I would avoid my past pedagogical mistakes and successfully navigate the challenges of setting up my classroom so that students of all races, genders, and backgrounds would experience full participation. I thought I had finally learned once and for all from the feedback I'd received from a Black student who pointed out that my practice of interrupting and reframing students' remarks felt like "white-splaining." I thought I'd corrected what an Asian American student had told me—that my efforts to create space for Black students to express their frustration about being asked to retell, yet again, the stories of their experiences with racism had made it so much more difficult for her to speak up about her own form of marginalization. In fact, no one, she said, had even noticed her presence during those conversations, let alone asked her to tell her own story.

I had listened, I had learned, each new year, hoping to get it right while my ongoing errors kept happening. No matter how hard I tried, I invariably confronted situations that I hadn't anticipated, requiring insight or experience that I didn't have. My training and position seemed to demand that I perform as the expert who could demonstrate how to address race correctly, but my experience as a white woman struggling to figure this out made me aware of how much I didn't know or understand in this arena. In addition, as a white law professor, for some students, I represented a system that is rooted in racism.

My attempts to sidestep the contradictions built into addressing race and avoid facing the limits of my capacity invariably failed. Once I had witnessed how people of color experienced the law school and the practices and norms of "justice" in the legal system, I couldn't unsee that reality, even if I didn't know what to do about it. My sense of personal legitimacy and integrity, along with my need for hope that change was at least possible, became bound up with my willingness to keep trying. Even if I feared making the same mistakes again, even if I found it difficult to remain in this uncomfortable place, I couldn't avoid the experience of having to deal with contradictory responses from students with different racial identities. These tensions resurfaced regularly in my interactions with students in and out of class, with my colleagues under pressure to address race, with the legal profession under scrutiny for its own racialized practices and its failure to hold others accountable for theirs, and with my BAC partners undertaking to tackle racism in the Broadway industry and the criminal legal system.

I have witnessed the replay of contradictions that have paralyzed change in predominantly white organizations as they struggle with how to become more equitable, inclusive, and just. Those reaching out to me for help in addressing race in their institutions have often been pulled simultaneously in opposing directions. Should they directly confront issues of race in their environment or instead seek to address these issues indirectly? Should they work inside institutions to address racism or create pressure for change from outside? Should white people support change in their institutions from their positions of power and influence or should they step back and empower those who are directly affected by racism? I have had to navigate these same tensions myself, as a white woman involved in addressing issues of race for my entire adult life. I had to learn that we can't avoid the contradictions that are built into our history, relationships, and institutions, but we can pay attention to when they're operating and learn to navigate them so they become an engine for change that leads to full participation.

That night at BAC's gala, as I took in the genuine excitement about what BAC had built, I realized that our collaboration had enabled me to straddle polarities that were so evident in the room: we shared a common humanity and commitment to anti-racism and full participation, and we were also struggling with and learning from our irreducible differences. We were striving to do better while realizing that failure has to happen en route to transformative change. Perhaps my acceptance of that struggle and my place in it made it possible to join that community.

Anti-racism work places people squarely in this space between the unacceptable status quo and the imagined world we would like to see in its place. Change agents are constantly striving to define and pursue what I call the "what might be": the short-term spaces and steps moving us toward a long-term vision of institutions that are anti-racist and fully participatory. The work with BAC, and with many of the organizations described in this book, involves figuring out how to pursue the "what might be": to close the gap between the "is" (the racist status quo) and the "ought" (the equitable and fully participatory institutions we imagine). I had learned this reformation of law's meaning from my law school mentor, Robert Cover,[9] and have translated it into a framework to support students and organizations in developing their own theory of change to guide their anti-racism work. In my work with BAC, it was thrilling to help artists and community activists join lawyers in putting their "what might be" into practice.

What Might Be builds on the recognition that anti-racism work requires acknowledging that paradoxical understandings and positions are an inherent part of this process. Embracing those paradoxes turns them into drivers of transformational change. Effectiveness and trustworthiness in anti-racism work depend upon creating the conditions enabling the navigation of the oftentimes stormy waters of paradox. Engagement with those contradictions, not overlooking them but learning what created them, and then finding ways to move through and beyond them is how anti-racism work can be sustained. The book offers stories and strategies for approaching the challenge of living with these paradoxes, which, by definition, force us to find resolution in new and unknown ways in order to address the embedded systems that sustain white supremacy and diminish the humanity of us all.

The first step in navigating the paradoxes of anti-racism involves identifying what they are and how they operate. In my work, I have focused on what I see as three persistent and related paradoxes that are built into anti-racism work and that form the foundation of effectively addressing them:

- The paradox of racialized power: Anti-racism requires white people to lean into their power to make needed change while simultaneously stepping back from exercising power in order to make space for people of color to lead.
- The paradox of racial salience: Effective anti-racism efforts must explicitly name and address issues in terms of race and racism while also proceeding in more universal terms rooted in shared interests rather than race.
- The paradox of racialized institutions: Predominantly white institutions must undertake anti-racism work while simultaneously being the target of it.

In order to appreciate how each of these paradoxes impacts the work of anti-racism, it is helpful first to further explore the significance of paradox in understanding this overall issue and then to delve into its specific relevance to racialized power, salience, and institutions.

Understanding Paradox

A paradox is a statement or proposition with two conflicting positions, both of which are true. For example, trust develops when people expose their vulnerability, but the willingness to be vulnerable requires trust. If members of a group working together on a project don't trust each other, they might be unwilling or reluctant to open up and show vulnerability, fearing that the other person will take advantage of their "weakness." Yet, unless they are willing to show their humanity, their humility, their capacity to be wrong and to be hurt, they cannot build trust. One side of the proposition calls for the other even as they conflict. Pursuing one without the other risks undermining the opposing prong of the duality.

A paradox can also involve thoughts and actions that interfere with each other, even as they depend upon each other.[10] In the midst of conflict, you may realize that your needs can only be addressed by working with your adversary, which requires collaboration that brings up disagreement about important issues, leading you back to conflict. The tension between interdependent opposites means that resorting to any one way of resolving or eliminating a conflict inevitably gives rise to its opposite.[11] Because the contradictory elements are built into the context, paradoxes cannot be resolved.

While the term "paradox" is often used interchangeably with the term "dilemma," it is important to differentiate the two. A dilemma is a necessary choice between mutually exclusive alternatives, each with advantages and disadvantages. British philosopher Bernard Williams offers the example of a person who is both lazy and thirsty.[12] The dilemma calls for choosing between competing exclusive values: Is remaining comfortably ensconced in place of more value than pulling oneself up and enjoying the satisfaction of slaking thirst? Both comforts are not simultaneously possible. Each option requires a trade-off, and choosing between the two is the only way to resolve the dilemma.

A paradox, on the other hand, involves choices that are contradictory but interdependent rather than mutually exclusive. Choosing only one side of the tension inevitably forces grappling with the other. The two poles are linked in a web of mutual interactions, contradictions that cannot be disentangled, avoided, or escaped. If you try to collaborate with someone you don't trust, you inevitably confront behavior or ideas that remind you of the reasons why you don't trust them, which leads you to either disengage or fight to get what you want; collaboration be damned! But if you avoid or battle with someone whose cooperation you need to achieve your goals, you fail to find the common ground that enables you to work together, and you end up stuck in the situation you hoped to change through collaboration.

Paradoxes are uncomfortable. Human beings like to know where they stand. They like conflicts resolved, messy situations cleaned up, and no dangling unknowns. Faced with a paradox, we typically try to ignore or resolve the quandary. But attempting to bypass or eliminate a paradoxical situation only ends up creating a vicious cycle that invokes the opposing force, undermining the effectiveness of any resolution. Choosing one side of a polarity triggers its opposite, entrenching each side in its own position. Trying to dismiss or sidestep such a conflict only gives rise to a new set of tensions.[13]

The etymology of paradox invites us to reconsider these counterintuitive responses to circumstances that seek to negate each other. The word's origin in Greek derives from *para* (beyond, contrary to, distinct from) and *doxa* (expectations, beliefs, or established opinions). The idea of resolving contradiction as being "beyond belief" arises from the way we learn to process information. Particularly in the West, we tend to make sense of the world by sorting information into what appear to be mutually exclusive categories that logically cannot coexist. But even if our thinking process holds discrete categories as opposites, that doesn't mean they cannot both exist, even if they work against each other. The idea of "paradox" challenges our way of thinking by inviting us to investigate what seems "contrary to belief."

Holding both sides of a paradox in the mind at the same time, rather than dismissing one or the other, opens up the possibility of thinking in a different way. Part of the exploration in this book is about loosening our belief in the capacity of our categories to serve as adequate guides in navigating the world of contradictions.

Paradoxes are built into the work of anti-racism. Conversations about race evoke, according to Law and Society scholar Mario Barnes, "the contradictory quality of simultaneously experiencing racial fatigue and seeing the need for more and better legal and empirical considerations of race."[14] What makes race and racism paradoxical is the need—and the possibility—of pursuing both sides of the polarity. Embracing only one side of these tensions without finding a way also to pursue the other will likely leave underlying structures unchanged and alienate key actors whose participation is necessary to alter the status quo. When the Supreme Court insists on colorblindness as the sole solution to racism, its unilateral approach instead heightens race's salience by ignoring its exclusionary operation and restricting the ability to reduce its significance in people's lived experience. In other words, we cannot deal effectively with anti-racism paradoxes by picking one side or the other.[15]

Navigating paradox demands an intentional set of strategies and capacities that harness the tension and push thought and action to a new level, beyond reproducing a futile circular process. How we deal with anti-racism paradoxes affects whether we are stymied by the contradictions or propelled by the tensions toward transformation. That shift could involve the transformation of the people in the paradox so that they can actually hold both sides of the contradiction. It could involve creating a context that makes it possible for the group or organization to maintain both sides of the tension. It could change the background conditions so that the contradiction is reduced. The transformation could involve a dialectical process that results in a new synthesis, a position beyond the conflict of opposing ideas.

With this understanding of how paradoxes operate in relationships and institutions, we can explore the basic paradoxes of anti-racism that underlie the efforts discussed in this book.

The Paradox of Racialized Power

White people holding positions of power in predominantly white institutions face the inescapable paradox of racialized power. On the one hand, we need to step up and take responsibility for addressing the racism operating in our own institutions and practices, for understanding its causes, for confronting the barriers and gaps in our own perceptions, and for acting to reduce racial inequity. Those leading predominantly white institutions bear the responsibility for making such concerns a priority in their work and their day-to-day interactions. On the other hand, white people trying to initiate positive change face constant reminders of what we don't and can't know, of when we need to include others in decision making, and of how to step back from exercising power so that people of color can directly influence decisions and practices affecting them.

As a white person in a position of power, I have grappled with how to contribute my perspective and promote change without dictating the priorities and solutions—and, in the process, pushing aside the insights of people of color. I know I have to offer my perspective without becoming the center of attention. My experience with BAC taught me that I have to share and even relinquish power in order to facilitate full participation in institutions by people of color whose experiences and identities have been marginalized and disrespected by the very design of the institutions they are part of. I've had to realize that I do not and cannot fully understand the experiences of people of color. I do not actually know what meaningful change looks like from their vantage point or how best to use my position to "include" them without replicating the dynamics I am seeking to change. At the same time, BAC's founders sought my involvement because I have expertise and resources they wanted me to contribute to enable their success. They asked me to offer my insight without dictating how to use it or displacing the expertise and voice of my colleagues of color. I've had to learn how to do this without placing the responsibility for teaching me on the shoulders of those who live day in and day out with the consequences of white supremacy. If I hoped to learn their perspective on what they need and want, and understand how they experienced institutions that needed to change, I needed to take responsibility for my own discovery if asking them focused attention on their race in a way that they did not want. Yet I also needed to respond to my own needs enough to remain engaged, even though I still had the power and privilege to walk away.

Effective anti-racism work calls for privileged people like me to hold up a mirror to ourselves and see clearly how our own power is operating and how our ways of working might further entrench racism. We have to do this even when the very dynamic of power and privilege predisposes us to avoid the discomfort and destabilization of confronting the injustice of existing arrangements. This understanding begins when we center someone other than ourselves. In our work with the Broadway Advocacy Coalition, those of us who are white have been willing to rethink how we exercise power so that it becomes possible to have a genuine say in what happens without being the person in charge. This process of reconfiguring power, explored more fully in chapter 6, is an ongoing struggle requiring people who currently hold power to be explicit about how we exercise that power at every step of the way. The paradox of racialized power requires that white people take responsibility for sharing and relinquishing that power, even while exercising it to make change, and to learn about racism without taxing those experiencing it with the responsibility for educating them.

People of color involved in efforts to change predominantly white institutions also have to grapple with the double-edged sword of involving white people with power in their efforts. They need to both work with and challenge the power of those who dictate decision making in those institutions. They might want to help white people understand that they have learning to do about race's operation, while protecting themselves from bearing responsibility for equipping white people and institutions to engage effectively with race and racism. The Black student I mentioned earlier, who brought to my attention my habit of jumping in and "white-splaining," later told me how hard it was for her to raise this issue with me. She said she'd thought about it for weeks before broaching the subject, and it took a lot of emotional energy to have the conversation. She said that she trusted me enough to take the risk to do something she had never done before with a white person in a position of power, somehow sensing that I would be willing to listen and learn. Yet she worried that calling me out might jeopardize our relationship and even undercut my willingness to write her a recommendation for a job. I have also heard such angst expressed by colleagues of color when they were faced with the necessity of calling on powerful white people to recognize ways they were misusing their power and step back. In assuming their power in this way, my colleagues may have been risking their position, but they were changing the rules so that their institutions could become more equitable.

People of color who assume leadership roles in a predominantly white institution can find themselves caught up in the paradox of racialized power in another way. While it's crucial to have people of color in leadership positions in order to move change forward, entrenched racism might undercut the capacity of those leaders to take the risks necessary to transform those institutions. If those leaders don't take steps to challenge or rescript the status quo, they may lose the trust and support of colleagues of color who believed their leadership would bring about genuine change. And if they push for systemic change despite the risks, they may then lose the support of powerful white people who are invested in the status quo and who might use their influence to push "troublemakers" out of those leadership positions.

These quandaries cannot be avoided by people of color pursuing change in predominantly white institutions. A Black administrator who agrees to serve on their organization's Diversity, Equity, and Inclusion task force then faces concerns from peers of color that their acceptance of that position had lent legitimacy to the leadership's adoption of cosmetic changes that left systemic racism intact, while at the same time, this administrator is pigeonholed by some white colleagues as a "race person" bending the rules to advance people of color. Students of color in higher education institutions can find themselves caught between not wanting to invest the time and emotional labor that accompany working with white people on anti-racism efforts and recognizing that without active leadership by people of color, anti-racism efforts cannot succeed. Faculty of color at predominantly white liberal arts colleges who assume the position of diversity officers often experience being asked to take responsibility for addressing issues of race and yet struggling to gain sufficient power to make real change within their institutions. But individuals and advocacy groups that try to avoid these quandaries by only acting as outsiders protesting racist conduct by predominantly white organizations risk being left out of the process of rethinking how those institutions make decisions and develop anti-racist practices.

If anti-racism's success depends upon white people ceding power wisely and willingly, the effort may well be doomed. In the words of Frederick Douglass, power "concedes nothing without a demand. It never did and it never will." But that statement can be tempered by examples of white people in positions of leadership who have shared and even given up power.

- I have been inspired by my college classmate and friend Andrea Levere, a white woman who used her position as the executive director of the national nonprofit Prosperity Now to increase the assets and power of marginalized groups, devoting her social capital, time, and energy to building the resources and sustainability of organizations led by people of color.
- James M. Grant, a white racial justice consultant, decided that he was "going to turn over my most beloved consulting gig to Black and Brown peers who have been doing this spectacular work with me as collaborators for the past decade. . . . The reality is that I have many Black collaborators who can easily step up to the leadership of this project and take it to the next level. All I have to do is stop hoarding the leadership berth."
- Jeanine Tesori, a white composer, has used her platform as a world-renowned Tony Award winner to open up opportunities for composers, writers, and artists of color to take center stage.
- Michelle Rhone-Collins, a Black woman who became CEO of LIFT, a program to break the cycle of poverty for low-income parents, described the process by which she succeeded the organization's founder, Kirsten Lodal, a white woman who had devoted twenty years to building LIFT. Rhone-Collins said her succession started "with the board's enthusiasm for creating space for a leader of color to take the helm . . . while Kirsten cultivated and championed my leadership. . . . Finally, rather than taking a seat on the board and thus hard-wiring deference in strategic decision-making, Kirsten took an advisory role, providing me with counsel and support."[16]

Each of these people has found ways to continue doing important and fulfilling work that keeps them involved and yet creates space for people of color to share or assume leadership.

Anti-racism efforts that do not enlist at least some white people will leave white supremacy in place. Despite a long history of white people standing in the way of change, genuine change cannot be made without their involvement. Understanding the paradox of racialized power is the underpinning for exploring the circumstances and strategies that can engage everyone needed to move anti-racism forward in institutions.

The Paradox of Racial Salience

When people in predominantly white institutions decide to tackle racism, what is the most effective way to frame their efforts? Should they explicitly target racism as the problem and proclaim anti-racism as their intention? Or should they avoid framing the work in terms of race, proceeding instead with more race-neutral or universal aims that tackle racism by adopting the principle that a high tide lifts all boats? Should they name racism as the problem or not name racism, focusing instead on issues affecting everyone working in an organization, such as fairness, accountability, improved communication, enhanced mobility, and overall well-being? While both of these ways of framing the problem and the goal are important parts of any effort to address racism, they also work against each other. This is the paradox of racial salience.

I have confronted this paradox in my scholarship. "Full participation" and "institutional citizenship"—terms I have used to frame the goal of enabling people of all races to thrive and contribute—situate race within a broader aspiration that applies to everyone. And yet, by not naming race explicitly, I have conveyed to some people of color that I am unwilling to talk explicitly about race, leading them to believe that I am not a trustworthy partner in anti-racism work. At the same time, I have been warned (mostly by white people) against using the term "anti-racism" because it will discourage some people who share my larger goals from participating. I have to find ways to express both the broader goal and the more targeted concern about racism. I cannot avoid the paradox of racial salience.

For many white people confronted with evidence of pervasive racial disparities in their organization, seeing and experiencing the enormity of the problem can produce a sense of urgency for transformative change. As organizational change researcher Marshall Ganz writes, "Because commitment and

focused energy are required to launch anything new, creating a sense of urgency is often the only way to get the process started."[17] Such urgency might
be triggered by a report highlighting racial inequities, a protest such as those
organized by Black Lives Matter, a lawsuit seeking a remedy for discrimination,
or a change in leadership that brings someone explicitly committed to advancing racial equity into a position of power within an organization. It took the
protests in the wake of George Floyd's murder at the hands of police to give
rise to the national racial reckoning that spurred many white people to acknowledge racism and make commitments to address it. Whether through
naming (such as through public reports), shaming (through protests and
public exposure), or blaming (through litigation that invalidates the discriminatory status quo), heightened concern about racism's presence and
impact plays a crucial role in getting predominantly white organizations to
prioritize anti-racism—a necessary step in any effort to advance change. The
efforts and process are set in motion when racism is explicitly identified, documented, and called out for its violation of values of equity, justice, and full
participation.

When white people acknowledge their own racial position and own up to
racism when it occurs, they help convey their seriousness about addressing
racism and the genuineness of their anti-racism undertakings, which in turn
builds trust among people of color. My own willingness to acknowledge my
race explicitly, along with how my racial background affects what I know and
how I can and should exercise power, has been a turning point in my working
relationships with students and colleagues of color. As one student shared in
an anonymous survey, "When you acknowledged your own racial identity, I
began to trust you to attend to mine."

Race consciousness is also needed to produce information about how race
is operating to exclude or marginalize people of color in an organization and
to understand what might be done to enable people of color to fully participate. As ample research on racism and its history has shown, effective change
in policies and practices requires naming the problem and establishing explicit
responsibility of those with power over decision making for increasing the
participation of people of color. In The Walls around Opportunity: The Failure
of Colorblind Policy for Higher Education, Gary Orfield provides compelling
evidence for the effectiveness of race-conscious strategies in desegregating
schools, at least for the brief period of time when these practices had the force
of law behind them. Orfield notes, "Color conscious policies, seriously implemented and backed by powerful sanctions and real resources, accomplished

changes that had been unimaginable a decade earlier. . . . Within the space of five years of active enforcement, the schools of the South had become the most integrated in the nation."[18]

And yet race-conscious efforts can also cut in the other direction, triggering countervailing responses that can limit their availability and effectiveness in promoting anti-racism. Making people aware of pervasive stereotyping, as researchers Michelle Duguid and Melissa Thomas-Hunt have shown, may have "the paradoxical effect of normalizing and naturalizing the expression of bias" because individuals feel less compelled to monitor what they say or do, and may also lead individuals to conclude that there's nothing they can do to change the pervasive reality.[19] Social psychologists Valerie Purdie-Greenaway and Greg Walton have identified a related race-conscious remedy that can produce a paradoxical response: the strategy of affirming the value of racial differences and providing programs geared toward including people of color can have the unintended consequence of increasing the tendency to categorize people based on their race and attaching stereotypes to those categories.[20]

Highlighting diversity as a goal in a group or organization can actually heighten underlying racial biases, with some studies suggesting that initiatives aimed at supporting people of color's access and success might prompt even those who genuinely value racial equality to discount the competence of people of color. In fact, research by Cheryl Kaiser and colleagues has shown that instituting diversity values and structures can lull organizations into believing that they have solved the problem, predisposing them to ignore, deprecate, or discipline Black and Brown people when they raise valid concerns about racism. Someone who complains about racist treatment can be labeled a troublemaker, a shirker, or someone playing the race card.[21] As Sara Ahmed puts it, "To become a complainer is to become the location of a problem."[22] Some people of color may even steer clear of programs designed to benefit them in order to avoid the risk of being stereotyped or stigmatized.[23] But to remain silent is to acquiesce in the invisibility of one's experience of indignity or injustice and to leave in place problems that are sure to resurface over and over again.

A common refrain I have heard in workshops organized explicitly to address racism or diversity is: "The people who really need to hear this are not in the room." This group includes well-intentioned white people who care about race but are exercising their power in ways that have unintended negative impact on people of color, as well as people who need to be held accountable for how they are actively perpetuating racist harm. Heightening awareness of bias can have the counterproductive consequence of discouraging white people from interacting with people of color or becoming involved in activities related to anti-racism. Studies finding that people of color are more likely to trust race-conscious efforts than race-neutral ones also show that race-conscious efforts sometimes increase white people's anxiety about cross-racial interactions and thus weaken their interest in interracial contact. Illustrating this point, as part of workshops I have facilitated, we have asked people to fill in the following sentence: "Because I am _____, I fear that I will _____." One of the most common responses for white participants is some variation of: "Because I am white, I fear that I will say something racist, or people will think what I say is racist." This fear, they acknowledge, has led them to stay silent when they are in cross-racial groups, particularly when issues involving race are being discussed. That silence feeds Black and Brown people's perception that white people don't accept their responsibility and are trying to avoid criticism. Efforts framed in terms of racism might, then, discourage white people who are in a position to facilitate meaningful change from participating. So, while explicitly naming racism is necessary in efforts to address inequality, doing so can also make it harder to engage white people in positions of power. Yet those who make decisions with racial consequences must be part of the process in order for meaningful change to happen.

Race is, as Stuart Hall observed, an organizing category of human history, experience, and difference,[24] but focusing on race alone risks overlooking or marginalizing the multiple intersecting identities of people within any identity category. Critical race scholar Kimberlé Crenshaw calls this intersectionality, pointing out that people who share a group identity have additional identities that differentiate them from each other—race, nationality, gender, age, and sexuality, for example. By focusing on one aspect of identity, an intervention may downplay the significance of another identity or define the entire group by the characteristics of its most visible or powerful representative. For example, Crenshaw writes, "because of their intersectional identity as both woman and of color within discourses that are shaped to respond to one *or* the other, women of color are marginalized within both."[25]

Organizations have often struggled with issues of intersectionality in their approach to affinity groups. Many organizations create groups with an organizing identity—Black, LGBTQ, Latino/a/e, Jewish, people with disabilities. This approach enables people to focus on a core identity but tends to downplay the experience of nonprototypical members of each group. As Audre Lorde observed in *Sister Outsider*, "Those of us who stand outside [the dominant power structure] often identify one way in which we are different, and we assume that to be the primary cause of all oppression, forgetting other distortions around difference, some of which we ourselves might be practicing."[26] While focusing on race as an organizing category can provide a much-needed community for marginalized groups, it can also make it more difficult to build the cross-identity alliances necessary to transform institutions so that they enable full participation for people, whatever their identity.

In addition to these contradictions rooted in different racial positions, new legal constraints imposed by the Supreme Court in 2023 on the use of race as a factor in college admissions decisions both limited the availability of race-conscious approaches and invited resistance to race consciousness in other contexts based on a desire to avoid the risk of litigation. The Supreme Court now treats any decision that takes race into account as suspect, equating efforts to consider race as a way to remedy racism and *increase* racial equity and inclusion for Black and Brown people with those using race to *exclude* people of color who have experienced historical and structural discrimination based on their race. Higher education institutions may no longer use diversity as a "compelling interest," justifying the use of affirmative action programs that factor in race in admissions decisions.[27] Those seeking to pursue anti-racism using race-conscious approaches face the question of when they can still do so legally, and whether their strategy will be challenged in court and upheld. The banning of the teaching of critical race theory in public schools in some states has also fueled fears about discussing race or racism.[28] White people already predisposed to avoid addressing race might use legal risk as a basis for resisting even lawful race-conscious approaches, thereby downplaying or overlooking the risks associated with failing to name and address racism.

Approaches to anti-racism that acknowledge and explicitly address race's salience will inevitably prompt countervailing responses, but so do approaches that avoid acknowledging and addressing racial salience. Approaches to reducing racial bias and inequity that proceed without explicitly naming race—what courts and commentators have called race-neutral approaches—can tackle some of the structural underpinnings of racism without triggering the retrenchment that race-conscious approaches sometimes provoke, but they also prevent organizations from identifying and tackling the dynamics particular to racial bias, hierarchy, and marginalization.

Legal scholars have encouraged the race-neutral strategy of opening up or removing blockages to full participation—rules and practices operating across the board that lock in or perpetuate racial inequality. Legal philosopher Joseph

Fishkin calls them "bottlenecks in the opportunity structure"—"the narrow places through which people must pass in order to successfully pursue a wide range of goals."[29] Bottlenecks are requirements for jobs, education, or other paths that lead to flourishing lives. These barriers operate to restrict access and participation by people based on their race without explicitly naming race as a factor in that decision-making process. These practices maintain racial hierarchy by perpetuating differences in opportunities based on race that were established when racism was both lawful and pervasive. They also work by giving people in positions to allocate resources and opportunities the power to make decisions that, whether deliberately or unconsciously, favor people like themselves and in this way to disadvantage or exclude people of a different race. Tests, credentials, recruitment processes, background checks, job references, admissions, job criteria—any basis for allocating opportunities and resources—might perpetuate racism not by explicitly using race as the basis for making decisions but by using processes and practices of decision making that insist on requirements that have not been made available on an equal basis to people of color or that permit white decision makers to act based upon unstated biases.

Universal or race-neutral strategies for pursuing anti-racism operate by removing those barriers and bottlenecks for everyone, thus making it possible, at least in theory, for anyone to get those opportunities, including people of color. The most obvious of this kind of race-neutral strategy would be a lottery for admissions to schools. Another approach might include removing criteria or practices that privilege white people, such as giving admissions preferences to applicants with parents who attended an exclusive college like Harvard, most of whom are white, or who participated in a sport that is not available in many high schools attended by youth of color. Inclusive facially neutral practices can avoid some of the counterproductive dynamics associated with race-conscious strategies for addressing racial disparities. Organizational sociologists have found that increasing and clarifying accountability and transparency in decision making appears to reduce racial bias in organizations.[30] When decision makers have to specify in advance the criteria they are using to recruit and evaluate candidates for a position, and then demonstrate that they applied those criteria fairly, they may be less likely to make decisions based on racial stereotypes.

At least in the short run, emphasizing commonality and the possibilities for racial harmony may make it easier to enlist the participation of white people concerned about issues cutting across racial lines, such as fairness and organizational effectiveness. In predominantly white settings where they experience marginalization, Black people and other people of color may prefer strategies that do not highlight their race and invite greater stereotyping. Race-neutral efforts also reduce the risk of legal challenges to anti-racism efforts by those asserting that race-conscious decision making is itself discriminatory.

Yet, race-neutral strategies give rise to countervailing concerns that mirror those accompanying race-conscious approaches. The Supreme Court's ahistorical embrace of colorblindness—the belief that racial group membership should not be taken into account, or even noticed, epitomized by Justice Roberts's 2007 statement that "the way to stop discrimination based on race is to stop discriminating based on race"[31]—locks into place exclusionary patterns, rooted in a long history of racism that can only be addressed by targeting race explicitly. The law's embrace of colorblindness encourages white people, already predisposed not to see racism, to believe that racism no longer continues to be a significant problem nor that they bear any responsibility for addressing it. When decision makers believe that they act in an unbiased manner and are engaged in meritocratic decision making, as sociologist Emilio Castilla has found, they will be less vigilant and more likely to express racial or gender bias in their decisions and interactions.[32] And when white people avoid talking about race, they actually appear more biased in the eyes of Black observers.[33] Purdie-Greenaway and her colleagues have shown that "norms or practices that appear identity blind to those comfortable within a setting can function as situational cues posing identity threat to a member of a stigmatized group."[34] In *Sister Outsider*, Audre Lorde describes how this "pretense to homogeneity" reinforces racial hierarchy:

> Somewhere, on the edge of consciousness, there is what I call a *mythical norm*, which each one of us within our hearts knows "that is not me." In America this norm is usually defined as white, thin, male, young, heterosexual, Christian, and financially secure. It is with this mythical norm that the trappings of power reside within this society.[35]

Without explicit attention to race and its relationship to power, race-neutral efforts leave in place biased norms and practices that perpetuate racial hierarchy.

The paradox of racial salience cannot be overlooked or avoided as institutions attempt to address racism in policies and practices. Race must simultaneously be named and not named in anti-racism efforts. Efforts to do only one and not the other only kick the can further down the road, and yet these two approaches work against each other. Martha Minow, legal scholar and former dean of Harvard Law School, has called the contradictions that accompany both naming and ignoring racism an example of the "dilemma of difference"—we may recreate difference either by noticing it or by ignoring it. The challenge we must take up is to avoid treating the paradox of racial salience—calling for us to pursue contradictory strategies together—as if it were a dilemma, posing a false choice between two mutually exclusive options. Both sides of the polarity have to be pursued.

Calling out racism and framing change in terms of promoting anti-racism in institutions are necessary to heighten awareness and facilitate trust and participation by people of color, even as it will be taxing and demanding to the very individuals it intends to help, but both can and must be employed. While it's crucial to create the urgency that can galvanize activism and identity safety for people of color, race consciousness also entrenches resistance and provokes white guilt, risking disengagement, resignation, and backlash. Highlighting race is necessary in order to make racism visible to white people and anti-racism action credible to communities of color. But as we have seen, this same situation can also prompt white people to reassert their power and privilege and some people of color to distance themselves from opportunities designed to benefit them. Race consciousness and race neutrality operate in tandem, and choosing one invariably triggers the resurgence of the other.

And yet, being mindful of the paradox of racial salience opens the door to harnessing both sides of the polarity. This happened to me in my work with BAC. A paradoxical orientation made it possible for us to create space enabling people in different racial positions to get the support they each need so that they can then connect across racial divides around shared goals. I learned how to be aware of how my racial identity affected my perspective and power, to accept my limits, and then to build on the strengths of what I could actually contribute within and across racial lines. I came to view the recurring conflicts not as threatening ruptures in our relationship but instead as the moments to double down on my learning and my commitment to my colleagues of color and to the larger goals we had come to share. Chapter 3 elaborates on the strategies that enable paradox to become this driver of learning and change. But to do that, it's also necessary to contend with the contradictions built into working within predominantly white institutions.

The Paradox of Racialized Institutions

How do anti-racism efforts seeking change within predominantly white institutions position themselves in relation to those institutions? Should they enlist those institutions as collaborators, working from the inside out and using the institution's tools and resources to advance the goal of full participation, with active involvement and leadership by those occupying positions of power within those institutions? Or should anti-racism efforts instead focus on mobilizing pressure to change from outside the existing power structure, whether through bottom-up collective action within the organization or by pressuring change from the outside?

In light of Audre Lorde's famous warning that "the master's tools will never dismantle the master's house,"[36] it might be foolhardy to expect institutions to change from within using practices that themselves bear the imprint of a racialized culture and measuring change based on embedded norms. And yet, given the centrality of predominantly white institutions in shaping people's lives and possibilities, their engagement cannot be avoided. Their active participation in anti-racism efforts is necessary both to change their own cultures so that they become more fully participatory and to catalyze change in the larger society. Anti-racism requires enlisting predominantly white institutions as drivers of change while at the same time destabilizing their legitimacy, pushing them to question themselves and be pushed to transform their own practices and share resources they currently hoard. These efforts must both pragmatically operate within the existing power structure of institutions that often marginalize people of color *and* push for more radical and transformative change. This is the paradox of racialized institutions—the changes required by predominantly white institutions to dismantle racism must also dismantle the very structure of those organizations as they are being introduced.

In their influential book called *Racial Formation in the United States*, Michael Omi and Howard Winant point out that institutions are central to "the process by which racial categories are created, inhabited, transformed, and destroyed."[37] My work has focused on institutions that are willing to undertake that transformation by explicitly connecting anti-racism to their mission in areas of education, justice, policymaking, and cultural and creative expression. Yet the structure of these institutions is itself rooted in a history of racism and the culture still largely led by white people. So, they continue to uphold the norms and practices that they are attempting to transform.

A contradictory relationship to racism and its elimination is baked into the legal system of the United States. The U.S. Constitution codified the opposing tenets of freedom and slavery, equality and exclusion, democracy and disenfranchisement. At particular moments in history and in the hands of jurists like Justice Thurgood Marshall, courts have taken up the role of equality's protector, particularly in the 1960s under the Warren Court. Activists of my generation—children of the 1960s and 1970s—grew up believing in the federal courts as the engine of civil rights and racial progress. I was inspired by civil rights advocates who used the law to expand access to housing, voting, education, and employment for people of color, breaking down barriers in ways that only the force of law could accomplish. Yet the legal system itself bears the imprint of white supremacy, as I learned in law school when I read decisions invalidating legislation aimed at remedying systemic racism because it went beyond the Court's constricted view of judicial power, or because the Court's narrow definition of racism was limited to overt and intentional discrimination by an identified individual. At critical points in our history, law has, in fact, functioned as a primary driver of white supremacy, stepping in to enforce and uphold racial hierarchy.

Law's paradoxical relationship with anti-racism has been part of the consciousness of Black activists and intellectuals from Frederick Douglass to Martin Luther King. In asking "which of the two, Freedom or Slavery, shall give law to this republic,"[38] Douglass came to embrace an abolitionist reading of the Constitution, even as he recognized the violent struggle it would take to realize those principles. In his *Letter from Birmingham Jail*, Martin Luther King invoked this paradoxical relationship between law and justice: "Law and order exist for the purpose of establishing justice, and when they fail in this purpose they become the dangerously structured dams that block the flow of social progress."[39] King viewed the willingness to defy a discriminatory law as a necessary part of making law consistent with justice over the long run. He operated from both within and outside of law, shining a light on law's injustice while using it as a tool for seeking justice. If the federal courts persist in standing in the way of anti-racism efforts, current-day advocates may well find themselves taking a position similar to that of Martin Luther King, encouraging institutions to proceed with race-conscious efforts needed to tackle segregation, no matter what the Supreme Court says.[40]

This contradictory relationship of law to racial equality has shaped how organizations deal with discrimination, mirroring these conservatizing and transformational tensions. Organizational sociologist Lauren Edelman argues that, sheltered by the weakness of equal employment opportunity law and the mechanics of the legal process, organizations tend toward cosmetic compliance, constructing their internal dispute resolution systems to be "minimally disruptive to the status quo."[41] They may adopt grievance mechanisms that give people a chance to complain but operate them so that they tolerate all but the most blatant forms of racism or use complaints submitted in good faith as starting points for an "independent investigation" that typically absolves the organization of wrongdoing and retrenches the racial status quo.[42]

Yet despite this track record, sociologists Emilio Castilla, Frank Dobbin, and Alex Kalev have demonstrated that organizational mechanisms that democratize decision making and institutionalize accountability can push organizations toward greater equality.[43] For example, procedures that decrease ambiguity in standards used to assess performance have the potential to reduce the expression of biases based on stereotypes. And creating roles within an organization that clearly confer responsibility for increasing full participation and reducing racism can also have a positive impact, particularly when those roles include a seat at the decision-making table.

Institutions of higher education share this paradoxical character of law to both promote and stand in the way of equality, which makes them simultaneously a driver and a target of anti-racism work. Public and private colleges and universities generally declare a commitment to diversity, social mobility, and cultivating knowledge and leadership in service of the public good. At the same time, predominantly white higher education institutions have, since their creation, been leading actors in enduring racial stratification. Initially founded as all-white male institutions, the wealthiest colleges and universities continue to use criteria that favor a body of mostly privileged and white students. They claim a disproportionate share of resources in comparison to institutions serving predominantly nonwhite communities. White students are increasingly concentrated today, relative to their population share, in the nation's 468 most well-funded, selective four-year colleges and universities, while Black and Latino/a/e students are more and more concentrated in the 3,250 least well-funded, open-access, two- and four-year colleges.[44] Higher education's racial exclusion and segregation have given birth to thriving historically Black and Hispanic colleges and universities, which initially provided the only way most people of color gained access to a bachelor's degree and have become the first choice for many students of color seeking an educational institution that values full participation.

In the face of this discrepancy and often in response to student activism, some higher education institutions have begun to confront the legacy of the racist histories embedded in their cultures and practices. Many predominantly white universities have undertaken major efforts to document their own complicity in enslaving Black people, leading to renaming buildings and awards, providing reparations, and providing funding for anti-racism efforts. They have resisted efforts to shut down affirmative action and, in the wake of judicial and legislative barriers to race-conscious admissions, some have moved away from standardized tests, such as the SAT, that produce disparate impact.[45] These institutions also provide the home for critical race theory, civic engagement, and leadership development of students and community members involved in anti-racism work. Yet, concerns about legal risk and political backlash are threatening yet another cycle of retrenchment in the wake of reform.[46] Higher education remains the site for both promoting equality and preserving privilege.

The institution of American Theater follows a similar paradoxical pattern. Theater has a crucial public-facing role in a democracy. As Oscar Eustis, the artistic director of New York's Public Theater, put it, "Theater is the essential artform of democracy . . . truth comes from the collision of different ideas. That and the emotional muscle of empathy are the necessary tools of democratic citizenship." And yet, the Broadway industry that began its history upholding and celebrating Jim Crow continues to be dominated by white theater owners, producers, and artistic teams and has only recently begun to hold itself accountable for addressing entrenched racism.[47] "The Visibility Report," published by the Asian American Performers Action Coalition in 2021, observes that "almost every gatekeeper, employer, and decision-maker in the NYC theatre industry is White," noting that "these are the industry leaders we are relying on to de-center Whiteness, to hire and promote more BIPOC [Black, Indigenous, People of Color] artists and administrators, to decolonize the workplace, and to institute anti-racist practices."[48]

Critical sociologist Victor Ray shows that organizations are not race neutral and that anti-racism requires understanding racialization processes that both reproduce and challenge racism—how social systems, norms, routines, hierarchies, and practices reproduce racial stratification and how internal organizing can alter those patterns of racialization and produce greater equality.[49] Organizational theorist Eduardo Bonilla-Silva has explained, "Racism is, above anything, about practices and behaviors that produce a *racial structure*—a network of social relations at social, political, economic, and ideological levels that shape the life chances of various races."[50] Institutions make social practices seem eternal and inevitable. While institutions have the platform and power to make needed change, those assets and privileges are the very things that can undermine it.

As a faculty member working inside a predominantly white educational and legal institution, and devoting much of my work to anti-racism, I am very familiar with the paradoxes embedded in such racialized institutions. While I love being able to bring people together, support the upcoming generation in becoming change agents, and share knowledge and resources with communities that want access to them, and I appreciate the influence I have by virtue of being part of a prominent institution, at the same time I am regularly reminded that institutions like the one I am part of often prioritize prestige over purpose, that they are comfortable with hierarchy, that they acquiesce in teaching, researching, and practicing in ways that preserve their own power, and that they resist transformational change. When they do undertake anti-racist policies, higher education institutions like mine often do so in ways that reproduce the racial hierarchy they have set out to dismantle. There are real limits on what I can accomplish as an insider, and so I continue to work with people who are deeply skeptical about the institutions of law and higher education and yet seek to work within and with them.

Institutions have the capacity to both resist and enable change. They reflect and perpetuate the norms of the broader culture, and they can also resist and redefine those norms. They incorporate categories such as race and, at the same time, can change the categories that organize how people interact with each other and what they value. They command and can share resources. They wield and can change the exercise of power so that people of color can participate in shaping the decisions that affect their lives. The paradox—that actions to initiate change also destabilize the institutions that undertake them—is part of what we must learn to navigate in anti-racism work.

The paradoxes of anti-racism that will be explored in this book—racialized power, racial salience, and racialized institutions—can shed light on why, as at many points in history, the policies and practices of institutions seem to be moving in opposite directions at the same time.

But hopefulness coexists with dismay when we see that the country's racist history seems to be repeating itself. Many of the changes prompted by the George Floyd protests have been cut back. For example, many of the DEI executives hired in the wake of that summer became the first laid off in the next economic downturn.[51] When I see events such as Donald Trump's success in building power by awakening the country's racist underpinnings, I know that the overt racism I had sanguinely characterized in a 2001 article as "largely a thing of the past" has emerged from its hiding place.[52] In many institutions, anti-racist rhetoric has not translated into real action. Progress has been met with backlash. The Supreme Court has taken colorblindness to a new level, overturning the decades-old validation of diversity as a compelling interest justifying affirmative action in admissions. The "anti-woke" movement on the right has targeted race-conscious programs, prioritizing relief from the pain of facing history over democratic commitments to equality and justice. The cycle of reform followed by retrenchment might seem to be relentless.

Yet on the side of hope, organizations as well as entire industries—Broadway, court systems, police departments, the tech industry, higher education—have publicly acknowledged their own racism and committed to change, many of them backing up their pledge with substantial resources. Racist attitudes in the United States overall have trended downward since the 1970s, with the younger generations leading the way through anti-racist attitudes and activism. Galvanized by George Floyd's murder at the hands of police, groups organized by people of color pushing for change have gained strength and momentum, using their voice to keep the spotlight on persistent racial inequality and insisting that predominantly white organizations make tangible and lasting change. Heeding these calls and cognizant of the demographic shifts underway (the nation is predicted to become a majority minority by mid-century), some white leaders of organizations and institutions have followed through on their commitments. People of color are slowly but increasingly making their way into positions of power and influence. These are signs of hopefulness that anti-racism efforts could produce lasting change.

The racism built into the structure, culture, and group interactions of American life is the context in which people and institutions have to undertake anti-racism efforts with the intention of bringing about full participation. How do we hold onto those values that support the belonging and contribution of people from all races and backgrounds in the face of enduring racism? How do we face these contradictions in ourselves, our institutions, and the larger society? What can we do to use these built-in tensions as springboards for broader transformational change? What will enable individuals, groups, and organizations to confront these paradoxes and remain engaged in anti-racism work over the long haul? These questions lie at the heart of the stories and strategies explored in this book.

The anti-racism paradoxes—and learning to navigate them—hold a key to the transformative change so desperately needed to address racism and advance full participation. An essential step in this process is understanding the dynamics and structures underlying the paradoxes and holding them in place. The next chapter will explore what keeps anti-racism efforts stuck. Understanding these patterns will lay the foundation for the rest of the book, which will explore strategies and stories showing ways to navigate these paradoxes of anti-racism so that they can drive transformation.

2

Stuck in Groundhog Day

WHEN I AM ASKED to speak with people in predominantly white organizations seeking help in pursuing anti-racism, I often start our conversation with a question: "How many of you have tried to address racism in your workplace and found yourselves bouncing back and forth, trying one thing, then another, only to end up right back where you started, or even a few steps back?" The show of hands is usually unanimous.

All too often, this is the experience of those who try to reduce racial disparities and increase full participation by people of color in their workplaces and institutions. Each of their efforts may have generated a short-term spike in interest that was then followed by a retrenchment—incremental steps forward followed by reverting to the status quo.[1] The pivotal moment when they realized they were stuck brought them to this point of looking for another way.

I've seen that moment of perceived paralysis again and again. When Lee, a white Broadway playwright, tried to address the racism that had been exposed in one of his productions, his suggested strategies revealed how little he actually understood about the issues facing people of color in his company and about how his own exercise of power perpetuated some of those problems. Peter, the white editor in chief of a law review at an elite school, was committed to increasing the participation of law students of color as authors, members, and officers, but his efforts elicited opposing objections—conservative white students balking at any considerations of racial diversity and Black and Brown students suspecting yet another example of "paying lip service" to the issue that would leave unchanged the exclusionary practices contributing to racial disparities. Jean, a Black professor of English, accepted a position as a dean for diversity at a major university hoping to increase the representation of people of color on the faculty and student body, but when she convened a cohort of students and faculty of color to take a leading role in the effort, she got pushback for letting white faculty members off the hook for failing to take responsibility for addressing racism themselves while increasing the burden to do so on those most affected by it. In each of these situations, those trying to initiate change were caught in a quandary that left them feeling both compelled to act and doomed to fail.

It's like they're trapped in the no-exit dilemma depicted in the popular feature film *Groundhog Day*. Each morning, the character portrayed by Bill Murray tries a new strategy for winning over the love of his life, only to find himself right back where he started twenty-four hours later, living the same circumstances over and over again. Like that hapless character, those attempting to address racial inequality in predominantly white organizations might repeatedly try a new "silver bullet" for solving their diversity problem only to find themselves back where they started—and having to start all over again. This cycle may repeat itself over and over as attempts to advance racial equity in organizations face countervailing forces supporting the reassertion of entrenched patterns and systems. After experiencing failure over and over, those who see the critical need for addressing racial inequity may begin to question whether meaningful change is even possible. As we will see in the stories and situations depicted in this book, those attempting to address issues and policies of racism in institutions and organizations often unleash dynamics that threaten to land them back where they started, or worse.

Judge Fein, a white trial court judge in a northeastern city, found himself facing the need to address elements of racism that seemed locked into place in the systems and roles in his own courthouse. His concerns were inspired by and aligned with the efforts of the chief justice and court administrator of the overall statewide court system who were attempting to address race as part of a larger culture change project they had undertaken. After reading a few of my articles and learning of my culture change work in other court systems, universities, and legal institutions,[2] they had invited me to work with a multiracial team to advance full participation in the overall state trial court system. Like many organizations I had worked with, this group had hit a wall in its efforts to reduce racial inequities within its system.

Like trial courts across the nation, racial disparities existed at every step of the legal process. Besides the overwhelmingly white composition of the judiciary in most states, there was evidence of unequal treatment based on race in levying fines and fees, charging decisions by prosecutors, assessing bail and jury selection, providing access to justice, sentencing decisions, and outcomes in civil cases. In New York State, for instance, the "Report from the Special Adviser on

Equal Justice in the New York State Courts," commissioned by the chief judge of New York in the wake of the national racial reckoning and released in October 2020, concludes with a sobering overview: "The sad picture that emerges is, in effect, a second-class system of justice for people of color in New York State. This is not new. In 1991, a Minorities Commission appointed by then-Chief Judge Wachtler declared 'there are two justice systems at work in the courts of New York State, one for Whites, and a very different one for minorities and the poor.'"[3] This assessment could be accurate in all fifty states. Not surprisingly, racial disparities also exist in overall trust in the justice system.

Before I started working with Judge Fein's court system, in response to the racial disparities documented in a series of reports, the leadership had tried convening conferences on racial diversity in the trial court, hiring a diversity director, holding implicit bias training, initiating listening sessions and cultural appreciation days with community members, distributing bench cards prompting judges to be aware of their biases, and beefing up the compliance process for investigating discrimination complaints. These efforts had yielded small improvements, followed by palpable backlash from some white judges who thought they were a distraction from their duties or even what they called examples of reverse racism. Chastened by the failure of these race-conscious strategies, the leadership had pivoted to race-neutral strategies intended to improve the overall fairness and effectiveness of the court system—by increasing promptness and productivity, reducing case backlogs, and modernizing technology and courtrooms. Again, there was little change in people's experience of racism, and the criticism from both sides had continued unabated.

Judge Fein, who had been part of the state court system for more than ten years, had participated in many of these unsuccessful initiatives. As I would learn through our work together, during his years as a trial court judge before the statewide initiative for change, he hadn't associated racial disparities with racism as he defined it—intentional discrimination by individuals of other individuals based on their race—and hadn't given much thought to whether he was playing a role in perpetuating them. Well respected and dedicated to his role, he had entered the courthouse each day believing that doing justice meant acting as an impartial umpire, evaluating cases on their merits as he saw them. He believed in the overall fairness of the judicial system and in his own unbiased treatment of those appearing before him or interacting with him in the court system. He had learned in an implicit bias training that people hold unconscious biases—preferences or stereotypes about people based on their identity—that disadvantage people of color.[4] Although he was troubled by research showing that "white people frequently associate criminality with black people without even realizing they're doing it,"[5] at heart he thought racism as he understood it was relatively uncommon and didn't believe his own behavior was biased or that people in his own court system were treated differently based on their race. At this point, he didn't think that it was the trial court's responsibility to remedy racism rooted in the larger culture. Judge Fein had entered this culture change process questioning whether there was much that he personally could or even should do about racial disparities that seemed inevitable in his daily interactions. Yet he was willing to try the various programs in the statewide initiative to address racism in the system.

However, like others, he had begun to express his frustration to the court leadership about this recurring cycle of forward movement followed by backsliding. This led him to be invited to participate in the collaborative process I was co-facilitating. Our project was aimed at building a community of change agents equipped to undertake effective culture change that would reduce racism and promote full participation and equity in the state court system. We were seeking the kind of institutional transformation that could move beyond anything that had yet been undertaken.

To launch this work, the trial court leadership recruited participants who held both formal and informal leadership positions at every level of the organization and were diverse by race, gender, role, and position. They included people with the power to make and implement policy and influence on-the-ground practice—judges and clerks with leadership roles in their local courthouses, chief court officers, human resources and compliance directors, chiefs of probation, and people with responsibility for education and training. And critically important, they included those who were actually experiencing racism in the court system—interpreters, community advocates, diversity officers, judges, and other people of color working in the court system.

As the first step in the culture change initiative, Judge Fein participated in a six-month process designed to build collective capacity to identify and act on racial inequities in the court. This workshop was different than the trainings he had previously experienced. Week after week, it asked him to interact with and learn about the concerns of people he had never had the chance to interact with outside of his role, and to continue these conversations both during and after the workshop sessions, even when they became uncomfortable. It asked him to connect research and studies about racism with his day-to-day experience and that of people with whom he interacted but had never engaged with about their experience in the trial court. It asked him to identify and act on ways he might be able to make immediate changes in his own context and identify concrete possibilities for longer-term change. Importantly, at the end of the six-month training, the workshop enlisted participants in a cohort that would, with ongoing support from the court, continue working on these anti-racism projects.

When Judge Fein started hearing from people he worked with about the racism that litigants and his colleagues of color regularly experienced in his court system, he realized that this was the first time he had faced up to the unacceptable conditions that had been hiding in plain sight. The enormity of these embedded disparities and their impact on people whose lives he so profoundly affected produced a sense of urgency in him for transformative change. But he also felt stuck in the patterns of interaction that discouraged confronting the contradictions built into the justice system. He wanted to take action but felt paralyzed by his preconceptions about the risks and realities of trying to make fundamental change as a judge. Making such change seemed unattainably utopian and beyond the scope of how he had understood his limited responsibility as a judge for the fairness of the overall system he worked within. He didn't see how he could even begin to address the systemic nature of the racial inequities he now couldn't ignore.

Judge Fein's story provides a context for exploring what can prevent any of us from facing the contradictions built into anti-racism work and reveals how avoidance strategies backfire and keep us trapped in an endless round of futile attempts to address the racism woven into our institutions. This chapter explores four interlocking patterns that keep people and organizations from effectively navigating the anti-racism paradoxes, often stuck on one side or the other:

- experiential segregation—the tendency of people occupying different racial positions to perceive and experience the same situations in different and often opposing ways
- scripted stuckness—the taken-for-granted narratives upholding patterns of understanding, interacting, and evaluating situations that predispose people to accept a racial hierarchy as given
- status quo bias—the tendency to resist change and opt for maintaining the current arrangements and choices over trying anything uncertain or new
- role rigidity—unquestioned acceptance of narrowly prescribed roles that leave responsibility for addressing racism to others

These underlying forces are not mutually exclusive; they reinforce each other. Being caught in their grip prevents people in organizations from bridging the tensions between the poles of the anti-racism paradoxes and from taking the necessary steps to escape Groundhog Day. Understanding each of these patterns provides the foundation for learning what it takes to break out of this vicious cycle.

Experiential Segregation

Judge Fein's interactions in the workshop for the state trial court system had forced him to realize that the world he experienced as a white person profoundly limited his own understanding and perspective. Like me, Judge Fein had grown up in a segregated, middle-class community surrounded by white people, with people of color present only at the margins of his life and typically in subservient positions. His elementary school was almost all white. His junior high and high school had some students of color, but a tracking system (assigning students to honors, regular, vocational, or special education tracks) had excluded most Black and Brown students from his classes and relegated them to classes with fewer resources and lower expectations. Judge Fein's teachers were almost exclusively white, and the curriculum offered almost no opportunity to learn about the history of slavery or the meaning of racism. He went on to a predominantly white college and law school, both of which were socially segregated. In law school, his close friends and study group members were white. The law school curriculum, taught almost exclusively by white faculty, had not required him to confront the systemic dimensions of racism in the legal system, nor did it set up an environment where students could interact about race, build racial literacy, or interact informally with people of a different race. His workplaces as a lawyer in private practice had been similarly populated mostly by white people who were basically oblivious to racial dynamics or their own impact on them.

Judge Fein's daily routines also afforded him few occasions to interact with Black or Brown people as peers—over 90 percent of the judges in his department were white. This contrast between the mostly white judiciary and the Black and Brown people who came before the court had not escaped his notice. Nor did the fact that every day he entered the courthouse through the entrance reserved for judges and lawyers, the privileged few passing through a streamlined vetting process, while litigants coming to use the court, primarily Black and Brown, passed through a metal detector under the watchful eye of court officers. But these disparities had not been disturbing enough to un-settle the overall positive view he held of the legal system.

Judge Fein's story illustrates an important underpinning of the paradox of racial salience: people occupying different racial positions tend to experience the same situations in different and often opposing ways, eliciting different and opposing responses. In a segregated and stratified world, perceptions of people with different racial identities develop from exposure to different in-formation pools and the meanings that get assigned to that information, lead-ing white people and nonwhite people to experience the same situations quite differently. For example, as a group, white people, on average, are more likely to view discrimination as an aberration: people are "colorblind" and interact with others without regard to their race. In contrast, Black people, on average, are more likely to hold that race discrimination is pervasive, that colorblindness is a myth, and that racial disparities result from the operation of systemic bias.[6]

Legal scholar Russell Robinson attributes this difference to what he calls "perceptual segregation"—the tendency of people with different racial identi-ties to, on average, "interpret the same set of facts through two radically differ-ent cognitive frameworks." This is why the language and strategies used to advance anti-racism often evoke different and conflicting responses from people of different races. Robinson writes: "While many whites view race-consciousness as an evil that must be strenuously avoided, blacks tend to see race-consciousness as critical to their survival in white-dominated realms."[7] This difference in perception helps explain why people of color and white people can end up polarized in their response to the same situations—as well as in their efforts to address racism.

People of different races also tend to define racism differently, with white people emphasizing that it means intentional exclusion based on race and non-white people more likely to define racism in terms of entrenched systems, structures, and power that disadvantage them. White people are substantially more likely to view the world as "colorblind."[8] For many white people, "to the extent that racism exists, it is in the hearts and minds of 'bad' people who unfortunately pass it on to their children." This kind of wrongdoing, as Kim-berlé Crenshaw notes, "is seen primarily as isolated actions against individuals rather than as a societal policy against an entire group."[9] Thus, white people frequently do not perceive the racial discrimination that Black people are see-ing and experiencing, contributing to a stark chasm of trust, not only interper-sonally but also regarding the justice system.[10]

People of color also differ from white people in their views about policies and practices related to workplace diversity, equity, and inclusion (DEI). A national survey conducted by the Pew Research Center found the following:

> Around eight-in-ten Black workers (78%) say that focusing on increasing DEI at work is a good thing. Just 1% of Black workers say this is a bad thing, and 20% view it as neither good nor bad. While majorities of Asian (72%) and Hispanic (65%) workers also say that focusing on increasing DEI is a good thing, roughly half (47%) of White workers hold this view. In fact, 21% of White workers say it's a *bad* thing.[11]

These racial divides are also evident in opinions about the need for reparations.[12]

Racialized differences in perception reinforce individual choices and public policies that perpetuate segregated interactions and institutions. As Judge Fein eventually realized, segregation is locked in place by separate and stratified housing, educational, and occupational structures, which perpetuate what sociologist Charles Tilly calls "durable inequality."[13] In *The Walls around Opportunity*, scholar and activist Gary Orfield documents that "where you grow up deeply shapes your life chances" and that "residential segregation is particularly harmful for students of color."[14] These enduring social patterns set up the circumstances that make it most likely that people of different races lead separate lives, form relationships with people of the same race, and perceive different races in hierarchical ways that preclude meaningful connection.[15] Judge Fein's experience of growing up surrounded by white people represents the norm. As Richard Rothstein and Leah Rothstein point out in *Just Action*, "every metropolitan area—north, south, east, and west—is residentially segregated, with clearly defined neighborhoods that are all or mostly white, and others that are all or mostly black."[16] Despite the rapid population growth of Latino/a/e Americans (the nation's largest minority), Asian Americans, and persons identifying as two or more races, by 2020, white people still live in mostly (and often largely) white neighborhoods. In *The Color of Law*, Richard Rothstein shows that government policies enacted in the twentieth century ensuring that Blacks and whites could not reside near each other continue to reinforce patterns of segregation today.[17] This may also account for the fact that "white neighborhoods are becoming more 'diverse,' mostly because they include more Asians and Hispanics, but not blacks."[18] In fact, zip codes often correspond to race and, for many, geography spells destiny.

As Judge Fein himself experienced, school segregation both drives and results from this residential segregation. A 2019 report from the Civil Rights Project documented a national trend toward resegregation that has persisted since the landmark decision in *Brown v. Board of Education* declared segregated schooling "inherently unequal": "In 2016, the typical white student attended a school in which more than two-thirds (69.3%) of his or her peers were also white," and the typical Black student and Latino/a/e student attended schools with about one-fourth white peers.[19] Reinforced by housing policies, separate continues to mean unequal. According to Orfield, "If you look at the high schools with the most resources and highest-scoring students, they tend to be in affluent white and Asian suburbs. These areas also have barriers even for families of color with sufficient money to buy or rent there, including discrimination by real estate and rental agents, by landlords, and by mortgage lenders."[20] Students also experience segregation within schools educating diverse populations. Racial disparities in opportunity and resources from preschool onward mean that the widespread use of academic tracking in high schools places white students, like Judge Fein, in classes predominantly with other white students. In my high school, even though Black students made up about 25 percent of the student body, there was only one Black student in my mostly honors classes throughout my entire high school career. Many educated whites interact with people of color as peers for the first time in college, if at all.

Occupational segregation maintains this spatial separation of whites and nonwhites. Thirty-seven percent of white workers have no African American coworkers, and 41 percent have no Latino/a/e coworkers. The higher people go in the organizational hierarchy, the more likely it is that they will be in positions where they interact regularly with mostly or only white people. Similar to the demographic makeup of Judge Fein's department, across the United States, 80 percent of all state trial judges are white. Nationally, the remainder is comprised of 7 percent African American, 5 percent Latino/a/e, and 8 percent other races. A 2023 report by the Brennan Center found that "in 18 states, no justices publicly identify as a person of color, including in 12 states where non-whites make up at least 20 percent of the population." The report also found that:

- There are no Black justices in 24 states.
- There are no Latino justices in 40 states and DC.
- There are no Asian American justices in 42 states.
- There are no Native American justices in 47 states and DC.

The study found that only 20 percent of state court justices nationwide are Black, Latino, Asian American, or Native American, while people of color comprise almost 40 percent of the U.S. population.[21]

During the trial court workshop, Judge Fein experienced a critical insight into his own experience of segregation through an exercise called "the Trusted Ten," introduced by one of my co-facilitators. Participants were asked to list ten people they trust, those they go to with issues or challenges or to talk to about important experiences. We then asked them to identify the race, class, gender, and other demographic categories of each person they had listed. Next, they were asked to examine any patterns they saw in the characteristics of their trusted ten. Finally, we discussed how those patterns might affect the way they themselves perceive the world. For Judge Fein, there was no way to overlook the fact that his world was defined and circumscribed by "whiteness."

I have used this exercise in workshops and courses at trial courts, with the performing arts community, in law schools, and for staff of legal institutions. In each situation, the results have been strikingly similar. People list mostly those who share their racial, social class, and educational identities. White people talk mostly to white people. Black people talk mostly to Black people. Latino/a/e people talk mostly to Latino/a/e people. Most people also name those mainly of the same socioeconomic class and educational background. And most are shocked to realize that they have few, if any, relationships of trust with people of different races. Many have never before noticed this pattern. Called "homophily" by social psychologists, this is the tendency to form strong social connections with people who share one's defining characteristics, such as race, gender, age, ethnicity, and socioeconomic status. It's not that Judge Fein hadn't interacted with people of color but rather that the nature and quality of those interactions had not prompted him to see the world through their eyes.

White people's limited interactions with Black and Brown people mean their understanding of the world comes from interactions with people who view the world from the same vantage point. According to a 2022 survey, "two-thirds of white adults had not discussed a single important matter with a non-white person in the previous six months."[22] Perceptual boundaries also give rise to informal social practices. People talk about race behind closed doors, mostly with people of the same race. People of color are likely to "cover," Kenji Yoshino explains, or "code switch," adopting behaviors that allow them to "tone down a disfavored identity to fit into the mainstream,"[23] making it easier for them to survive and succeed in predominantly white institutions.[24]

Because they are embedded in segregated and often unequal environments, people of different races are exposed to different sources of information. White people are shielded from information showing the disparities in resources and power associated with white as compared to nonwhite spaces. And because people of color have no choice but to interact in institutions led by white people, they often have to pay attention to white people's views and norms. Those experiencing racism may well share that information only with people from their own racial group, knowing from previous experience that white people were more likely to dismiss their concerns and pressure them not to complain publicly about racism. Russell Robinson observes, "Stories of perceived discrimination are often told in all-black settings, sometimes as a means of group therapy, sometimes as a means of entertainment, and sometimes as a little bit of both." Summarizing extensive research, Robinson concludes that white people's "relative invulnerability to racial discrimination in most workplaces enables them not to think about race. The different social positions of blacks and whites explain the general differences in attentiveness to race."[25]

White people who grow up in homogeneous white communities are also less likely than nonwhite people to be exposed to the history of enslavement and its continuing legacy in the aftermath of Reconstruction up to the present day, a history I did not learn when I was growing up. Recent successes of the reparations movement have begun to change public consciousness about slavery and segregation by engaging institutions in learning about their own history of racism, along with providing long-overdue steps to acknowledge and redress past wrongs.[26] Yet, at the same time, this effort has been met in some states with a countervailing push to enact legislative bans on teaching critical race theory and to ban books that expose students to America's racist past and present.[27] Access to accurate and unvarnished history in education plays a crucial role in shaping how people perceive racial inequality and the government's central role in reproducing it.

Experiential segregation coalesces into what Susan Fiske and Shelley Taylor call "schemas"—broad cognitive structures that help organize, interpret, and retrieve information. Schemas are built from messages we absorb from our interactions, environments, and reward structures. They operate as the blueprint for how we read and interpret new social interactions. They serve as what William Sewall calls "tools of thought" helping people make sense of new circumstances.[28] When facing ambiguous situations, people tend to fall back on their schemas, based on past experiences, to fill in the gaps in their information.

Ensconced in a segregated world, many white people view disparities in the treatment of Black and Brown people through racial schemas that frame discrimination as exceptional rather than pervasive. They do not notice or question the dramatically diminished resources and opportunities that frame the lives and aspirations of Black and Brown people. They do not identify their own racial position in interactions involving the exercise of power. This is what legal scholar Barbara Flagg calls the "transparency phenomenon"—"the tendency of whites not to think about whiteness, or about norms, behaviors, experiences, or perspectives that are white-specific."[29] With only white people as their reference point for norms and expectations, they remain unaware that characteristics, traits, and behaviors they assume to be neutral, natural, and fair are, in fact, closely associated with whiteness. For many white people, people of color simply lie outside their circle or measure of concern. Even if they do interact beyond racial lines, their scripted interactions within status hierarchies do not prompt them to face up to the human impact of accepting racial disparities as normal.

Judge Fein's experience in the workshop we did for his trial court had shaken the views and comfortable assumptions he had developed in his segregated world. Never before had he heard firsthand stories of people's experience with racism in the courthouse nor understood their frustration with white leadership who did a lot of talking without taking any meaningful action. He listened as a Black judge talked about being periodically mistaken for a defendant by lawyers and occasionally by staff. He shared the dismay of an interpreter who worked with Spanish-speaking defendants and regularly overheard lawyers saying racist things about the clients they were representing. His understanding deepened as people of color in positions throughout the court system reported day-to-day experiences of racist jokes, slights, and insinuations that they didn't "belong." Judge Fein was beginning to question, as legal scholar Patricia Williams puts it, how it could be "that so many well-meaning white people have never thought about race when so few Blacks pass a single day without being reminded of it."[30]

Once Judge Fein faced up to the overt and subtle racism in the court system and the impact of accepted practices on court users and personnel alike, he could not ignore the racial realities that stood in stark contrast to the image of justice he believed in. "By staying silent and doing nothing, I am really complicit in an unjust system," he found himself admitting. That realization—that the full participation values he was committed to required transformational change—had been an important first step in his breaking out of perceptual segregation and beginning to act as a catalyst for change.

Judge Fein had come to realize the limits of his racial understanding and the whiteness of his trusted relationships. He had heard from court users about disrespectful and racially tinged interactions with court officers, clerks, judges, and lawyers—prosecutors and defense counsel alike. He had learned to talk about race with other white people and across the racial divide. He had started to ask more questions, pay more attention, listen with more empathy, and learn more about the troubling experiences of people of color in the courthouse. He had started to bridge the divide caused by experiential segregation—a step toward navigating the paradox of racial salience.

Scripted Stuckness

But becoming aware of systemic racism does not necessarily translate into trying to do something about it. Judge Fein still regarded race and racism as societal problems beyond his own reach or responsibility, believing that they played out in an arena largely outside the scope of his role as a judge. He didn't think much about his own race, or believe that racism affected him personally or the way he worked. No one had ever questioned or challenged him based on something he said or did that reflected racial insensitivity or complicity in a racialized system. For him, racism described the attitude held by people who were overtly biased or the experience of those who were discriminated against by them. Although he had learned about unconscious bias in implicit bias training, he doubted whether he could do anything to reduce bias he wasn't conscious of. He didn't think there were racial disparities in the outcomes of his own decisions and hadn't thought to test his assumption of unbiased treatment. Although he had read reports highlighting concerns about the harmful and racist experiences of those brought into the judicial system, he didn't connect that information to his own daily interactions or responsibilities.

Judge Fein had comfortably operated within the limited arena of his assigned place in the court system. The scene was set for him by who appeared before him each day, with his interactions prescribed by the rhythms of his caseload and the rituals of the courtroom. Like most judges, he interacted informally mostly with other judges and with his law clerk. He knew very little about other people who worked with him in the court system—court clerks, court officers, interpreters, administrative assistants—those whose daily interactions had a profound impact on the people using the court system. The dominant cultural narratives—"We've come a long way"; "People who make the effort can lift themselves up by their bootstraps"; "Equal access and opportunity are hallmarks of our society"; "Racism is abhorrent but now largely a thing of the past"—reinforced Judge Fein's assumption that the legal system was basically fair and that racial bias was the exception.[31]

During the months of our work together, the underpinnings of Judge Fein's assumptions and practices had begun to crumble. Conversations with people of

color working in the court system revealed to him that his actions, his expectations of lawyerly behavior, his impatience with people representing themselves
in court, and his tolerance of inhumane conditions in the courtroom and corri-
dors all meant that people, particularly people of color, experienced his courtroom very differently than what he had presumed.[32] For the first time, Judge Fein
had begun to see that as a white professional in a position of power, he had been
stuck in a script that limited his perceptions and understanding. And in conversations with his colleagues of color, he learned that they had a very different experience of the same situation, more like one of "weary recognition."[33] This led him
to face the contradictions between his ingrained belief in the system's fairness and
the lived realities of those at its mercy. He began to recognize that his perceptions,
interpretations, and beliefs had been framed by a broader cultural narrative that
normalized racial hierarchy and encouraged white people to view people of color,
particularly Black people, as the "other." Like Judge Fein, many people in predominantly white institutions occupy positions in a status hierarchy organized to
reflect the prevailing norms and ethos of their institution and profession, reinforced by such assumptions and beliefs of the larger culture.[34]

Narratives are how we make meaning of the world around us. The stories
we are told and then tell ourselves, about ourselves and each other, make up
the script that structures the way we interact and interpret situations. These
scripts, rooted in the dominant values and themes, operate as invisible filters
through which people perceive the world. They structure where and how
people of different races interact. Such frames operate as "a cultural model that
is top of mind" for most people, what researchers at the FrameWorks Institute
describe as "a patterned mode of thinking that appears almost automatically
and serves as a lens through which people evaluate incoming information."
These frames often reside in the general culture but are also reflected in and
shaped by the news media. These narratives predispose people like Judge Fein
to focus on individual personal failures as the cause of enduring racial
inequality and racist attitudes, including white people who deliberately treat
people badly because of their race and nonwhite people who haven't tried hard
enough to "pull themselves up by their bootstraps."[35] This individualistic ex-
planation for the inequality and outcomes they see predisposes them to overlook the structural and systemic factors behind those outcomes. Individualism
is part of the narratives that influence how people make sense of the racial
hierarchies they observe and how they view their own roles in sustaining that
narrative. These narratives also shape how they treat people of color in their
day-to-day interactions.

The given script in an organization defines people's expectations for themselves and for those occupying different positions in their world. The prevailing language reinforces the value assigned to people in the situations defining their place, and it defines what people take for granted and think of as normal. In the culture of organizations, these narratives dictate who might be expected to be in positions of influence and how they should act. For Judge Fein, seeing white people in power and people of color as court officers, clerical staff, and defendants seemed normal in the court system, as did the exercise of that unilateral power and the vastly unequal resources that accompanied these different racial positions. Unwritten rules guided interactions, and the resulting scene appeared as natural as the air we breathe. As sociologist Mary Douglas explained, "When institutions make classifications for us, we seem to lose some independence that we might conceivably have otherwise had."[36]

In her book *Caste: The Origins of Our Discontents*, Isabel Wilkerson offers a way to understand the underlying scripts sustaining racism. She writes that the social divisions of a "caste" system are "the invisible structure that created and maintains hierarchy and inequality. But caste does not allow us to ignore structure. Caste is structure. Caste is ranking. Caste is the boundaries that reinforce the fixed assignments based upon what people look like. Caste is a living, breathing entity. It is like a corporation that seeks to sustain itself at all costs."[37]

Many of the scripts marginalized people—outcastes, in other words—operate within were written by white people, such as the laws that govern their communities and literature circulating in the popular culture that supports the dominant narrative. It is not surprising then that people of color are more acutely aware of white people's scripts than the other way around. They have developed what W.E.B. Du Bois called "double consciousness—this sense of always looking at one's self through the eyes of others, of measuring one's soul by the tape of a world that looks on in amused contempt and pity."[38] People in nondominant groups may also internalize the dominant script, enabling them to operate within the assumed racial hierarchy. And they may also develop their own scripts, rooted in shared history and experience, prompting them to distrust white people's intentions as a way to protect themselves from harm: "The societal narratives around them may force minority group members to stay extra vigilant, often fearful of fulfilling the narrative script prescribed by the majority."[39]

Alan Jenkins, the founding director of the Opportunity Agenda, a social justice communication lab, explains how the same information given to people with different racial narratives leads to disparate conclusions and policy responses:

> Upon hearing that "African Americans are incarcerated at more than 5 times the rate of whites," audiences for whom the prevention and equal justice narrative is most prevalent typically conclude that people and policies in the criminal justice system tend to target and treat African Americans more harshly than whites for the same conduct, requiring systemic reform. Audiences for whom the law and order narrative is salient are most likely to conclude that African Americans are more disposed to commit crime, that targeting those communities is therefore justified, and that if any reform is needed, it relates to the personal choices and "culture" of African American individuals and families.[40]

As Wilkerson points out in *Caste*, because cultural scripts about race ordinarily operate outside our awareness, that makes them all the more powerful. Like the air we breathe, we cannot and do not question them. "The high triumph of institutional thinking," Douglas noted, "is to make the institutions completely invisible."[41] Whether we are white or nonwhite, the scripts we live by are based in narratives we have received from our families, our education, the media, and the dominant culture, and the beliefs and attitudes embedded in them have crystallized into a set of assumptions that shape our day-to-day interactions.

Stuck in racialized scripts, white people are unlikely to perceive, let alone question, the limits of their own way of understanding race and racism. Their point of view operates as the only point of view, leaving them unable to even notice, let alone acknowledge or grapple with, a different way of understanding or interpreting experience. Reinforced by the fact that white people often occupy positions that don't require them to contend with the opposing perspectives of people of color, racial scripts keep people stuck in habits of mind and practice that reinforce the status quo.

Status Quo Bias

When Judge Fein became aware of the script he had accepted without question, he began to see the importance of redefining the way he conducted his work in the trial court. Nonetheless, that developing awareness of the narratives that normalized his court system's disparities and injustices did not immediately translate into questioning or disrupting his habitual roles and

position. Up against Judge Fein's genuine commitment to creating a more equitable justice system in his court was his perception of the risks and losses—
both for himself and for the court—associated with such change. Recognizing
racial inequities in our workplace, our community, and our world can upend
our lives as we question the legitimacy of the status quo that supports us and
that we benefit from, at least in the short run. Maybe it was tempting for Judge
Fein to maintain the wall between his newfound understanding of the injustices of the system and the personal benefits that accrued to him from continuing to regard that system as basically "fair and worthy."

In addition, the small steps he felt he could comfortably take himself paled
in comparison to the scope of the problems. He was seeing that the more he
learned about, talked about, and acknowledged the racial disparities in his
court system, the more frustrated his colleagues of color seemed to get, knowing that despite his new awareness, Judge Fein and the trial court leadership
would remain reluctant to take significant action.

In light of his more comprehensive understanding of the anti-racism paradoxes, Judge Fein recognized that while his growing knowledge and power
had better equipped him to take action, it also heightened his awareness of the
risks of doing so. What if his efforts backfired? If nothing he tried to address
racism in his court worked, that could undercut his perceived legitimacy as a
judge, and along with it, his reputation. This kind of concern about the potential impact on one's position of undertaking meaningful change is status quo
bias, the strong inclination to avoid making change, which perpetuates the
current state of affairs.

Status quo bias comes into play even for white people who see racism as a
serious problem they genuinely want to address. Psychologists have identified
both cognitive and motivational explanations for status quo bias. The status
quo can seem to be a fact of life, like the state of nature. This is "just the way
things are." Without even being aware of this assumption, we can simply believe that there is no other way to do things than the way they are currently
being done. The status quo just *is*. Some racial scripts can feel so hardwired,
built into the system, that they seem "natural." Even though the current reality
results from previous human choices, it seems impossible to imagine the world
any other way.

This way of thinking arises from what John Jost and Mahzarin Banaji call
"system justification": "the process by which existing social arrangements are
legitimized, even at the expense of personal and group interest."[42] Like Judge
Fein, those who have worked hard to achieve their position and performed

well within that system are likely to be invested in considering that system fair and just, believing that it works well enough for most people and is the least bad system they can imagine. These assumptions are core to the way they see themselves, feel safe, and justify the position they occupy. They shape how those in the system respond to information and initiatives that question the legitimacy, fairness, and justice of the existing system. Even for those who are not thriving under the status quo, it can actually be more painful or anxiety producing to see the system as unjust or illegitimate than it is to accept their own unfavorable position in that system. Legal scholar Matthew Tokson provides evidence that judges may resist changes that will add time and effort to their decision-making process or that will force them to face up to the incorrectness or bias of their earlier decisions.[43]

Assuming that maintaining their place in the racial hierarchy is the best way to protect their own interests, people with power maintain the status quo and avoid taking steps that would limit or share that power. Having hoarded opportunities for education, employment, and other social goods in ways that led to the current circumstances favoring them, they may assume that, given the chance, people of color might turn the tables on them with the aim of reversing the racial hierarchy.[44] Stuck in a zero-sum mindset, they may believe that if they give up or share that power, they will be worse off: "If things are getting better for Black people, it must be at the expense of white people." That assumption, documented by Harvard Business School professors Michael Norton and Samuel Sommers in an article titled "Whites See Racism as a Zero-Sum Game That They Are Now Losing," translates into fear of sharing power, perhaps the most obvious version of status quo bias prompting some white people to resist change.[45] As Heather McGhee, policy expert and author of *The Sum of Us*, demonstrates, "The logical extension of the zero-sum story is that a future without racism is something white people should fear, because there will be nothing good for them in it."[46] In a pathbreaking article, critical race scholar Derrick Bell pessimistically observed: "Whites may agree in the abstract that blacks are citizens and are entitled to constitutional protection against racial discrimination, but few are willing to recognize that racial segregation is much more than a series of quaint customs that can be remedied effectively without altering the status of whites."[47]

But the assumption that retaining power over people of color is the only way to protect and advance their own interests actually prevents many white people from recognizing that they too are impoverished by a poverty wage economy that traps whites, along with people of color, in low-wage jobs and enriches only the owners of wealthy corporations.[48] Rethinking the distribution of power, a crucial step in enabling people to navigate the paradox of racialized power, is a theme running throughout this book and is addressed specifically in chapter 6.

People in Judge Fein's position may also be paralyzed by their inability to envision what changing the status quo would look like and how it might succeed. Judge Fein might have understood the warning, summarized by critical race scholar john powell, that "distributing benefits based upon institutional practices in which hierarchy and group norms are embedded merely reproduces domination at deeper and more subtle levels."[49] But he couldn't imagine a pathway leading to more fundamental change. He didn't know of a better system of justice than the one he was currently a part of, and he had no blueprint for building a different one.

The incentive structures further cut against facing up to the contradictions embedded in the status quo. Wading into unfamiliar terrain and uncertainty, Judge Fein was experiencing the kind of personal conflict built into working within racialized institutions—how to question and at the same time embrace the institution and practices he felt committed to serving. If Judge Fein and his colleagues took on responsibility for racism in the way judges, prosecutors, and clerks exercised their power, would they be abandoning their historical role as passive umpires? Judge Fein was facing the uncertainty associated with the complexities of addressing entrenched racism in any predominantly white institution.

In my work with student editors of several elite law reviews, I have documented similar trepidation about changing the rules governing how they define their selection practices and publication priorities.[50] For example, if the Yale Law Journal's editors were to decrease reliance on traditional measures of success for selecting editors and articles and instead focus on making their journal more accessible and able to address pressing issues such as racism, would they risk diminishing its prestige and impact according to conventional standards?[51]

Under conditions of uncertainty and ambiguity, people tend to fear the consequences of admitting that they don't know what to do or, even worse, of making a mistake. Failure could mean rejection and humiliation. In the absence of what Harvard Business School researcher Amy Edmondson calls "psychological safety," people will often avoid taking action that risks conflict or failure. Over the course of his investigations during the six-month workshop, Judge Fein learned that this fear was widespread in the court system, particularly in relation to race. As he told me, "I hadn't realized that no one felt safe talking to me or others if they were having problems or witnessing issues that needed to be addressed. They felt they were supposed to know what to do, and if they admitted that they didn't, they were afraid that they would lose status or be publicly criticized. It was better to keep your head down and just go along." Some trial court leaders in Judge Fein's court system resisted efforts to document patterns of racial bias, worrying that this information could be used to criticize them publicly or to take action against them, rather than as a way to improve. Culture change is hard to pursue when failure is a risk that people in an organization are not willing to take.

The cultural tendency toward individualism also contributes to status quo bias. When the responsibility for an outcome lies with each person alone, one is faced with becoming a hero or a villain, which invites short-term solutions that can be put in place quickly, even if they are bound to eventually not work. The pressure to show immediate results can discourage the necessary sustained involvement in change that will produce significant results only down the line.

Status quo bias holds in place unquestioned and unchallenged policies and ideas that normalize racial inequality. This pattern was evident in the drafting and enactment of the GI Bill after World War I. In *When Affirmative Action Was White*, Ira Katznelson documents how this program, which put millions of working-class veterans through college and into new homes and the middle class, was administered through restrictive and discriminatory policies and practices. "Written under Southern auspices," Katznelson writes, "the law was deliberately designed to accommodate Jim Crow by assuring that the programs were directed not by Washington but by local white officials, businessmen, bankers and college administrators who would honor past exclusionary practices." As a result, thousands of Black veterans were denied housing and business loans, as well as admission to whites-only colleges and universities. Instead, most were channeled toward traditional, low-paying "Black jobs" and small Black colleges, which did not have the funds, facilities, or programs to handle the flood of eligible Black veterans. Though separate, Black colleges were hardly equal.[52]

Policies sustaining the status quo in a world set up by and for white people become, in the words of sociologist Daria Roithmayr, "locked in." Roithmayr points out the economic, structural, social, and political costs of switching to new, more inclusive rules, even when the existing rules have been shown to be ineffective and unfair.[53] The continued use of the LSAT by law schools to determine admissions—in the face of ample evidence that these tests lack predictive value and produce racial disparities in the student body—is a case in point. Even after elite law schools stopped participating in *U.S. News & World Report*'s ranking system (published to inform prospective students' choice of law school) because it did not fairly reflect what law schools most value, the institutions continued to rely on the LSAT. Belief in the LSAT as the best available measure of ability has produced what legal scholar Lani Guinier called a "testocracy," i.e., reliance on a measure that does not actually predict success as a lawyer and that excludes from selective universities and law schools students who do not have the privileges of wealthy white applicants.[54] However, if elite law schools abandoned the use of the LSAT, they would lose the efficiency of relying on the test's administrative network and "would have to pay to construct, validate, monitor, and administer any replacement test."[55] So, in favor of status and economy, the status quo is preserved.

When people seeking change in predominantly white institutions face the enormity of the problems and the predictability of backlash in trying to change the status quo, they may feel overwhelmed by a sense of hopelessness about change. Yet, as civil rights advocate Bryan Stevenson points out, "hopelessness is the enemy of justice."[56] To stay engaged, those who seek change have to find ways to balance skepticism with hopefulness, developing resilience in order to respond effectively to uncertain conditions—a topic covered in the book's final chapter. But even that response might be impeded when change agents get caught in too narrowly defining their role, the pattern I call role rigidity.

Role Rigidity

Judge Fein's initial view of what he could and should do when he witnessed racism in the judicial system had been shaped by how he had learned to define his role as a judge. As noted, he had come into the workshop conceiving of his judicial role as one in which he used his technical skills of adjudication to treat people fairly, judge each case on its own merits, and "judiciously" apply precedent to the situations presented by each case. Other than consciously avoiding overt bias in decision making, he had considered it beyond the role of a judge to try to address systemic disparities. As one of his colleagues put it: "Our job is to call balls and strikes—nothing more and nothing less."

This narrow view of the judicial role is shared by many judges, which accounts for the tendency to overlook or dismiss their responsibility for racial disparities in the court system. In their analysis of this issue, Matthew Clair and Alix Winter found that many judges were indeed aware of the evidence showing that Black and Latino/a/e defendants were treated more punitively than whites and that discriminatory treatment by others in the system—court officials, lawyers, and police officers—contributed to these disparities. Nonetheless, most retained a passive stance in their role, not questioning the disparity. They instead adhered to "noninterventionist strategies, which do not deal with possible differential treatment by other actors or the disparate impact of the criminal justice system."[57] Clair and Winter point out that a minority of judges did adopt an interventionist stance, raising questions about their own differential treatment of defendants and acknowledging that tendency in some of their colleagues. These judges were also interested in "addressing the disparate impact of their own decisions and of the process as a whole." But, except for these outliers, the noninterventionist strategies of the majority of judges "help to explain the reproduction of racial disparities in the judicial system."[58] Status quo bias combined with role rigidity predisposes judges "to fall back on their legal training and acculturation, which includes the historical role of judicial passivity as a marker of impartiality and judicial assistance for litigants as a marker of bias."[59] A sobering historical example of this noninterventionist stance in the face of inequities, described by renowned legal scholar Robert Cover in *Justice Accused*, is that of judges in the pre–Civil War era who, acting on their fidelity to a narrow conception of their role, were willing to enforce laws and contracts enslaving people.[60]

This kind of narrow conception of their professional role as judges is a clear example of role rigidity, but the tendency is evident in all professions, along with its impact of impeding anti-racism efforts. As MIT social scientist Donald Schön recounts in *The Reflective Practitioner: How Professionals Think in Action*, professionals tend to exercise their roles as defined by technical expertise in solving discrete problems: "Hungry for technical rigor, devoted to an image of solid professional competence, or fearful of entering a world in which they feel they do not know what they are doing, they choose to confine themselves to a narrowly technical practice."[61] As a result, lawyers, teachers, directors, actors, doctors, police officers, professors, and managers—professionals in general—are socialized to shun responsibility for dealing with the "swamp"— Schön's metaphor for important, complex, and messy problems, such as racism. Role rigidity leads people to ask, "Is this problem within the scope of my technical expertise and my preconceived role as a professional?" That narrow conception of their role contributes to the belief that there is nothing they have the power (or right) to do outside their job description, which means they must simply accept any contradictions or injustices they might perceive in the larger system. And if they do notice a human concern that isn't amenable to a solution discoverable through their technical expertise or a systemic problem calling for a redefinition of their role, they might be inclined to simply say, "It's not my job."

Such prescribed roles do not invite, equip, or require those who enact them to ask questions about whether the larger system within which they operate is functional, fair, and just for everyone involved. And rigid alignment with these roles certainly does not encourage action as change agents. For myself, as a teacher of civil procedure—a required course for entering law students about the legal processes used to resolve conflict—role rigidity predisposed me to teach students to argue cases within the existing adversarial system and to master the same legal doctrine taught by most civil procedure teachers. This narrow role conception cuts *against* using this required course to equip students, as part of their professional socialization, to address issues of unequal access to justice that undermine the legitimacy and fairness of the judicial system itself. It discourages students from focusing on the human (but not legal) needs of people affected by the system, or the impact of legal doctrine on the communities that bear the brunt of their decisions. Legal education teaches future lawyers to accept and operate within a system that they know to be dysfunctional and unjust rather than equipping them to use their power to change that system. And the same status quo assumptions delimit the avenues of action that might be taken by those operating in other institutions and organizations.

A white theater director I worked with assumed this narrow stance toward his role when his show reopened after the Covid-19 pandemic subsided, and he was asked by company members of color to address the racist practices they had previously experienced during the production. During a workshop I cofacilitated with this company, he explained his frustration and his understanding of the boundaries of his role: "I am a director, not a social worker. I am here to produce a show of high quality that makes money. How can I do that when I am being asked to handle issues far beyond my job description, and which I didn't even know existed before now?" Like Judge Fein, role rigidity had clouded his perception and tied his hands.

Many in predominantly white institutions occupy organizational or professional roles that do not equip or encourage them to enter the risky and uncertain territory of organizational and social change. Like Judge Fein, they may see the need for change, but the way they define their expertise and professional roles disables them from acting on those values. However, avoiding the issues by hiding behind roles does not relieve people in power from the responsibility to address ongoing racism. Rigid role definitions that prevent people from addressing racism in their system only perpetuate the cycle of Groundhog Day.

What does it take to stick with the possibility of progress toward anti-racism in the face of experiential segregation, scripted stuckness, status quo bias, and role rigidity? When fear, possible failure, discomfort, and backlash seem an inevitable part of the effort, how can we resist the urge to give up, retreat, or take the easy way out? What supports us in moving toward greater equity and full participation in the face of racism embedded in the status quo? How can people interested in pursuing anti-racism become what Deepak Bhargava and Stephanie Luce call "practical radicals" who "let go of habitual patterns of understanding the world, take in the whole field of experience with fresh eyes, and find new ways of acting that can disrupt dysfunctional systems"?[62] The next chapter takes on the possibility and challenge of doing just that.

3

The Promise of Paradoxical Possibility

HOW DO GROUPS discover ways to connect across experiential divides so it becomes possible for them to find common ground? What can be done to resist the gravitational pull of the status quo, reinforced by racial narratives discouraging change? What might enable people in an organization to reconfigure their roles and relationships so that they can navigate the paradox of racialized power? Short-term, one-shot reforms have proven insufficient to push back against the pressures that produce the vicious cycle of reform and retrenchment. How do we overcome the tendency to treat the two sides of the anti-racism paradoxes as mutually exclusive choices, when both are necessary to make real the values of full participation? Meaningful change in the face of these countervailing forces requires a committed and sustained effort over the long haul. Given the paradoxes inherent in anti-racism efforts, can people working in predominantly white institutions find ways to destabilize the racial status quo and open up possibilities for genuine and lasting change?

Escaping Groundhog Day requires learning to move forward with commitment and determination, accepting resistance and failure as part of the process, yet knowing that small successes can create momentum for significant change. These efforts include searching for ways to better understand and live with the contradictions in the process, discovering where the conditions giving rise to those contradictions can be changed, and finding ways to demonstrate that undertaking anti-racism efforts is in the best interests of institutions. Treating those tensions as opportunities for learning and triggers for transformation is key. Even as we struggle with the paradoxes built into anti-racism efforts, continued engagement with these contradictions is the only way to close the gap between rhetoric and reality.

This kind of reflection-in-action is hard work against the odds, but it can be done. I have seen it happen and experienced it myself in organizations I have worked with. It might begin with a culture change process like the one Judge Fein undertook with his colleagues in the trial court. That process provided a vehicle for building relationships with people in different racial and organizational positions while learning how to work together to advance full participation despite their differences and distrust. Judge Fein became part of an ongoing community of change agents that called upon its members to assume responsibility for transforming an unacceptable status quo.

The process Judge Fein experienced in his trial court brought together people of different races, positions, and backgrounds who recognized that they didn't know how to address racism in their court system and were willing to invest time and energy to figure out what to do about it. It began by setting up opportunities for the group to learn more about each other's experiences. As they took the time needed for these conversations to occur, they built the capacity to engage across racial difference. Early on, the group committed to ground rules that invited open dialogue among people who had been working together, in some cases for years, but had never really communicated about themselves or their experiences with the justice system. As the trial court's overall leadership team—the chief justice and court administrator—shared their own struggles and mistakes in dealing with race, they set a tone that invited others to take similar risks. This willingness of white leaders to speak openly about their own racial identity development is an example of the kind of vulnerability that research professor Brené Brown deems crucial to making meaningful change.[1] They did exercises and worked on small projects together, and they began to share more openly and take the risk of speaking about race across racial lines.

Judge Fein started to notice when and where race seemed to be playing a role in his own court; he also began to see the differences in perception and experience of people with identities and backgrounds different from his own in a culture that had afforded him what feminist scholar Peggy McIntosh described as "white skin privilege: an invisible package of unearned assets that I can count on cashing in each day, about which I was 'meant' to remain oblivious."[2] He began to realize how little he knew about the communities of color that were home to the people appearing before him in the court and how little say those communities were having in the way the court did its work. The workshop sessions themselves were giving him a taste of the kind of environment he wanted to experience as part of the trial court's day-to-day operation— people talking openly across race and position about their struggles and perspectives in a community formed around the commitment to change. This was in stark contrast to the segregated and detached dynamics that had been characterizing his daily interactions in the court system. He moved from a stance of passivity to one of curiosity and collaboration, and he began to connect these racial dynamics to other issues that were affecting the quality of justice he was providing. Judge Fein had begun the work to escape the vicious cycle that had kept him and his workplace trapped in Groundhog Day.

When we suggested that participants in our workshop try a small experiment in their everyday work environment, Judge Fein asked his leadership team, which included a Black court clerk and a Latino/a/e court officer, to start observing the dynamics of the courtroom, comparing treatment and outcomes in cases involving people with different racial identities. When they first started working together, this team had to go through their own process of sharing differences in perceptions and experiences, learning how to speak openly and vulnerably with each other for the first time. Judge Fein's doubts about the possibility of change were tempered by glimmers of hope. Determined now to figure out how he and his colleagues could institute the desired change, and what role he could play in moving toward that vision, Judge Fein was ready for the next step.

When our six-month workshop series ended, the chief justice of the state-wide system, who had also taken the workshop and made anti-racism a priority, charged all of the participants with further responsibility for undertaking a culture change process within their own sphere of influence. At this point, knowing more about his position and his aim, Judge Fein was willing to assume the risks entailed in the next step in this effort. Despite the discomfort he felt in unscripted roles, the pushback he anticipated from white people in the court who didn't want to talk about race or racism, the concerns of some about going beyond their conventional professional roles, and the criticism he knew he'd receive from colleagues of color if the effort failed to produce any substantive action, he was ready to try.

He began by assembling a group of judges who would review and discuss each other's data over the previous two years to identify and help each other understand racial disparities in their sentencing practices. His own participation in this process prompted him to stop considering traffic convictions in sentencing, when those convictions would exponentially increase the sentence of Black men for "driving while Black." Taking that step would strengthen his resolve to resist the daily pressure to spend as little time as possible on sentencing, recognizing that succumbing to that pressure only increased the likelihood that decisions would be biased. He began using his judicial opinions to change the narrative, acknowledging the unfairness of the rules he had to follow and eventually engaging the court in a wider discussion about the system's unfairness and bias.

Judge Fein had realized that transformative change would require taking the initiative beyond the walls of the court system, involving both community members affected by the trial court's racialized practices and decision makers like prosecutors and police officers whose behavior contributed to the unacceptable racial inequities. He visited other systems and countries that used restorative rather than punitive approaches to public safety and began a dialogue in his own court about ways to move in that direction. He realized that systemic change would require learning more about the communities of color affected by the court systems and owning up to the limits of solving social and economic problems with punitive measures. And he was inspired to try experiments that would shift power and resources from courts to communities. The necessary systemic changes would not happen overnight, but participating in a community of change agents had taught Judge Fein that he could begin moving his court toward a more just and equitable judiciary by creating a space designed to build trust, face up to challenges involving race, identify common concerns, take action, and remain engaged in the face of struggles and failures.[3]

Efforts like these, based on recognizing the anti-racism paradoxes, can use those paradoxes to drive learning and effective change. They can explore and build upon what I see as four critical and interlocking strategies that characterize effective anti-racism efforts. These are:

- learning to live with contradictions and complexity
- committing to a long-term process of rescripting the racial narrative
- taking small steps toward big changes
- building a multiracial community of change agents

These strategies are what is required to begin moving individuals and organizations toward anti-racism practices and policies, and they are critical in sustaining that effort over the long haul.

Learning to Live with Contradictions and Complexity

"The law had been presented to me as all about being right or wrong, and it's been so deeply ingrained in me to be *right*. What would it mean to take the risk of acknowledging my own fallibility, questioning my role as it's currently defined, admitting that the system responsible for administering justice is un-just?" That was Judge Fein's concern when we first began working together. Over time, he had come to accept that there were no easy answers and that meaningful change required resisting the temptation to simply impose a solution and then retreat to safer ground, hoping things would somehow just work out.

I'd had a similar realization about my own role in pursuing anti-racism in the classroom and in my work with organizations. I had to be willing to live with uncertainty about how issues of race might manifest and the limits of my ability as a white woman in a position of power to meet those challenges without trig-gering a new, unforeseen version of the very issues I was trying to address. I had to find ways to accept and learn from the contradictions, failures, and messiness I inevitably experienced. I eventually realized I had to shift from a stance of "getting it right" to one of staying in the struggle, learning from my own and others' failures, forgoing the urge to insist on an immediate resolution, and being simultaneously more understanding and more accountable in the face of my own and others' mistakes. I had to accept uncertainty and discomfort as something to be acknowledged, valued, and embraced. I call this "a failure theory of success"—treating mistakes as inevitable and failures as information that helps increase racial literacy, accountability, and efficacy. That stance en-abled me to be open to learning from issues when they arose, engaging myself and others explicitly in understanding the contradictions, and sharing power with my collaborators as a way of broadening the perspective of everyone in-volved. When I was able to maintain that stance, I found that the people of color I was relating to were much more willing to trust me and to collaborate, leading to some of the most rewarding relationships and projects of my career.

Social psychologist Carol Dweck might frame the willingness to embrace uncertainty and learn from failure as a shift from what she calls a "fixed" to a "growth" mindset.[4] When we view the challenges presented by the paradoxes inherent in anti-racism work through this lens, we see that when those with a fixed mindset face the uncertainties inherent in navigating anti-racism's para-doxes, they more readily conclude that resolution is not possible and are there-fore less likely to invest the effort and time to learn from others and explore ways to improve relationships and interactions. In contrast, those with a growth mindset understand uncertainty as a prerequisite for positive change and thus regard failures along the way as opportunities for learning and im-provement. This is what Judge Fein was developing.

Transformation requires embracing what people naturally seek to avoid—remaining in uncertainty, accepting our lack of control, and recognizing the necessity of conflict and error as part of the process of resolution. It also sometimes includes acknowledging the impossibility of resolution, at least in the short run. It requires living together in that uncertainty, not blaming or turning against each other in frustration at not knowing "the solution." Adam Kahane, conflict facilitator and author of *Collaborating with the Enemy: How to Work with People You Don't Agree with or Like or Trust*, calls this "stretch collaboration"—embracing both conflict and connection, remaining willing to experiment with different perspectives and scenarios and open to willingly change ourselves in the process.

As Barry Johnson, author of *Polarity Management: Identifying and Managing Unsolvable Problems*, notes: "Fear of getting stuck in the opposite pole gets you stuck in your pole."[5] However, paradoxical possibility requires remaining open and attentive to both sides. Paradox is not a problem to be solved but a both/and polarity to embrace. Sticking with one pole over the other surfaces the limitations of that side of the polarity. Unless the other side of the polarity also kicks in, the one-sided situation inevitably leads back to Groundhog Day. To gain and maintain the benefits of one side of the polarity and reduce its risks, you must also pursue the benefits—and deal with the risks—of the other.

Reframing racial conflict through the lens of paradox is an "aha" moment for many of the people I have worked with. Because both sides of the anti-racism paradox affect the capacity to address race as it actually operates in personal experience and in organizations, learning this both/and approach opens doors to unanticipated possibilities. It is possible to both lean into power and step back from power, even though doing so may well produce conflict and tension. It is possible *both* to focus on race *and* to not focus on race in the way organizations address racial disparities and pursue full participation.

This both/and approach is what Johnson calls "polarity management." Learning how to see the picture from the vantage point of the other polarity requires temporarily suspending your typical way of thinking. When you trust that you'll be able to return to your own understanding of reality after you try shifting to an opposing perspective, you can open yourself to a better, and perhaps new, understanding of the whole picture. In learning to work effectively in the midst of complexity and contradiction, you have to move back and forth from one side of the duality to the other. Judge Fein learned to say to himself: "If I let go of trying to resolve these conflicting racial experiences, I can better understand them and how they interact. Then I can actually make sense of my situation, uncomfortable as it is."

Johnson uses the difference between catching a ball and juggling as a useful analogy for understanding this process: "Juggling is like a polarity to manage because it is ongoing. The objective is to keep one ball in the air at all times while rotating through the three balls. . . . In juggling, the absolute interdependence of opposites is very clear. The opposites are both throwing and catching with the same hand."[6] Recognizing the work of anti-racism as juggling a paradox shifts the focus away from each side trying to prove it is right or defend its intentions to instead creating a context open to exploring what can be learned from the contradictions, from recognizing value in both sides, seeing the power and limits of each polarity, and viewing them from a stance of inquiry rather than battle or retreat. Seeing contradictions as inevitable in anti-racism work allows the tensions to be framed as necessary drivers of understanding and change. Kenwyn Smith and David Berg, scholars of paradox, call this process the art of balancing forces in such a way that "they do not cancel each other out, and each side shoots sparks of light across their points of polarity."[7]

White people seeking to pursue anti-racism have much to learn from people of color about this ability to hold the complexities with what critical race scholar Mari Matsuda calls "multiple consciousness." As outsiders, people of color have had to learn how to move back and forth between working outside of an unjust and racist system that marginalizes and oppresses them and working within that system in order to survive and promote change. Building on W.E.B. Du Bois's juxtaposition of the ideal and the actual, expressed by the idea of double consciousness,[8] Matsuda offers multiple consciousness: "a deliberate choice to see the world from the standpoint of the oppressed." This, Matsuda urges, is "the pathway to a just world," one that is "accessible to all of us," with people of color leading the way. She provides examples of people of color strategically shifting back and forth between "their consciousness as a Third World person and the white consciousness required for survival in predominantly white institutions." With this "characteristic duality," they see and, where possible, act on their awareness of "life under patriarchy and racial hierarchy," while also shifting to "where most people stand," using the dominant system when necessary to meet their needs and those of their community. Matsuda calls upon white change agents to also develop this habit of mind.[9]

For white people who have not yet acknowledged their own racial position, the complexity of taking this step can be more challenging. As Martha Minow notes in *Making All the Difference*, it involves first recognizing that what we might previously have thought was a universal perspective is actually our point of view and that we don't know what any situation might look like from other perspectives. Shifting back and forth across the perceptual divide of race requires the intentional effort to step out of our own perspective and learn about the perspective of people of color.[10]

Over the course of the workshop, Judge Fein began to develop the kind of multiple consciousness Matsuda was calling for. For example, when he got to know a woman of color in the group who was working in the court as an interpreter, he heard about her daily experiences of being both essential to the system's functioning and made to feel invisible and undervalued. Until that conversation, Judge Fein had assumed that by providing interpreters for non-English-speaking litigants, the judicial system was responding appropriately and even with consideration. But this interaction revealed the gap between what people in power, mostly white people, perceive and how their actions are experienced by those in their midst who are treated as outsiders. He further learned that racism also permeated the interactions of interpreters with lawyers and court officials, who were sometimes overheard making disparaging comments about non-English speakers, who were perceived to be incompetent and suspected of being untruthful. Judge Fein realized that he had never in his career paid attention to interpreters' interactions in his courtroom, and he had no idea what it was like for a defendant to experience the courtroom through the filter of an interpreter. This realization prompted him to undertake a more sustained inquiry into the experience of interpreters and those they served in the court system. While the group wasn't sure how to address the problem, they were at least now aware of the consequences of tolerating these inequities in the system. This was a step toward figuring out how to improve the treatment of non-English-speaking people and their interpreters.

That inquiry also opened up a dialogue about what had prevented Judge Fein and his judicial peers from noticing this problem before. Still believing in the justice of the system, Judge Fein was able to step into the shoes of people who experienced that same system as profoundly unjust, toggling back and forth between his own perspective and theirs. He realized that he rarely had an opportunity to see what justice looked like from vantage points other than his own.

As white people, particularly those in positions of power, acknowledge that we are operating with a particular worldview that often prevents us from perceiving the one-sidedness of our understanding, we are able to be more open to competing views without trying to arrive prematurely at a conclusion or resolution. Learning to live with that kind of uncertainty is a necessary step in the process of addressing racism in institutions and organizations. Doing anti-racism work requires building an environment in which it is possible for people to be uncertain, to take risks, to make mistakes, to be open to and explore unfamiliar ways of viewing situations.

Creating this kind of open environment that accepts uncertainty and resists premature resolution requires adopting a stance of humility. As Paolo Freire wrote in *Pedagogy of the Oppressed*, "dialogue cannot exist without humility. The naming of the world, through which people constantly recreate that world, cannot be an act of arrogance. Dialogue, as the encounter of those addressed to the common task of learning and acting, is broken if the parties (or one of them) lack humility. How can I dialogue if I always project ignorance onto others and never perceive my own?"[11]

In the context of relationships, humility, as one report focusing on addressing racism in the medical field states, entails a "lifelong commitment to self-evaluation and critique" that is the underpinning of "redressing the power imbalances" and creating "mutually beneficial and non-paternalistic partnerships" with directly affected individuals and communities.[12] For groups and organizations, Amy Edmondson calls for "situational humility"—creating settings that communicate willingness to learn, openness to new ideas, and acknowledgment of limitations and knowledge gaps.[13] At the level of governance, humility means that "policy-making begins with an acknowledgment of the prevailing uncertainty and is thus built as a continuously iterative process, in which actors are willing to (and allowed to) change their mind as new information arises."[14] I call this process institutional mindfulness—setting up a process that systematically examines decision making and outcomes in an organization to assess whether people of every race and background have the opportunity to succeed and thrive.[15] Building this capacity for reflection supports the shift from binary win/lose, right/wrong thinking to a focus on learning from conflict, failure, and conditions of uncertainty to address anti-racism at every level: within individuals, groups, organizations, and communities.

This step from a fixed to a growth mindset, from seeking certainty to accepting ambiguity, from imposing one-sided quick fixes to navigating paradox, is daunting. The pressure to find quick fixes and the worry about failure make it tempting to retreat to the sidelines and step out of the struggle. In the face of the huge hurdles and recurring setbacks in anti-racism work, how can individuals and organizations remain hopeful and stay engaged in the long-term systemic change needed to address racism?

Committing to a Long-Term Process of
Rescripting the Racial Narrative

In each situation where I have observed people in predominantly white institutions undertaking sustained and effective engagement with the anti-racism paradoxes, that process has happened when enough of those involved realize that if they are serious about escaping Groundhog Day, the transformative change they seek requires commitment to the long haul. Trial and error have taught them that there is no silver bullet, gentle nudge, or quick fix that will produce the necessary culture change to address the entrenched problems of racism. Often triggered by mobilization by people of color and their allies who speak up publicly about racism, something happens to make the racial inequities—and their impact on those directly affected by them—more widely visible and the disconnect between professed values and practices no longer tolerable.

Sometimes, public protest is a necessary catalyst to awaken the commitment to long-term change. As Martin Luther King proclaimed in *Letter from Birmingham Jail*: "Nonviolent direct action seeks to create such a crisis and foster such a tension that a community which has constantly refused to negotiate is forced to confront the issue. It seeks to dramatize the issue so that it can no longer be ignored." This was King's call for "a type of constructive, nonviolent tension which is necessary for growth."[16] It was that kind of tension produced by the national protests in the wake of George Floyd's murder that induced some institutions to publicly acknowledge their own racism and commit to reparations and anti-racism goals aiming at long-term culture change. These long-overdue commitments were a direct response to public pressure—a fact underscored by the backsliding that took place in many institutions when that pressure subsided.

Sometimes, data-driven critiques by organized groups within an institution provide the momentum and support that prompt leadership to undertake systemic change. I witnessed data playing this role in my work with the editors of the *Yale Law Journal*. It was sustained, data-driven public criticism of the journal's' homogeneity, coupled with concern about the publication's declining relevance and legitimacy, that compelled the journal's leadership to rethink its selection processes and begin prioritizing scholarship that addressed pressing social justice issues.[17] Sometimes, the push for change comes from litigation that overtly challenges the legality of discriminatory practices, particularly when the case forces someone in a position of leadership to take responsibility for addressing racism or to step aside for new leadership willing to pursue change.[18]

In the state court system that Judge Fein was part of, the "something" calling for culture change involved a combination of external pressure and an internal awakening to the widespread need for more humane interactions within the court system. Public reports documented patterns of racist interactions and persistent racial disparities experienced by Black and Brown trial judges, lawyers, and court users at each step of the judicial legal process. In the face of a groundswell of critique from both inside the court system and the public, the leadership of the state court system finally understood that they had to respond to the racism with systemic change, that they could not address race and bias without rethinking the internal practices of each local courthouse as well as the court system overall. Recognizing the truth of the maxim that "culture eats strategy for breakfast," they saw that commitment to creating a system that afforded justice with dignity meant they couldn't settle only for piecemeal programs or individual accountability for racist incidents. Moving toward an equitable justice system required changing the culture of the statewide trial courts. That meant finding ways to involve those directly affected by racism in the decision-making processes of the court system. It meant shifting the overall climate of distrust and cynicism at every level of the state justice system so that people would be willing to speak openly and have difficult conversations. It meant identifying the prevailing assumptions and stereotypes that predisposed people to tolerate inhumane treatment, as well as uplifting examples of people in power using their positions to highlight the unacceptability of that treatment and undertake efforts to change the system. It meant incorporating efforts to promote full participation and equitable justice into people's understanding of their roles. In other words, they had to engage the entire system of the trial court in rescripting the racial narrative.

Judge Fein's personal experience illustrates the transformational character of this rescripting process. Forced to confront the disconnect between his own deeply held commitment to justice and his new level of awareness of the system's injustices, Judge Fein ventured into the risky yet rewarding territory of inviting questions and challenges when confronted with troubling disparities and injustices. In doing so, he shifted from a stance of operating on his own, individually responsible for his own actions in his courtroom or his chambers, to working collaboratively to identify the source of problems in the whole system and then brainstorming alternatives.

Even though that process inevitably exposed conflicts he hadn't even known existed, he was able to begin identifying opportunities for a new way forward, treating day-to-day decisions across the system as choice points for reshaping the racial narrative. He expanded his understanding of his own role by questioning practices that seemed unfair, disrespectful, or biased. For example, were people who were unfamiliar with the court system provided information in a form that they could understand? Was there room in the process for them to ask questions and get help? And why were people of color getting charged for more serious offenses than white people arrested for the same offenses? By asking questions himself, he was making it safe for others to do the same, rewarding those who surfaced problems or conflicts so they could be addressed. He and his colleagues pushed the court system to start gathering information on such discrepancies as a matter of course, and he began using periodic staff meetings within his court system to think together about those results. He developed relationships of trust with people of color by inviting feedback on a regular basis and committing to making changes based on that feedback, acknowledging when he made mistakes and remaining involved when conflict arose. Even while fielding criticism from valued colleagues for departing from time-honored conventions of detached neutrality, he began to reimagine ways to involve those most directly and adversely affected by the court system so they could communicate how it was affecting them, and then explore alternative ways to address problems that could be better handled in the community.[19] Judge Fein had started down the path toward becoming one of those "interventionist judges" Matthew Clair talks about, willing to question the status quo and acting to correct the injustices that seemed built into the script.

Over time, Judge Fein began to see small but meaningful changes: issues involving race and racism became subjects of explicit reflection and problem-solving; the small group of judges who examined patterns in their sentencing observed a decrease in those disparities over time; community-led pilot programs gained support, albeit on a small scale, for a restorative approach to criminal offenses; and the trial court made racial equity a pillar of its new strategic plan. Alongside these modest improvements, the reflection process also forced Judge Fein to face the glaring gap between these incremental changes and the systemic disparities built into the prevailing system.

Judge Fein's efforts illustrate what can happen when people in a predominantly white organization begin rescripting the racial narrative. That process goes beyond simply acknowledging that there is a problem. It involves taking the steps that create the conditions for surfacing the prevailing narrative—the taken-for-granted assumptions that normalize racial inequality—and building a constituency for systems change. This happens when organizations put in place recurring cross-racial reflection that makes visible the prevailing culture and the practices locking it in place. It requires asking: How are people of different races and backgrounds experiencing day-to-day interactions? Who is thriving and who isn't, and what explains differences in perceptions and outcomes? Whose voices and well-being matter? What happens to people in different identities and positions when they struggle or fail? Asking such questions makes visible the gap between the "ought" (what the organization says it cares about) and the "is" (the realities of what people of different races and identities experience). This awareness opens up the space for challenging the assumptions that normalize racial hierarchy, and it builds momentum for transformational change (the "what might be").[20]

Rescripting the racial narrative to change the culture of organizations requires the kind of perspective-taking and self-examination exhibited by Judge Fein. It requires changing the way power is exercised so that those directly affected by racism become part of redefining the practices and values. This transformative framework opens up possibilities for bridging experiential divides, overcoming status quo bias, sharing power, and integrating the process of addressing racism into the roles and structure of the organization.

Most predominantly white institutions have yet to make a genuine commitment to rescripting the racial narrative. Elite law schools like my own are not yet seriously addressing how the prevailing culture alienates and marginalizes people of color. Change has taken place largely around the edges: awarding anti-racism grants supporting one-time efforts of law students or creating teaching tools to support faculty willing to address race and racism in their classrooms. These efforts, though valuable, preserve sacred cows that maintain the racial status quo—teaching practices that haven't been changed in over a hundred years, admissions criteria that emphasize selectivity (like high test scores) over leadership potential, and hiring and promotion practices that devalue real-world impact through scholarship, teaching, and engagement. Concern about precedent and prestige—both individual and institutional—keeps many people from opening up a dialogue that would make visible how law schools need to change if they are to meet the demands of a world in crisis. Although it's possible and important to rescript the narrative in subcultures forged in classrooms, clinics, and programs, there is not yet a critical mass of insiders with power—deans and tenured faculty members—willing to engage over the long haul and do the hard work of rescripting the racial narrative in law schools.

However, even when predominantly white institutions are not committed to long-term change, there are ways to build spaces within them and with the communities surrounding them in which steps to rescript the narrative can take root. Those small-scale transformations can serve as steps to larger change as long as change agents remain engaged in the work required to move organizations toward a culture promoting full participation.

Taking Small Steps toward Big Changes

The changes Judge Fein was able to initiate in his own court were a promise of what might be possible on a broader scale in the statewide court. That context of change could serve as what adrienne maree brown, activist and author of *Emergent Strategy*, might call a "fractal." In her use of the term, a fractal is a microsystem, a small-scale version of the world you want to see happen more generally, a pattern "developed at a small scale that can reverberate to the larger scale." As she points out, a fractal can be an "invitation to practice the world we want to see in the current landscape."[21]

The six-month workshop for leaders in trial courts was itself a fractal, a space where race could be renegotiated, relationships could be reconfigured, power could be shared, learning could substitute for defensiveness, and change experiments could be pursued. And each of those experiments was a fractal, like the group of judges Judge Fein formed, in response to a workshop assignment, to review and assess past court decisions, demonstrating a way of practicing law from a new perspective. The leadership workshop also provided a context for connecting such fractals so that the patterns could reverberate beyond their original locus of practice. The process enabled participants to experience and witness versions of their own hoped-for transformation at a scale they could manage, without the illusion that this small step would solve the overarching problem. This creation of "fractals" offers one strategy for organizations to take small steps toward larger transformation.

Navigating the paradoxes of anti-racism requires this kind of transformative incrementalism. Because racism is baked into the current culture, it is necessary to rescript the standard and entrenched operations in every context to avoid perpetuating the status quo. Yet the risk is that wholesale efforts to change the system all at once will overwhelm participants and invariably run out of steam. You have to find a way to "chunk" the issue into workable bits, so it is both manageable and still disruptive of the status quo. Chunking involves identifying a challenge or opportunity that is big enough to make a difference and small enough to accomplish. A crucial aspect of this chunking process involves defining the scope of what you can achieve at any particular point along the way, and then defining success in terms of meeting those goals. If change initiatives are measured against whether or not they eradicate racism, they of course fall short. The test could instead be whether these incremental steps are moving in the direction of more transformative change, laying the foundation for the next round of experiments, and building momentum and support for staying in the work over the long haul.

Law professors Charles Sabel and Michael Dorf label this process of learning from successes and failures "experimentalism." Local actors come together to figure out complex problems, try new things at the local level, and then participate in peer reflection. The willingness to experiment, reflect, learn, and try again is what opens up the possibility of feeling the way toward more fundamental change.[22] Adam Kahane, the author of *Collaborating with the Enemy*, calls this approach "scenario planning": inviting collaborators to "take a step forward, observe what happens, and then take another step," which produces "a set of radically new shared narratives of alternative possible futures . . . and new working relationships among the protagonists."[23] The key question in trying out possibilities, as critical race scholar Patricia Williams puts it, is "how do we cultivate the muscle of radical imagination needed to dream together beyond fear"? She has connected this insight about creative experimentation to anti-racism work:

> To a very great extent we dream our worlds into being . . . I believe that racism's hardy persistence and immense adaptability are sustained by a habit of human imagination, deflective rhetoric, and hidden license. I believe no less that an optimistic course might be charted, if only we could imagine it.[24]

This is the process Judge Fein was engaging in his court.

However, not all small steps move in the direction of transformative change. Some incremental steps simply appease crusaders for change that something is actually happening and ultimately preserve the status quo. An experiment might sometimes simply replicate the power dynamics that operate in the larger system and thus deepen the polarities built into the anti-racism paradox. Engaging in this strategy in a way that addresses racism thus requires differentiating small steps that reinforce the status quo from those that lay the foundation for larger-scale change.

In the same light, it's crucial to assess whether efforts to address racism in an organization or system are moving in a direction toward larger goals or simply letting off steam. In taking small steps it is important to differentiate quick fixes that reinforce the status quo from the cultivated experiments that lay the foundation for broader transformation. Doing this involves building ongoing reflection and assessment into regular practice, tracking process and progress, and providing accountability for sustained movement in the direction of equity and full participation.

How do we keep our small-scale efforts moving forward and contributing to broader transformation in the face of status quo bias? Meeting these challenges requires building a community of change agents—the fourth and final pillar of paradoxical possibility.

Building a Multiracial Community of Change Agents

What makes it possible for people and organizations undertaking anti-racism work to stay in that work over the long haul? How do people in organizations build connections with others, especially with those experiencing racism, that make it possible to see the whole picture? What supports them in embracing the need to rescript the racial narrative and sticking with the process as they move from system justification to grounded experimentalism? How do they resist acquiescing to the demands of the status quo as they build the conditions that enable change? The response to each of these questions lies in creating and sustaining communities of change agents, both within and outside one's organization, who are in a position to help push for and support needed transformation.

The culture change Judge Fein and his state court system undertook provided the opportunity to experience the power of joining with others to create effective change. The state court's most senior leaders had committed their own time and energy to design, initiate, and participate in this transformative process. Those in the statewide six-month training experienced people in different racial and organizational positions who were ignited by the need for change, and the processes they went through during the training helped cement that commitment to change. They could count on talking regularly with others committed to change about issues relating to race and how they were tackling them in their own workplaces. The understanding they developed in relationships like this informed and deepened their power and reach as change agents. Such a framework for sharing ways of addressing personal and systemic challenges encourages and sustains people in working together to address issues of racism in the culture of their organizations.

As we have seen, as Judge Fein built this community in his own court, people in different racial positions and roles got to know each other as people and to learn together how to grapple with the challenges of racism they all faced in their work. Until then, judges had mostly interacted with judges (who were mostly white), clerks with clerks (who were also mostly white), court officers with court officers, administrative assistants with each other, and so on. Many of the participants had never before heard, much less understood, what people in different racial and organizational positions were experiencing in their everyday interactions. And now, together, they were facing issues of institutionalized racism.

Careful attention was paid to creating an environment that encouraged people to speak openly and confront the contradictions that surfaced, while providing them with opportunities to increase their racial awareness and communication tools that enabled them to learn with and from each other. They shared the reasons that led them to work for the trial court and to participate in the workshop, along with the fears that had prevented them from discussing sensitive issues, particularly race. The dialogue shifted back and forth from focusing explicitly on race and racism to addressing problems of more general concern. One of the participants, a woman of color, said something many in the group could relate to: "I want to feel like I belong in this workplace. I don't want to work in an environment where people stab each other in the back, where no one cares about how others in the office are doing." Both within and between meetings, participants shared stories and perspectives. It is this kind of community environment that allows for insights and possibilities that support people in a workplace to begin making inroads into anti-racism.

Building this kind of community of concerned individuals allows people to come together and directly confront racism in their organization. And it lays the foundation for the necessary broad participation in long-term culture change. In this context, Judge Fein's understanding of his role as a judge began to include responsibility for addressing racism and advancing full participation as part of his regular work. He could collaborate with others in the system to achieve goals he couldn't pursue on his own, and he now knew that he could work toward the goals he had become a judge to advance. And his supportive community of change agents now included other judges who had combined their responsibilities on the bench with efforts to address systemic inequities, as well as members of the court at every level.

Although the six-month leadership workshop that launched Judge Fein's commitment to anti-racism did not itself produce culture change in the court system, he was able to see it as a small-scale version of what he hoped could develop in the trial court overall. He'd had the chance to build trust with Black and Brown people directly affected by racism and to learn about his own position in the racial narrative. He'd observed this multiracial group's commonalities amid their differences in perspective and position. He'd developed his own personal "board of directors"—a group of people who shared his values and were willing to be "loving critics" who would speak up when they observed issues with his conduct and whom he could consult when he confronted racism or resistance to change in his court system.[25] He'd built an informal working group within his own courthouse and could enlist them in identifying and brainstorming about barriers to full participation that were within their reach to address.

The workshop had prepared members of that group to deal head-on with complex problems that Judge Fein had previously sidestepped: What do you do when issues of race come up in the context of a case? How do you recruit people of color to work in the court system when their community does not trust that system? How do you involve people in that community in designing ways to deal with conflict that they might be in a better position to address? Although they did not feel ready to solve these problems for the institution as a whole, they were ready to take small steps in that direction in their own court.

While Judge Fein created his community of change agents essentially from the top down, initiating and guiding the process, communities of change agents have also coalesced within organizations among those who have mobilized change from the bottom up. These could be groups organized by race, shared interest in organizational change, or both. Groups like this can provide a context of support for people who are struggling to navigate the contradictions they face related to racial identity in their workplace or in the challenges they face in their roles in anti-racism work in an organization. They can also operate as fractals, creating experiments that explore the kind of culture and organization members want to see, and then using that to energize broader institutional experimentation and change.

As I have learned from my participation in a group of white change agents engaged in advancing anti-racism, support and accountability groups made up of those who share racial and/or cultural identity can be invaluable in helping those engaged in anti-racism work stick with the work in the face of challenges, learn from each other's failures and successes, and stay accountable while taking risks. Support groups like this might be formed within an organization, but sometimes change agents seeking to disrupt racism can only find support outside the structure of their own organization to develop strategies that might act as levers to initiate the needed change. Joining with others, they can develop the insights and creativity to envision new possibilities and get the support they need to implement them.

This is how the Liberal Arts Diversity Officers (LADO) Consortium got started. Shirley Collado and Mike Reed founded this racially diverse consortium to address the frustration they had experienced in their work as diversity officers in liberal arts colleges. Shirley and Mike envisioned LADO as "a convener, a bridge, a force that brings different minds and activists together to do things that they couldn't do themselves." LADO is now comprised of people from across the country in positions responsible for promoting diversity, equity, inclusion, and belonging in the liberal arts colleges where they work. Each of them had run into a wall of contradictions in their own institutions. While they had formal responsibility for increasing and addressing diversity, they had little authority to effect real change. Even though diversity was part of their institutions' rhetoric, it never seemed important enough to prioritize actions to support it. As these change agents together acknowledged and confronted the limitations in their roles, they figured out ways to use their collective power to create openings for change in each of their institutions.

LADO's role in catalyzing and supporting transformation within participating institutions led its members to build and fund cross-institutional initiatives for change. One effort involved a ten-year collaboration among liberal arts colleges and research universities, funded by the Mellon Foundation, called the Creating Connections Consortium. C3 (as it came to be known) aimed to increase full participation on the faculties of liberal arts colleges, which had struggled to attract faculty of color from research universities. Shirley Collado remembered initially asking, "What if we thought way bigger than our places [colleges] and started thinking about the solution, about the whole pathway . . . providing these connecting points, [since] very few research universities were even advising their graduate students of color around all of these things?" C3 became a cross-institutional collaboration that built relationships across these institutions and provided mentorship, information, fellowships, and support at each step along the pathway into the professoriate. C3's final report summarized the results:

From 2013 to 2023, C3 supported the professional development of nearly 2,600 participants from 70 [higher education institutions]. Of the 103 undergraduate fellows who have graduated, seven have received PhDs, 14 have received either a JD or master's degree, and 22 are current PhD students. At the time of this report, C3 postdoctoral fellows have obtained tenure-track positions at an astonishing rate of 83 percent (24 of 29), and half are currently at liberal arts colleges (LACs). Notably, all C3 LACs now employ a greater percentage of racialized faculty members.

Shirley Collado attributed this success to the multiracial, cross-institutional community of practice that C3 developed: "Partnerships are really what propelled the beginning of C3; the vision has always been collaborative, an increase in faculty hiring across the participating institutions, along with the placement of a diverse group of postdoctoral students into tenure-track faculty positions."

And yet, C3 also revealed the challenge of attempting transformational change at the institutional scale when authority is decentralized and accountability is lacking. As Collado later observed, "A big barrier to all of this [is] the governance structures and requirements. . . . So that's a big thing to think about: What sets of practices really move the needle, which we learned from C3, that need to be fundamentally addressed? In other words, we must continue to reimagine how we conduct business on our campuses so that the processes and outcomes value all constituents."[26] LADO has continued to support its members in pushing for culture change on their campuses, at a time when the entire DEI field is under siege.

Like LADO's effort to increase full participation in liberal arts colleges, Judge Fein's court system continues to be a work in progress. As is true of its surrounding culture, entrenched racial disparities remain, undermining the quality of justice and the legitimacy of the system. As he knows, the kind of change needed to approach a genuinely equitable and just system will require sustaining the change process for decades, weathering leadership changes and the inevitable slide toward retrenchment. The promise lies in viewing the culture change initiatives as launching pads rather than destinations.

The four practices identified in this chapter to support the work of anti-racism, though each daunting in and of itself, actually work in synergy. Building the capacity to live with contradictions and complexity makes it possible to stay involved in the face of mistakes and setbacks. What is learned through that process can support the need and desirability of committing to rescripting the narrative over the long run. Small wins along the way help build momentum and staying power. And supporting each other in community is an essential driving force for undertaking, learning from, and navigating the paradoxes of anti-racism as we build the narratives that make anti-racist organizations possible, desirable, and worth the struggle.

This chapter has offered the promise of possibility and what it can take, both for individual change agents and for those working in predominantly white institutions, to move forward with change efforts in the face of the paradoxes built into anti-racism work. This possibility of change is evident in the culture change efforts launched in various contexts across the country. But the long history of failed reform efforts attests to the fact that there are many forces working against anti-racism practices in institutions.

The remaining chapters of the book focus on the critical question of how to advance the goal of full participation for individuals and groups pursuing anti-racism in predominantly white organizations. Each chapter offers a different strategy or approach that change agents can use, individually and collectively, to stay on the pathway of paradoxical possibility—bridging opposing perspectives and exercising power and enlisting their institutions in both reimagining themselves and facing up to the ways that they continue to perpetuate racism.

People of color have been at the forefront of the fight for racial equality and full participation, but the question remains: What can motivate white people to embrace this challenge? We turn to that question in the next chapter.

4

Forging Linked Fate

WHEN BRITTON SMITH set out to find Broadway artists with clout and visibility who could help the Broadway Advocacy Coalition get its anti-racism work off the ground, Jeanine Tesori was at the top of his list. A world-renowned, Tony Award–winning composer of Broadway musicals, Jeanine is a white woman with a track record of social justice activism and mentorship of people of color. For years, she had been showing up when it mattered to people of color and long before it became fashionable to be "anti-racist." She talked, wrote, and spoke out about race. She developed new venues that brought people of color and their work into a field that hadn't been taking them and their work seriously. She played a major role in developing two now-thriving projects: Encores Off-Center at New York City Center, which she cofounded to promote change, and A Broader Way, an arts empowerment program for young women. She has used her platform to bring in, mentor, and support people of color and women. Jeanine Tesori is the real deal.

Jeanine and Britton share the view of theater's role in addressing racism that the great Black American playwright August Wilson spoke about in his 1996 speech at the prestigious Theater Communications Group, "The Ground on Which I Stand." Wilson starkly depicted racism's operation in every aspect of the theater industry. As a member of the Black community, Wilson pointed out the intertwined connection between his experiences in theater and in American society as a whole. For both theater and democracy, "the abuse of opportunity and truncation of possibility" for people of color define "the work that is necessary to alter our perceptions of each other and to effect meaningful prosperity for all." In a statement underlining this centuries-old pattern, Wilson continued: "The term black or African American not only denotes race; it denotes condition and carries with it the vestige of slavery and the social segregation and abuse of opportunity so vivid in our memory. . . . The problematic nature of the relationship between white and black for too long led us astray in the fulfillment of our possibilities as a society. We stare at each other across a divide of economics and privilege that has become an encumbrance on black Americans' ability to prosper and on the collective will and spirit of our national purpose."[1]

Wilson coupled his unflinching critique of racism with an unwavering belief in American theater's transformative power. He claimed "the ground of the American theatre on which I am proud to stand," which his artistic ancestors "purchased with their endeavors . . . with their pursuit of the American spirit and its ideals." Wilson believed in American theater's "power to inform about the human condition." He invoked "its power to heal, 'to hold the mirror as 'twere nature,' to the truths we uncover, to the truths we wrestle from uncertain and sometimes unyielding realities." Declaring that "we have to do it together," he called upon those "who are capable of these noble pursuits" to meet "at the crossroads, in equal numbers, prepared to do the work of extending and developing the common ground of the American theatre."[2]

Wilson's message—that the nation's prosperity as a whole depends upon coming together across the racial divide to address the roots of racism—rests on the recognition of how our fate is linked across the racial divide. Fates are linked because the situation of Black and Brown people cannot be remedied without changing the overall rules and power dynamics that affect everyone. While those practices and policies causing "abuses of opportunity and truncation of possibility" might most acutely affect Black and Brown people, they also impinge upon the fate and fulfillment of other groups in ways that have been overlooked or simply accepted. Fates are linked because people who engage in practices that dehumanize others also undermine their own well-being and humanity. The social circumstances diminishing Black and Brown people impoverish the overall well-being of white people as well, and solutions cannot be effectively realized without both groups collaborating, reaching across the divides of different positions, identities, and interests. Prosperity and democracy require this "both/and" approach—*both* confronting racism *and* pursuing full participation for everyone.

In his book *Behind the Mule: Race and Class in African-American Politics*, political scientist Michael Dawson first used the idea of linked fate to explain why Black individuals with different class and geographic positions continue to identify as a cohesive group for purposes of political and social action.[3] Dawson posits that this homogeneity results from the perception that the life chances of an individual Black American depend on the status and fortunes of

Black Americans as a group—in other words, the fate of one person is linked to the fate of the whole group. Political scientists have since adopted the concept of linked fate as a general analytical tool, and social movement activists and change agents have deployed it as an organizing framework to build solidarity.[4] When racial equity efforts seek to mobilize people in different racial positions and with diverse perspectives in support of interdependent interests, reframing those interests in terms of linked fate facilitates the pursuit of a shared agenda without losing the explicit focus on race and racism. In any organization facing issues of racism, recognizing that the fate of whites and nonwhites is interwoven becomes indispensable in discovering a way to sustain anti-racism efforts over the long haul.

When people of different races see that their own well-being, their ability to thrive, and their capacity to realize their values can only be achieved by embracing the "both/and" concerns that lead to fundamental change, they discover the trustworthy "why" that is the prerequisite to effective collaboration across racial divides. Recognizing linked fate serves as a framework for making visible and credible the shared needs and challenges of people occupying different racial positions, without glossing over differences in their interests and power. It also opens up a process by which people of different races and identities can collaborate to address shared needs and challenges as they become apparent, even as they experience the conflict built into these collaborations.

What is it that enables white people and people of color to come together around their linked fate? This question is such an important one, both for white people seeking to address racism and for people of color striving to build a cross-racial coalition. What is it that would lead white people to be willing to make change, to see that it is in their own interest to tackle racism, and to share the power and resources they currently hold in order to make that happen?

This chapter explores what supports the development of linked fate and the challenges involved in perceiving and trusting that process and perspective. This exploration then culminates with three conceptual tools that help people of different races come together around their linked fates and bridge the challenges and polarities built into anti-racism efforts so that the work they do together can bring about transformative change. These three tools are:

- the miner's canary: learning how the experiences of people of color reveal concerns that affect everyone in an organization

- the solidarity dividend: identifying shared benefits that can be reaped by coming together across race
- stretch collaboration: facing the necessity of working together despite racial distrust as the only way to avoid irreparable harm to values each group holds dear.

White People and Linked Fate

For white people at the bottom of the economic and social hierarchy, the connection between their interests in fundamental change and those of people of color may seem easier to make and believe. For example, in *Practical Radicals: Seven Strategies to Change the World*, Deepak Bhargava and Stephanie Luce describe a convening, organized by Community Change in 2008 when Deepak was serving as executive director, that brought together "an unusual coalition of grassroots groups working with different constituencies and issues under the frame of 'linked fate.'" Deepak was deeply moved by how "white rural farmers connected their own experience of struggle to that of undocumented workers. Both were harmed by the same set of U.S. trade policies. These shared stories forged a new sense of 'we.'"[5]

Many of the white law students who are most committed to anti-racist work have shared with me that they have experienced poverty and hardship growing up and have come to see a direct connection between the dynamics of racism and those that perpetuated their own impoverishment. And I have heard over and over from some of my white students and colleagues most committed to addressing racism in the criminal legal system that their interest has arisen directly from having a family member or close friend who has experienced incarceration. Ironically, it has been the exponential increase in overall rates of incarceration in the United States, rooted in a racist narrative, that has led to more white people being directly affected by this oppressive system and coming to see their interests bound to those of Black and Brown people who have historically been targeted by the criminal legal system.

Prison abolitionist Ruth Wilson Gilmore, and author of *Golden Gulag*, powerfully illustrates linked fate at work in her analysis of police violence: "Behind the sturdy curtain of racism that makes killing after killing after killing of Black people newsworthy, noteworthy, and yet not change anything, the police are killing lots of other people too. If we can stop the police from killing Black people, other people won't be killed."[6] In *The Sum of Us*, author and policy expert Heather McGhee points out that policies and practices based in racism act against the interests of all involved. This "racial bargain," as she terms it, "distorts our politics, drains our economy, and erodes everything Americans have in common, from our schools to our air to our infrastructure."[7]

What about the realization of linked fate by white people who occupy positions of relative power and privilege? Jeanine Tesori's story provides some clues about what linked fate looks like and how it develops for those who look like they might have more to lose by dismantling racialized power structures. Asked in an interview about the source of her interest in anti-racism, Jeanine spoke about her early childhood experiences of feeling like an outsider herself.[8] "I had Amblyopia, so one of my eyes turned in completely, and I had glasses at 2 and an eyepatch, and it made me incredibly tough on the playground. I knew as a kid that I was ugly, everyone affirmed it, and so I got a really great sense of humor because of it." She became an observer of behavior from a young age. "I was looking at the world literally through glasses and an eyepatch."[9]

Jeanine also grew up in a "really strict, very difficult household," often butting heads with her father. But she also saw and got from him the importance of the pursuit of excellence and a practice of empathy that would shape her entire orientation. A physician with a home office, her father opened their family home to people who were too sick to go to the hospital. "He always said, 'The hospital would kill them; I have to watch them.'" That often meant that "we would go downstairs and sleep on the couch. It was not a big deal. That's what you do. It's a value system I learned." It's not uncommon for white people in positions of privilege who genuinely care about racial justice to trace their commitment to their early life experiences with family members—through experiencing trauma that taught them lessons of empathy (as in my case) or through witnessing their parents' religious principles, spirituality, political activism, or professional integrity.

"The thing that has always interested me," Jeanine observed, "is the invisible person—the person who society has deemed not worthy of being the protagonist, someone not worthy of holding the center." Jeanine learned herself to be willing to be visible, having been taught to "really lean backwards—to do my thing, be in the background, and not call attention to myself." It was through her encounter with two inspiring Black performers—Lena Horne and Linda Twine, who would become her mentor—that Jeanine learned the importance of really being present. When Jeanine was nineteen, she saw Linda Twine conduct. "She is this beautiful African American woman who was in complete command with all of the men on stage looking at her every move, and then I knew it was all possible. I had never seen anything like it in my life. And I just thought, what is this? I want to be a part of that." The rest of her career has been a process—through both her artistry and her activism—of pursuing the complexity, contradictions, and joys of engaging with the stories of outsiders "trying to find their way in who have been bruised by the system."[10] Her own sense of purpose and fulfillment took her down the path of grappling with racism as an integral part of her work.

How Jeanine's commitment to racial equity developed, and what it meant for how she approached her role as a white composer, is beautifully illustrated by the story of her involvement with the opera *Blue*, "an intimate portrayal of a Black family living in Harlem, whose world is ripped apart when they become victims of a gross injustice."[11] This project began when Jeanine was commissioned, for the third time, by Francesca Zambello, Glimmerglass Festival General and Artistic Director, to write an opera. For this commission, Jeanine recalled, "she just said, 'I want a really political opera.' She knew that my appetite was for complicated issues and trying to find out what's dangling at the end of them."[12] Agreeing that the opera would address contemporary issues surrounding race, Francesca emailed Tazewell Thompson, a Black director and playwright with five NAACP Awards and two Emmy nominations, asking for his ideas on a list of possible librettists. At that time, in 2016, aware of the same events and experiences that had given rise to the Broadway Advocacy Coalition, Tazewell was feeling, as he would later recall, "traumatized, depressed, disgusted, angry, in fear of getting up in the morning and walking through the streets of Manhattan. I felt more than ever that I was a moving target." For him, "the opportunity to write the libretto for this opera . . . felt like fate."[13] Although he had directed opera, this would be his first libretto. Instead of recommending others for the job, he responded, "What about me?"

Rejecting the well-worn and exclusionary path of requiring prior experience before giving someone their first opportunity at something new, Jeanine asked to meet with Tazewell. She listened, read the work he'd done as a playwright, and learned about his experience as a Black man growing up and living in Harlem. It was, in Tazewell's words, "a match." Based on their conversations, some of which revealed Tazewell's personal experience, they decided to create an opera that would tell the story of a Black family living in Harlem.

"Around the same time," Jeanine recalled, "I was doing a lot at the Columbia Law School and with the Broadway Advocacy Coalition." Through that work, which included a concert accompanied by workshops and panels, she met and spoke with Black police officers and heard personal stories about what they

called the "blue line for people of color in uniform." She described her experience to Tazewell: "I've not seen that story before, of an officer of the law who
is also part of the community, and what happens to them when they're not in
uniform."[14] Instead of having the father be a jazz saxophone player, Jeanine
asked, "What if the main character is a cop?" Tazewell's initial response was,
"Absolutely not. I did not want to write about a police officer." He went on,
"But despite myself, I soon recognized the irony, the tension, the glittering
possibilities of personal conflict and heartache for a father whose son is murdered by a fellow officer," and the story became about, in Tazewell's words, "a
Black man in Blue."[15]

Jeanine observed with excitement that "*Blue* became an opera with ten
people and all are opera singers of color." In the process, *Blue* also became a
vehicle for engaging with opera's contradictions. In Jeanine's words, "This
opera is about being part of the solution *and* part of the problem." *Blue* provided a vehicle for reaching white audiences while transforming opera itself,
embracing all that made it a medium that could have an impact. "We were
bringing an epic story to the epic stage of the opera, which honors the epic
nature, the joy and tragedy of these stories. There was a time in opera where
it was just the gods that were brought on, and then it was mortals, but then it
was only some mortals. And now what we're asking of opera is to look at all
mortals, to really look at contemporary life with its joy and its tragedy, and
bring that to the operatic stage." Jeanine feels "a pull to the epic story, and to
people I feel have maybe not gotten equal time downstage center. I'm really
interested in that, in seeing people have agency. What this ended up being was
more Greek than I thought it would, because I don't know that a Black man in
this country doesn't have his fate somewhat sealed." She hoped that the opera
"might reveal that and make us wonder."[16]

Keith Kellogg, who played the father in *Blue*, took this a step further:
"I think that the significance of this piece really lies in the opportunity for our
audiences that are predominantly white to have this experience and see things
from our perspective and how we really are seen as people of color in America." *Blue* also changed Keith's perspective of what opera could be. "I've been
singing and I've been singing for years, and I've been all over the world singing.
And opera just became a routine. And then we were hearing all the news about
Black bodies being killed and police violence. Here I was, traveling the world
doing all these amazing things while people who looked like me were being
murdered." Keith had even considered quitting opera because "it wasn't serving a purpose for me." But, he said, "*Blue* changed that for me—knowing that

I could tell a story like this and it reached typical opera audiences who don't get to feel this."[17] As a story that "exposes the systemic racism that seeps into everyday American life like poison," for both Jeanine and Tazewell, "*Blue* is a story that needs to be told in the opera world."[18]

Jeanine and Tazewell became not only collaborators but also close friends. She learned from his personal experience of racism as a Black gay man in America and his powerful narrative drawing on the work of James Baldwin, Ta-Nehisi Coates, and Claude Brown: "This story is rightfully his. The poetry in *Blue* comes from Tazewell's heart." Tazewell also contributed stories he learned by consulting friends, Black and white, asking them, "How do you prepare a son for what awaits him? Do you have 'the talk' about how to survive and thrive from day to day? All the Black parents said yes. The white ones said it had never even entered their thoughts." Tazewell shared that, working with Jeanine, he refined the craft of writing an opera libretto: "I learned how to edit rambling sentences down to select bites that would allow the music to enter, how counterpoint is used, and the dramatic musical effect of repeating lines and using active verbs." And Jeanine used her musical technique and skills to "harness the power of the narrative as it meets the music" and to "spotlight the multi-layered story in the opera of this family's experience."[19]

Jeanine and Tazewell also traveled around the country as part of a series called *Breaking Glass: Hyperlinking Opera and Issues*, a five-episode podcast that explores social justice through the lens of opera. Together, they spoke with audiences about police violence and racism, and about the role of music and opera in tackling these issues. Jeanine described the impact this had on her: "We went to all of these cities discussing blackness in white spaces, particularly African American involvement in something like opera, which is typically Euro-centric." For Jeanine, "it just cracked the world open. I was the only person not of color on the panels. It was great to have to just shut up and listen and learn; it's really changed me."[20] Jeanine emphasized the importance of her own humility in the collaboration: "I had to open my ears and know this is not my story." Jeanine prefers that publicity center on Tazewell, not her. "My job on this is to illuminate what I think this sounds like, but I am not the author of this story." Jeanine is absolutely clear that "Tazewell has the underlying rights to the story because it is connected to his experience in the world. That, to me, is what reparations looks like."[21]

Jeanine's story demonstrates what it looks like for a white person to become deeply engaged in and integral to a project that involves race and to use her power, her platform, her gifts to create the space for the leadership, stories, and voices of Black people. That cross-racial collaboration made it possible for a story about racism to tackle racism and, in the process, to transform the medium of opera itself.

Author and anti-racist facilitator Frances Kendall writes in *Understanding White Privilege* that white people must take on racial equity work "because our lives depend on it—our physical, psychological, spiritual, and economic lives."[22] At certain points in history, white power holders have come to this realization. The Kerner Commission, a largely white group convened by President Lyndon Johnson in the wake of racial uprisings that swept the country in 1967, warned white America that pursuing its present course, yielding "two societies, one black, one white—separate and unequal," would sustain "the continuing polarization of the American community and, ultimately, the destruction of basic democratic values."[23] When white people heed this warning and see their fate bound up with that of people of color, transformative change becomes possible.

The story of Jeanine and Tazewell attests to that possibility. It is one example of successful cross-racial collaborations sustained by mutual recognition of linked fate. Before probing what enables organizations to create conditions fostering this kind of long-term commitment to just, inclusive, and anti-racist institutions, it's important to identify cross-racial collaborations that get stuck in the anti-racism paradoxes and end up preserving the racial status quo.

Short-Term Self-Interest vs. Long-Term Linked Fate

It is a Thursday evening in the late fall of 2021, and I am in a Zoom meeting with a group of white people involved with the creation and production of a play that had enjoyed a long run on Broadway until the Covid-19 pandemic shut everything down. Lee, an award-winning writer for Broadway and the author of that play, had reached out to me during that long shutdown after hearing me speak on a panel in June 2021. That event, titled "What Now Part II: From Ally to Action," was an online forum organized by the Broadway Advocacy Coalition as part of its series aimed at building momentum to address racism in the theater industry.[24] Lee told me he had attended the forum to try to understand more about the issues being brought up because one of his own productions had recently been pinpointed as a locus of racist practices. Our conversation would lead to that Zoom call in the fall of 2021 when Broadway was opening again, and Lee and the group of concerned white artists involved with the play he had brought together wanted to know how to address these ongoing issues.

This examination of racist practices on Broadway had been set in motion a little more than a year earlier, in June 2020, by the publication of an online letter, "We See You, White American Theater." Forged by some of the most prominent and respected Black and Brown artists in theater, and prompted by the national racial reckoning following George Floyd's murder, that letter had focused on the entrenched racism evident at all levels of the industry.

While the letter attested to the authors' continued commitment to the importance of the American theater, it was also calling out white theater makers for their role in perpetuating "the ongoing national assault on Black bodies, Black artistry, and Black values." Standing together in the legacy of August Wilson's "The Ground on Which I Stand," the letter was turning a spotlight on practices that "un-challenge white privilege, inviting us to traffic in the very racism and patriarchy that festers in our bodies while we protest against it on your stages." More than just a statement clarifying the issue, the letter presented a twenty-nine-page list of demands, including equitable BIPOC presence and acknowledgment both on- and backstage, an anti-racism code of conduct along with ongoing training and enforcement for violations, equitable hiring practices, changes in directorial, programming, and curatorial practices in order to credit BIPOC work, and changes in funding, compensation, budgetary transparency, and parity.[25]

When Lee first read the "We See You" letter, he recognized its searing truth and had joined in the righteous indignation it expressed. The problems of racism and the efforts to address it were not new in his life. His parents had been activists in the civil rights movement, and when he was growing up, his family's dinner table conversation had often included the topic of racism. In college, he'd joined many demonstrations against racism and police brutality. In his earlier professional work, Lee had contributed time and money to events that used theater to focus attention on racism. He thought of racism as something other people did and experienced and of himself as part of the solution rather than part of the problem. Lee was, he believed, on the right side of history, in a position to act on behalf of the "victims" of racism.

After the publication of the "We See You" letter, Lee had attended protests, donated money to the Black Lives Matter movement, and spoken out publicly about racism in the theater industry. He had been about to announce his allyship with the letter writers when Black and Brown members of the company producing his current show sent a letter of their own to the production team,

documenting similar experiences and demanding change. That letter impli-
cated Lee in indignities and erasures that had been happening under his watch.
Black and Brown actors had received notes from white directors of the show
saying that they should act less "urban" and play their roles the same way their
white predecessors had. The suggestions of Black artists for how roles written
for people of color could be more authentic had been disregarded. And en-
semble members of color who were experiencing unsafe and racist conditions
had learned that they had nowhere to go with their concerns other than to the
all-white management, who had already shown that those with complaints
about racism would risk being labeled as troublemakers difficult to work
with. While this letter had not yet been posted on social media, the signatories
made clear that in the absence of concrete action, it would be, which would
expose the letter's targets—high-profile white writers, directors, and producers—
to the glare of the public spotlight.

Lee reached out to several people of color in the production to apologize
for what they had experienced and for his part in allowing it to happen. He
expressed his solidarity with their cause, asking if they could meet to talk. To
his dismay, one of them responded on behalf of the group, saying that given
the white leadership's past failure to take any action to address the racism that
Black people and other people of color had experienced on a daily basis in his
play's production, they didn't feel comfortable meeting with him and the other
members of the all-white creative team until they did their own work. That
was when Lee contacted me, remembering the online forum where I had described my own efforts to navigate these challenges and hoping I could help
him and other members of the all-white creative team process the letter and
figure out what they could do to bridge the chasm exposed by their colleagues
of color.

During our first conversation, it became apparent to both of us that when
Lee approached his colleagues of color, his concerns revolved around a desire
to feel better about himself and to relieve the discomfort accompanying his
guilt and fear. His initial questions were based on what some have referred
to as "virtue signaling"—publicly demonstrating that he was a good white
person. They were essentially focused on: "What can I do to let the people of
color in my production know about my efforts behind the scenes to push management? And how can I communicate that I am on their side?"

Such initial reactions are common for white people, who have grown up in
largely white spaces set up and led by white people (parents, teachers, politicians, religious leaders, etc.). Even though Lee, in his position as a playwright,

had shared space and time with Black actors, like Judge Fein his usual day-to-day interactions exposed him primarily to white people and white culture. So, despite his personal history of responding to racial inequity, his power and privilege insulated him from seeing and understanding the issues faced by people of color in his productions and his own role in perpetuating those issues. As a result, in response to his apologies and requests for dialogue, the people of color in his production conveyed that "once again the white folks are managing to focus the attention on themselves."

In *Why Are All the Black Kids Sitting Together in the Cafeteria*, Beverly Daniel Tatum, renowned psychologist and former president of Spelman College, summarizes a body of research documenting the developmental mindsets that white people experience as they become cognizant of their place in the cycle of racism. At that point, shame and fear like Lee's would be a predictable stage in white identity development—the experience that unfolds for white people when they begin understanding "what it means to be white in a race conscious society."[26] Tatum notes that when white people become aware of their own racial identity and the degree to which racism has affected their lives and those of people of color, they typically experience racial stress, accompanied by a desire to avoid this discomfort and return to blissful ignorance. In the same vein, decades earlier James Baldwin had pointed out that white Americans regard racism as "a disastrous, continuing, present condition which menaces them, and for which they bear an inescapable responsibility. But since, in the main, they lack the energy to change this condition, they would rather not be reminded of it."[27]

In the months following the letter demanding change, the management of the company doing his show—in part prompted by Lee's urging—hired a diversity consultant and held listening sessions with company members of color. But to those seeking significant change, these seemed to be largely cosmetic gestures, aimed at simply checking "the diversity efforts box" while leaving in place an all-white leadership structure and unilateral decision making that prevented meaningful accountability leading to change in policy. It appeared that the "White American Theater" had taken refuge in the safest course of action—staying out of the line of fire with the hope of eventually returning to "normal." The theater company management's response to the letter only further fueled overall distrust of white leadership's willingness to take responsibility for genuine change.

Racial justice scholar Derrick Bell exposes the disingenuousness of efforts like this, pointing out that they are operating on what he calls "the interest-convergence principle," assuring that "the interest of blacks in achieving racial equality will be accommodated only when it converges with the interest of whites."[28] This dynamic predisposes white people to cooperate only so long as they believe that it is in their narrow self-interest, jumping ship when they have to share some aspect of their power, entitlement, or privilege. They may proclaim shared interest with those calling for diversity, equity, and inclusion, but when white people believe that the change will cost them resources, limit their power, or push them beyond their comfort zone, they willingly sacrifice the well-being of people of color to advance their own self-esteem and security. Bell's interest-convergence principle makes it unsurprising that the management in charge of Lee's production were fine with diversity as long as it contributed to the production's marketability and attracted broader audiences without resulting in any "loss, inconvenience, or upset to themselves or other whites."[29]

In a *Harvard Business Review* article titled "Getting Serious about Diversity: Enough Already with the Business Case," Robin Ely and David Thomas conclude that most companies touting the business case for diversity have instead adopted a "simplistic and empirically unsubstantiated version" that does not do the hard work required to achieve a learning orientation. Organizational leaders who likewise promote the "business case for diversity" have been known to draw the line when proposed programs give rise to calls for changes in resource allocation, hiring practices, decision making, and accountability. Moreover, Ely and Thomas warn, "when company diversity statements emphasize the economic payoffs, people from underrepresented groups start questioning whether the organization is a place where they really belong, which reduces their interest in joining it."[30] When diversity programs are set up to pursue short-term profitability, benefiting the "haves" at the expense of the "have nots," it's no wonder that many Black people distrust white people's self-proclaimed allyship. Such white-centered policies undermine the cross-racial trust needed to identify and pursue linked fate.

Lee's initial paralysis in the face of contradictions he could not resolve might have led him to conclude, as had so many others, that there was no workable response for him to make as a white person in a leadership position except to seek comfort in a narrow definition of his role and responsibility. Not recognizing the paradox of racialized power would keep him stuck on one side of the polarity. Retreating to the sidelines in the face of uncertainty and racial stress would be an example of what author Robin DiAngelo calls "white fragility," the tendency of white people to react defensively when accused of racism and simply withdraw.[31] And yet, naming and rejecting the option of retreat doesn't help white people figure out how to move forward constructively in the face of unavoidable contradictions.

Lee genuinely wanted to join his Black colleagues in pushing for anti-racist practices, but he was caught in the crosscurrents often faced by white people in leadership positions. Pulled in conflicting directions, he wondered if he should just step back. He said, "I've witnessed so many conversations in Zoom rooms where white leadership in the theater world, afraid to do the wrong thing, are admitting that they're now reluctant to say or do anything." But for Lee, failing to notice and act to address the experiences of those around him is what got him in trouble in the first place, leaving him feeling that if he didn't take action he would be, in some significant way, failing himself.

Despite the temptation to withdraw, Lee knew he had to remain engaged. Besides his genuine concern for the well-being of people of color in the company presenting his work, he also realized that his integrity depended upon facing up to his own place in the hierarchy named in the letter. He couldn't simply retreat to the sidelines and try to avoid the issue. But where and how would he start? "Maybe I could threaten to close the show. Or I could go public with these concerns, and if that had an impact on the show's financial success, that could give me some leverage. But I don't have enough of a relationship with people of color in the production to find out what they might even want me to do." How could he deepen his own and others' understanding of what needed to be done?

Lee had reached a crossroads much like the one many well-intentioned white people face when they attempt to address racism in their predominantly white institutions. How can they address problems they don't understand, especially if those experiencing racism firsthand don't trust them enough to speak frankly about those experiences? And could staying engaged require a level of power and resource sharing that white people in power might not be willing or able to sustain? For the group of white people in his production that Lee had pulled together to consider these issues, the questions became focused on how they could learn to bridge the gulf revealed in the "We See You" letters and how their collaboration would affect the production as a whole.

As Lee had learned, neither he nor the system he was part of had developed ways to interact with those directly affected by racism that could generate more workable solutions. Before changes could be instituted that would effectively address these interwoven concerns, trust had to be built among all those involved. In any organization addressing racist practices, a shift in perspective in the direction of linked fate depends on developing relationships of trust, yet such changes can be difficult to bring about and sustain, as we saw in chapter 3, especially when the inevitable challenges and contradictions surface.

Becoming Trustworthy

How does trust develop in the context of the distrust born out of experience? As political economist Charles Sabel observed in "Studied Trust: Building New Forms of Cooperation in a Volatile Economy," "if trust is absent, no one will risk moving first, and all will sacrifice the gains of cooperation to the safe, if less remunerative, autonomous pursuit of self-interest."[32] When groups facing mutual threats or challenges hold a tradition of suspicion about each other, whether grounded in history or stereotypes, how can they come to see the other as trustworthy enough to explore and act together on their linked fate? How can they learn rather than run from their collective past so that they can reinterpret their relationship going forward and cooperate, notwithstanding the inevitable tensions and risks experienced by everyone involved?

People of color face a double bind when it comes to trusting and collaborating with white people who express interest in anti-racism work. Changing systems and cultures that disadvantage them cannot occur without the efforts and cooperation of white people, and yet that interaction carries considerable risk. As Adam Kahane points out in *Collaborating with the Enemy*, alongside one dictionary definition of collaboration—"to work jointly with"—is the other more sinister one: "to cooperate treacherously with the enemy." It can be dangerous to cooperate with people you do not trust, whose interests and perspectives are different from and even contradictory to your own, and who might exercise their own power to maintain benefits for themselves from the conditions and practices that you seek to change. Collaboration also risks being co-opted or losing the ability to push for change in other more confrontational ways if dialogue fails.[33] The specter of racial discrimination lurking behind these efforts makes cross-racial collaboration risky. There is always the chance that the initial optimism will fade into yet another episode of unacknowledged racism, with the dispiriting, even retraumatizing, sense of futility when white people end up continuing to hold onto power.

But people of color interested in transforming predominantly white institutions cannot achieve their goals only through protest, exit, or coercion. They must interact with white people who have the power to change the rules, or at least with the institutions and policies they have historically put in place. This is the unavoidable paradox of racialized power at work. In *Sister Outsider*, Audre Lorde warns against retreating into isolation and despair, acknowledging that tackling racism, sexism, and homophobia means "doing the unromantic and tedious work necessary to forge meaningful coalitions, and it means recognizing which coalitions are possible and which coalitions are not."[34]

Lasting cross-racial collaborations require willingness on the part of (at least some) white people in power to take steps necessary to build trust. And this requires, as legal scholar Martha Minow points out, that "the majority itself changes by sharing power, accepting the members of the minority as equal participants and resisting the temptation to attribute as personal inadequacies the legacy of disadvantage experienced by the group."[35] This change happens when a group of white people in an institution come to understand the perspective of their nonwhite colleagues and begin to explore how they themselves might be shortchanged by clinging to narrow self-interest. Lee realized that his own writing would remain inauthentic and offensive to an audience he really wanted to reach unless people of color were full participants in the creative process, and that the responsibility for calling out management's prioritizing of the bottom line over the health and safety of company members extended beyond people of color to him. When white participants reinterpret their interests as aligned with those of people of color, as Jeanine Tesori did, they take steps toward becoming trustworthy collaborators willing and able to work jointly and mutually with people of color in a leap across the trust divide.

Yet how do people in an organization work together across race to identify common concerns and aspirations when they can't trust each other enough to reveal what they most deeply care about but when that vulnerability itself requires trust? As those who study how trust develops have shown, trust is not a static or unchanging quality but can be cultivated and grow through interaction that changes the narrative and assumptions that have produced mistrust.

For Lee, building trust with his colleagues of color had to begin with himself and his relationship with his white colleagues. Taking responsibility first for learning about racism in his company and working through his own fear and shame helped him uncover more trustworthy values and motivations for engaging in anti-racism work. This led him to identify and invite into the learning process white people he trusted, those who had also expressed concern about the issues of racism raised in the letter and who genuinely cared about the integrity of productions on Broadway and the quality of life of those involved in them. This group that Lee convened began meeting regularly to discuss situations each of them had experienced or observed themselves and to learn together from publicly available sources about how racism operated in the theater industry. They recognized that they could not ask their colleagues of color to treat them as allies without first increasing their own racial literacy to develop a better understanding of the experience of people of color in their productions. They read books and posts, watched videos, listened to podcasts, and discussed past racialized interactions they had tolerated without question. They started to brainstorm about what they, as concerned white people, could do to support change in their own situations. This willingness to take responsibility for what they didn't know, and to build their own racial literacy without expecting or relying on their colleagues of color to educate them, was an important basic step in cross-racial trust building.

Over several months of exploration, Lee and his white colleagues in this group discovered how little they knew not only about decisions that affected the quality of their productions but also about the quality of life of most of those involved at all levels in their Broadway productions. They had simply accepted the usual practices and policies as the norm. But now, together, they were taking the crucial step of owning up to the legitimacy of the accusations and distrust detailed in the "We See You" letters, acknowledging their own past failure to act. They recognized that up to that point, they had been inviting people of color into a conversation set up and led by those in power, those who saw the world from a predominantly white perspective. They saw that they had been making unilateral decisions about how to address issues of race without involving those directly affected.

This process enabled Lee and his group to move beyond defensiveness and narrowly defined self-interest and begin to see the situation from the perspective of their Black and Brown colleagues. As Lee considered what he might have done to contribute to the issues they had raised, he thought back to the negotiation of his contract when he overlooked the opportunity to insist on more equitable casting as part of the deal. In fact, it hadn't even occurred to him. He also revisited the script he wrote from the vantage point of the letter writers and realized the legitimacy of their authenticity concerns. He hadn't consulted with, much less enlisted, a cowriter of color as part of the process, nor had he checked in with Black and Brown actors about their experience performing the script.

After their extensive self-reflection and education, the members of this group realized that the next step in their process would be to find a way to meet with interested colleagues of color. The initial meeting of the interracial group that convened was facilitated by an artist of color trusted by everyone in the group, who set up a Zoom conversation once he learned about the work already undertaken by Lee and his white colleagues. Together, they established ground rules for their interactions to ensure that anyone who experienced marginalization or threats to their identity due to their race would be respected and have agency over when and how to participate. This shift in how the rules of the road were developed and practiced helped build what social psychologists Valerie Purdie-Greenaway, Claude Steele, and colleagues call "identity safety." Establishing that Black and Brown racial identity would be valued in the situation was basic in building trust.[36]

The dialogue started by establishing that together, the group would be confronting issues of race and power within their own interactions, within their theater companies, and in the industry as a whole. In the initial meetings, white participants asked their Black and Brown colleagues what they wanted and needed from the dialogue, and the group built its agenda around those responses. Lee's white cohort shared concrete information about what they had been doing, including questioning their own actions and inaction. They reported that they had learned to listen differently—not to defend themselves or decide how to fix things but rather with an ear toward genuinely understanding what mattered to the Black and Brown colleagues they worked with.

As their meetings continued, Lee and his group listened to what Black and Brown people had experienced in productions they had been part of; they consulted data showing systemic patterns in the industry that negatively affected people of color; and they identified practices that had a negative impact cutting across race. They invited and accepted criticism about their failure in their positions of power to correct inequities and oversights. One of the most important points of feedback for Lee came from a woman of color in the group. She recounted an interaction she'd had with him about a scene in his script that was subtly reproducing racist stereotypes. She said that at the time Lee had responded defensively and brushed aside her concerns, so she decided that her efforts were futile; now she was seeing that something had changed in him. She acknowledged that he was listening differently and inviting the kind of input she had tried to offer earlier, and he was accepting that there were problems with his script stemming from his failure to respond to this kind of mutual exchange in the past. Together, Lee and his white colleagues were recognizing the admittedly contradictory need to step back and accept responsibility for past inactions while at the same time stepping up and taking positive actions grounded in the needs and concerns of those directly affected by such oversights.

These meetings opened the door for everyone in the group to begin re-thinking how their productions could achieve full participation. Accepting responsibility, listening to learn, and staying engaged in the face of criticism and feedback had become their building blocks of trust. Practicing this through repeated and ongoing interaction, they began to rewrite their own piece of the history of American theater.

People of color in the group expressed surprise at the encouraging reactions they were receiving from Lee and his colleagues, noting that they hadn't thought this kind of exchange could even be possible. But could it last? One Black artist wondered aloud "if it's true, or if they were hopping on a ride at an amusement park because it was the thing to do." Everyone in the group knew it would take time for those in positions of power to unlearn past patterns of expecting deference to their perspective and decisions. Building deeper trust in the group would depend on repeated experiences of success in dismantling both the habit and the assumption that white people would treat race as some-one else's problem, would insist on being right, and would inevitably bail out if change became uncomfortable.

In any organization, trust is built by navigating the paradoxical process of requiring collaboration among people who do not trust each other while at the same time engaging in the very collaboration that will itself help build that trust. Initially, trust exists alongside distrust, and collaboration alongside con-flict. As the ability to maintain connection and commitment to doing so are experienced and demonstrated over time, trust grows. As participants remain vulnerable in the face of uncertainty, genuinely seeking to fulfill their inten-tions and their responsibilities to the group, trust grows. The process requires dedication, patience, and a deep recognition that individuals of any color at all levels of an organization are, in Martin Luther King's words, "tied in a single garment of destiny."[37]

The successful process in the group Lee convened exemplifies what Charles Sabel calls "studied trust." When a process of trial, reflection, error, and further reflection ends up forging trusting relationships, a new narrative enables a group to "reinterpret their collective past, and especially their con-flicts, in such a way that trusting cooperation comes to seem a natural feature, at once accidental and ineluctable, of their common heritage."[38] When groups commit to this process, backed by a credible pledge to act on what they are learning, perspectives and values formerly perceived as contradictory can become entry points into the transformation necessary to understand and act on linked fate.

As we saw in the cross-racial collaboration unfolding in the group Lee had convened, discovering linked fate is not a one-shot deal. Lee and his white colleagues had started down this path by reflecting about their own experience as individuals in positions of power, viewing the situation through the lens of history and the perspective of those directly affected by racism. Trust between them and the Black and Brown members of their companies who went through that process with them developed as it became clear that the reflective insights they brought into their conversations were coupled with action. This is what Paolo Freire in *Pedagogy of the Oppressed* calls praxis—"reflection and action on the world to change it."[39] As mutual trust grew in this group, they found themselves moving beyond entrenched positions and into that shared praxis.

As sociologist Roger Gould posited in his book *Insurgent Identities*, collective identities can develop across race and class when people in different racial positions uncover a common set of needs or grievances that undermine each group's thriving and success and discover that these are sufficiently pressing to motivate action.[40] An intentional process of inquiry and action facilitates the development of these collective identities. When systemic inquiry followed by practice followed by further inquiry becomes part of the culture of a cross-racial group or institution, the growing recognition of linked fate serves as the engine of transformation.

Conceptual Tools for Forging Linked Fate

Recognizing racial disparities in an organization can also reveal patterns of injustice or dysfunction affecting everyone, regardless of race. Identifying this level of linked fate can reframe issues to bind together those who care about race and those who care about an issue not explicitly related to race. This framing enables people and organizations aspiring to institutional change to *both* make race central *and* make situations not explicitly connected to race relevant to everyone involved. This "both/and" framework also invites the involvement of those who might not initially participate in or support an effort defined solely in terms of anti-racism. As a driver of transformation, this understanding of both/and can serve everyone in an institution or community, especially as they seek to bridge the polarities built into the anti-racism paradoxes.

The three conceptual tools summarized at the beginning of this chapter can support cross-racial groups in the process of discovering their linked fate: the miner's canary, the solidarity dividend, and stretch collaboration. Each of these approaches provides a way to use linked fate to help people and organizations navigate the anti-racism paradoxes. The perspective offered in the following illustrations can help guide groups stuck in a zero-sum struggle to reframe issues in ways that reveal reasons to act together. They also provide ways of asking questions and analyzing information that inform decisions about where to pursue change, both to have maximum impact and to motivate emerging collectives to work together over the long haul. Exploring each of these in contexts where cross-racial groups forged linked fate offers some guidelines for moving beyond apparent divisions into a cooperation that serves all involved.

The Miner's Canary: What Affects Those Racially Marginalized Affects All

In 1987, when Dr. Freeman Hrabowski was hired by the University of Maryland, Baltimore County (UMBC) as vice provost for academic affairs, he found himself on a campus no one was proud of. He had been recruited to help this predominantly white commuter school, with little research funding and a self-image as a mediocre institution, improve students' academic performance with the goal of making UMBC into a full-fledged research university. During Hrabowski's first week on campus, the administration building was taken over by the Black Student Union, and he began to sense an important aspect of the school's underlying problem. Hearing from a Black secretary that sit-ins like this had been happening every year, Hrabowski set out to learn more about why. Protestors told him that many Black students and faculty viewed their campus as racist and indifferent to the concerns of minorities. They reported that "when black and white students were in the same class, black students typically received lower grades than white students. Since the teacher was white, it must be racism. What else could it be?"[41] White faculty members responded defensively, and the resulting situation threatened to bring about the paralyzing cycle often created by the paradox of racial salience.

As a Black man, Freeman Hrabowski was no stranger to racism. The great-grandson of an enslaved person, Hrabowski was a veteran of civil rights marches, having been spit on and arrested as a child by the infamous Bull Connor in Birmingham, Alabama. He himself had faced barriers of racism and inadequate academic preparation, overcoming them with the help of supportive parents and mentors to obtain his master's in mathematics and his PhD in higher education administration. Hrabowski's personal commitment in all the positions he held in his professional life had been not only to build success in academic institutions but also to increase educational equity—in particular to assure the full participation of Black and Brown people in the fields of science, technology, engineering, and math (STEM). With that intention in mind, he set out to bridge the divides he believed were holding back Black students at UMBC, affecting the community as a whole.

Hrabowski launched a rigorous and systematic inquiry aimed at understanding the source of the problem. He learned that up to that point, no Black student had ever received above a C in a core biology or chemistry class, and almost none had earned an A in any upper-level science course. Recognizing the necessity for the school "to look in the mirror and ask, what are we not doing," Dr. Hrabowski enlisted people at every level of UMBC to investigate the source of the problem. What was undermining Black students' success, and what could be done to enable them to succeed? Rejecting the more typical deficits frame, which would have focused on identifying inadequacies in students' preparation or skill level, the inquiry instead probed the aspects of the overall environment at UMBC that might be contributing to the underperformance of Black students.

Hrabowski and his team undertook a set of data-driven inquiries, looking at the factors and practices promoting achievement for all students and, in particular, for Black students. They examined who was and who wasn't succeeding academically across different disciplines and demographic identities. They looked at what was going on in the classroom, for Black students and for students overall. They assessed the impact of faculty members' expectations of academic success for students and inquired about the kind of support available outside the classroom. They investigated the differential rates of academic and social isolation and the impact of isolation on academic performance for Black students and students in general. They looked at students' access to information about and support for academic success, such as how to develop good study habits, reach out for tutorial assistance, form study groups, and communicate with their teachers. They determined the impact of financial need on academic performance. In the end, this inquiry process revealed the source of the problem not in individual students or faculty but in the institution's culture—the web of norms and practices, which included a system of expectations, rewards, and patterns of interaction that produced the defeatism and racism that affected all students and faculty.

Lani Guinier and Gerald Torres, authors of *The Miner's Canary: Enlisting Race, Resisting Power, Transforming Democracy*, would regard the Black students who had been struggling at UMBC as "canaries in the mine." Just as canaries taken underground by coal miners signaled when the air had become toxic, the experience of Black students at UMBC was revealing a much deeper and pervasive problem affecting all students at the school. By addressing the injustices and indignities experienced by Black people, the system will be better able to live up to its aspirations and values for many others. Guinier and Torres write:

> Those who are racially marginalized are like the miner's canary. Their distress is the first sign of a danger that threatens us all. It is easy enough to think that when we sacrifice this canary, the only harm is to communities of color. Yet others ignore problems that converge around racial minorities at their own peril, for these problems are symptoms warning us that we are all at risk.[42]

As Guinier and Torres point out, issues affecting a much broader group are frequently most visible in their effect on people of color, because their lack of resources and marginalization make them more likely to reveal serious problems and the consequences of inadequate policies and practices before their impact surfaces for others struggling within the same culture. The experiences of Black students in the STEM fields at UMBC were indicating deeper problems affecting many other students as well.

Hrabowski was convinced that starting with and learning from Black students' experiences would not only address racial disparities at UMBC but also introduce ways to improve the culture supporting all students. His initial focus as vice provost for academic affairs became increasing Black student enrollment in the STEM fields. When philanthropist Robert E. Meyerhoff approached him with the idea of creating a program that would aim to support UMBC students in attaining excellence in those areas, Hrabowski had the support he needed. The groundbreaking Meyerhoff Scholars program, aimed at increasing diversity in the STEM fields, was launched in 1989 and would eventually lead to broader institutional change. Constructing an environment on the foundations of high expectations and strong support, the program combined community building, financial resources, program staff to provide ongoing advising and monitoring, summer internships with leading researchers, and, perhaps most unique and effective, building a positive academic environment on campus.

After Hrabowski became president of UMBC in 1992, he set out to engage the entire university community in applying the lessons learned in the Meyerhoff program. His research had shown that Black students were not the only ones at UMBC who were not succeeding in the sciences. Seventy percent of all freshmen in chemistry were receiving below a C, yet somehow, faculty had regarded that fact as simply a sign of rigorous courses doing their job of "weeding out" unqualified students. What Hrabowski was seeing at UMBC was a microcosm of a problem he knew existed in institutions of higher education across the country. National research showed that, along with the 20 percent success rate of Black and Latino/a/e students, only 32 percent of whites and 42 percent of Asian Americans who started out in science would remain. To Hrabowski, it was clear that "something is wrong with the culture of science, technology, engineering, and mathematics (STEM) on our campuses."[43] He used the Meyerhoff experience as the miner's canary that would produce collaborations within UMBC so it could transform itself.

This was the starting point for learning what needed to change in the institution to create an environment that provided more effective support for all students. Organized around the idea of empowerment and full participation, the Meyerhoff program became the cornerstone for broader institutional transformation that enables people, whatever their race or social position, to succeed, thrive, advance, and contribute to the thriving of others. With Meyerhoff's success came calls at UMBC for broader implementation of its program components to include empowerment of other groups, including women and students transferring from community colleges. What had begun with Hrabowski's efforts to support students of color in the STEM fields had ended up benefiting all students, an example of linked fate in action.

Bill LaCourse, the dean of the College of Mathematical Sciences at UMBC, is one of many white faculty and administrators who, inspired and supported by Hrabowski's emphasis on values, joined an effort he might not have championed had it been framed only in terms of racial disparities. LaCourse had been a first-generation college student and like about 50 percent of UMBC students, he had transferred to a four-year school from a community college. "I had dropped out of college a couple of times before completing it," he said. Now, drawing on his own history, he felt passionate about exploring what could support students in their college experience. "How can they come here and feel wanted? How can they come here and feel like they're part of the community? What can we do to inspire them to solve or overcome challenges when they have a lot of other things that challenge them every day anyway?" The positive impact he was seeing with the Meyerhoff program looked like it might help answer some of those questions. "The Meyerhoff's a wonderful program. How do you make every student that comes in the door have a

Meyerhoff experience?"[44] And he was willing to pursue that for the success of all his students.

For years, LaCourse had watched students in his large, gateway chemistry classes not pay attention, move to the back of the room, and eventually disappear. These included a disproportionately high number of Black students. He began to realize that his approach to teaching—the usual reliance on lectures, tests, and quizzes—invited passivity in all students and contributed to stereotypes about science and students alike.

Supported by an atmosphere created in the Meyerhoff program that meant "you could try something, fail, and not be blamed for it," LaCourse began experimenting with innovations in the teaching of science. He created scenarios where the students take on role-plays that enabled them to "discover for themselves the concepts that we used to make them memorize." They then focused on community building by forming peer cohorts where the students could ask questions, get T-shirts that supported a sense of community, and meet early on with respected people in their field who believed in them and cared about their success. "This drove the participation rates in classes much higher. For quite a large number of students, community- and cohort-building actually had some of the biggest impact." The upshot was that "we were able to cut the failure rate in freshman chemistry in half."[45] The lessons LaCourse learned enhanced the effectiveness of his teaching for all students and contributed to their academic success.

"Inclusive excellence" became UMBC's watchwords, orienting its community around the priorities of shared values and full participation of students from all backgrounds. Recognizing that what adversely affects the "miner's canary" in any institution also affects others provides a way to initiate broader changes that benefit everyone. Identifying linked fate had made it possible for people with different racial backgrounds and positions to recognize shared needs and work together for systemic change. UMBC's culture change process, grounded in learning from the experience of Black students, has transformed the school into a dynamic, highly respected institution that fashions itself as "unabashedly aspirational." With the mantra "success is never final," UMBC has become a nationally recognized innovator in STEM education, particularly for groups who have been historically shut out of those fields. According to the National Science Foundation, UMBC graduates more Black students who go on to earn PhDs in the natural sciences and engineering than any other college. The Meyerhoff program has been replicated in institutions across the country.[46]

Linked fate can develop, as it did at UMBC, by engaging in sustained reflection that reveals that the conditions causing people of color to struggle actually undermine everyone's ability to thrive. Acknowledging and insisting on the systemic change needed to address the toxic experiences of people of color, the Meyerhoff program reframed anti-racism efforts to show that what benefited one group on campus benefited everyone. This is what the authors of the "We See You" letter called upon white theater people to do as a response to the problematic conditions harming people of color and people in the theater industry overall. Addressing the conditions preventing full participation of those at the margins will enable others who have been harmed by those conditions to participate as well.

The Solidarity Dividend: Recognizing Common Interests to Achieve Common Goals

In *The Sum of Us*, Heather McGee persuasively points out that the dominant racial narrative keeps white people from seeing that "the economic benefit of the racial bargain is shrinking for all but the richest." Cross-racial collective action, she writes, makes "gains available to everyone when they unite across racial lines," including "higher wages, cleaner air, and better funded schools." She calls this the "solidarity dividend"—the benefits of linked fate that result when disparate groups that share common interests join forces across the racial divide to achieve outcomes that are possible only by working together.[47]

An example of the effectiveness of this process has begun to emerge in the theater industry in the efforts to eliminate the exhausting but accepted work practice known as "ten out of twelve," described in industry sources as "an allowance of a twelve-hour work day, so long as no more than ten of those hours are active working hours." Put in place decades ago in collective bargaining agreements negotiated by Actors Equity, the trade union representing professional actors and stage managers in the United States, this practice typically has actors rehearsing from noon to midnight, with a two-hour dinner break. For technicians and stage crew, these days easily turn into twelve out of fourteens and, as others in the profession testify, "it's 14 out of 16, if you're lucky."[48]

The unhealthy and counterproductive character of this practice has been widely recognized yet accepted as a given. But signaling the advent of a new perspective, in 2020, a website hosted by a newly formed organization called No More 10 out of 12s described the impact of the practice in this way:

In trying to uphold the spirit of "the show must go on," theatre practitioners in professional and academic settings have repeatedly pushed themselves far beyond their physical and mental limits, jeopardizing both their health and their future. Nonetheless, the ten-out-of-twelve was a staple concept for putting up a show. . . . It is the air we have been breathing for generations.[49]

Of course, these kinds of hours are not limited to the world of theater. They come with the territory in many fields, from law to consulting to health care to corporate America.[50] Eating at your desk, working late into the evening, and being "on call" make up the accepted work ethic, held in place by the understanding of the necessity to "do whatever it takes or lose your job." Millennials and organizers across these fields have challenged such practices for their negative impact on overall health and well-being, as well as noting the additional and often invisible impact on people of color and those with childcare responsibilities, especially if they must rely on their jobs as their only and often inadequate source of income.[51]

The Parent Artist Advocacy League (PAAL) was founded by Rachel Spencer Hewitt, a white actor committed to supporting those in the performing arts and media who have responsibilities as caregivers, typically of children and elders. In 2019, Spencer Hewitt organized a summit focusing on the impact of the ten out of twelve and six-day workweek. Framing the purpose of the summit, she wrote:

> We love immersing ourselves in the play. We love being consumed by the work. When the work starts consuming us, we can't produce as well anymore. We can't take care of ourselves, our family members. That's where we can draw these boundaries. Because I love producing in the theater, we have to abolish the 10 out of 12.[52]

In a similar vein, in the spring of 2020 the executive board of the Theatrical Sound Designer and Composer Association began organizing to abolish the ten out of twelve, having determined that it was an issue that designers, stage managers, and tech personnel wanted to prioritize. These groups had not connected with each other or in fact gotten much traction until the "We See You, White American Theater" letter and the movement it inspired.

One of the demands of that letter was the call for the elimination of ten out of twelves, making explicit the relationship between white supremacy and these practices of owning people's time: "When these practices are in place, the growing and nurturing of the BIPOC family structure is imperiled. Many

BIPOC artists have been forced to make a choice not to have families. For Indigenous artists and other peoples recovering from genocide, these practices are extremely detrimental."

Tony-nominated composer and sound designer Lindsay Jones, a leader of No More 10 out of 12s, wrote that the "We See You" movement provided "a slap in the face to American theatre culture: if you won't make these changes for yourself, then do it for the BIPOC community." Jones's group, together with the organizers of PAAL, rallied around the "We See You" movement's leadership and ethical imperative. As Jones put it: "We started walking down this road, and we would meet people and say, Hey, do you want to come aboard?" The group that coalesced discovered, "Wow, we're really passionate about this. And that's how we all came together as a group to really start to talk about these issues and figure out what we could do about them." That is how the No More 10 out of 12s' efforts became a multiracial movement. Groups that had been launched by white people reoriented their advocacy to support the leadership of the "We See You" coalition.[53]

This collaboration has been highlighted by artists of color as an example of how a coalescing of groups builds the solidarity needed to accomplish their aims. Several features account for its success. First, the leadership and interests of people of color, mobilized by the "We See You" movement, anchor the coalition, while actively aligning with white-led organizations. That means those directly impacted by racism are shaping how issues are understood and addressed, identifying where and how the systems are failing them and what changes are needed to create settings where they and others can thrive. In support of that, as a white-led organization, PAAL's attention to the role of race facilitated the development of solidarity across racial groups. Its public commitment to making anti-racism "the central pillar to caregiver support," recognizing that BIPOC communities are exponentially affected by that gap, attracted activists who might have been less likely to mobilize around the concerns of Black people alone. The solidarity dividend enabled the collaboration to straddle both sides of the paradox of racialized power.[54]

A second reason for the success of this coalition is that it grounded its work in the narratives and testimonials of a multiracial group. Posted on their website and featured in presentations, these narratives provide the context necessary for those involved at any level of the theater industry to experience, or at least imagine, the perspectives of those living with the ten out of twelve. By juxtaposing stories of people with different racial identities, the coalition demonstrates both the commonality of people's experiences and the particular ways that racism amplifies the impact of these inhumane expectations. Sharing how people with different identities and positions experience long hours and lack of caregiver support also builds connections across racial divides and facilitates a cross-racial embrace of linked fate.

A third component of this success is that white-led organizations have contributed resources needed to produce rigorous studies documenting the consequences of the ten out of twelve on health, safety, and productivity. This kind of research buttresses the information gleaned from personal narratives and provides data that each organization can use to highlight its own members' situation and the collective impact of these problematic practices. The data also provides a way for institutions to build ongoing accountability for the impact of these practices and receive recognition when they implement demonstrable change.

Finally, by featuring on the No More 10 out of 12s' website the companies and leadership that are experimenting with alternatives, the coalition demonstrates their impact and provides a road map for others to follow. More than fifty companies and academic institutions have eliminated the ten out of twelve, and a few have also eliminated the six-day workweek. The growing list includes New York's Public Theater, Baltimore Center Stage, and a number of theater departments at prominent colleges. The website also provides a variety of scenarios and tools that have been used by these productions to implement their changes. Concrete actions with results are fueling the movement's momentum and sustainability.

Changes in the ten out of twelve were initiated by two white-led groups initially organizing around a concern without direct relevance to race. But the realization of linked fate became clear as Black and Brown activists called attention to racism's foundational role in both perpetuating the problem and driving the need for change. When issues of inequality were addressed, the solidarity dividend paid off for everyone. Recognizing common challenges and understanding common needs and priorities pave the way toward the collective identity of linked fate. However, when that commonality does not exist, a third working principle of linked fate must come into play: stretch collaboration.

Stretch Collaboration: No Choice but to Fight and Collaborate

What if the only thing that connects people across race and power is the recognition that neither group can achieve its goals if they keep fighting with each other? What if the groups at odds define the problem itself differently and profoundly disagree ideologically but cannot avoid, neutralize, or defeat each other? Can linked fate operate to enable these groups to get beyond the impasse and collaborate in the midst of conflict? Adam Kahane offers a path forward in situations involving profound and entrenched disagreement. He calls this "stretch collaboration." Those involved may not share values or a sense of common purpose, or even agree on the definition of the problem, but they do agree that the status quo is unacceptable and that other ways of pursuing their interests have not worked. They do share the understanding that they cannot get where any of them want to or have to go without stepping out of the destructive and polarizing cycle to find a way to cooperate with those they distrust and disagree with. As Kahane puts it: "Collaborating with diverse others cannot and must not require agreeing on a single truth or answer or solution. Instead, it involves finding a way to move forward together in the absence of or beyond such agreements."[55]

Stretch collaboration offers a framework that can move intensely polarized racial groups toward linked fate. Kahane focuses on the effectiveness of actually bringing people in conflict together without the expectation that they will identify a shared goal or solve the problem. Instead, they agree to generate and try out different scenarios to see what happens as a result of each one. What Kahane learned through this work is that "the most robust collaborations are those that different actors support for different reasons. . . . People who have deep disagreements can still get important things done together."[56] And along the way, the trust and mutual respect that emerge can help sustain lasting collaboration, notwithstanding enduring conflict.

The Reimagining Public Safety Collaborative in Ithaca, New York, is a vivid illustration of stretch collaboration, revealing how racially polarized groups can continue to work together while remaining in conflict, propelled by their shared sense of necessity. As in so many cities across the United States, protests after the murder of George Floyd erupted in Ithaca, uncovering the long-standing tensions between law enforcement and communities of color that had a history of being overpoliced and subject to police violence. In the wake of ongoing daily demonstrations nationally and continued killings of Black people by police, the governor of New York issued an executive order that required each local government "to examine and reconcile past experiences of marginalized populations who have experienced disproportionate contact with the public safety system based upon national tragedies and unresolved local issues."[57] Any city seeking funding for a proposed program had to file a report and recommendations with the state legislature. Ithaca's mayor and county administrator, a person of color with roots in the community, took up this challenge in earnest.

Engaging the facilitation services of the Center for Policing Equity, a national nonprofit focused on racial justice in law enforcement practices, he set out to bring together local law enforcement personnel with members of the community who were deeply concerned about ongoing racial conflict in interactions with the police. Despite their opposing perspectives, backgrounds, experiences, and ideologies, the one thing both groups shared was having lived through recurring episodes of this destructive conflict.

This uneasy coalition deliberately began its work without any concrete goals in mind. They just started gathering information, sharing experiences, and generating competing ideas for possible solutions. Black and Brown community members expressed profound and irreconcilable distrust of law enforcement. Their experiences of racism and violence when they called the police had led some community members to turn to self-policing when they faced threats to their safety, rather than risk another dehumanizing encounter with police. Many of the community participants had called for defunding the city's police department and instead employing community-based organizations trained to address the mental health, drug treatment, and poverty concerns underlying many police encounters. In response, law enforcement participants expressed frustration about the lack of public understanding of their work and protested the unfairness of blaming police for inequities caused by the lack of government investment in mental health services, housing, and jobs for communities of color. Their sense of futility about working with people who sought to abolish their positions was met by the sense of futility in the communities of color about changing a department that used tactics that instilled such fear and distrust in them.[58] Both sides were stuck in a paradox: they had to simultaneously work together in the attempt to maintain public safety while at the same time knowing they were in conflict about who was the cause of the violence that was keeping them at odds.

As the group met over the months, occasionally they found consensus about the causes of the problem and the goals, but more often they did not. Yet the group stayed together, agreeing to disagree and to keep going nonetheless, trying out ideas and solutions, gathering data, and reflecting on their experience. Despite tremendous and ongoing friction, they continued to listen to each other without trying to reach agreement. In doing so, they opened themselves up to further conflict but also to unanticipated connection. Eventually that friction began to produce some creative possibilities along with a willingness to keep going, even though no one yet was satisfied.

A year after beginning the process, this conflict-ridden collaboration produced its initial report to the city along with its recommendations, with the explicit stipulation that the document was to serve as a report on a process rather than as a final set of solutions.[59] In response, Ithaca's government proposed a set of recommendations: placing armed police under a civilian deputy manager of public safety, experimenting with reliance on unarmed community staff to handle mental health crises, instituting community-led cultural competency training, and committing to support pilot programs that would test the efficacy of new forms of community-led public safety.[60]

Viewed as unacceptable by some in the government and non-negotiable by others, further disagreements erupted. Some law enforcement personnel resigned from the group, some community members publicly protested, and the district attorney challenged the ethics of the contract with the Center for Policing Equity.[61] But despite this turmoil, the work of the group continued, held together by a newly elected mayor, and by their shared understanding that their fate was linked in both conflict and collaboration. Even those who were most critical remained engaged in the process—showing up for public forums and participating in the deliberations of the committee set up to implement the recommendations of the initial report. That process gave rise to experiments trying out some of the recommendations on a small scale. These included a new data dashboard that would increase police transparency and accountability by publishing weekly data on arrests, prosecutions, and case outcomes from law enforcement agencies in Tompkins County, broken down by race, along with the creation of an unarmed response unit staffed with civilians and mental health workers from the community who would be the first responders for behavioral health and other related crises. These experiments gave people a chance to build trust and see concrete movement toward transformational change, even as the larger policy recommendations of the report remained contentious and unresolved.[62] Despite the challenges and apparent failures, the dialogue about community trauma and healing continues, with members of the group reiterating that "this is an ongoing, evolving process" that requires continued participation by police and community stakeholders.[63] There was hope even in face of failure, and one Ithaca resident managed to encapsulate perhaps the only way to respond to this quandary:

As a Black man, I'm wary of any changes like this, because the history of policing in this country is fraught with examples that show me the odds are stacked against me. But I do know this is important. Because what it *does* do is take this kind of dialogue a step forward—where it's no longer about safety through policing, but instead reverts the focus back to safety for the community. I know the folks involved in this process actually listened to the voices of many community members I trust, many folks who look like me and feel the way I do—traumatized, at times hopeless, wary, often scared of the repercussions of purely existing in a society historically pitted against them—but still believing there's a chance we can do better, one day.[64]

Even in organizations with ongoing racial conflict and distrust, the kind of stretch collaboration evident in Ithaca demonstrates that there is value in continuing to work together and building trust, even as they remain wary of each other's motivations and methods. Stretch collaboration requires spanning the opposing sides of the anti-racism paradoxes—seeing the world differently, holding different kinds of power, having opposing views about whether positive change is even possible—while also recognizing that the only alternative is a destructive downward spiral serving no one and hurting everyone. That realization alone opens the door to the possibility of acting on linked fate.

Each of these three different conceptual tools for forging linked fate has its own version of reflective practice, and each calls for a both/and approach that tethers concerns about race to other critical human and institutional goals. Going through a reflective process of forging linked fate builds trust among people of different races, grounded in discovering mutual benefit. Framing anti-racism around genuinely shared interests creates momentum that can help people escape Groundhog Day and fuel the pursuit of paradoxical possibility.

In each of the scenarios leading to the discovery of linked fate, it is evident that there are key change agents who facilitate the process that bridges distinct and opposing groups and perspectives: Hrabowski at UMBC, the founders of No More 10 out of 12s, and the mayor of Ithaca, New York, along with scores of everyday leaders cutting across racial lines. Leaders like these act as translators across the divides of experiential segregation. They shift the focus of groups that are in conflict toward the values and goals that connect them. They help those stumbling toward mutual understanding to communicate, explore common experiences, and achieve collaborative successes through small experiments they try together.

These people are the organizational catalysts who play the pivotal role of helping people stay connected when they confront the paradoxes of anti-racism. And they use these tensions to find their way into paradoxical possibility. These individuals, who inspire and provoke innovative change in institutions, facing head-on the legacy of racist policies, are the subjects of the next chapter.

5

Building Bridges, Weaving Dreams

WHEREVER I HAVE SEEN anti-racism take root in a predominantly white organization, it has happened when pivotal people have facilitated a long-term process enabling individuals with different racial identities and perspectives to connect, coalesce into a functioning collective committed to closing the gap between the vision and the actuality, and remain engaged over time. They have fostered critical inquiry that makes visible the ways that the status quo reproduces racial hierarchy and exclusion. They have helped people with different racial identities find overlapping and shared interests and build trust across racial lines. They have provided concrete opportunities for people to augment or redefine their conventional roles so that they can address systemic issues. They have found ways to involve people who may not yet have recognized their linked fate but whose participation is required to make lasting change. They have helped others reconnect with the values and vision that may have initially brought them into the organization and rekindle the belief that change is possible. They have enlisted and inspired others to join them in these efforts and found ways to sustain that involvement, even when it's difficult. They have crafted an environment that enables people to take risks and reminds them of what might be possible if they are willing to experiment in the present while imagining the future they hope to create.

These people are what I call organizational catalysts, those who knit together diverse individuals, roles, identities, and perspectives in order to advance shared goals related to anti-racism. They orchestrate paradoxical possibility, finding ways to bridge the experiential gaps dividing people in different racial positions, inspiring and galvanizing them to move forward together despite the inevitability of struggle and failure. In previous chapters, we have seen the power of this role in operation. Judge Fein, realizing that the culture in his court had bred his own tolerance of racial inequities, used his position to enlist other white judges in a multiracial exploration of policies and practices that might better support racial justice. Jeanine Tesori collaborated with artists of color to make it possible to link opera to the project of transforming the racial narrative for predominantly white audiences. Lee, galvanized by the insights of Black artists about ongoing racism in the theater industry, helped forge the cross-racial collaboration dedicated to building equitable productions. Freeman Hrabowski, guided by his passion for addressing racial inequities in higher education and his dedication to promoting full participation across race, gender, and socioeconomic class, launched the model initiative at the University of Maryland, Baltimore County, increasing the enrollment of students of color in the STEM fields while uplifting the academic performance of the institution as a whole. These are the dream weavers who, by bridging the polarities that have previously kept them and their organizations stuck in an unacceptable racist status quo, have forged interracial relationships that have endured as they pursued anti-racist policies together.

Organizational catalysts are individuals with knowledge, credibility, and influence, motivated by values related to equity and justice, who connect people in positions where they can leverage change. Merriam-Webster defines a catalyst as "an agent that provokes or speeds significant change or action." Organizational catalysts bring together people and resources in new ways that make change toward greater equity both possible and desirable. In concert with others, they put into practice Webster's definition of organizing—putting "persons or things into their proper places in relation to each other," and they thereby "arrange elements into a whole of interdependent parts." In anti-racism work, organizational catalysts bridge worlds that usually have been segregated by systems, structures, and narratives that discourage people from working together across racial divides. They know how to communicate with people who speak different languages and operate on different assumptions. They help those involved in countering racist practices in institutions develop their own theory of change tailored to their particular situation. They guide the process of understanding, as my mentor Robert Cover put it, the "is" (the problematic way things are), the "ought" (the world they want to see in its place), and the "what might be" (the ways they can work together to close the gap between the "is" and the "ought").[1] They inspire people to participate in change efforts that previously may have seemed unrealistic and futile. And they involve people in ongoing interactions that keep them engaged over the long haul.

Organizational catalysts play an essential role in activating and sustaining the process of rescripting the racial narrative. They forge that "small group of thoughtful, committed citizens" that, as Margaret Mead told us, "can change the world." They can create a foothold to push for and enact change, even in predominantly white organizations that have not yet acknowledged the need to rescript the racial narrative.

There is no formal job description delimiting the functions of the organizational catalyst. Rather, they integrate anti-racism work into the current responsibilities of their job or position, redefining their role in order to encompass and address both tasks. They may head an organization or project, as Freeman Hrabowski did. They might, like Judge Fein or Jeanine Tesori, be in a job without formal organizational authority over policy but in a position to use their influence to inspire others. Or, as we will see in this chapter, they might be change agents from inside or outside an organization who understand the context in need of change.

Organizational catalysts are versed in qualities, skills, and practices that enable them to activate and sustain change across racial divides. As previous chapters have illustrated, they might be white people who have formed relationships of trust across the racial divide and made racial equity a priority as an expression of their own values and responsibilities. They might be people of color who have decided to work in predominantly white institutions to advance racial justice and full participation. Racial identity does have advantages and drawbacks in how effectively someone can promote change. People of color in positions of influence may find it easier to build credibility and trust in their efforts to address racism, but they may also have to contend with the racial stereotypes that set a high bar for success and can make mistakes more costly. And when white people promoting anti-racism can help other white people develop their racial literacy and take responsibility for addressing racism as part of their jobs, they may also be constrained by their limited racial understanding and credibility with people of color. When organizational catalysts of different races work together, they can bridge these divides more easily.

The most effective organizational catalysts I have studied and worked with have a history of multiracial collaboration, themselves having gone through a personal process of learning and transformation. They have managed to redefine their conventional roles so that they can advance racial equity as part of their day-to-day work and pursue projects that include racial equity as a core focus. They have found ways to build bridges across relational chasms, envisioning the world they want to see, experimenting with how they might get there, and continually reconnecting short-term decisions to long-term hopes and dreams. These are the qualifications and the strategies of an effective organizational catalyst doing the work of anti-racism in an organization.

This chapter looks at several exemplary organizational catalysts, the qualities and capacities they bring to their work, and the strategies they use to overcome the barriers of experiential segregation, scripted stuckness, role rigidity, and status quo bias and help build lasting multiracial collaborations that rescript the racial narrative of their organizations. These strategies include:

- building cross-racial partnerships
- using proximity to promote transformation
- creating cohorts that support sustainable change over time

These three strategies enable organizational catalysts to build bridges across experiential divides and weave dreams that inspire transformation toward full participation.

Building Cross-Racial Partnerships

"How do we get our students to work together when they are so used to trying to win an argument rather than learn from each other?" Lani Guinier was open-ing our conversation in her usual way, immediately pinpointing the issue. We were meeting to discuss a conflict that had just arisen between two students in the class Lani and I were teaching together at the University of Pennsylvania Law School. "They each seem so intent on being right that they keep talking past each other," she went on. "What will it take for them to shift gears, to focus on understanding each other's perspective, even when they deeply disagree?" Lani—tall, vibrant, alive with ideas, humor, and vision—had become my clos-est friend and colleague at Penn. When she first joined the law faculty, I had been teaching there for two years, and she had sought me out to help her navi-gate the language and culture of the institution, determined to translate her pathbreaking ideas about voting rights and racial justice into legal scholarship and pedagogy. We developed a deep friendship filled with conversations about work, our families, and our social change commitments. And now, recognizing that learning from each other in the crucible of cross-racial partnerships like the one she and I had developed could model and support a multiracial learn-ing community, she had invited me to co-teach with her a class titled "Critical Perspectives in the Law: Race and Gender." We had framed the course so that it would bring together students with different racial backgrounds and gender perspectives and give them the opportunity to build relationships across their experiential divides.

Both of us were well aware of many students' frustration with how the culture of the law school consistently sidestepped issues of race and gender. Hungry to acknowledge their particular life experience and incorporate that into the development of their professional identity, many had asked for a class like the one we were now offering. In response, Lani and I were determined to create a space that would take on hard questions and invite disclosure, conflict, creativity, and connection while also rekindling the hopes and values that had first called many of them to law. We had structured situations for our students where their cross-racial interactions would be frequent, sustained, and facilitated by the two of us, enabling them to learn from their differences and push each other to incorporate that learning into future efforts to promote racial equity. I would discover later that social psychologist Patricia Gurin and her colleagues had been developing a similar process that involved institutions across the country in groundbreaking pedagogy. In *Dialogue across Difference: Practice, Theory, and Research on Intergroup Dialogue*, they provide empirical support for the effectiveness of the very kind of dialogue Lani and I were using to promote communication, collaboration, and problem-solving among diverse racial groups.[2] They argue that intergroup dialogue accomplishes the "dual, sometimes seemingly contradictory objectives" of simultaneously fostering "a capacity for collaboration and broad democratic engagement" while also acknowledging "differences, inequalities, and conflicts." These dialogues work when they are facilitated and collaborative, strive for understanding rather than agreement, deal explicitly with issues of power and inequality, and provide for frequent, sustained, and engaged interaction and problem-solving.[3]

To help build a collaborative learning community, Lani and I required students to pair up, preferably with someone they didn't know, to co-facilitate a class focused on a project or issue that mattered to each of them individually. As we had anticipated, this mostly resulted in cross-racial pairs, along with the inevitable misunderstandings and disagreements that arise when two people from different races with limited prior knowledge of each other's cultures and experiences must work together on issues they each feel invested in. We were prepared for that, knowing that the challenge would not only shed light on the social dynamics of racism in our culture but also provide the opportunity for the two of us to offer what we had learned together in our cross-racial relationship.

Two of our students signed up to co-facilitate a class on affirmative action, which was even then a topic of heated debate not only across the nation but also in the law school. Even though twenty-five years later the Supreme Court would change the terms of that debate with its decision barring affirmative action in admissions,[4] the dialogue between these two students surfaced tensions that would continue to frame anti-racism efforts.

A few days into the assignment, Verna, president of the Black Law Students Association, and Evelyn, a white woman leading the Penn Women's Law Group, asked to meet with us to help resolve their deepening conflict over how the class should be conducted. Verna wanted to set up an experience in class that would provide white students with a sense of how it felt to be Black at Penn. In a prearranged agreement with a few Black students chosen to facilitate the process, the discussion of affirmative action in the class session would allow only the voices and opinions of the students of color to be heard; the white students would be interrupted or not allowed to speak. Then, the performance of everyone in the class would be evaluated on the quality and level of their participation. "I think this will help white students better understand what it's like to be Black in this kind of discussion and situation," Verna said, "and in the law school in general. That might get across the need for affirmative action to level the playing field by bringing more students of color to the table." Verna was searching for a way to communicate the impact of the law school culture on students of color and the importance of sufficient representation for people of color to feel like they can be full participants in the law school and in any organization.

Lani listened intently as Verna spoke, and then sat back to express her reservations. "I had a class last year when students tried something like this, and it resulted in a level of polarization and distrust that stayed with the group from that point on."

"I am willing to take that risk," Verna said, with an edge of hope and passion in her voice, "if doing so might get white law students to see how they are benefiting from a system stacked in their favor."

Evelyn was almost in tears as she said that the process Verna was proposing seemed more aimed at shaming the white students than at identifying commonalities among people of different races, which was what Evelyn wanted to do. "Maybe this topic is just too hard to speak openly about without alienating people. What if we just discuss the viewpoints expressed in the readings instead? Or try to find points of agreement among our classmates? That seems like the safest way to go."

Neither student was budging in her perspective or ideas. Evelyn said Verna was being rigid, negative, and unwilling to work things through. Verna countered that Evelyn was too sensitive and focused on self-protection, willing to paper over disagreements and wanting to talk more than act. Their communication gap was in line with studies showing that, in cross-racial interactions, societally privileged groups want to focus on commonalities while members of less privileged groups prefer to focus more on differences that exist alongside commonalities.[5] Initially, both of them had wanted to work with each other, but now their interactions had left them wanting to withdraw to their respective corners. Stuck on either side of this polarity, they could only see the situation from their own vantage point. Lani and I had to do something to keep their collaboration alive despite the tension and distrust.

Whether in a classroom, a workshop, a staff meeting, or a project get-together, this situation is a microcosm of a common interracial dynamic that organizational catalysts might encounter when they initiate conversations to address policies and issues related to race. How can those in boundary-spanning roles offer tools—ways of interacting—that help people shift from a stance of defensiveness to one of curiosity to understand those with a different racial perspective? How might they build the trust needed to work together toward solutions everyone involved could embrace? And how do they create settings that people of different races will experience as "identity safe," where differences in group identity are seen as a source of advantage and value, not disadvantage and threat?[6] Building this kind of understanding can be especially challenging when there is any level of urgency in a situation, as many organizational catalysts find out (and as Lani and I certainly did).

Unlike Lee, who could first get his white colleagues together to uncover their issues and conflicts over a period of time, Lani and I were faced with the immediacy of this situation for our students. Understanding that it was part of our role as catalysts of cross-racial dialogue to offer opportunities to learn courage and resilience, we asked ourselves some basic questions: What practices could we use to help Verna and Evelyn understand the underlying dynamics of their conflict so they could make more aware and intentional choices about difficult cross-racial interactions? How could we equip them with ways to keep the lines of communication open, take care of themselves individually while not withdrawing from their struggle, and figure out how to put that learning to work not only in facilitating the class but also in the professional arenas they would each be working in in the future?

Lani and I had discovered that students relied on each of us differently, primarily but not exclusively in ways that correlated with race. Lani was more of the disrupter—someone who started many sentences with "my problem is . . ." and really pushed everyone to speak out about the embedded racism they saw around them and to question themselves if they had automatically accepted their predominantly white law school's definitions of success. Black students were more likely to seek her out when they needed support and guidance from a person of color who had also experienced racism firsthand. I tended more toward enabling students of different races to fully participate in the space, building environments that promote cross-racial collaboration, and helping white students and sometimes students of color navigate their own challenges in cross-racial relationships so that they could succeed in conventional terms and become effective and transformational change agents. Both ways of facilitating were necessary to develop an effective multiracial group ready to undertake change.

Well-versed in arenas of interracial conflict through both personal experience and study, Lani laid the foundation for building a relationship between the two students. "Let's first acknowledge what's happening here," she began. "This is hard work, maybe harder than you had expected." They both nodded. "I've been there many times, and I know it's possible to find a way through."

Verna and Evelyn looked doubtful, so I asked, "Have you had a chance to identify what you each want out of working together on this topic—what your own goals and worries might be? Have you each had a chance to consider how your own background, experiences, and identities might affect how you are interacting with each other and with the issue of affirmative action?" They looked at each other and, seemingly a little surprised, turned back to us and shook their heads no. "It's really hard to jump right into a hot-button issue like affirmative action," I offered, "without first having a sense of who you are talking to and why it so deeply matters to them."

Lani and I suggested a self-reflection process as a first step. Either on their own or with someone they trusted, they could reflect on a set of questions that would provide a critical perspective on their experience. These would include: What do you think accounts for the different ways you are each approaching this class? What are you each feeling and needing from the other? What are you each assuming? What experiences and cultural messages might explain how you came to hold these assumptions? What do you want to know from each other that might help you understand your differences and work together?

These questions would help prepare the two students to have a necessary and difficult conversation about race. In their bestselling book that would later feature these same practices, *Difficult Conversations: How to Discuss What Matters Most*, Douglas Stone and his coauthors point out that this kind of reflective process invites people to become more aware of the triggers that may be operating in their conflict.[7] These might include the nature of the relationships involved, the truth of what is being said, and the identities at stake for the participants. This kind of reflection can help those in conflict prepare for and deal constructively with situations that might be fraught with personal risk by inviting them to shift into the growth mindset that Carol Dweck talks about, enabling them to treat mistakes as opportunities for learning and problem-solving rather than as failures.[8]

The questions we posed to Verna and Evelyn are the first step toward what Lani would call developing racial literacy—engaging in practices that enable people of different racial backgrounds to better understand and navigate the exigencies and dynamics of race as part of addressing racism.[9] Racial literacy involves self-inquiry about how racial background affects the way those with different racial identities might differently experience the same situation. That includes how race intersects with other identities, such as class, gender, religion, and so on. This personal dimension of racial literacy relates to what critical race scholar Rhonda Magee calls "a deeper and more nuanced capacity to perceive and to understand how race and racism operate in our own lives and in the lives of others."[10]

The interpersonal dimension of racial literacy involves understanding how to interact with people of different racial backgrounds and identities, including when there is misunderstanding and mistrust. Racial literacy requires learning to discern when racial issues, whether explicit or unrecognized, are occurring in relationships and institutions and to understand how the history and culture have given rise to that situation.[11] It develops in part through a process of what social psychologists call "perspective taking"—"imagining the world from another's vantage point or imagining oneself in another's shoes to understand their visual viewpoints, thoughts, motivations, intentions, and/or emotions."[12] Research has shown that in addition to reducing unconscious expressions of racial bias, perspective taking helps create, maintain, and strengthen social bonds in cross-racial relationships.[13] And it also involves understanding how individuals might use their power to influence others' understanding and willingness to address racism and advance full participation. This kind of race-conscious work has taken on even greater importance in the post–affirmative action environment.

The systemic dimension of racial literacy involves understanding the many ways racism is deeply embedded within and constituted by relationships of power and in society as a whole.[14] Whether the context is personal, interpersonal, or institutional, racial literacy is critical in rescripting the racial narrative. This is what Lani and I were inviting our two students to do: to develop the racial literacy that would help them understand the institutional arrangements and power dynamics held in place by racial conflict. Rather than them being stuck inside a dynamic they couldn't understand or reshape, we wanted them to consider race as a "diagnostic," the miner's canary alerting them to the source of the problem. And we hoped that referring to the dynamics of our own experience would help them discover a path toward linked fate.

The opposing points of view evident in the class plans Evelyn and Verna were each proposing might have seemed irreconcilable to them, but we knew that if they both understood that they were experiencing the inevitable contradictions stemming from their different racial positions, they might be motivated to explore what was giving rise to those differences. We hoped to help them understand how they could, from their different vantage points, see the impact of race while also understanding cross-cutting concerns rooted in commonalities. Cultivating their ability to hold this paradox would require us to help them acknowledge what they didn't know, build enough trust between them that they could risk showing their mutual vulnerability, and provide perspectives that demonstrated to each of them that working together, despite the tensions, could benefit them both.

After the students left her office that day, Lani said, "If we can get them to turn this around by helping them understand and cultivate racial literacy, I think that will be a transformative experience for them. And it might also set them up to instigate a similar dynamic for the rest of the class." Grappling with this situation was exactly what we had hoped could happen in this class we were facilitating together.

This cross-racial bridge-building role was not new for Lani. For years before our work together, she had built relationships and credibility across the racial and gender divide, relishing the role of connecting people in these different worlds. She had worked as a leading civil rights advocate for a decade, first in the Justice Department and then as the head of the Voting Rights Project at the NAACP Legal Defense and Educational Fund, developing cross-racial coalitions that linked the fates of Black and working-class white communities. Since coming to Penn, her writing and speaking about race and gender, as well as about legal education, had attracted students across the racial and gender spectrum. Her office door was always open for students interested in any of these issues, and she worked tirelessly with student organizations to make law school more relevant and meaningful, especially for women, people of color, and students focused on social justice issues. And she brought journalists seeking to rethink the role of the media in a democracy together with people from diverse communities to promote a national conversation about race. In each of these contexts, Lani was a catalyst in the larger project of transforming democracy.

In all of these situations, she played the role of the consummate "social connector," someone who, as political theorist Danielle Allen would put it, is skilled at creating "bridging ties," linking people together across demographic cleavages. According to Allen, bridging ties foster the egalitarian social relations that are fundamental to democracy. They enable diverse and divided communities to coalesce into a connected society enriched by difference.[15] People who serve as social connectors also facilitate the capacity of diverse groups to deal constructively with conflict. Reaping the insights and innovation that can come from cross-racial interactions relies on individuals who, like Lani, are adept at creating the conditions that support cross-racial relationships. These were the skills and practices we each had spent years developing and that we were working to cultivate in our students.

Becoming an Organizational Catalyst

Our personal backgrounds were the wellspring of the work Lani and I were able to do together. When she was growing up, Lani's home, as she writes in her book *Lift Every Voice: Turning a Civil Rights Setback into a New Vision of Social Justice*, "spanned the experience of two families of immigrants—Eastern European Jews and West Indian blacks." She and her sisters—children of Eugenia Paprin Guinier, a civil rights activist, and Ewart Guinier, a lawyer and union organizer of Jamaican descent—were what their mother called "bridge people," living in two worlds, an identity Lani would eventually carry into all her work.[16]

Because of this family background, Lani grew up celebrating both Passover and Easter and learning about multiple cultures. "Both my parents educated me and helped expose me to different cultures and perspectives," she wrote, but as she puts it, she felt like "both an outsider and an insider." The relatives on her mother's side were initially upset that Lani's mother had married a Black person and, despite the fact that they loved Lani, some of their attitudes toward her still bore the mark of racism. She recounts the story of her white maternal grandfather lovingly giving her a bath and telling her that though he would "scrub and scrub . . . you are still dirty. I scrub your elbows and knees, but I can never get you clean." Lani understood that "he wasn't being malicious. He was making an observation from his limited perspective, but it hurt, nevertheless." By the time she was in junior high school, Lani identified as Black, discovering the power of her own Black culture and identity as a source of strength and community. She would later write: "It was my black father's experiences with discrimination that provided the organizing story of my life."[17]

But Lani's parents had both educated her in the art of communication across the worlds she traveled between. Her mother, she writes, "schooled me diligently in the lessons that nothing you do by yourself or to benefit only yourself really matters." Her father schooled her in the power of storytelling by peppering Lani and her sisters with tales from his childhood in Linstead, Jamaica. These stories, "chock full of details about scarcity and making do without enough money," were "uplifting tales of triumph." His experiences of racism, first as an undergraduate at Harvard and then later when he unsuccessfully sought work at the *New York Times*, would become Lani's life lessons in never being silenced. She learned from him that she was what he liked to call "a virago," in its original meaning, a brave and heroic woman. To Lani, this meant someone who spoke up and held people's feet to the fire.[18]

Both of her parents underscored the importance of words: "Listen carefully to those who know more, whether simple folk or polished intellects. Learn from rather than internalize criticism, develop allies, and then speak truth to power." Lani did just that, learning how to speak as a lawyer, a scholar, a teacher, a storyteller, a public intellectual, and an organizer, anchoring all these modes of communication in the language of relationship building. Having honed the practice of building bridges across racial divides, she personified the role of an organizational catalyst.

For myself and many white people I've encountered who have become organizational catalysts, the pathway to that role was more circuitous. Like Lani's, my family nourished my passion for justice. I heard about my father's experience of anti-semitism as a Jewish boy growing up in Germany under Hitler's rule and connected it to the discrimination experienced by Black people in the United States. Both of my parents expressed support for the civil rights movement and encouraged my volunteer activities in high school, most of which involved providing mentorship or support to Black and Brown children. But unlike Lani, I didn't see my parents genuinely living the anti-racism they preached: their cross-racial interactions were only with people working for them in traditional hierarchical ways—in our home doing domestic work or with employees working for my father's family business.

I have been thinking about race and racism since I was a little girl. I'm still not really sure what made racism such a personal and pressing issue for me. Maybe the injustice and power abuse I experienced in my own home somehow primed me to care about race because even as a white person, I was acutely aware of how it felt to be on the receiving end of such abuse. As a child, it became my role in the family to mediate conflict and to do whatever I could to narrow the gap between the myth of our perfect family and the reality of the abuses of power I witnessed and experienced. Growing up, I was constantly on the lookout for the "what might be." I said to myself countless times, "It doesn't have to be this way." How could I bridge the gap between rhetoric and reality? Doing that volunteer work in high school, mostly with Black children, I witnessed another chasm—between the democratic ideals I learned in school and the lived experiences of the Black people I was meeting. It was somehow the same dissonance I felt in my own family.

As an adult, my interest in addressing race has remained profoundly connected to my sense of purpose and my passion. But the emotional urgency I felt to step in and fix things, to "get it right," at times distorted my judgment, led me to take up too much space in my interactions about race, and triggered those directly impacted by racism. I had to learn to navigate this tension between purpose and ego, trying to heal both myself and my world.

Until I got to know Lani and then created the Critical Perspectives class with her, I had never been in a work situation or project led by people of color, nor had I experienced a genuinely mutual collaboration with a nonwhite colleague. When Lani invited me into a space that she had created with a group of mostly Black and Brown students, for the first time I had the chance to be part of a process that wasn't set up according to white people's rules. The experience was destabilizing and transformative.

It was Lani's blend of love, respect, and critical thinking that invited me to expose my vulnerability and ignorance, sometimes without even realizing that that was what I had fallen into. I learned to use those moments of paralyzing surprise—when I said something that revealed my ignorance or my racial stereotypes or biases—as opportunities to listen, take responsibility, and build trust within that group.

When Lani and I were teaching together, how we addressed each other's missteps was a model for students to see the value of taking risks and learning from mistakes. Recognizing the limits of my experience, as we taught together I was able to step out of the role of being the all-knowing "expert," the one who knew how to address an issue, or the one who solved the problem herself or with other white people in power. I also experienced Lani doing the same thing with me.

For the first time, I began to feel authentic in cross-racial contexts, aligned with and able to act in a way that was consistent with my love of connecting people with each other and with my desire to make a positive difference in the world. As a result, I began to experience a shift in my relationships with many of my students and colleagues of color as they more willingly opened up about their experiences of racism and their hopes and dreams for themselves. This rigorous training is what helped prepare me to build bridges as an organizational catalyst. I also learned—and continue to relearn—the value of having a person of color leading this work and the importance of cross-racial facilitation. What I learned from Lani was that the only way I could effectively and justly address issues of race was in cross-racial partnerships.

Communicating across the Racial Divide

Lani and I knew that the struggles we had experienced with each other in building our own cross-racial collaboration could help Evelyn and Verna connect across their racial divide. We also hoped they would use their experiences as a springboard for the conversation they would co-facilitate in class. When they returned for their next meeting with us, Lani began by asking them to share what it had been like for each of them, on their own, to reflect about their personal stories. "And if you're willing, sharing something of those experiences might help make sense now of the different ways you are each approaching the class, and that could provide a basis for finding common ground." As they each responded, it was clear how helpful it had been for them to think about the differences in how they experienced race when they were growing up and how that could be affecting their responses to each other.

Then, building on that understanding, we asked them what any of that background might have had to do with why they signed up to facilitate the class on affirmative action. We were in effect inviting them to take the next step in developing racial literacy. We were asking why was that topic important to each of them? How did it relate to their own story? In retrospect, I see now that these were questions that would become even more important to engage with after the Supreme Court's decision barring the use of affirmative action in admissions. They each talked about why they wanted to grapple with issues of affirmative action, sharing their fears and hopes about working on this issue with someone who came from such a different background, especially after the conflicts they had already experienced with each other. They also made it clear that concerns about affirmative action had affected each of them before they got to law school, albeit in different ways, and that questions about it continued to come up regularly at Penn. In light of all that, Lani and I asked if they were still willing to have this conversation about affirmative action with each other, and if so, what might they hope to achieve? How much of their concerns about affirmative action were they ready to share with each other, and how would they navigate the conflicts that might surface as they talked?

Verna nodded and began. Her whole demeanor changed as she described how it felt to have peers or faculty regularly assume that she was only at Penn because of affirmative action. "I worry that other people think I don't deserve my place. And if I am not at the top of the class, I sometimes question whether I belong myself." She sighed and continued. "I am genuinely torn. Affirmative action hasn't really worked, and yet we need it. Without it, this place would be even more white than it is."

Evelyn had been listening intently to Verna as she spoke and seemed genuinely moved by her story. "Wow, I feel terrible about what you've experienced. And I share your ambivalence about affirmative action. I too worry about the stigma it attaches to people of color. I don't know how to respond to the resentment expressed by some of my white friends, who believe that affirmative action is what kept them from getting into the college of their choice." Verna nodded with understanding but then countered, "The stigma comes from racism built into the culture and the admissions process, not from affirmative action. I don't feel comfortable speaking openly about this with people who have not acknowledged their own racial privilege." Evelyn seemed a little taken aback by what might have been intended as a personal criticism and was about to speak when Verna went on. "But I want to find a more constructive way to fight about this, to convey my perspective about race and affirmative action to the class and to people I hope to influence when I am in policy positions in the future." Although they were finally talking with each other, Verna and Evelyn still seemed caught in a polarized debate.

Lani's intervention at this point arose again from our own experience together. "Your conflict reminds me of when Susan and I had to work through our own frustrations with each other about how we each spoke about race and affirmative action." Several years before, Lani's nomination by President Bill Clinton to serve as Assistant Attorney General for Civil Rights had been withdrawn—what Lani dubbed her "disappointment"—partly due to the opposition of mainstream Jewish organizations to her stance on affirmative action. "Susan and I had spent many hours together processing that experience. And I remember losing patience with her for pushing me to translate my concerns so that my Jewish allies could understand what I was saying."

As Lani went on, it was clear that both students were visibly moved by her story. "I felt like why should I try to understand where *they* are coming from? But through talking with Susan, I was able to acknowledge that I hadn't been communicating effectively except with those who already agreed with me. If I wanted to build coalitions with a broader group, I had to be ready to listen to them so that I could figure out the points of connection. Susan was challenging me to use language that spoke to the people I hoped to reach about how problems long identified by people of color actually affected Americans of all races. She helped me see that I could talk about race and at the same time find points of common concern with those white people who questioned the fairness of the current system, even if they couldn't yet see how racism was operating in this system. It was worth the struggle—Susan and I came to realize that we had to worry about *how* we talk about race, not *whether* we talk about it. We *had* to talk about race."

Our willingness to have our own vulnerabilities revealed seemed to break the ice.[19] Verna and Evelyn started asking each other questions with genuine curiosity about how the other thought. And now, neither of them was skirting the issue of race. "The editorial board of the law journal just had a meeting to discuss the issue of affirmative action," Evelyn said. "We're trying to decide whether to adopt any kind of policies, including adjusting our selection practices, to increase the participation of people of color on the law journal. And there is an upcoming meeting with the editorial boards of law journals at other schools to discuss the same issues and decide what policies, if any, we should collectively adopt. These aren't easy issues for me to come to terms with, and none of us have resolved this yet."

Verna perked up. "The Black Law Students Association [BLSA] has also been having internal discussions about the law journal's lack of diversity." As the association's president, Verna said she would be guiding the development of its public stance on that issue. "Talking about this with Evelyn and the class could help BLSA better understand how to reach a broader audience with our message about the importance of affirmative action."

Even as they continued to view the issue through different and still conflicting lenses, Verna and Evelyn were engaged in "stretch collaboration," willing

to explore how they might move forward together. We walked through different scenarios for how they might frame their class discussion on affirmative
action, each providing a critical perspective and anticipating where the conversation might lead. By the end of our session, they were ready to co-lead a
dialogue with the class that could take the students through a process similar
to what they had gone through themselves. They hoped to demonstrate how,
moving through apparently intractable positions, they had arrived at being
able to find value both in Evelyn's desire to make it safe for people to speak
openly and in Verna's commitment to moving from talk to action.

The class these two students created bore the earmarks of a successful
cross-racial dialogue, designed to encourage listening and reflection, practice
in critical awareness and perspective taking, and the ability to engage in constructive conflict as well as collaborative action. During the conversation in
the class, Verna and Evelyn were each able to intervene at critical junctures to
invite constructive conflict and learning, posing questions like "What are the
recurring arguments that keep us stuck in this debate?" "What are we assuming about who deserves to be at Penn?" "What personal experiences are underlying the different positions people are taking?" "How might we reframe this
issue to focus more directly on our shared interests?"

The context Verna and Evelyn had created through developing and deepening their understanding of process and dialogue had a significant impact on
the law students' understanding of how to address racism in their practice.
One student later commented: "When everybody has a different experience,
the only way you are going to even understand the problems is by listening."
This is what Lani and I had learned and what we had aspired to teach.

The question another student posed has become even more pressing in
light of the changed legal landscape limiting affirmative action as an option
in higher education. That student wrote: "The class broke away from 'affirmative
action is good' or 'affirmative action is bad' and instead, turned to 'what do we
need to do to make higher education fully accessible to people of color?'" This
is the question that faces organizational catalysts working to bridge the racial
divides that get in the way of effective collaboration aimed at bringing about
full participation in institutions caught in the anti-racism paradoxes.

The experience Lani and I had in formulating and teaching the Critical
Perspectives class is one example of how to promote change in any context
seeking to address racism. Although organizational catalysts take different
pathways into the role, they share an intentionality about cultivating the capacity to address race, learn from failures, and reap the benefits of cross-racial

partnerships. Partnerships built on both personal and professional bonds can break down the barriers that so often paralyze people whose experiences of race have led them to interpret the world differently. In a relationship of trust, they can learn from those differences rather than magnify them. Such partnerships may be formed of individuals who are the facilitators of dialogue in an organization, or they may emerge within groups of people who work together. Whatever arena they are operating in, effective cross-racial partnerships function as the organizational catalyst to enable diverse groups to sustain relationships that lead to collaborative action. They provide the connective tissue that brings people with different backgrounds and identities together despite the paradoxical tensions that drive them apart.

One need not identify as a leader in an organization in order to build cross-racial partnerships that can become the building block of broader change. Students and coworkers who care deeply about those around them, whatever their position or identity, can help build a community that values other people's well-being and sense of belonging. Even though they are not in front of the room or seeking to make broader change, by proactively connecting across difference, they are developing cross-racial relationships of trust that are the building blocks of anti-racism.

In their book *Just Action*, Richard Rothstein and Leah Rothstein describe one such grassroots cross-racial initiative that led to successfully crossing racial boundaries. Tonika Johnson, a Black social justice artist and photographer, set out to build connections between mostly Black homeowners living on the South Side and white homeowners living on the North side of Chicago. Tonika grew up in Englewood on the South Side where annual income is less than half the city's median level. As a teenager, she went to a racially mixed but still mostly white high school on the North Side. Struck by "how different from Englewood were the communities she observed in traveling to school," she decided to use her skills as an artist to bring these two separate worlds together.[20]

Tonika had discovered that certain houses on Chicago's South Side were what she called a "map twin" of a house on the North Side, each with an identical layout and with street locations mirroring each other. However, there was very little social interaction between white and Black people in these neighboring communities. This project, called "Folded Map," became the basis of her experiment to bridge these two racially distinct communities. Tonika sent letters to the residents of these map twins asking if they wanted to meet. Many agreed, meeting at each other's homes and touring each other's neighborhoods—most visiting each other's neighborhood for the first time.

Discovering many more commonalities than they expected, they started meeting regularly and developed enduring friendships. They also documented and began to speak publicly about the systemic racism that accounted for the dramatic racial disparities in infrastructure and investment in the Black and white neighborhoods. Along with its goal of racial healing and cross-racial relationships, Folded Map became "a visual investigation of disparity and inequity in Chicago," said Tonika.[21]

House twins became block twins and began collaborating on neighborhood projects. During the Covid-19 lockdown, they began regular Zoom meetings and started a quarterly newsletter. Their projects moved from neighborhood beautification to creating new activist groups that could take on issues such as police harassment and racial differences in shopping and neighborhood amenities. They created a Folded Map Action Kit to invite Chicagoans "to expand their understanding of segregation and use as a tool for racial healing." Though only a beginning, efforts like this initiated by everyday people can build the cross-racial relationships needed to navigate the paradox of racial salience and fuel collective action.

Changes like this, by those directly affected by systemic racism, can come from those who are already working in the contexts in need of change—like Lani and me in teaching law students and like Tonika impacting a local community. But what if those who have experienced the ways an organization is affecting people of color have been excluded from participating in the work of the organization? Efforts to address racism built into the policies of social systems and large organizations can sometimes be addressed effectively only by enlisting the participation of someone from outside the organization who has directly experienced its impact and can communicate the need for change to those in a position to take action within the power structure.

Using Proximity to Promote Transformation

In 1977, the entire Rhode Island prison system was declared unconstitutional. The findings determined that the mostly Black and Brown people incarcerated by the Adult Correctional Institutions (ACI), as the statewide system was called, were, in the words of the presiding judge Raymond Pettine, "forced to live in a state of constant fear of violence, in imminent danger to [their] bodily integrity and physical and psychological well-being, and without opportunity to seek a more promising future." Judge Pettine attributed this inhumane regime to "a deeper dysfunction" in the entire prison system: "an attitude of cynicism, hopelessness, predatory selfishness, and callous indifference that tolerated these conditions and that appears to infect, to one degree or another, almost everyone who comes in contact with the ACI."[22]

After spending over a decade waiting for prison officials to do something about facilities and conditions that were "unfit for human habitation," Judge Pettine had appointed Allen Breed, at that time the director of the National Institute of Corrections and former commissioner of the California Youth Authority, as "special master," a role designated by a title that had been in use for centuries. Tasked with investigating and remedying the unacceptable conditions, Breed was to act as the "arm, and the eyes and ears of the court" with responsibility for monitoring and assisting in the implementation of a massive reform of the Rhode Island prison system.[23]

I was still in law school when Allen Breed hired me as his assistant, and the work would be unexpectedly eye-opening for both of us. A white man with sparkling blue eyes, a thoughtful demeanor, and a good heart, Allen had spent his adult life trying to reform the criminal and juvenile justice system from the top down and the inside out. Based on that experience, he knew that personal contact was key to making effective change in a system. So, soon after he was appointed to his role, Breed set out to meet the people incarcerated in ACI, hoping to enlist their cooperation in tracking compliance with the court order. Arriving in the dining hall, with corrections officers lining the walls, he took his position at the podium onstage and, looking out at a sea of mostly Black faces, started by introducing himself and his role. "My name is Allen Breed. I want to let you know more about the court order and my role in enforcing it. I have been appointed by the court as special master." Before he could go any further, a Black man sitting in the front row spoke up: "Does this mean we have to call you 'master'?"

Until this interaction, none of us working to enforce the court's order had made the connection between the term "master" and slavery's legacy. Limited by seeing through the lens of the white world we each occupied, we were oblivious to how the title would be heard by Black people forced to live in prison conditions that had been declared racist and inhumane. We had failed to understand how, even in our choice of words, we were invoking the legacy of a system of slavery that was still impacting their lives. For organizational catalysts working in any system, understanding the context from the perspective of those experiencing entrenched racism is crucial in order to avoid getting things wrong, breeding mistrust, and overlooking critical aspects of the very system they are trying to change.

In his book *Usual Cruelty: The Complicity of Lawyers in the Criminal Injustice System*, Alec Karakatsanis documents the pervasiveness of demeaning practices in the criminal justice system that are simply ignored or not even noticed.[24] He reports that the custom of requiring an accused person to appear in court shackled and confined in a glass box is accepted as the norm by prosecutors, defenders, clerks, court officers, and judges, perhaps not even questioned until an "unusual" (meaning white and privileged) defendant appears in the same restraints. Operating within narrowly defined roles that keep them at an emotional distance from the Black and Brown people who are affected by their actions and decisions, white people in power can remain ignorant of and unmoved by the human consequences of their own practices. Caught up in their own context and conditioning, they fail to even notice treatment that, if they were to pay attention, would trouble them. This detachment might explain why the term "special master" remained in use by courts until 2022, when the national racial reckoning following George Floyd's murder triggered its removal by the very association that represents "special masters."[25]

In the same way, unless they involve those who experience the effects of racist practices, predominantly white organizations can unwittingly tolerate rules and systems sustained by the momentum of history and culture. Effectively addressing racism requires getting close enough to the problem to gain a new perspective and rethink assumptions. In a widely viewed TED Talk, public interest lawyer Bryan Stevenson tells us that "we have too many problem solvers and too many politicians whose solutions are not working because they're too distant." Stevenson says that in order to be a "responsible influencer" it is necessary to get close to the problems: "When you get proximate to problems you see things and you hear nuances and details that you cannot see from a distance." Proximity is indispensable in developing workable solutions informed by knowledge of how racism is, overtly or covertly, affecting everyone in a system seeking change. And as Stevenson points out, proximity also changes those who are acting as organizational catalysts. "When you get close to problems, you will learn you have power that you didn't think you had. Being a witness in a place of despair can be transformative." Proximity, as he sums it up, is "one of the most important steps we can take to change the world."[26]

Yet over the years that I had been teaching Lawyering for Change, a course intended to help students explore how they could use their law degrees to promote social change, I was continually brought face-to-face with students' disconnection from the communities they planned to represent.[27] In one of his online reflections about the class, Oliver, a white student interested in human rights, wrote that "growing up in an environment in which I experienced hardships from behind a glass wall" had prompted him to wonder, "how can I negotiate from my comfortable distance the social problems I seek to tackle?" Another student, Jenna, echoed Oliver's concern: "How do I deal with the fact that I am and always have been separated from the people and communities most affected by the issues I am passionate about? As a law student and as a white, cisgender, relatively affluent, able-bodied woman, I can intellectualize and diagnose and genuinely do my best to be a change maker. But I can't make out the actual faces. I lose the granularity and the humanity of the individual experiences."

The angst that students in my class were feeling about this disconnect cut across race. Kris, a Black woman with family members who had experienced incarceration, saw that being in law school was changing her in ways that worried her: "I am losing my connection to my community. I feel myself changing the way I talk and even the way I think. I am even further from the people I am trying to help than I ever was." Instead of helping students discover how they would bridge this gap as lawyers, the experience of law school was exacerbating their sense of alienation. Despite my intentions in offering Lawyering for Change, something was still missing that would help students find their way back to pursuing social justice and anti-racism in a way that could actually change an unfair system.

Clearly, it hadn't been enough for me to just tell my students that as lawyers, it would be important to collaborate with the communities they would be representing, nor for them to hear from lawyers who represented those communities, nor for them read about the link between racism and mass incarceration. Even though by that point I had collaborated extensively with people with firsthand experience of racism and incarceration,[28] my own secondhand descriptions of the knowledge and insight I had gained did not seem to dislodge the messages my students had absorbed from the larger law school culture. That left them at risk of following in the footsteps of so many lawyers and policymakers who give lip service to centering the voices of those directly affected by racism but fail to build the functional relationships necessary to make good on that commitment. As Stevenson would counsel, transformative proximity requires that those directly affected by a system are in the room, shaping the conversation as full participants. Since one of the main areas of interest for the class was learning about the impact of the legal system on people of color, we needed to hear from someone who personally understands, from the inside, the system that needs transformation, and someone who could effectively communicate that perspective to students at Columbia Law School.

This led me to reach out to Alejo Rodriguez. Alejo is an Afro-Latino writer, activist, published poet, teacher, mentor, and change leader. Born and bred in the Bronx, he has a master's degree from New York Theological Seminary, serves on numerous boards, and is in demand as a public speaker. Alejo has been featured in news articles and documentaries for his transformational work in the criminal legal system. He also spent thirty-two years in prison.

I first met Alejo when I was working with the Broadway Advocacy Coalition's Theater of Change. Given BAC's aim to use the power of storytelling to dismantle the systems that perpetuate racism, its founders had realized early on that they would need to build partnerships with those directly impacted by incarceration, as well as with those who were knowledgeable about policy and law and could bring resources to the effort. That became a core part of my role as BAC's policy director and co-designer of the Theater of Change course and methodology.

After a presentation about the Theater of Change at a conference on using artistry as a vehicle for activism, Alejo had come up to me brimming with excitement. "I love what you're doing. I know the power of storytelling. While I was in prison, writing down my story is what kept me sane and alive. And now I'm supporting other people after they're released to push for change in the justice system by telling their own stories." I felt an immediate connection to Alejo and what he was doing. And as we continued talking, I understood more deeply why he was drawn to this work. "I work with a reentry organization supporting individuals coming home from Rikers Island," he said. "I spent some time there myself." Rikers is New York City's largest jail. In 2017, a scathing commission report found that for decades Rikers had been imprisoning people in violent and inhumane conditions, fueling what would become a successful campaign for policymakers to commit to closing it.[29] It was clear that Alejo understood from the inside what all of us connected to BAC felt so urgently committed to changing. "Are you interested in exploring how the Theater of Change might help advance your goals?" I asked, and was thrilled when he responded with enthusiasm.

Alejo subsequently joined the board of BAC, and the Theater of Change brought him on as part of the facilitation team. As I got to know him, I realized that he would be able to reach my students in ways that I could not. And I could see that there might be mutual benefit in connecting my law students who were concerned about the link between racism and criminal justice with those who had themselves experienced the dehumanizing conditions of the "justice" system and were now seeking to change that system so rooted in racism. I invited Alejo, along with two others, Devon Simmons and Isaac Scott, who had also been in prison, to speak to the students in Lawyering for Change. Alejo had already been working with public defenders around the country to help them build trust and mutual collaborations with the people and communities they represented and advocated for, so he could speak directly to these students' interests and concerns. What I would see happen in the class would make it clear that the best way to effectively transform any system in which racism is a concern is to learn with and from those who directly experience its impact.

When Alejo, Devon, and Isaac came to my class, they began by introducing themselves with a little about their background. Then, knowing the value personal stories could have for this multiracial class, Alejo invited students to speak with each other: "Please take a few minutes to talk to the person next to you about your relationship to the criminal legal system. What experiences have you had yourself in this arena? How do you see yourself in relation to the justice system?" When he asked the class what had come up when they talked, one Black student shared the story of getting "the talk" from his parents when he was eight years old about what to do if he was stopped by police. Another described regularly having his ID checked when he entered Columbia Law School while his white peers entered without question. A white student talked about working in a public defender's office and watching lawyers, in the face of an ineffective and overburdened system, become desensitized and cynical about their roles.

Alejo nodded as they spoke. None of these experiences were unfamiliar to him. To underline the point that was becoming clear, he said, "Did you know that the United States incarcerates more people than any other country in the world? And did you know that 75 percent of those incarcerated in New York State come from seven neighborhoods, including Harlem and the Bronx, where I grew up? Nationally, a little over 60 percent of adults in the United States know a family member who has been to jail. For Black people, that number is closer to 80 percent. These statistics are not just academic for me. I spent thirty-two years in the New York State prison system."

Alejo stopped for a moment, allowing the students to process the dissonance they might be experiencing between their view of this speaker as someone with considerable education, knowledge, and leadership skills in contrast to what might have been their preconceptions of someone who had spent time in prison. For some of the students, this was the first time they were directly in touch with a person who had experienced the school-to-prison pipeline, and they were about to get a firsthand account of what that meant. "In my own life," Alejo continued, "I have experienced a sequence of failing institutions, from public schools that didn't educate me to inadequate health care to utter lack of decent employment opportunities. As a young Black man, I got caught up in a culture of apathy. I saw that no one cared about me, so I didn't care about anyone else.

"So now you might be wondering what made it possible for me to be speaking with you at Columbia Law School and working with lawyers and policymakers to change the system." I saw people nodding around the room. Alejo continued: "When I was in prison, incarcerated individuals could still use federal financial aid to pay for college courses offered inside. So, ironically, in prison I had the chance to get the education I never received outside. I worked in the metal shop during the day and went to class at night. I took a poetry class and started to write."[30] Poetry became Alejo's vehicle for expressing his anger and frustration with the racism and abuse he was witnessing daily in prison. "I was using my writing to sort through some real shit. My anger. My distrust of anything institutional. My questioning of myself. Writing became my way of sledgehammering these walls." Anger became inspiration, and writing became a way for him to connect to a world beyond the bars of his cell, as shown in this excerpt from one of his poems written at that time, "Sing Sing Sits Up the River."[31]

How sparrows still remind me there's a spirit
free. And that it breathes.
Even where winters are the coldest
& holidays are just a thing from another life.
Even in this cold that burns,
the sun kisses my forehead
as if I were as pure
as a day breastfeeding in my mother's arms
How unimaginable,
how freedom comes alive
touching the sun
between bars.

Education and personal expression became Alejo's way to discover his power in the world. "I read anything I could find that critically analyzed systemic oppression. Anger became insight, and that insight was understanding why I chose to involve myself in volunteer programs outside of what was mandated or why I spoke up not just for myself but also for others locked up." Even while living in the chaos and daily violence of the prison system, Alejo earned an associate's degree, a bachelor's degree, and a master's degree. "For me, education was the resource that got me mobilized to reimagine who I am." He learned American Sign Language and, for eight years, worked with deaf people in prison. He took a course in legal research, started an Alternatives to Violence Project, taught classes, and served as an informal mentor, "paying forward" the support that was being given to him along the way.

By offering his vivid stories and insights, Alejo was the catalyst my students needed to understand more fully the system they wanted to affect with their work. He invited them next to begin rethinking the relationship between law and justice, between lawyers and communities directly affected by incarceration. To illustrate the problem, he talked about his own experience of lawyers, of their failure to listen to him, about their unwillingness to face up to the chasm between how law is written and how law was lived by those at its mercy.

"All in all, I made eleven parole appearances and served fourteen years over my minimum," he told the students. "Each time I sought parole, I was denied for the same reason I was convicted. Whether I was suitable for release—the programs I participated in, my rehabilitative transformation, remorse, and insight—didn't seem to matter. And the legal help I was getting was no help at all."[32] Seeking to convey the disrespect that characterized his treatment by the "legal advisors" he was given, Alejo continued: "Imagine being called for an interview without being told the job you're applying for, no job description, no indication of the skills or qualifications they're looking for. Just go in there and *sell* yourself. The process is so arbitrary that many people who make parole can't even say for sure what swayed the interview in their favor. It was fumbling around in the darkness. But did it have to be that way?"

Alejo's experience of lawyers' detachment and lack of genuine concern continued after he was out of prison. When activist lawyers learned that Alejo had spent time in Rikers and could tell a powerful story about his experience there, they pushed him to speak publicly at protests and advocacy events about his dehumanizing experience. "They asked me to go to speaking events, like the 'Close Rikers' campaign. But I knew that if the demonstration goes wrong, I could be back in Rikers. They didn't seem to care. They wanted my voice, but they didn't want *me*." Through his story and his presence, Alejo was conveying a vivid cautionary tale that educated these law students about how *not* to represent and work with those they sought to assist. One student later wrote,

"What I could imagine from Alejo's story was the feeling of being used as a tool by those activists who failed to look into his eyes and sincerely say, 'We want to help you; what do *you* need?'" In organizations seeking change, this is the value of hearing the stories of those impacted by racism, so that the question "What do you need?" can lead to action in a context of shared understanding.

Alejo had invited my law students to envision a relationship that centers the voices and insights of those directly affected and builds genuine partnerships. By inviting everyone in the room into his personal story, he had created the proximity necessary for these law students to rethink what their own relationship might be to those they intended to serve in their legal careers. Alejo was using impact storytelling—combining personal narratives with a systems lens that places those stories in a larger context. Rather than emphasizing his individual experience of trauma, he drew the attention of these law students to the context and root causes that perpetuated racism and the system of mass incarceration. Hearing his story was an "aha" moment awakening them to their responsibility for changing a "justice" system that was, in fact, unjust. They began to question the gap between law on the books and law on the ground. They saw things about the criminal legal system that had escaped them and their criminal law professors as well, and they realized the importance of learning with and from people like Alejo.

Alejo was demonstrating an important quality and practice of organizational catalysts, a kind of 3D insight based on combining stories from personal experience with policy and data analysis, providing the credibility needed to reach people at all levels in a system or organization. Alongside his master's degree and publication record, he had, as he puts it, "a PhD from the streets." With his feet firmly planted in two worlds Alejo was multilingual, able to adapt his mode of communication to the context. While he could speak about policy, government programs, and research when it was needed and relevant, he remained tethered to the concerns of those most affected by incarceration. He could not and would not disassociate himself from the reality he was studying, assessing, and attempting to transform. Like others he works alongside in this process, he knows, "I have to be the change I want to see."

Alejo's ability to find strength in his vulnerability opened the floodgates in the class, in particular for students of color and first-generation students, who had been struggling to find their footing in law school. He listened intently to the raw pain and emotion as they described their law school experiences. Stella, the daughter of immigrants, said she had experienced law school thus far as "soul-killing," strangling her voice and disconnecting her from the community she cared about and those she sought to represent. This was the first time in our class that students who had family members and friends who had been incarcerated shared those experiences with each other. One of them told Alejo, "I couldn't help but cringe and fear what people in the class and in law school here at Columbia would think about some of my friends and family." By situating his story in the narrative of race and systemic injustice, Alejo had made it possible for these students to share experiences they had never before revealed in law school. He invited all of them to express their own truths and to understand how they could shift their relationship with communities affected by incarceration from being saviors to being collaborators.

Just as Allen Breed and I had to learn the impact of language like "master" in perpetuating embedded stereotypes, all three of the formerly incarcerated leaders in the class with us that day wanted the students to recognize ways that unquestioned language built into law and policy perpetuated dehumanization. To support this point, Isaac read a passage from "Open Letter to Our Friends on the Question of Language," written by Eddie Ellis, a widely respected formerly incarcerated advocate for human justice:

> When we are not called mad dogs, animals, predators, offenders and other derogatory terms, we are referred to as inmates, convicts, prisoners and felons—all terms devoid of humanness which identify us as "things" rather than as people. These terms are accepted as the "official" language of the media, law enforcement, prison industrial complex and public policy agencies. However, they are no longer acceptable for us and we are asking people to stop using them.[33]

To encourage students to see this call as something they could respond to immediately themselves, Isaac urged them to follow Ellis's plea to "get progressive publications, organizations and individuals like you to stop using the old offensive language and simply refer to us as 'people.'"

One white student later commented: "The class was highly instructive; the presenters showed me that the people who know best how to identify the shortcomings in the law or in society are the people who have been failed by America's institutions repeatedly in their lives." Another said, "I think that when we're able to acknowledge our limitations as lawyers, we create space to learn from others. This is why it is critical that we engage with individuals who have been impacted by the criminal justice system and allow them to guide our thinking about the system and ways to reform it." Yet another reported that the conversation with Alejo "has shaken me and left me reading every case differently since."

As the class session was ending, Alejo invited the students to dream with him: "What would a human-centered relationship between lawyers and directly affected communities look like? How might voting rights lawyers working on felony disenfranchisement collaborate with formerly incarcerated advocates to build genuine political participation with the knowledge, awareness, and trust that entails? How might we keep this conversation going after we leave today?" As part of Lawyering for Change, students had been assigned to project groups focused on advancing change in areas ranging from mass incarceration to education to immigration to environmental justice. For those focused on reducing mass incarceration, this invitation was an exciting opportunity to rethink the projects they were already engaged in by directly involving formerly incarcerated advocates as partners. The three leaders who spoke in class that day had fueled students' enthusiasm by suggesting ways they might connect with those they knew and worked with who would be interested in doing that. They said that the students might continue this conversation, not only with them but also with other formerly incarcerated leaders who were part of their community. Through communicating the system's impact on them, they had enlisted the students in imagining a different kind of relationship with people directly affected by an unjust legal system and had inspired them to embrace their roles as lawyers working within the system while at the same time trying to change it.

Sometimes, a system needs to bring in an organizational catalyst like Alejo, who is an outsider but personally understands that system's impact on people of color. When an organization is trying to address racism but is stuck in self-limiting ways of framing or understanding the issue, an outsider with insider knowledge can introduce effective transformative thinking and actions. But, for this impact to last, one-time proximity is not enough. People working inside institutions have to find ways to enable people directly affected by racism to become part of the ongoing change process.

My role and that of organizational catalysts operating inside institutions is to use the legitimacy and leverage of our position to introduce such change agents and sustain their involvement with organizational insiders. I was able to sustain change initiated in that class by introducing Alejo to student leaders, faculty, foundations, and policymakers and locating resources to support his continued collaboration with them. And eventually he would be hired by Columbia to work with students and faculty on reimagining legal education and the role of lawyers in working with communities affected by racism and incarceration. I helped Alejo create a new course and program, titled Breakthrough Advocacy Through Transformative Learning Exchange (BATTLE), which I co-teach with him, bringing together law students and formerly incarcerated advocates to learn with and from each other and to pursue projects aimed at transforming the criminal legal system.[34] I have played an analogous role with Devon Simmons, using my position, contacts, and knowledge to support him in creating and directing the Paralegal Pathways Initiative (PPI), a program that enlists law students to help those returning home from American prisons find sustainable careers. PPI does this by refining the existing talents of formerly incarcerated people, who often gain legal research and litigation skills while inside correctional facilities. These examples illustrate how an insider with influence can bring outsider catalysts into spaces they would not otherwise be in, thereby acknowledging and supporting the importance of their expertise. The dream of racial equity in organizations depends on weaving positive change in partnership with those most adversely affected by the present system.

Creating Cohorts for Sustaining Change

Organizational catalysts seeking lasting change must find a way to sustain cross-racial collaborations and proximity, ensuring transformation in the wake of struggle and setbacks. How do organizational catalysts find ways to sustain their own efforts to make change over the long haul? This can happen when they construct a diverse community of people who are themselves equipped and committed to change in the larger organization, building in strategies for sustainability from the start.

One example of this cohort approach comes from the University of Michigan's effort to increase the participation of people of color and women on its faculty.[35] As the recipient of a grant from the National Science Foundation, an initiative called ADVANCE at the University of Michigan committed to institutional transformation that would change academic climates so they would become inclusive, welcoming, and supportive of women and people of color. Abby Stewart, a psychology professor and founding director of UM's ADVANCE project, spearheaded the ADVANCE initiative at Michigan, finding in this work a way to broaden her role as an academic to include social activism, as well as to pursue intersectionality theory as a way to bridge race and gender.[36] As an integral part of her role as a professor, Abby committed herself to "working on institutional change within higher education and in particular in her own institution," recognizing early on that this kind of culture change could only happen if she enlisted and sustained a diverse group of people from fields spanning the university who could catalyze change in their own departments. The cultivation of such organizational catalysts became one of ADVANCE's core strategies for sustaining change—creating, equipping, and supporting diverse communities of change agents, and then placing them in positions where they could advance full participation of first women and then people of color, one step at a time.

To implement this strategy, Abby created STRIDE (Strategies and Tactics Recruiting to Improve Diversity and Excellence). Drawing on the networks and relationships she had developed through years of interdisciplinary collaborations and institutional change work, she recruited faculty members respected as researchers in their fields who also had a track record of mentoring diverse junior faculty and graduate students and who cared about racial and gender equity. One STRIDE member later recalled: "I was a little bit skeptical that a committee could do anything effective. But after I heard Abby I changed my mind and agreed to be on the committee. . . . There was a lot of information about the climate at U of M, and that made me feel that the problem was larger than I thought."[37]

After one of their initial meetings, another STRIDE member recalled, "We sat in this room and asked the question, 'Now what do we do?' We had good intentions but were completely ignorant about the problem. We all had our gut feeling that there is underrepresentation of women and people of color in the sciences at the faculty level, but how do you prove that to a real skeptic?" It turns out, he discovered, that "even the people who are not convinced that we have a problem recognize that the numbers are low but think that this something beyond their control. They disregard the fact that the climate within the department is part of the problem. When a person says 'I had nothing to do with it,' that is what we need to attack right there."

The STRIDE members wanted to know what would be important to communicate, and what would be the most effective way to reach those they hoped to influence. Abby helped them answer these questions, leading them through a weekly learning process over the course of a summer to build a community that understood the problem, knew how to talk about it persuasively, and had concrete examples of what could be done about it. She grounded that process in their lived experience as faculty members: "Universities require people to make a lot of judgments of merit—all day, every day. We evaluate each other constantly: Is this a good talk? Is this student accomplishing what I hoped they would? We read and write reviews of papers and grant proposals. We read and write letters of recommendation. We evaluate students. We think we do this fairly and well. Are we right? Not really!" Abby then provided the STRIDE committee with the social science explaining why people's forecasts about others are likely to be wrong and to reflect widespread schemas and biases built into our thinking.[38]

With her support, the STRIDE group studied social science research explaining racial and gender exclusion, shared stories about their own experiences, and developed strategies for communicating effectively with their peers about what they had learned. Abby helped STRIDE members learn to use the credibility of science, combined with stories, as the way to legitimate racial and gender bias as a serious problem.

STRIDE developed into a space where people cared about each other, developed the courage and know-how to act on their own values, and became invested in each other's success and well-being as change agents. The trust that developed encouraged people to speak openly, even about themselves: "In spite of having extremely different races and backgrounds, women, men, engineers, scientists, medical school people, we all bonded very quickly. So we didn't hold anything back and started using examples of things that had happened in our own departments." STRIDE became a community with a common mission and shared vocabulary, engaged over the long run in supporting each other's efforts to promote change. They then set out to educate colleagues in their respective fields about how gender and race were operating in their own departments and to support them in adopting evidence-based practices that would increase participation and promote equity.

After the summer, STRIDE members began meeting with department chairs, search committees, and deans, not only as part of the faculty hiring and promotion process but also in response to racial and gender issues that had been raised with STRIDE members by faculty and graduate students. "With the chairs, we learned to figure out something that bothers them, like attrition, and connect that issue to concerns about race and gender." With Abby's support, the group continued to meet to brainstorm about strategy, provide moral support, and develop tools that others could use to promote full participation. Eager to expand their impact, over time they developed spin-off groups to equip and support additional change agents in pursuing gender and racial equity in their departments and fields.

Abby's creation of a sustained process for learning and community building turned out to be crucial to getting potential change agents to the table, keeping them involved, and fueling their continued involvement. This process equipped STRIDE members to become multilingual communicators in their worlds, like Alejo was in his—able to marshal data, stories, and strategies for change. In commenting on the changes at UM to expand diversity, one member of the team said, "STRIDE played a very important legitimizing role. They were well-known scientists on the campus who got it, after training. They then wanted to tell people about it. They played a hugely important role in legitimizing it."

STRIDE has demonstrated its staying power; it is still in existence after two decades. Facing pushback or burnout, STRIDE members could turn to a cohort of support that mirrored their values and helped them remain engaged in the face of setbacks and failure. The impact went beyond changing policies to changing the overall culture of the school. One participant reported, "Now when I overhear something or I am part of a conversation I know I have to speak up, when before I might have recognized it but I didn't say anything. I am exercising that moral leadership." STRIDE became a community of organizational catalysts, with lasting presence and impact. These workshops have led departments to adopt strategies, tactics, and resources that have increased their hiring of diverse faculty. In 2020, the provost charged all schools and colleges on the Ann Arbor campus to use STRIDE's workshops to orient their faculty search committees.[39] STRIDE's values and practices have been exported to new initiatives: a cohort supporting new faculty in launching their careers at UM; a group tackling retention issues facing BIPOC faculty; a cross-institutional network developed by the National Science Foundation, providing an additional layer of community support for sustaining change work at UM.

In some organizations the cohort anchoring change is organized around racial identity, at least at the outset, as we saw with the Meyerhoff program at UMBC. Sometimes a multiracial group serves as the organizational catalyst, coalescing around a shared goal, such as creating full participation in the institution, department, or community, as we saw with STRIDE and in Judge Fein's court. Sometimes, the cohort brings together people from inside the institution and people from the community as we did with BAC in the Theater of Change and in the course created by Alejo called BATTLE (Breakthrough Advocacy Through Transformative Learning Exchange), which included law students and community advocates affected by incarceration. Just as BATTLE was built on combining cross-racial facilitation and proximity to create cohorts committed to lasting change both within Columbia Law School and in the justice system, all of these successful efforts were led by a group of organizational catalysts willing to sustain the effort over the long haul.

The three practices offered in this chapter—building cross-racial partner-ships, using proximity to promote transformation, and creating cohorts that sustain change—help organizational catalysts build trust across racial divides and weave together collaborations that can advance collective aims over the long haul. Cross-racial partnerships in such contexts enable people with very different racial experiences to communicate with and learn from each other as they ad-dress their differences in perspective, experience, and power. Such proximity opens the possibility for those directly affected by racism to influence how power is exercised by those in decision-making positions, even as it challenges the legitimacy of that power. Organizational catalysts create contexts that pro-mote and sustain change, providing ways to take small steps in the short run that make anti-racism work doable and desirable, even as they highlight the necessity of comprehensive, long-term transformation. These catalysts create collabora-tion among people who have built trust with different constituencies and who can work together over time. This longevity is what enables the tensions built into the anti-racism paradoxes to become a source of learning and change.

Powerful and transformative as they may be, the collaborations built by organizational catalysts can also be fragile. They require some source of sustenance in the face of the pressures working against them. That support might come from those in leadership positions within the organization. It might come from groups, working inside or outside the organization, that offer sup-port and accountability for anti-racism efforts. Without some combination of these supports, even successful change efforts may founder over time.

Whether or not that critical support for anti-racist practices develops is a function of power. But the way power currently operates within an organization can cut against the ability of organizational catalysts to effectively address rac-ism. These undermining effects can happen especially in predominantly white institutions where those in power are still operating with a zero-sum mentality that defines interests narrowly and prevents people from discovering the linked fate that can lead to changes in racist practices. How can those dedicated to change move forward with building bridges and weaving dreams in the face of institutions that are set up to maintain the status quo? Answering that question requires rethinking how power is exercised, the subject of the next chapter.

6

Repurposing Power

THE MALL OF AMERICA, the largest shopping mall in the United States, opened in August 1992 in the mostly white suburb of Bloomington, Minnesota. It soon became a destination not only for tourists on shopping sprees but for local teens looking for a place to hang out, particularly during the winter with below-zero weather. Boasting fast food, video games, and thrill rides, it was a magnet for youth—white kids from the suburbs, one of whom portrayed the Mall to a reporter as "a place to see and be seen, meet friends, get a date, or a job," and Black teens from urban areas, one of whom described the Mall as "the safest place you could be, not like a park, party, or out late at night in the streets." Another Black teenager explained: "Saturday night, we come to the Mall. This is about the only place we can kick it. Everybody gets together and has fun; everybody in the neighborhood, everybody in the city, people you went to school with. It's more fun than seeing them on the streets."[1] Within a couple of years of its opening, on Friday and Saturday evenings three to four thousand young people, most of them Black and from neighborhoods in Minneapolis, were pouring out of the public transportation terminal, built expressly to serve the Mall, and onto the 129 acres of commercial offerings.[2]

As the number of teenagers congregating there on weekends grew, so did Mall officials' concerns about their impact on tenants and shoppers. Groups as big as fifteen to twenty kids, at times swelling to as large as fifty, were traveling through the megamall together, sometimes blocking the entrance to stores and escalators. One night, when a fight involving a gun broke out among a group of teenagers, the situation made headlines in the local media. Mall representatives assured the public that this incident was "isolated" and that kids were mostly just doing "junior high stuff."[3]

However, the racial tension underlying the situation was apparent in the remarks of one white shopkeeper who worried that many of his older shoppers were "scared away" by the teenagers who were wearing what he perceived to be "gang-related apparel." He went on to make his point more explicitly: "A lot of people are not used to seeing large numbers of minority kids." When some members of the Black community expressed concern about racist responses to the teenagers' behavior, Mall officials acknowledged that "'gang' has become a word used as a judgment of black youth." The police chief agreed that the concerns were overblown. "Gang activity isn't running when you are supposed to walk and swearing. By and large, it's pretty peaceful. They are going to the Mall on the bus because it's cheap. They are getting a burger and fries and a drink and having fun, and then they go home. Do they wear baggy clothes and silly looking colors? Sure, but they are kids."[4]

But Mall leadership began worrying that the teens' rowdy and unruly behavior would discourage customers from coming to shop. "People were getting the perception that weekend nights were not a night to come out," one Mall spokesperson was quoted as saying. To deal with the issue, the Mall leadership soon exercised its power with a show of force, redefining the purpose of its security officers from public relations to policing behavior. Made up of mostly young suburban white men who had never been around Black people before, the "Mall Security" began their operation carrying handcuffs, pepper spray, and batons. As one supervising officer described his work: "Our attitude was, 'We are going to war.' I was part of the quick response team. We would walk around in black jumpsuits and boots, and intimidate troublemakers." The Mall officials invoked their right as property owners to evict anyone from the premises for any reason—a policy that had only recently been upheld by the Minnesota state courts—authorizing the security officers to arrest teenagers for trespassing if they returned after being asked to leave or if a Mall guard decided that they had been disorderly.[5]

Not surprisingly, some of the teenagers claimed that the security guards were singling them out for scrutiny because they were Black, and they were not the only ones who held that view. The county attorney reported that he had watched guards on Friday and Saturday nights order young African American males off benches while making no such efforts with adults or white youth, and either the kids "did what they were told or there was a fight."[6] By 1995, the Mall was stationing security guards every ten feet in certain areas and equipping some officers with trained dogs.

One weekend in the early spring of 1996, several security guards used physical force on three Black girls, ages fourteen and fifteen, accusing them of blocking the entrance to an escalator and using "foul language." After the girls yelled,

"You are prejudiced because we are Black!" the conflict escalated. The officers physically restrained one of the girls and sent her handcuffed to the county's juvenile detention center. The Black community's anger about the treatment of their youth boiled over with charges of racism, and the parents of the three girls sued the Mall for discrimination. As tensions escalated between mall officials and the community, news reports about these incidents signaled to the world that the Mall of America might not be safe for anyone. The Mall's "power over" strategy of trying to control the kids using force had backfired.

The term "power over," first used in 1924 by management theorist Mary Parker Follett and later elaborated on by social theorist Steven Lukes, refers to a relationship in which individuals or groups in positions of dominance use coercive or manipulative tactics to impose their will on others.[7] Using force, threats, promises, or manipulation, those with "power over" get others to follow their rules and do what they want. "Power over" typically operates within a hierarchical power structure in which a small group makes decisions affecting a larger one, and it is built on the belief that power is a finite resource, meaning that in order to preserve power in a situation, it has to be hoarded and used to prevent others from gaining power.[8]

In the situation at the Mall of America, as those in power used their legally enforceable property rights to protect their economic interests, they escalated racial conflict, increased negative publicity, and drew concern from the greater community. How could Mall leaders redefine how they exercised power and thus their relationship with the communities of color affected by their decisions? Doing that would require everyone concerned to work together to discover creative solutions.

Such an opportunity was presented at a meeting convened by the Metropolitan Council, a group coordinating policy and planning for the Twin Cities area. That meeting was attended by the Mall's leadership team, all of them white, by representatives from the mayor's office and the police department, and by leaders from the Black community who had been critics of the Mall's initial response. That group of Black representatives included members of the local Urban League, members of the Urban Coalition, a nonprofit group in Minneapolis founded to address racism and issues of social and economic inequality, and leaders from Club Fed, a group led by Black people and made up of eighty youth-serving organizations located in the Minneapolis-St. Paul area.

Club Fed had worked with Mall of America employees the previous summer on a series of events for kids who lived in public housing in Minneapolis-St. Paul and had built a good relationship with some of the Mall of America staff, including those in leadership who were at the meeting. "They realized that those same kids, the kids who they had had fun with over the summer, were the ones hanging out at the Mall of America on evenings and weekends," Club Fed's president reported. That realization opened the possibility of shifting the question from "What do we do to control those unruly kids?" to "How are we treating the kids who are part of our community? What can we do together to connect with them so they can be safe, avoid trouble, have fun, and also get their needs met?" In response, a Mall official at the meeting quipped, "We need more moms here," and the idea took hold. "Mighty Moms" was born, a response to the issue framed in terms that were important to both the Mall and the community advocates.[9]

With resources provided by the Mall, Club Fed hired, paid, and supervised a team of teachers, counselors, clergy, parents, and moms who were from the same communities as the teenagers coming to the Mall, people the teens could trust. These Mighty Moms walked the Mall on Friday and Saturday nights, diffusing any potential conflicts and interacting with the kids, many of whom they already knew. Instead of using authority to force the kids to either comply with the rules or leave the Mall, their strategy was to connect with them, asking them about their lives—how is school, how are things at home, what's going on outside school, where are your friends? Building relationships of trust rather than premised on authority was key. As one Mighty Mom explained, "It's a gradual thing. You can't just walk up to the kids. They have to see you all the time, and then you can feel free to walk up and talk to them. Most are looking for someone to talk to and listen to them." If there seemed to be a need, the Mighty Moms sometimes would put kids in touch with resources and, when they felt it would help, speak with their family members.

An additional contribution of the Mighty Moms was that they explored ways to prevent or diffuse tensions between the kids and Mall security officers. If there were a conflict, the Mighty Moms would often step in before the situation got out of hand, reaching out to kids they knew in the group to establish a human connection and find out what was going on with them. They talked with the kids about choices they could make to minimize clashes with security. One Mighty Mom reported the importance of simply educating kids about the consequences of getting in trouble with the authorities. She said, "I had an opportunity to take a kid to the side and say, 'Look, this is what can happen. You don't want this to happen to you.'"

And the Mighty Moms could also explain the experience and behavior of the kids to those working in security who might otherwise have jumped to unwarranted conclusions about danger and intervened with force. "I was paired to walk the Mall with someone who had no idea what my experience was," one Mighty Mom said about her own interactions with a white security guard. "Getting to know me gave him insight, and let him know, hey, all people are just people. They are learning from us how to talk with minority kids."

The Mighty Moms had the kind of power needed to adequately address the issue at the Mall—the ability to understand the situation from the perspective of everyone involved, to communicate effectively, and to persuade those involved that responding in this way would be more successful than "power over." Community members and Mall leadership agreed that the Mighty Moms' involvement was keeping many situations from escalating. The group soon received accolades from the African American mayor of Minneapolis, Sharon Sayles Belton, who fondly recalled growing up with women in her community watching over the behavior of all the children. In response to this new program, she said, "Who better than moms? It's called tapping into the community for solutions."

The community group recruited by Club Fed was starting to imagine ways that the Mall could use its financial resources and access to physical space to respond to the needs identified by the kids and their communities, including the lack of adequate places for kids to hang out in their neighborhoods. That issue was becoming a citywide concern, leading Mike Bazerman, a professor of youth studies and youth development at the University of Minnesota, to write a suggestion: "Let the Mall contribute some money to create a wider variety of alternatives for kids in their community and in the downtown area. There's lots of money coming into the Mall. Let them put it back in safe and viable experiences, and involve kids in the planning."

It looked like the Mall's leadership was considering those ideas and, in responding to the community as part of the solution, was genuinely respecting the interests and needs of community members of color. Could it be that the Mall of America was moving away from a zero-sum approach to power toward one that located the power for decision making within the full array of those with the knowledge and understanding to address tough problems involving race? There were signs that the Mall's leadership was interested in upholding mutually agreed-upon values, values that the social and political culture of the area subscribed to. If that inclusive approach took hold, the Mall and the local community members would be engaging in a participatory, collaborative, and equitable way, in what Follett and Lukes might both regard as "power with."

In contrast to domination and control, "power with" opens the way to collective action that includes all groups affected by and responsible for a decision or situation. "Power with" starts from the assumption that one person or group cannot fully understand and should not be in a position to dictate what's best for another. In "power with" contexts, everyone affected by a situation shares in decisions and actions related to it. Together, they identify what they are aiming for in a solution and consider how best to achieve those aims while supporting each other in individual and collective goals.[10] This does not necessarily mean that all decisions are made collectively but rather that the way power is delegated is determined by everyone involved and those agreements are continually revisited to assure that "power with" remains the overarching modus operandi. Enacting this kind of "power with" is what the Mighty Moms could have exemplified.

The Mall leadership had the chance to take the crucial step of reconfiguring the way they exercised their power. The Mall could not change its relationship with the youth and their community using a "power over" approach. They needed the community members' expertise and collaboration to develop a long-term solution that would go beyond the Mall's narrow economic and commercial interests and ensure that the project would advance values of equity and mutual respect. When those with "power over" face up to their linked fate with communities of color, they have the chance to be intentional about what Lukes called "power to": the capacity to act in furtherance of those goals by those with the necessary knowledge, commitment, and legitimacy, particularly those directly affected by the problems sought to be addressed. "Power to" poses the question: Power for what purpose? Repurposing power means arranging relationships and resources to move from narrowly defined self-interested aims to equitable ones, which necessitates moving from "power over" to "power with."

The changes at the Mall of America initiated by Club Fed seemed to promise a move to "power with." But in June 1996, barely two months after the Mighty Moms program was initiated, a family visiting the Mall from Portland, Oregon, found themselves caught in the middle of a fight in the food court between groups of Asian American and Black teenagers. Feeling unsafe, the parents, in their words, "raised a big stink." Although the fracas didn't make the local news, the Mall authorities reacted, reasserting their "power over" the kids and the community. They instituted a curfew barring people under sixteen from the Mall on Friday and Saturday nights unless they brought a parent or other adult over the age of twenty-one with them, a policy many in the Black community viewed as once again targeting people of color.

Mall leadership hired men from the same community as the Mighty Moms to serve alongside them as Dedicated Dads; both groups were now charged with responsibility for enforcing the curfew. This redefined role replaced the relationship-building aspects of the Mighty Moms with a focus on avoiding disruption. The program had become, in the words of one Mighty Mom, "security with a soft touch" and a "PR program to sell the community on the parental escort policy." After this shift in power, one of the Mighty Moms commented, "The purpose of us being there now is to determine who is underage and escort them down and out of the Mall. It's a waste of our talents. We should be there walking around and talking to people. We don't have that with the community anymore." The Mighty Moms had turned into a purely symbolic way to preserve the status quo. The number of kids hanging out at the Mall dropped, but as one former Mighty Mom asked, "Where are these kids on the weekends? I have no idea. The Mall's concern for them evaporated when the escort policy drove the kids away." In the face of challenging circumstances, the Mall had abandoned "power with" and resumed "power over."

Yusef Mgeni, president of the Urban Coalition, publicly chastising the Mall leadership for divorcing themselves from the problem, declared: "They are merely displacing the problem to some other part of the community." The Minneapolis *Star Tribune*'s editorial board, critical of the Mall for imposing the curfew, labeled the policy unfair and predicted it would land teenagers "somewhere less attractive, less supervised, less safe." Calling attention to the economic benefits reaped by attracting young people to its public space, the editors wrote that the Mall "owes its young customers and its community" a commitment to provide "a safe and congenial place where young people can mingle and generally experiment with the modest freedoms of adolescence." The editorial beseeched the Mall to devise more creative and pioneering solutions by working closely with community leaders—perhaps quintupling the Mighty Moms cadres—instead of multiplying the number of Mall security guards.[11] All of this to no avail. "Power over" policies remained in place.

The Mall's leadership had missed the chance to repurpose its power. Shifting to a "power with" collaboration could have redefined their relationship with those who were now their critics. They could have engaged the city's youth, community members, and government agencies in addressing a shared long-term concern: the well-being of young people in the community. Instead, the Mall had reverted to exerting its "power over" the community and the teenagers, pursuing its narrow concerns about public relations and profitability at the expense of building trust and community well-being.

In order for people in predominantly white organizations to address issues of power in a way that sustains anti-racism work over the long haul, it is necessary to reconfigure the way they exercise power so that cross-racial learning and accountability can continue to drive the pursuit of linked fate. Without shared power, white people in "power over" positions are likely to downplay the concerns of people of color, making it likely that they will revert to preserving a zero-sum status quo at the expense of pursuing collective well-being. Repurposing power in the context of anti-racism means redefining relationships and reallocating resources to move from narrow self-interests to shared aims, forged by recognizing linked fate and pursued collectively through mutual learning and accountability. This chapter lays out three crucial dimensions of repurposing power:

- what forms power assumes to either maintain or transform situations involving racism
- how knowledge and expertise become participatory and genuinely shared so that they can advance anti-racism
- where and by whom decisions governing an organization or project are made so that constituencies of color and values relating to equity can have genuine impact

Recognizing issues of power and naming them is the first step in reconfiguring relationships so that people of different races and power positions can work together to address the racism embedded in our institutions.

The Challenge of Moving from "Power Over" to "Power With"

Power lies behind all decisions involving race. As Lani Guinier and Gerald Torres explain in *The Miner's Canary*, "In saying that race is linked to power, we suggest that it is linked to more than the way an individual experiences power. We mean that the distribution of resources in this society is racialized and that this racial hierarchy is then normalized and thereby made invisible."[12] Even when people in predominantly white institutions have embraced "both/and" values that make anti-racism work worth the effort and risks it entails, they can fail to address how the prevailing power arrangements affect whether that commitment holds up over time.

Meaningful change in organizations committed to addressing racism and advancing full participation requires confronting how power operates in ways that undercut that commitment. Freeman Hrabowski and his white colleagues were able to transform a predominantly white institution into a driver of inclusive excellence only through genuine collaboration in which the experiences of Black students could serve as the "miner's canary" for the whole institution. In the wake of the "We See You, White American Theater" letter, Lee discovered that power sharing with Black company members, based on a mutual commitment to human-centered values, was a prerequisite to making his anti-racism efforts trustworthy and effective. The "power with" processes used to forge linked fate—connecting interests to values affecting the well-being of everyone in an organization—can be sustained only if they are built into the organization's explicit understandings and agreements about how decisions will be made and who is in a position to make them.

When propelled by increased calls for accountability, those in power in an organization may have accepted the necessity of addressing racism, but that does not necessarily mean that they will share that power when, as happened at the Mall of America, they are confronted with disagreements about priorities or situations that affect the bottom line. Simply inviting a diverse group of people to develop common aims does not assure that those experiencing racism will have a genuine say in pivotal decisions that affect them and their communities, or that diverse teams will value the insights of people of color. Nor does proximity guarantee that people of color will have the chance to speak up and be heard when those with "power over" make choices inconsistent with agreed-upon aims. When organizations with embedded hierarchies attempt collaborative means to solve problems, they might fail to set up the conditions required for less powerful people to fully participate. There is always the looming risk that they might end up using their power to co-opt members of the community and defuse the pressure for change by making only symbolic gestures, not investing the time and resources required for genuine change.

The disempowerment of the Mighty Moms revealed the hazards of trying to move predominantly white institutions from "power over" to "power with." As happened there, when the interests of those in power diverged from the values supporting anti-racism, it was easiest to revert to "power over." When push comes to shove, unless there are countervailing constraints leading them to do otherwise, those with "power over" are likely to advance their immediate interests at the expense of the human-centered values that might prevail in a "power with" process.

Any cross-racial group seeking to advance values at odds with racism has to determine how to reconfigure power so that it will be exercised to advance those aims. As Lukes points out, power is value-dependent. The way it is exercised enables or constrains a group's ability to act on and advance the values animating anti-racism efforts—equity, well-being, belonging, thriving, connectedness, full participation. This is what "repurposing power" to address racism in an organization means—setting up or rearranging the exercise of power in a way that advances the stated values that those who have come together are pursuing, assuring continuity in forging linked fate over the long haul. Trying to pursue anti-racism without repurposing power in this way keeps people stuck in the paradox of racialized power, maintaining "power over" by those in charge even when they face challenges that expose the limits of their capacity and commitment to achieve those collective aims.

How do those genuinely interested in advancing change in an organization or group step out of this counterproductive cycle? Staying the course in addressing racism in institutions requires full participation by people of color, those whose fates are most directly affected by racism. This often involves changing the way decision making operates in an organization that is used to decisions by fiat. Navigating change that is transformative means using collaboration in the way a group makes decisions, redefining who is part of the decision-making process, and ensuring that everyone involved is held accountable for sustaining and supporting changes based on shared decisions. That is the description of functional "power with."

But if "power over" is the habitual response when problems arise, how is it possible to sustain a transition to "power with"? Making lasting changes in the power structure of predominantly white organizations depends on making power's exercise visible, so that people in different positions can understand and shape how power is and should be operating. Lasting change also depends on instituting a process of accountability to make sure that there are ways to question those exercising "power over" and to monitor whether they are supporting and enabling "power to."

The very meaning of the word "power" is relevant here. Power is the ability to make things happen, or to prevent things from happening. As Lukes points out, the etymology of the word actually straddles two distinct conceptions of power revealed in the Latin roots from which the English word derives: *potestas* and *potentia*. *Potestas* refers to being subject to the power of another. Those who cannot act to get their voices heard are subject to the power of another and thus power-less. *Potentia*, on the other hand, signifies the power to exist and to act—what Lukes calls "power to."[13]

Because "power over" is so endemic in predominantly white organizations, it is a common misunderstanding that "power to" essentially means "power over." This overlooks the importance of "power with" in building the "power to" achieve equitable aims. "Power with" operates not through coercion or manipulation but through influence: sharing perspectives, knowledge, and needs that enable a group to change its course of action through a process of learning. Those with "power over" can set up situations where they use "power with" to achieve their goals. And those without "power over" can exercise "power with" by influencing others in the service of their aims.

But when "power over" supplants "power with," the shared aims that are achievable only through collaboration are compromised. I witnessed an example of this when I first started working with a group of students at Columbia on an ongoing project to reimagine the *Jailhouse Lawyers Manual,* a handbook published by law students to help provide those who are incarcerated and unrepresented by lawyers with knowledge and information to pursue their legal claims. This group's express intention was to make the manual more understandable and accessible to those who needed it by involving, as codesigners in transforming the language, layout, and content, those who had themselves experienced racism and incarceration. But eager to produce immediate results, the student leaders began meeting and making policy decisions without the participation of the directly affected coauthors. They proposed changes in the manual's format, started planning the training of incoming editors, and divided up responsibilities for the editorial process—all without the participation of any people directly affected by incarceration.

Without realizing it, they were exercising "power over" the project, making decisions without including those who had themselves experienced incarceration and the impact of the legal process—despite their explicit commitment to sharing power with those with that firsthand knowledge. As a result, their initial ideas were jargon packed and inaccessible—replicating the manual's incomprehensible and bias-ridden style of communication that they had so genuinely wanted to transform. These students had assumed the default position of "power over" even when they conceived of the project for the purpose of implementing "power with." When this gap between their stated values and their practices became apparent to them, they realized that they had to be intentional about interrupting their internalized habit of exercising "power over" and instituting processes to assure the full participation of those most knowledgeable about and affected by the issues addressed in the manual. Owning up to the ever-present risk that they would reassert their "power over" the direction of the revisioning process, the manual's leadership created a position for a formerly incarcerated person on the editorial board and set up the drafting process so that it couldn't proceed without the coauthorship of every chapter by someone with firsthand experience of incarceration.

Revealing the way power is being used and misused, as happened with the students, is a necessary step toward making "power with" sustainable in an organization. Power can be expressed in different yet interrelated ways, helpfully analyzed in a widely cited article by activist John Gaventa called "Finding the Spaces for Change: A Power Analysis."[14] Gaventa's ideas about power developed in the course of his work at the Highlander Research and Education Center, a nongovernmental organization that enables ordinary citizens to understand and challenge inequalities of power and to participate in shaping the institutions governing their lives. Gaventa describes three different but interrelated modes of expressing power that reveal the underpinnings that must be considered in the transition to "power with" in an organization: visible power, agenda-setting power, and invisible power.

The most direct and observable form, *visible power*, involves decision making about people, practices, and policies in an organization. Visible power often overlaps with authority—positions that carry official decision-making responsibility, backed by the ability to enforce those decisions. Those with visible power determine the concrete allocation of benefits, sanctions, and privileges within an organization—such as hiring, firing, and resource allocation. Visible power can be exercised as "power over," as, for example, when Mall of America officials imposed a curfew on the community and when security officers forced teenagers in groups larger than two to disperse or face expulsion. Visible power can also be exercised as "power with," such as when the Mall shared responsibility with Club Fed for deciding who would be hired as Mighty Moms and what their roles would be, decisions affecting people and policies that were made with the participation of the community members who might be directly affected by racism.

A second level of power, what Gaventa describes as *agenda-setting power*, determines the ground rules for the operation of visible power. Agenda-setting power is exercised by those who determine and uphold the governing norms and practices, the "rules of the road," of a situation or organization. It affects *how* the rules governing decisions are made, *which* issues or concerns are prioritized, *how* issues are framed and by whom, *what* information will count to inform decisions, and, perhaps most importantly, *who* gets to participate in making the rules and setting the priorities and terms for decision making. Agenda-setting power is vividly illustrated in "Why the 'Haves' Come Out Ahead," the title of legal scholar Marc Galanter's widely cited article. Galanter explains that repeat players with the power to shape the rules governing courts' process can stack the deck so that the law is likely to promote their own interests over the long run.[15] This form of power may be hidden from those who are not part of the decision-making process, leaving them unable to perceive, understand, or even recognize how norms, policies, and practices are established. Kept in the dark, they might not even be able to imagine that there could be a different way.

In the context of anti-racism work, making agenda setting visible is crucial to shifting from "power over" to "power with." When agenda setting includes people of color, issues of importance to them are more likely to become priorities and the unstated rules favoring the status quo can be exposed and redefined with their perspectives in mind. The Mall of America's leadership never took that step, foreclosing the possibility of genuine collaboration with the community.

Gaventa's third mode of expressing power, *invisible power*, is about the ideas and beliefs that shape how people think about their place in the world, their understanding of the meaning of events and decisions, and their orientation to what is valued in the context in which they find themselves. Invisible power, as the term indicates, typically operates beneath the level of anyone's day-to-day awareness, nonetheless shaping decisions they make, how they understand and exercise power, and what they believe is possible and desirable for their well-being. Invisible power is embedded in the culture of an organization through the norms, decisions, and practices that dictate, for example, how new people are socialized into the organization, what kinds of information carry weight, and which behaviors receive encouragement and reward and which elicit negative consequences. Invisible power shapes people's status in an organization, what sociologist Ceceilia Ridgeway defines as "their sense of being valued by others and the society to which they belong." Ridgeway explains that "status is based on widely shared beliefs about the social categories or 'types' of people that are ranked by society as more esteemed and respected compared to others."[16]

In *How to Be an Antiracist*, Ibram X. Kendi explains the invisible power behind the origin story of racism that legitimated the exercise of white people's power over nonwhite people. As he points out, "experts" versed in faux science developed categories that organized people into racial identities, and then assigned value and status based on those categories. This kind of invisible power embedded in prevailing beliefs and values, developed when white people held exclusive power, made concepts such as the meaning of racism, definitions of expertise, and standards of merit seem natural or unchangeable.[17] They became part of the "script," making intolerable treatment of other human beings seem proper and inevitable.

For projects grounded in linked fate, each level—visible power, agenda-setting power, and invisible power—must be reconceived through a "power with" lens to repurpose that power to sustain anti-racism over the long haul. Addressing racism in the context of linked fate requires those in power to bind themselves to the mast of power sharing, committing the organization to exercising power in ways that will uphold the values of the group they are sharing power with. This means setting up modes of action, decision making, and accountability that limit "power over" in favor of "power to." With such structures and practices in place, those with "power over" have to pay attention to the perspectives and concerns of everyone involved, including people of color whose viewpoints may have previously been overlooked. Even when short-term risks or costs might otherwise tempt those "at the top" to advance narrow self-interest at the expense of shared long-term values, they are restrained by the power-sharing structure they have agreed to.

This doesn't mean that every decision in an organization has to be made collaboratively with everyone involved. A pilot doing an emergency landing of a plane on the Hudson River does not need to have a dialogue with crew and passengers about choices. Likewise, there can be critical circumstances that require immediate action with no time for consultation or situations that are sufficiently straightforward that they do not require input from others. But in general, in a "power with" context, decisions about when to delegate power and to whom are made collaboratively and evaluated in terms of whether "power over" is needed to achieve collective aims. How have organizations that have successfully built and sustained "power with" done that in addressing anti-racist policies? And how can power sharing with people of color be sustained in predominantly white institutions?

Uplifting Undervalued Knowledge

When Ras Baraka was elected mayor of Newark, New Jersey, in 2014, the city he loved had been grappling for decades with the problems of poverty, racism, and violence, with Black and Brown neighborhoods bearing the brunt of the harm. Decades of government policies with vast racial discrepancies in funding for housing, transportation, taxation, and education had fueled white flight to the suburbs, depriving Newark, like many other cities, of adequate jobs and public resources, leaving behind an economy too eviscerated to support the now predominantly nonwhite population. This systemic neglect contributed to increasing levels of crime and violence in impoverished communities. The typical power-over response—increased control by police—made residents feel even less safe. Born and raised in the neighborhoods he now sought to support as mayor, he had personally experienced violence used both by community members and the police. In taking on this issue in his role as mayor, Baraka was building on the social activist legacy of his father, Amiri Baraka, a world-renowned beat poet and playwright, and his mother, Amina Baraka, a poet and social activist, both of them relentless voices for social and political reform in his hometown of Newark.[18]

In 1967, the uprisings over racial injustice that erupted in cities across the nation also engulfed Newark. A commission appointed by New Jersey's governor to investigate the causes of the violence there found that the mostly white Newark Police Department had for years used excessive and unjustified force, racial profiling, and unnecessary stop-and-frisk policies and had made a racially disproportionate number of arrests.[19] The Newark uprising, four days of conflict that resulted in twenty-six deaths and hundreds of injuries, mostly of Black people, was a tragedy remembered by Newark's beloved historian Clement Price as "a racial upheaval by a Black community that had long suffered discrimination in employment, housing, and civic empowerment."[20]

During that uprising, Ras Baraka's father was arrested, severely beaten, and jailed. Two years later, Ras was born and raised, as he puts it, "amidst struggles and triumphs. I played on dirty mattresses in abandoned lots and witnessed my friends beaten by police or murdered by poverty and drugs in the hands of people they know."[21] When he was nine years old, Baraka witnessed his father being beaten by police, this time in New York City. Later, in Newark, home from college one summer, he stepped in to protect his mother from the police when she protested his brother's arrest. Baraka was handcuffed and taken to a back room in the city jail, where he was beaten by the police.[22] After college, he returned to Newark and, inspired by his father, engaged in protests, wrote and published poetry, became a teacher and principal in a neighborhood school, and worked with a group of local activists pushing for police accountability and systemic, community-led solutions to violence. Eventually, as a city council member, he began reframing violence as a public health issue.[23]

Despite determined efforts of activists to hold the police accountable and prioritize the needs of their community, by 2013, Newark was still holding its long-standing place on the list of the ten most dangerous cities in the United States, a continuing testimony to the failure of reliance on punishment as the solution to problems rooted in racism, poverty, and untreated mental health and substance abuse issues.[24] Determined to make real institutional change from within the political power structure, Baraka ran for mayor, buoyed by a groundswell of community support. Just three weeks after his election in 2014, the United States Department of Justice issued a report revealing a "stark and unremitting" pattern of abuse, misconduct, and discrimination in Newark's police department. Baraka was now in a position to do something about it.[25] "There's violence that happens *in* our community," he acknowledged in an interview, "and there's violence that happens *to* our community."[26] He was convinced that the solution was not going to come from further enhancing the power of the police but rather from drawing upon the power of the entire community to discover and create systems to support public health and build community well-being.

When organizations face complex problems like racism and public safety that cannot be solved through "power over" approaches, their ability to figure out what to do and who needs to be part of that process depends upon rethinking the way they define expertise. Expertise allocates power to those designated as experts. Whose knowledge is seen as legitimate affects how issues are constructed and how power is experienced. The status of "expert" confers authority in both senses of the word: who is an "authority" respected for their skill, knowledge, and experience with the issue at hand, and who has "authority" with a mandate to determine the questions asked, the information credited, and the solutions proposed and adopted.

The approach of vesting power and authority to deal with those problems in experts defined only by their occupational roles (like police) or educational credentials (like a PhD in criminology) rests on a series of faulty premises: that the criminal justice system has an agreed-upon purpose, that expertise is neutral, that technical or professional knowledge can provide the information needed to address complex problems of racism, and that the criminal justice system as currently defined is the appropriate arena for solving problems of public safety.[27] Questions that have been portrayed as scientific, objective, neutral, and technical actually involve the exercise of invisible power—normative choices about political values at each step. And, as sociolegal scholar Monica Bell observed, "most legal and policy approaches that proceed under the banners of racial justice and economic justice reveal a breathtaking cluelessness—or, perhaps, a willful flattening—of the nuanced realities that ghettoized African Americans face on a daily basis."[28] Accepting conventional experts' "power over" problem-solving hides from public scrutiny the way this power is being exercised and, in the process, devalues the knowledge located in communities of color and excludes those communities from participating in the normative choices that most directly affect them.

As Baraka did, anti-racism efforts have to figure out how to involve all the groups with a stake in the issue, especially those who have firsthand experience with the impact of racism on their community. These experiences equip them with a reservoir of ground truth—"personal knowledge of how these systems actually function, interact, fail, and change."[29] The challenge, framed elo quently by Monica Bell, is to figure out how to "hold space for both the (bounded) expertise of academics and technocrats and the (bounded) expertise of the people who could benefit most from the achievement of racial and economic justice, those who will suffer most if it continues to elude us."[30]

Some of the strongest examples of repurposing power come from people of color like Ras Baraka, those who have attained positions of formal power within a predominantly white institution and have still maintained their connections with and accountability to Black and Brown communities. Based on his work as an activist, Baraka knew that the knowledge, relationships, and commitment required to redefine public safety resided in Newark's neighborhoods. He also knew that these community members needed first to have the chance to build their capacity to take up this challenging role. Doing so would require investing in the process of developing community capacity, summarized by sociologist Robert Chaskin and his colleagues to include: "(1) a sense of community; (2) commitment to the community among its members; (3) the ability to solve problems, and (4) access to resources."[31] Baraka set out to assure the recognition and resources that this work warranted so that the community could take up his call to "build belief and ultimately the courage to transform, to move from what we know to what we can imagine." In his new position as mayor, Baraka could now provide the resources and legitimacy to make that happen.

He began by asking: Who had the expertise to adequately define the problem and then figure out how to respond? What did expertise mean? How did existing approaches to expertise need to change for problems involving racism to be effectively addressed? By asking these questions, Baraka was opening up the space to expand definitions of expertise to include those with the ground truth and legitimacy needed to reimagine public safety. In one of his first efforts to address those questions, he reached out to Aqeela Sherrills, who had a proven track record of success in violence prevention and community healing in Los Angeles, primarily through engaging those with "on-the-ground" experience. Growing up in the LA projects where survival was a daily challenge, Sherrills had himself become a gang member when he was a teenager, as a way to get protection and support. Seeking a different life, he left for college, where he had a transformative experience that led him back to his home community to work as an activist addressing gang violence. In the 1990s, he helped broker peace between the Bloods and the Crips in LA, and when he lost his son to gun violence in 2004, he redoubled his commitment to community-based public safety, becoming a nationally recognized expert in this arena.[32]

At Mayor Baraka's behest, Sherrills came to Newark and began his work by pulling together a group of local organizers and community members, those who were already involved in impromptu street teams trying to stem the tide of violence. Many of them had also grown up amid gang violence and understood Newark's South Ward, where violence within the community and in interactions with police was most prevalent. The street team members were part of the communities they sought to heal and knew many of the young people at risk. One of them captured the urgency of their work by reporting a conversation he'd had with a group of local eleven- to thirteen-year-olds: "We asked them to envision what Newark would look like if there were no crime and violence. No one could envision that world. That is what we have to change." These street workers knew how to spot when conflict could explode into violence. Many of them had turned their own lives around, some only after incarceration, so they knew what kinds of support enabled young people of color to pursue a different path.

Sherrills began by assuring them: "My charge from the mayor was to come to Newark to build out infrastructure, put systems in place, and then turn this program over to you," which is what he would do over the next seven years. Up to this point, the Newark street teams hadn't received the kind of recognition and support that could allow them to broaden their impact in the community. They had been largely on their own in figuring out how to navigate the intense situations they were facing, with little opportunity to learn with and from people experienced in dealing with such situations, and no access to those with the power to address the systemic underpinnings contributing to violence. Baraka's recognition and the work of Sherrills would lead to the kind of support that would enable their unique knowledge of the problems to make real inroads into solutions. This pilot project would grow into the Newark Community Street Team (NCST), a pillar of the mayor's community-led violence prevention movement. Its guiding principles would be expressed as:

"Safety is not just the absence of violence but the presence of well-being and systems that support the most vulnerable among us." Starting in the South Ward, the work of the NCST expanded into other Newark neighborhoods and would eventually become the centerpiece of a national coalition to build community-based violence reduction programs around the country.

Sherrills set up a process and systematic training to nurture and develop the on-the-ground expertise of what would become the NCST. As documented in a narrative evaluation conducted by the UCLA Social Justice Research Partnership, Sherrills enlisted Dr. Aquil Basheer, the founder of the Professional Community Intervention Training Institute and author of *Peace in the Hood*, to lead a four-week, interactive training program to hone the skills of NCST members to deal effectively with the issues and the people they regularly encountered in their work.[33] They learned, in Basheer's words, how to "normalize, stabilize, and get resources" for young people at risk of experiencing violence and "how to serve as a nexus with the public safety system," including families, teachers, law enforcement, and government agencies.[34]

Basheer's aim "to restore besieged communities so they become self-reliant and can determine their own destiny" had the intention of "empowering individuals to be activists and leaders, as well as turning around the mindset of individuals who use violence as a means to an end, both gang members and others."[35] NCST participants in the training were also learning from those with prior experience in community-led violence prevention. As those who had been out on the streets shared their intuitive knowledge about how to address the challenges in their neighborhoods, they were building their confidence as experts in anti-racism and violence prevention. They also learned how to involve nonprofit and government organizations in constructive collaborations, which could provide resources needed for community members to heal from trauma and tackle the underlying causes leading to violence.

By the time this group hit the streets as the now fully-fledged Newark Community Street Team, they knew what they knew, they knew what the police didn't, and they were ready to put that expertise into action, building trust with the people in the community, knowing where violence was likely to break out, knowing how to step in to defuse conflict, and understanding what government and private actors could do differently to address the underlying causes of the violence in Newark's neighborhoods.

In any process seeking to address complex problems involving racism, it is crucial to redefine expertise to include the knowledge and skills of those directly affected, as Baraka did in Newark. That strategy involves recognizing the knowledge and skills of those who have experienced racism and its effects and opening the way for community-led initiatives that grow out of that collective knowledge. And as happened with NCST, it also requires investing time and resources in building a community's capacity to make their tacit knowledge explicit and equip them to speak with authority about what they know. Establishing this kind of context in which to share knowledge, develop confidence in that knowledge, speak up, and raise issues that require change is an effective example of cultivating "power with."

This redefinition of expertise also empowered people of color in the Newark community to hold accountable those retaining "power over"—in this situation, the police and city officials—ensuring they used that power responsibly, in keeping with mutually defined goals. To do this, the Newark Community Street Team convened and facilitated a biweekly Public Safety Roundtable, providing a space for community members to identify problems, inform how those problems would be framed, and build relationships with the police and others from government agencies who were interacting with youth on the street. Police department representatives, New Jersey's attorney general, and other Newark officials regularly attended and participated actively in these meetings. The NCST had created an effective "power with" situation, which meant that those in "power over" positions had to listen to, respect, and respond to the concerns of the community. This forum became a way to make visible the agenda-setting power of the police and to create community accountability for the exercise of that power. As noted in the UCLA report about this effort, one resident said, "We don't got to like the police, but we do gotta co-exist. If we know we are strong, we can get along as equals. And that's the important word. Equals." Community members interviewed in 2024 about their experience with the Public Safety Roundtable went further: "We need this," one woman in a focus group declared, "because we gotta get started talking to each other somewhere." Observing that law enforcement maintained the majority of the financial resources, another community member observed, "We could get them to share if we just start talking." Embracing the responsibility that accompanies this shift in power, a third community member concluded, "This way, we can be accountable to ourselves."[36]

In any institution serious about tackling intractable issues relating to racism, it is important to provide support and recognition for those with "on-the-ground" expertise, building trust and capacity to collaborate with those having "power over." This means providing people of color who are willing to become part of change work with the opportunity to cultivate the capacities they seek for themselves. These efforts build the power of the "experts" on the ground to define and address problems in a way that creates the avenue to cocreated and effective solutions.

Sharing Expertise

Newark's success in making the community a genuine partner in reimagining public safety was part of a comprehensive strategy that enabled the city to reduce its crime rate to the lowest level in five decades. Another crucial partner in the process was Rutgers University in Newark. Around the same time Baraka became mayor, Nancy Cantor stepped in as chancellor of Rutgers-Newark. A white woman who is the child of activists herself, Cantor is a nationally recognized leader in building partnerships between higher education institutions and the urban communities they occupy. Recruited by historian Clement Price, a distinguished Rutgers professor and longtime resident of Newark, Cantor grounded her leadership in a vision and mandate to use the power and expertise of the university to address Newark's needs as they were defined by that community. She made redefining expertise central to the university's contribution to revitalizing the city. This initiative would bring another dimension of response to the redefinition of public safety in Newark that Mayor Baraka had undertaken.

Adopting what she calls an "outside-in" strategy, Cantor brought faculty members, staff, students, and alumni together with residents of the Newark community, including members of the Newark Community Street Team, for sustained periods of extensive collaboration to define shared challenges and propose ways to address them. One of the many programs inspired by these dialogues was the Anchor Initiative, launched by Cantor to enlist faculty members and students in reimagining this major university's relationship to its surrounding community, which also meant committing to improving Newark's health and well-being, as defined by that community itself.[37]

As part of the Anchor Initiative, the School of Criminal Justice at Rutgers created the Newark Public Safety Collaborative (NPSC), committed to supporting the Newark community by lending its expertise to address the problems in the university's "own backyard." The criminal justice researchers who launched NPSC were bringing their own form of expertise to the situation— the ability to analyze the causes and contexts for community violence by using the technological and statistical skills of their discipline, their knowledge of the academic literature on crime, and their prior experience working with police departments. But they knew that these proficiencies were far from sufficient for understanding the multifaceted and complex problem of violence in Newark, let alone knowing how to successfully address it.

Members of the Rutgers research team were aware of the limitations of "experts and their technocratic solutions," which have been "woefully unprepared to address deep, systemic injustice."[38] They knew that defining expertise only by academic credentials, disciplinary knowledge, and positions of authority would overvalue particular forms of knowledge, such as statistical analysis. Without community participation, they might focus on what's measurable (reported crimes or recidivism rates) and fail to notice the ways that existing data and analysis replicate racialized policing patterns. They might also steer clear of more complex, multifaceted issues, such as changing culture, that resist statistical analysis or technical solutions. In fact, their very expertise might lead them to misdefine the problems they were seeking to address and misunderstand the systems that held those conditions in place. In so doing, they would undermine the trust of the community they were working with and the legitimacy of the very institution charged with addressing public problems. They were determined to avoid the pitfalls of what scholar-activist Harry Boyte calls "a cult of expertise," aware that those who are culturally acknowledged experts can reinforce racial hierarchy often without realizing that they are doing so, shaping inquiry and ideas without knowing what they don't know.[39]

In a conversation with the author reflecting on the Anchor Initiative, Cantor explained the challenge facing the Rutgers researchers: "NPSC really had to prove itself as useful and not as the classic academics coming in, directing things, and then treating the project as a 'one and done.'" A thought leader in the adoption of engaged scholarship, Cantor understood all too well the tendency of researchers to act unilaterally and define issues in ways that fail to include the perspectives, knowledge, and needs of those closest to the problems.[40]

The usual way data had been used to address crime in Newark and across the country was by placing the information gathered in the hands of law enforcement to guide where the police should target their efforts. As the presumed "experts" on public safety, measured by arrest and crime rates, law enforcement had exclusive access to this statistical information, which then led them to stop, frisk, and arrest people in particular areas, often those inhabited mostly by Black and Brown people.[41] In this way of using data, members of Black communities were typically regarded as the "perpetrators" or "victims" and had no role either in deciding how to reduce violence or in questioning how police were responding to the crime data. The Rutgers researchers would set out to change how their data would be used to address public safety.

Instead of using only their data to formulate solutions, the collaboration that the researchers convened was a conjunction of expertise, organized around the experiences and wisdom of those, like the Newark Community Street Team, who had firsthand experience working to reduce violence and the biggest stake in arriving at solutions. In addition to representatives from the Newark Community Street Team and other community-based organizations, this working group included police officers, utility company representatives, developers, local business owners, and school officials. They regularly came together to participate in a dialogue informed by an innovative statistical technique called Risk Terrain Modeling, in which information revealed by research is presented to participants in an accessible form designed to invite a collaborative problem-solving process. For the Newark Public Safety Collaborative, this meant presenting information focused on increasing public safety in neighborhoods experiencing violence and crime. Community members, rather than researchers or police, could then identify the problems that mattered most to them, refocusing the researchers' data analysis for the purpose of problem-solving.[42]

The next step would be formulating how to address these concerns. Knowledge of the neighborhoods and the problems was paired with statistical data to inform where and how to tackle particular issues. This process of using data to support the involvement and actions of community members in addressing problems came to appropriately be named Data Informed Community Engagement (DICE).

In their interactive exchange with the community, the Rutgers researchers used their data to highlight the locations where violence was clustered: convenience stores, vacant lots, and ATMs. The community groups then offered information that helped explain the dynamics behind that data. For instance, when the researchers asked what lay behind the high incidence of crime in these particular locations, community members filled in the facts: "Most shootings are related to turf conflict, often over drug deals, and convenience stores are where drug buyers are solicited. They're open late, which makes it easy to hang out, and it's easy to come and go without being noticed or questioned." Other areas of concern were also identified and supported by data. Poorly lit streets and abandoned lots exacerbated problems. Students going back and forth to school at predictable times were vulnerable to violence in areas where gangs were active. Auto theft wasn't reduced when the police ticketed cars double-parked while community members ran into a store on a quick errand; instead, distrust was deepened.

This intermediary role of using data in dialogue with community perspectives and knowledge exemplifies a shift from "power over" to "power with." This kind of shift can happen when people with knowledge in a particular profession or discipline ask, "How does someone with my expertise collaborate with those who bring a different perspective and kind of knowledge?" The interactive listening and learning that the Newark Public Safety Collaborative facilitated made it possible for those who had grown accustomed to one kind of expertise and way of answering questions, even when that approach wasn't working, to open themselves up to appreciating and respecting what others knew. This "power with" approach to expertise allowed the researchers, the local community, and local agencies to set a common agenda, pool their knowledge, and explore what information and strategies could produce community safety and wellness.

In an organization or system that is unintentionally having an outsized negative impact on communities or employees of color, the ability to address these problems effectively requires redefining expertise to include everyone with relevant knowledge and putting that knowledge on a level playing field. This happens both by lifting up the knowledge of those with on-the-ground expertise, as Baraka modeled, and by limiting the power of those with conventional expertise to dictate the questions posed and the methods used to answer them. By sharing power in this way, the Newark Public Safety Collaborative was practicing the kind of humility, discussed in chapter 3, that creates paradoxical possibility—turning anti-racism's contradictions into drivers of learning and transformation.

Using the data provided by NPSC through DICE, the Newark Community Street Team was able to "chunk" its efforts—focusing on the issues and areas pinpointed, such as ensuring safe passage for children walking to and from school and identifying other locations where the team could interrupt conflict before it erupted into violence. Responding to data showing the relationship between poorly lit streets and increased violence and crime, other community-based organizations moved the Newark Public Works Department to partner with the local utility company to fix or replace streetlights in problem areas. Community development organizations teamed up to purchase abandoned properties, turning vacant lots in high-risk areas into usable, maintained spaces with library boxes, stages, and murals painted by local artists and young people. And representatives from the Newark Police Department started engaging in conversations with community members to discuss ongoing needs, such as paying attention to vacant properties near schools where drug dealers might connect with students walking by. This previously unlikely teamwork, informed by data and shared expertise, is an effective example of repurposing power.

The Rutgers researchers had used their expertise not as "power over" but rather as a way to invite others with varying knowledge, skills, and resources to advance the shared goal of public safety. They equipped the community groups with data to buttress their intuitive knowledge, amplify their voice, and reorient how law enforcement and other government agencies defined their roles. The police began to see the value of decentering their role in public safety, limiting law enforcement "expertise" to those situations, defined in collaboration with the community, that required policing to avoid or minimize harm so they could begin shifting responsibility and resources to the communities who had on-the-ground expertise in public safety. An array of government and private actors began to take responsibility for working with the community to invest in the well-being of areas of the city that had previously been ignored and to address issues ranging from quality education to community economic development, from affordable housing to community health.

In 2015, Ras Baraka signed a consent decree, settling a class action lawsuit challenging police misconduct by agreeing to implement body cameras, police training, data sharing, and other practices designed to increase transparency, integrity, and community-oriented policing. In 2016, he reached out to Nancy Cantor and Rutgers-Newark to conduct research on gentrification and housing displacement that would become the basis for the mayor's Equitable Growth Advisory Commission, one of many collaborative initiatives concentrating on equity, economic development, and neighborhood revitalization. By June 2020, Newark had redirected $12 million annually from its police budget to programs, like the Newark Community Street Team, that were designed to address the root causes of violence and steer resources to trauma recovery and community healing. As of 2022, Newark had reduced its crime rate to the lowest level in five decades and did not even appear on the list of the one hundred most dangerous U.S. cities.

And yet, Baraka acknowledges the long road that remains ahead. In his 2022 State of the City Address, he called Newark's efforts "a constant work in progress," acknowledging that "the task that lies ahead of us is enormous."[43] Redefining expertise to prioritize working with communities offers one important way of remaining engaged with issues involving racism, an example of what Baraka called "the radical imagination that forces us to believe in each other."

The narratives offered throughout this book show that, although there are challenges and pitfalls, it is possible to navigate the paradox of racialized power to sustain forward momentum.

Newark's reconfiguration of who holds the power of expertise is a good model for how those in positions of power at all levels of an organization can use that power to recognize and cultivate the expertise of those closest to the problem of racism. By redefining expertise, they begin to shift "power over" based on position or credentials or race toward "power with" in creating a community of experts who are bringing together the different forms of knowledge required to address the complex and entrenched problems racialized institutions face in their transformation. When all those determined to address racism in an organization are invited to reconfigure power by sharing expertise, shared knowledge as the basis of "power with" becomes a successful operating principle that can sustain itself over time.

Sustaining "Power With"

What can those working in or with predominantly white institutions with a history of exercising "power over" do to change this dynamic in a sustainable way and ensure credible commitments to sharing power? As we have seen, changing interracial power dynamics requires finding ways to make sharing power an explicit focus of attention and, where possible, to build power sharing and collaboration into the structure of the project or organization. Seizing the moment when commitment to shared values is at a high point, those with "power over" can commit themselves to power-sharing arrangements to sustain this effort by creating an infrastructure of ongoing cross-racial problem-solving, risk-taking, and resource sharing. This strategy involves building what I call an "architecture of inclusion," making decisions visible at every level, including formulating the rules of the road, shaping the narrative and incentive structure, and assuring collaboration when complex or contested issues arise.[44] These efforts can set up overall governance in an organization to assure cross-racial collaboration, ongoing reflection, and mutual accountability.

Predominantly white organizations can sustain the move from "power over" to "power with" by building agreements and accountability into the structure of the organization. This way of guaranteeing collaboration and shared decision making with those affected by racism makes it possible for white people in positions of power to take responsibility for anti-racism work while also limiting their ability to act in ways that (deliberately or not) would advance their own interests at the expense of declared intentions and shared values. With these guardrails in place, if those in "power over" positions do overstep or fail to step up, built-in "power with" processes make it necessary and possible for them to learn from those mistakes and failures while remaining engaged. The contradictions inherent in having to both step up and step back can, in this way, become a source of energy and learning. Such strategies for sustaining "power with" make it possible to stick with anti-racism efforts despite the inevitable challenges.

Building this architecture of inclusion sometimes begins when those who have already been instrumental in anti-racism work, and who are committed to ongoing collaboration with communities of color, are placed in leadership roles that provide the opportunity to change the way power is exercised in an organization. At Rutgers-Newark, faculty members who were part of the Anchor Initiative were on the diverse committee charged by Nancy Cantor with rewriting the criteria for faculty promotion so that it included crediting research and teaching done in collaboration with communities of color as a valued form of scholarship that could be a basis for awarding tenure. Ras Baraka used his mayoral "power over" to change the culture of the police department by signing a consent decree binding that department to collaborate with advocates and community members. He also ensured "power with" by building funding for community-led public safety into the regular budgetary allocations of the city and by creating a civilian review board, composed largely of people representing communities of color, to address issues of police accountability.[45] In any context, organizational catalysts seeking to sustain change that they have cultivated in "fractals"—microspaces of equitable decision making— can bring those practices into an organization's overall power structure, as a way to introduce bottom-up change.

Legal contracts can also serve as vehicles for ensuring power sharing and equitable relationships in an organizational structure. In the entertainment industry, some artists have built into their contract a provision requiring participation by people of color at critical decision points in a production and ensuring that they have the bargaining power to enforce this. When Frances McDormand won an Oscar for Best Actress in 2018, she used the platform of her acceptance speech to promote this practice. "I have two words to leave you with tonight. Inclusion rider," she said, underlining her support for making hiring practices in the industry more equitable.[46] The term first introduced in 2014 by Stacey Smith, the director of the Annenberg Inclusion Initiative, refers to a contractual process for hiring and casting that expands and diversifies the candidate pool, encouraging the inclusion of those who have been traditionally underrepresented in productions, which means people of color. The agreement also provides for tracking progress and accountability for sustaining forward momentum. Following Frances McDormand's call to action, writers, lead performers, directors, and other white people with market "power over" have begun using that power as they are setting up their contractual relationships to require collaborative decision making involving people of color in hiring, casting, and conflict resolution. They are also building into their contracts provisions for information sharing and ongoing reflection about the processes used to make decisions and the impact of those decisions on people of color and other groups that have previously been excluded or marginalized.

White people can also repurpose their influence into serving "power with" by using their knowledge and expertise to support the autonomy and exercise of power by people of color. The work of Andrea Levere, a classmate of mine at Brown University, is a concrete example of how this can happen.[47] Andrea is a white woman with infectious energy who has been interested in social justice for most of her life. After graduating from college, she got a fellowship to help organize primary health-care centers in Appalachia and west Tennessee and then went to work in the region for a nonprofit legal services organization as a health-care organizer. She watched these "outstanding organizations fail" because "people didn't know how to finance them and people didn't know how to manage them." She decided to go to Yale School of Organization and Management, where she realized "that finance was the scarcest skill for people interested in social and economic justice. And that's what I wanted to do."

Andrea's focus on racial justice developed on the job, working on financing inner-city development, low-income housing, and small businesses. As she collaborated with small businesses owned by people of color, she "heard their stories and particularly began to understand the reality of how they could not access capital." As her work expanded, she began to see that entrepreneurs of color were "not being well served by their accountants" and it became clear to her that "many of our sources of capital were profoundly discriminatory."

At some point, Andrea realized that working transaction by transaction with people who were trying to navigate the existing discriminatory landscape was not going to make the necessary change: "We need policy change." And so she joined a national nonprofit called Prosperity Now, rising from director of economic development to become president, orchestrating the organization's mission of reducing wealth inequality. "If we wanted to truly address issues of poverty and discrimination, we must focus on building wealth, not just income." Over the course of twenty years, Prosperity Now developed the entire asset-building field, supporting the self-determination and economic prosperity of low-income people and communities of color.

Andrea recognized that in order for this work to be successful, capacity building and power sharing with people of color had to be built into the fabric of the organization. "One of the lessons I learned very early is that the way to really diversify your staff is to have people at the highest level who are people of color. So, I built a diverse executive leadership team who could then attract an even more diverse workforce." With the knowledge and expertise of this multiracial leadership, Prosperity Now "built out a robust program on racial wealth equality."

Asked why people of color were willing to partner with her and even to join her white-led organization, she responded, "One of the critical factors in my success was something that Bob Friedman, who founded Prosperity Now, taught me: the power of a generous brand. That means not thinking that the way you advance yourself, your work, or your organization is keeping the credit. The reality is, even when I built the organization to eighty-five people, I knew that if we were going to address wealth inequality, we need as many partners as possible to join us. So it's to say don't try to take the spotlight for yourself. It's to say, 'let's share credit. Let's share resources.' Somebody offers us funding. It's not just for us. Let's figure out how working with others gets us to our goal more quickly than just working by ourselves. And that ends up rebounding back to you." Sharing power was built into the DNA of Prosperity Now.

Andrea identified a second factor in Prosperity Now's success: coming up with a metric to measure wealth inequality. "We worked with two respected economists to develop two measures that helped to transform this field: One was the metric of asset poverty. And the other, which was the most powerful, was called liquid asset poverty. The definition of liquid asset poverty was the inability of a family to exist at the poverty level for three months if their main source of income was disrupted. And our ability to show this data point by race changed everything." The organization's resources and visibility attracted the attention of the head of the NAACP's Economics Unit, who became interested joining Prosperity Now with his team based on his belief, Andrea recalled being told, that "this work addressing wealth inequality and building assets was the most significant strategy to help reduce the racial wealth divide." After joining Prosperity Now, that team created a program called Building High Impact Nonprofits of Color (BHINC)—a comprehensive leadership development and capacity building initiative to both raise the profile of organizations led by people of color in cities around the country and expand their access to funding.

Prosperity Now is now led by a woman of color, and Andrea moved on to working with a cohort of nonprofits led by people of color by helping them assess their financial sustainability and increase their "unrestricted net assets," also known as "equity" in nonprofit accounting. After Andrea stepped down as president, when Prosperity Now was about to launch a new cohort of BHINC, they reached out to Andrea: "They came to me and asked, 'would you add financial management training to our program and also conduct financial assessments of the strengths and weaknesses of each of these organizations?'" Andrea agreed, and this new BHINC cohort launched in the Twin Cities and Seattle the week after George Floyd was killed by the police. "As a result," Andrea recalled, "all these organizations had the benefit of renewed attention and commitment."

One of those organizations was Build Wealth Minnesota (BWM), led by Executive Director David McGee with a mission of reducing the racial wealth divide by helping Black families become homeowners. After going through the BHINC training and financial assessment process with Andrea, BWM's leadership asked her for help in building a program that could directly address the disparity in homeownership between whites and Blacks in the Twin Cities, which at that point had the greatest racial disparity in homeownership of any major city in the United States. As Andrea recounted in an article written for Bridgespan, BWM had helped more than three thousand families become homeowners and learn to create and manage budgets effectively but "hit a funding wall when it decided to lend directly to its clients." McGee explained, "We were too tiny to get the funding necessary to lend at scale." This is not unique to BWM, McGee added. "It is common among nonprofits led by people of color who do the work in successful, outcomes-based programming. Finding funding to take our work to scale seems to consistently elude us."[48]

Andrea worked with McGee to create a clear goal with a complementary fundraising strategy. "We asked ourselves to set a realistic goal for our impact: Could we reduce the homeownership disparity by 15 percent? How many new Black homeowners would we need? I came up with the name '9000 Equities,' because we were aiming to help 9,000 new Black homeowners buy their homes in the Twin Cities." Reaching this goal "not only would build financial equity for homeowners but would be creating broader equity in the community."

The next step was to identify the type of capital BWM needed to achieve this goal and to create a prospectus to begin to fundraise. They worked together to raise the equity, or "net assets" as it is known in nonprofit accounting, which was essential to leverage the debt so that they could create a mortgage pool—a pool of capital they could use to provide mortgages for potential homeowners who were not receiving the type of underwriting assistance they needed in the traditional marketplace. Andrea described how this process unfolded:

> In one of the very first conversations, they were told by a major foundation in the Twin Cities that they needed a one-to-one debt to equity ratio— every dollar of debt needed a dollar of net assets. I knew from years of experience that the traditional ratio was four-to-one for most community leaders. I was able to intervene and get this changed so that they were able to go forward. I then made introductions to other funders, particularly national funders, who, in light of the national racial reckoning, had made major financial commitments to invest in racial justice. All these activities also helped raise their profile with funders who knew them as well as those who met Build Wealth MN for the first time.

Over the past several years, this collaboration has raised $12.5 million in net assets to leverage enough debt capital to create almost 1,000 new Black homeowners. Andrea's role was a crucial component of this Black-led organization's growing visibility and power. Her behind-the-scenes support—building capacity, offering ideas and strategies that can captivate audiences, speaking truth to power, sharing her social capital—models how white people can repurpose power to advance racial equity and full participation.

Another strategy for building "power with" into an organization is including on its board of directors community members with direct experience of the work or issue being addressed, enabling them to influence codes of conduct, leadership selection, and other accountability measures. The Workplace Project, an organization dedicated to fighting workplace abuses and exploitation of immigrant workers on Long Island, used this strategy to ensure that the people who experience those abuses have the power to address them. The organization was initially led by Jennifer Gordon, a self-described "white woman, highly educated, English speaking, connections-to-donors, much respected founder." In her book *Suburban Sweatshops: The Fight for Immigrant Rights*, she acknowledges that the attributes she brought to the organization also unwittingly concentrated power in her hands, both within the organization and in her interactions with outsiders.[49] She also points out that the contradictory set of risks to the project because of her position in the organization—that she would either stay too long or walk out prematurely—meant recognizing that the Workplace Project's sustainability depended upon finding a way to navigate these imbalances of power.

In response to these concerns, Gordon hired an organizer from the immigrant community, and together, they set up a committee comprised entirely of the workers who were immigrants. Provided with training and support, that group laid the groundwork for a board of directors made up of immigrant workers, who became active participants in decision making, reflections, and priority setting. When Gordon decided it was time to leave the organization, the immigrant-led board made and enforced the decision about who would replace her as executive director.

Yet another way of reconceiving "power with" that organizations can consider in addressing the impact of racism is modeled by a graduate program created jointly by Vanderbilt, a predominantly white, resource-rich university, and Fisk, an HBCU originally set up to serve Black students when they were excluded from white institutions and that describes itself as "resourceful." The shared goal of these two universities, to increase the number of underrepresented minorities earning PhDs in STEM fields, could not have been achieved without the mutual dedication to go beyond the barriers in their own institutions that they could not bypass or change. Vanderbilt faced barriers in exclusive admissions and other institutional policies that made it difficult to recruit and retain students of color. Fisk contended with inadequate support for research, limited opportunities to work in labs that would enable students to prepare for their doctorate, and insufficient information about the requirements and process of reaching the PhD for students who, almost without exception, were the first generation in their families to pursue higher education.

The two institutions created the Fisk-Vanderbilt Master's-to-Ph.D. Bridge Program, which would benefit both schools and equalize power through ongoing collaboration and learning.[50] That program created a long-term partnership between Fisk and Vanderbilt, aimed at "preparing underrepresented minorities for success as they traverse the critical Masters-to-PhD transition." Students complete their master's degree at Fisk, with mentorship and support from both Fisk and Vanderbilt faculty, and then transition to complete their PhD at Vanderbilt. Two codirectors, one each from Fisk and Vanderbilt, are the primary leaders for obtaining internal and external funding and directing the program's goals. The admissions, steering, and student government committees involve equal numbers of members from Fisk and Vanderbilt. The mentorship teams for STEM program participants consist of a faculty member from each university. The Bridge program has redefined the selection criteria for admission, abandoning the usual application measures based only on test performance and proven ability and supplanted them with one that identifies applicants with unrealized or unrecognized potential, with the intention to invest in cultivating that potential. This partnership has also catalyzed the development of long-term mutual relationships among faculty at both institutions and stimulated changes in the way programs in each institution operate. The Bridge program has evolved into a national model for truly mutual institutional partnerships between colleges and universities that are predominantly white and those that serve primarily students of color.

The Fisk-Vanderbilt program is an example of what Nancy Cantor calls a "third space," a concept originated by literary theorist Homi Bhabha. Cantor and her collaborators have described third spaces as sites of interaction "where established and often unequal relationships of power and expertise can be shifted to acknowledge what each member of the partnership brings to the table."[51] This hybrid space affords the chance for participants to forge equitable relationships attentive to issues of power. As an example of a third space, the Fisk-Vanderbilt Bridge program created its own environment, governed by values and practices set up to enable full participation, even as it worked within existing institutions. In the Bridge program, even though Vanderbilt holds more economic and political power than Fisk, the organization and design of the Bridge program guarantee equitable power sharing. Third spaces like this require both parties to work together to reach decisions and provide opportunities for cross-racial groups to interact under structured conditions of equality. As demonstrated by the success of the Fisk-Vanderbilt partnership, a third space can become an opportunity for repurposing power exercised by predominantly white organizations so that change advancing anti-racism can be effectively pursued and sustained.

While none of the strategies to address racism described in this chapter will insulate an organization from the larger culture in which predominantly white institutions still continue to hold disproportionate power, studying and following proven models of change can help an organization make valuable inroads. Even when those with "power over" undermine or eliminate efforts to equalize and share power, those involved in the work of anti-racism can create communities of practice that make it possible to stay engaged, have hope, and build momentum for broader change. As Ras Baraka has so poetically stated, in the face of the forces that might lead some to lose hope, "We believe anyway. We join hands across neighborhoods and wards. We learn each other's languages and eat each other's foods. We break these artificial barriers and cross these imaginary lines. WE show the world what the future looks like."[52]

7

Anti-Racism over the Long Haul

"DO YOU HAVE a few minutes to talk about an exciting opportunity that just came my way?" Alejo posed the question to us at the end of a staff meeting for our Center for Institutional and Social Change. It was late June 2023, and he was now working at Columbia, collaborating with student leaders, faculty, and staff to change the way lawyers and legal systems interact with communities affected by racism and mass incarceration. We had found a way to turn his impactful appearance in my Lawyering for Change class into a position at the Law School that would situate him to transform the lives of both law students and community members directly affected by incarceration and had the potential to involve him in institutional policymaking that could drive broader culture change, especially in areas of anti-racism.

Knowing Alejo's track record for creativity, I was eager to hear about this new idea. With a mischievous smile, he asked, "Do you know what one of the nation's most popular high school team sports is?" While my mind was sorting through football, basketball, and soccer he announced, "Speech and debate! And these teams produce many future lawyers and leaders." He went on to tell us that, as might be expected, kids of color have usually been closed out of these teams. "But this dude just reached out to me with a way to change that. He wants to explore how his work with speech and debate clubs to develop community leaders among students of color could be connected to our efforts here with the law students and formerly incarcerated leaders."

Jonathan Conyers, the man who called Alejo, had turned his own life around in high school through his participation on a speech and debate team and was now part of a group making that opportunity available to young people at risk of becoming caught up in the criminal justice system.[1] "Our partnership with him could mean that our law students and formerly incarcerated advocates could work with high school students of color—especially those in communities affected by mass incarceration—who might become interested in pursuing law as a result."

As Alejo talked about how this collaboration could multiply the impact of the work he was already doing with young people of color in law schools, I started to get excited. "Building these relationships between high school kids of color and law students who work with formerly incarcerated leaders could be one of the best ways I know to get Black and Brown people into law schools." Without skipping a beat, Alejo replied, "Yes, and these are the ones who need to be at the forefront of reimagining legal education—something you and I both know is way overdue." I left the conversation with a sense of hope and determination, confident that we were part of building a foundation that could spur broader change and help bridge the nation's racial divide.

As I reflected on Alejo's idea over the course of the day, larger developments came to mind that buttressed that sense of hope. Alejo and other directly affected advocates were gaining visibility in and influence on the public dialogue about racism and the justice system. Organizations led by people directly impacted by incarceration seemed to be gathering momentum and coalescing into a national movement pushing for fundamental change. An essay called "Participatory Law Scholarship," written by legal scholar Rachel López and published in the *Columbia Law Review*, heralded the emergence of a movement to produce legal scholarship in collaboration with authors who have no formal legal training but have gained expertise in the law through lived experiences.[2] And some policymakers at the local and national level were prioritizing community-led change and creating places for people directly affected by racism and incarceration at the policy table.

The day after my conversation with Alejo, I opened the news to catch the headlines. The decision had just come down from the Supreme Court, holding that the affirmative action practices at Harvard and the University of North Carolina violated the Constitution's equal protection clause. Cross-racial groups on the front lines of anti-racism were reeling in response. The Supreme Court had affirmed its allegiance to colorblindness, notwithstanding the voluminous evidence that this way of addressing racism actually reinforces patterns and practices of racial exclusion. The Court's opinion exemplified the flawed assumption that the full participation of Black and Brown people, supported by affirmative action, could only happen at the expense of others—read: white people. And counteracting the opinion's impact on the racial narrative would be made more difficult by the emerging success of state laws that prevented schools from teaching their students about the country's racist history.[3]

Yet again, I was reminded of Martin Luther King's calling out of law's paradoxical relationship to justice, demanding that the injustice embedded in our legal system must be revealed "with all the tension its exposure creates, to the light of human conscience and the air of national opinion before it can be cured."[4] My hope from the previous day's conversation evaporated.

Experiencing these two events within twenty-four hours—Alejo's opening the door to full participation by people of color in higher education's promise and the Supreme Court's closing off the use of affirmative action as a strategy for doing so—reminded me that as a society we are in the midst of the polarizing paradoxes. Just as anti-racism practices seemed to be gaining momentum the nation was also veering backward, with those in positions of power standing in the way of bridging the divide. Poised on the edge of these competing perspectives, we could be on the verge of either moving forward into a more racially just and equitable society or falling back into one with a scarcity mindset that is antidemocratic and even more racially polarized.

So, where do we go from here? What do these contradictions mean for anyone who is in a position to address issues of racism? How do we navigate this stark dichotomy so that anti-racism efforts can unfold into full participation? Doing this requires finding ways to stick with anti-racism work over the long haul.

History has shown that any kind of systemic change that can transform a racialized social and economic order requires dedicated ongoing engagement and struggle. That was the lesson of the abolition movement, the civil rights movement, and any efforts I know of that have produced lasting culture change within organizations. Every one of the stories in this book that has led to a positive and lasting impact has been about people and groups who remained engaged and committed over many years. Freeman Hrabowski worked at UMBC for thirty years, making it possible for institutional transformation and full participation to take root and cultivating leaders to sustain those values. This effort has served as a catalyst for positive change at schools around the country. Ras Baraka started his change work in college, and over decades, working with community members and leaders, began transforming the City of Newark into a place that provides communities of color the opportunities they need to flourish. Newark's public safety innovations became a centerpiece for federal government initiatives to center directly affected communities in public policymaking. It took decades for Andrea Levere to build Prosperity Now into a multiracial driver of economic policy transformation aimed at closing the wealth gap.

But all of these successes have been hard-won, as anyone involved in this work knows. Each success is built on the bricks of failure. The efforts of Judge Fein and his colleagues to increase fairness in the court system, though yielding important incremental improvements, have yet to produce the kind of change they now know is necessary to make fairness and justice a reality for people of color in the court system. There will always be a balancing act between the progress that can be made at the local level and the need to find ways to impact systems more broadly and policy at the national level.

With racism as entrenched and multifaceted as it is in our society, failure along the way is inevitable, but as the saying goes, "fail often, fail forward." The key to success is not being defeated by the failures, even those as crushing as that Supreme Court decision barring affirmative action in higher education admissions. Remaining committed in the face of failure and trying out new ways of working in response to the lessons learned are what enable the transformation of those institutions that continue to operate in ways that perpetuate racism. That is what sticking with it for the long haul requires.

Building a community of people who want to work and learn together to create change is part of what makes it possible to remain engaged in the struggle. As we saw in Newark, even though distrust and conflict persist between police and community members, they continue to meet, brainstorm, and experiment with ways to heal the trauma the community has experienced and change the way police interact with communities of color. This is what carries them forward in the face of the paradoxes that persist in their experience of reimagining public safety: community members and police officers continually holding opposite interpretations of incidents involving police (the paradox of racial salience); disagreement over whether mental health crises should remain within the purview of police, risking violence, or shift completely to community members who lack authority to use force if necessary (the paradox of racialized power); and conflict about whether the police department is or could ever be anything other than racialized (the paradox of racialized institutions). The success of this process in achieving "what might be" remains to be seen, but the fact that people who experience public safety from opposing perspectives continue to engage with each other offers hope that their efforts can be successful. Their sense of linked fate, notwithstanding their enduring conflicts, makes it possible to try to understand what underlies their opposing perspectives and to explore the possibilities for developing new ways of working that redefine how power is exercised and problems solved. Ultimately, it is this capacity to stick with challenges in the face of uncertainty, resistance, and struggle that differentiates cosmetic from transformative anti-racism work.

Because Alejo has been willing to persist in the face of troubling obstacles, he has been able to make inroads into more fundamental changes at Columbia, despite the entrenched habits of a system burdened by bureaucracy. His position at Columbia started with lengthy delays in getting paid, an unnecessarily opaque and intrusive background check, and relentless questions about his criminal record, despite the fact that he had been hired because of his expertise as a formerly incarcerated person. Alejo was able to turn these barriers into learning opportunities for the institution. Building on the trust and the track record he had developed with student organizations and community leaders, he has launched a trauma-informed lawyering initiative in partnership with a Columbia Law School clinic to build the capacity of future lawyers to work equitably and effectively with people and communities affected by mass incarceration, and he is collaborating with a national organization that enlisted Alejo to help make this innovative framework available to legal advocacy organizations and government agencies around the country. The reason why Alejo is able to enact this transformative change is because he is committed for the long haul and has the support of faculty members who share that long-term commitment.

As Ras Baraka pointed out, "We are a constant work in progress. The world is certainly being pushed backward. And there needs to be equal and opposite force in the other direction." This movement toward full participation is not a step-by-step process or a linear sequence. Change doesn't happen in an orderly or predictable fashion in any context, but especially not in the work required to address an issue as entangled in history and culture as racism. We enter the work from different points and perspectives and move in different sequences, knowing that the process is messy and never-ending, even as we find ways for clarity and closure along the way. Locating ourselves within that is a critical part of the work.

Locating Yourself in the Situation

Just as Judge Fein in the trial court system and Lee as a Broadway playwright had to go through a process of self-reflection as part of building their capacity to address race, it is necessary for any of us wanting to be effective change agents to engage in some kind of reflection-in-action that allows us to discover how our own personal story affects our interactions involving race and our roles in doing anti-racism work. As a white person with limited exposure to the experiences and perspectives of people of color, Lee had to go through a process of acknowledging his part in perpetuating harm experienced by people of color in his company, taking responsibility for building his racial literacy, and changing how he exercised his power as a playwright and influencer of public opinion. I have found that for myself, as well as for my students and others with whom I have worked on anti-racism efforts, that kind of self-reflection, when it is combined with taking action, strengthens the perceptual and emotional muscles needed to navigate the paradoxical divides of racial identity, power, and position. Reflective practice cultivates our ability to accept uncertainty, approach uncomfortable situations with curiosity, discover what we don't know, and hold the contradictions and complexities of racism in a way that allows them to transform our own understanding. Being aware of our feelings, needs, and perspectives enables us to perceive those of others without projecting our interpretations onto them. Without that level of insight, our reactions and patterns are more likely to get in the way of being effective in anti-racism work.

My own self-reflection helped reveal some of the experiences that lay behind my deep passion for anti-racism work. As a child growing up in a home with a loving yet emotionally abusive parent, I found ways to stay safe by being the one who solved problems, mediated disputes, and tried to repair harm. Anti-racism work was another arena of conflict in which I tried to close the gap between the ideal and the actual version of reality. But this personal motivation also led to some of the tensions I experienced in my relationships in this work. The same needs that drew me into anti-racism work, coupled with my socialization as a lawyer, meant that I frequently was first in a group to propose *my* ideas, *my* solutions, and *my* knowledge of the system. *I* wanted to be the problem-solver. This urgent need to "fix the world" often made it hard for me to leave space for those directly affected by racism to speak, generate ideas, and act for themselves. As someone who grew up feeling powerless, it was difficult for me to recognize the power I was exercising over others through this behavior. Once I recognized this dynamic and its source, I could begin to understand what was going on in my unsuccessful interactions with others in anti-racism work and to seek ways to change this pattern.

The primary support that made this growth possible was building strong relationships with the people of color with whom I was working closely on projects aimed at making change. Sustaining those relationships required continuing to do my own work, but grounded in genuine caring and commitment, they are what supported me in becoming a trusted collaborator able to sustain the work needed over the long haul.

This personal work, on my own and with others, helped me identify the roles that I can best fulfill in the work of anti-racism, as well as the ways I can be most effective and do what I find meaningful. As a middle child who grew up mediating conflict and an intellectual type relishing the power of ideas, I love connecting people through their shared interests and their overlapping desire to facilitate positive change. I derive joy in helping others discover and act on what they care about most. Because of my experiences as a child, holding the tensions built into paradox and maintaining relationships amid contrary perspectives and truths is second nature. And for the same reason, being the warrior—on the front lines of protest—is not. For any of us, the avenue to being most effective in anti-racism work is finding the passion, calling, and unique skills our life experience has equipped us with, and then bringing that into our work with others.

What made working with Lani Guinier so rewarding for me was that, in addition to our shared values and love of our students, we brought different strengths and predispositions to our work together. This was due in part to our different racial identities and family histories. As the oldest of three children in her family, Lani was the one in charge. Her experience growing up was part of the training that made her the courageous combatant who could speak truth to power, inspire, advocate, and shake people up. Lani, as she put it, could "not let anyone get away with lazy or loose arguments."[5] She unflinchingly unveiled racialized power, critiquing insider Black politicians along with white liberals exercising "power over" when they had no connection to the communities they purported to represent. She brought that radical candor to her interactions with those she worked with, and she sometimes relied upon me to keep people engaged in our collaboration and support their "growth mindset" even as they felt destabilized by her critique. Our roles complemented each other and made our anti-racism work sustainable for us and our students.

There are many different roles to play in anti-racism work, each offering essential tools in the pursuit of paradoxical possibility and each carrying with them their limitations. George Sanchez, an American studies professor at the University of Southern California, loves designing and building communities to support full participation for people working both inside and outside predominantly white institutions. That, combined with being a warrior who stands up for his values and getting things done, enables him to bridge the tensions in serving both roles of "power over" and "power with." Yet, straddling "power over" and "power with" is challenging in racialized institutions that have many layers of authority that resist sharing power. When change agents assume positions of formal power, they have to navigate the contradictions built into using the power they now hold. They have to become part of the institution in ways that will limit what they can do. So, they have to simultaneously build up their own leadership to make change from the inside and enlist the leadership of people who will push them from the outside or from the bottom up, holding them accountable to those values.

This book provides many examples of people working to make change from the bottom up or outside in. As a poet, storyteller, and visionary, Alejo draws vastly different worlds together into learning communities animated by a shared vision. Straddling the paradox of racialized institutions, he is both a disruptor, able to discern and decry the dehumanizing practices of predominantly white institutions, and a dreamer, able to reimagine those institutions as a way to support full participation. The researchers who started the Newark Public Safety Collaborative at Rutgers use analysis, operating behind-the-scenes, to help weave together different kinds of knowledge and expertise in support of community-led problem-solving. I have used my position on the faculty to invite experimentation, create community that connects people interested in change, build the capacity for students and community advocates to be able to lead change, mobilize support when the need to speak out arises, and work with institutions that genuinely want to pursue full participation. Those of us seeking to transform institutions from positions outside formal leadership must face the challenge of sustaining these small-scale efforts and parlaying them into broader policy and culture change in our organizations and in the larger society.

No single strategy will work to produce transformative change. People in different roles have to depend upon each other to navigate the limitations and contradictions built into any single approach.[6] It is helpful for the members of any group seeking long-term change in predominantly white institutions to understand the roles they each can play to support the work and stay true to the group's purpose. It is also helpful to maintain flexibility in those roles. Tools such as Deepa Iyer's Social Change Ecosystem Map and Ariel Fox's Big Four Profile (Thinker, Dreamer, Lover, Warrior) can guide change makers in learning their strengths and limitations, understanding the roles they can most effectively play in a group, acknowledging how race operates in shaping those roles, and figuring out ways to learn from and collaborate with each other.[7] Organizational catalysts, in their work of building bridges and weaving dreams across racial divides, also play a crucial role in supporting people's discovery of their place in the work. Skilled in understanding how power operates in groups and organizations, they can help a group identify its position within a larger organization or system and support the recruitment of collaborators needed to make change. Reflecting on our personal background and what we uniquely offer the work is a crucial and ongoing part of building the change communities that can navigate the anti-racism paradoxes and effectively galvanize experiments that aim for full participation.

Concerted cultivation of our capacity to hold these paradoxes, both as individuals and in the groups and institutions we work with, is one basic and important way we can prepare ourselves to stick with anti-racism work. These capacities include listening, perspective taking, developing racial literacy, systems thinking, impact storytelling, and learning to have difficult conversations involving race and racism. "Concerted" effort means being deliberate and systematic about cultivating these capacities in ourselves, as well as doing this work in concert with others. This is the kind of capacity building that Verna and Evelyn experienced at Penn when they learned how to talk with each other about affirmative action from their different racial vantage points. In the post–affirmative action era, this will be a critical ability in our efforts to continue pursuing anti-racism and full participation in institutions within the scope of the Supreme Court's ruling. When groups involved in change work combined those efforts with concerted cultivation of their capacities as change agents, as the Newark Community Street Team did, they can build multiracial communities that experience joy amid struggle and have the resilience to persist come what may.

Zooming In and Zooming Out

Lani Guinier was a brilliant and pragmatic visionary. She advanced big ideas and long-term goals demanding fundamental change in our society, such as making the political process genuinely participatory, higher education truly democratic, law actually accountable for racial justice, and public conversations about race commonplace. And she also proposed and enacted transformative changes that could happen in the short run. She did this by galvanizing experimentation and turning the classroom, the courtroom, and the court of public opinion into laboratories for democratic experimentation. Moving back and forth between the "is" and the "ought," she used these microspaces of justice to create the "what might be," finding ways to straddle the tension between the dual role of institutions as perpetrators of racial inequity and beacons of democratic possibility. Sticking with change over the long haul requires this ability to link small steps with big goals.

I can imagine how Lani, if she were alive today, might invoke creative experimentation in response to the decision of the Supreme Court in 2023 to dismantle affirmative action in college admissions. She would probably begin a class or an article by pointing out the enduring relevance of her condemnation of the Supreme Court, expressed in "From Racial Liberalism to Racial Literacy" on the fiftieth anniversary of *Brown v. Board of Education*, for resorting to colorblindness "as the way to forbid government actors to remediate societal discrimination," changing the impact and purpose of *Brown* "from a clarion call to an excuse not to act."[8] She might urge public readings of Justice Sotomayor's and Justice Jackson's ringing dissents in *SFFA v. Harvard*,[9] urging us to use these opinions to create "a novel and potentially interactive pedagogical space, one that, with the right technology and a democratizing agenda, could spark a lively conversation among, and with, a decidedly non-professional and non-elite audience."[10] She would warn against leaving it to the Supreme Court to define equality and justice, reminding us about the power of social movements to breathe meaning into constitutional values and the necessity of limiting the reach of the Court's regressive ruling.

But Lani would also call upon us to use the constraints imposed by the Court as a new clarion call for creativity and problem-solving. She would likely guide us toward finding and creating opportunities to reimagine what higher education should look like, to redefine merit as cultivating potential rather than rewarding past privilege, and to use community-led examples to inspire continued collaboration and mobilization for systemic change. In *Tyranny of the Meritocracy: Democratizing Higher Education in America*, Lani offers illustrations of how small-scale change has led to transformative change with democratic merit. In the book, she features the University Park Campus School at Clark University in Worcester, Massachusetts, built by a long-term partnership with the surrounding public school district and providing free, high-quality education to the racially diverse and struggling community; the Posse Foundation, an organization that identifies promising urban public school students who would not otherwise be admitted to selective higher education institutions and creates cohorts, "posses," to support the success and thriving of those students; and Uri Treisman's "calculus clubs," an interracial, peer-to-peer learning model that produces a collaborative space that "changes you, and in turn you change a community, a bureaucracy, a culture, a government, a world."[11] Lani pushed anyone interested in anti-racism to couple their critique of systemic racism with an affirmative vision of the kind of institutions we want to see and experiments that embody that vision. That kind of envisioning process helps provide the inspiration and urgency that can sustain anti-racism work in the face of backlash and failure.

Such examples of change hold the promise of genuine impact on a relatively small scale, but the gulf between these fractals appearing on a local level and what's happening in the larger, still racist world can make the odds of sustained success seem remote and the enormity of the problem feel overwhelming. This tension between digging deep into institutional and place-based work and yet zooming out to push for broader cultural and political change is inescapable. And it can be even more difficult to sustain hope when steps in the direction of anti-racism provoke backlash and backsliding. Impatient about the pace of change and concerned about the future, my students often ask me how I remain committed in the face of such odds. This is an important question for anyone wanting to stay engaged over the long haul.

One strategy that has worked for me, and for others I know who have been effective in sticking with the work despite the challenges, involves intentionally moving back and forth between the micro and macro levels of change. A group I am working with might begin by looking at a situation involving race in an organization first with a wide-angle lens, so to speak, surveying the long-term vision, the field of possibility, the need for change, the systemic barriers, and the opportunities that might exist for bringing people in different racial positions together around a shared goal. This overview might include mapping out different types of power needed in the situation—first-order power to make decisions, second-order power to set the agenda, and third-order power to shape the racial narrative. It could also chart choice points—opportunities to make decisions or structure interactions in ways that could either increase or decrease full participation.[12] Choice points offer the chance to locate experiments in an organization in situations where they have the potential to have broad impact in the future. Choice points could be personnel decisions or leadership changes, an organization's response to a conflict or crisis, the planning process for an upcoming event or workshop, or strategic planning opportunities. With this big picture in mind, we can then pick a particular focus for attention and experimentation based on opportunities for collaboration, interest in participation, and prospects for impact—our "what might be."

Once we have decided on a focus, we can then zoom into creating this fractal or experiment with change. I imagine this process like using a telephoto lens to zoom in on the details of a specific situation in which transformative change can happen on a small scale. Staying focused on that small yet transformative space, making it a place where we can have concrete impact, build relationships that matter, and connect across differences feeds our souls and keeps us going. This fractal is a platform upon which to develop the next experiment, drawing on the lessons learned and relationships forged during that first fractal.

Every so often, it's important to zoom back out, using the wide-angle view to relocate our small-scale effort in the larger context. This enables us to understand how that larger context shapes and impacts the sustainability of our small steps. This can help identify choice points that might position us to enact another small-scale change or to seize opportunities to influence relevant policies or practices that could enable others in the organization to apply the approaches developed in the fractal that enabled it to succeed. Looking at the greater context might help us analyze where the work of our fractal can have the most leverage to advance full participation in the culture and structure of the overall organization. This zooming out can also help us see if we are failing in our stated purpose to affect change in an organization or if our efforts reveal the limits of change within the existing institutional arrangements. We can then assess whether to keep going or shift gears, zooming back into the same fractal or a different one in which we develop another experiment that seems worth trying.

Freeman Hrabowski used a strategy similar to this to support his long-term goal of full participation at UMBC. As his story revealed, when he learned about the problem triggering protests by Black students, he zoomed out to understand the overall picture, enlisting help to document the patterns and policies that were having a negative impact on Black students and to analyze their relationship to broader institutional practices and problems. He identified a key point for intervention and then focused in, creating the Meyerhoff program as a small-scale experiment to increase students' participation and success in the STEM fields, starting with Black students and then expanding to other students committed to diversity. While tracking the success of that effort, he periodically zoomed out to consider other areas in the larger institution where versions of the Meyerhoff program could be applied to enhance student success and increase full participation. Zooming out further to consider the national higher education landscape, Hrabowski saw the need and the opportunity for the UMBC model to cultivate full participation to be put into practice by colleges and universities across the country.

Zooming in and zooming out is a way to make progress without losing sight of where it is you want to go. This enables change makers to experience success in the short run, along with the positive reinforcement that brings, while making sure you are not succumbing to the temptation to use quick fixes and cosmetic changes as a substitute for institutional transformation.

Building the Architecture of Paradoxical Possibility

This book has highlighted both the necessity and difficulty of learning to navigate the contradictions and tensions built into addressing racism. We have to incorporate into our regular practice the multiple consciousness that moves us back and forth across the dualities, as Mari Matsuda exhorts us all to do. We have to sustain collaborations among groups that see the world differently and deeply disagree. We have to both work within institutions and build movements outside of those institutions that will push them to change. We have to address race and racism head-on while also changing the "rules of the road" that undergird racism and affect a much broader group. How do we build the architecture and the support structure that can sustain the multiracial collaborations necessary to achieve this paradoxical possibility?

We have seen examples of those support structures throughout the book—the "personal board of directors" who can keep people like Judge Fein and Lee tethered to their values, the cohorts of change agents that Abby Stewart was able to build at the University of Michigan. Sharing and learning from efforts like those described in this book—both the successes and the failures—are an important part of the work of institutional transformation.

The kind of support and learning I have primarily focused on in institutions is also occurring in cross-institutional organizations set up to build community and collaboration among people doing anti-racism work in the same field, such as the national Liberal Arts Diversity Officers group, supporting those on the front lines of college diversity, and the Community Based Public Safety Collective, the national organization of community groups involved in reimagining public safety with an anti-racism lens. The Anchor Institutions Task Force has developed into "an action-oriented learning community of nearly 1000 individual members in the U.S. and abroad," which is helping "anchor institutions, particularly higher education and medical institutions, to improve the economic, social and civic health needs of communities." In *Learning to Improve: How America's Schools Can Get Better at Getting Better*, Anthony Bryk and his coauthors have documented the development of what they call "networked improvement communities" in the field of K–12 education. Through reflection, comparison, and data analysis, these learning communities enable teachers, parents, and educational leaders to improve their practices to achieve more effective and racially equitable educational classrooms and schools.[13] If the institutions we are part of do not have—or are not ready for—a community of people interested in promoting anti-racism, we can align with change agents facing similar challenges in their institutions, supporting each other as we push toward full participation.

These cross-institutional collaborations have even greater impact when they coalesce into a national movement that links bottom-up institutional transformation with top-down policy change. This is what happened with the Community Based Public Safety Collective. Once the local "reimagining public safety" initiatives joined forces and launched a national dialogue, the Justice Department embraced this community-driven, collaborative, equity-focused approach to public safety and enlisted directly affected community advocates as advisors, capacity builders, and codesigners of national policy. As a result, Congress enacted the Bipartisan Safer Communities Act, authorizing the Department of Justice to award $100 million in grant funding to local communities for community violence intervention. Building on Newark's example, the DOJ has committed to "building the community infrastructure that is so vitally needed and required," seeking to "bridge long-standing divides, build the bonds of trust, and create a true, shared safety."[14]

But public policymakers also use "power over" to shut down institutional efforts to address racism. What can we do to maintain hope and keep pushing forward in the face of countervailing legislation and judicial opinions? During times of public policy retrenchment, it's crucial to maintain the institutional practices and communities pursuing the "what might be," using these external barriers as drivers of creativity and commitment. Coalitions and third spaces, operating both within and across institutions and bringing together people committed to anti-racism and full participation, keep anti-racism values and constituencies alive. This is what a group of college presidents has done, launching an informal network, called Education for All, which has grown to nearly 150 presidents, mostly from community colleges. It is serving as a space where people can brainstorm together, commiserate, and craft their message in ways that can reach people who resist efforts framed in terms of anti-racism but genuinely care about students' full participation. In my own law school, I have been heartened by the multigenerational collaborations that have developed to sustain ongoing change, particularly those that are student led, with institutional resources and support. These collaborations provide much-needed affirmation to students whose sense of belonging could easily be undermined by efforts to shut down anti-racism work. They also provide laboratories for cultivating and spotlighting students' leadership and have become a source of hope and inspiration for all of us who are involved in this work. These efforts maintain momentum for those committed to full participation so that these constituencies are ready to step up when the public policy pendulum swings back toward addressing racism.

But what about the many institutions that don't acknowledge the problem of racism or that lack a critical mass of people in positions of influence who care about this issue? What about the places that have retreated from confronting racism and instead adopted policies that block effective efforts to support full participation and anti-racism? In these situations, some form of outside pressure is necessary to remind those in power of the risks they face by *not* addressing racism and to mobilize actions to advance full participation. Mobilization by student groups, actions led by community activists, and other kinds of public protest often are the catalyst that initiates this process. In Newark, for example, the transformative institutional change work inspired by Ras Baraka and Nancy Cantor happened only after years of protest by both students and the community, along with litigation leading to findings of and remedies for the racist practices of the police department. Another example involves a cross-racial, cross-generational organizing effort in Texas, described by Obi Afriyie, a Black community organizer with the NAACP Legal Defense Fund (LDF), in his remarks at a conference celebrating the seventieth anniversary of *Brown v. Board of Education*. "A lot's happening in the Lonestar State, where over 160 anti-education, anti-queer, anti-Black, anti–people of color bills were introduced in the Texas legislature in one session." Students and community members felt personally attacked by this onslaught, which was "super-draining and super-isolating" for students, faculty, and staff of color. Instead of retreating, however, the attack on racial justice instead became the occasion to build community across, race, class, and gender lines:

> LDF led a charge bringing together grassroots community organizations, graduate students, professors, fighting against bills . . . to abolish critical race theory, tenure, and DEI. This was a rapid-response mobilization. You had students, law students, undergraduate students who were in the middle of their spring semester holding teach-ins every single night, printing out copies, hosting advocacy days, busing students in from various parts of Texas.

Obi located the greatest hope for change in "building up what young people in these spaces see themselves as. Hopefully the young people we are working with today are the leaders of the movement down the line. I always say I am organizing to work my way out of a job. . . . That's the mindset we all need to have. These are long-term fights."[15] Movement building that takes place outside of institutions and cultivates new leadership is crucial to catalyze change within those institutions. Ras Baraka started his journey to institutional and political leadership as one of those young people protesting racist policies and practices.

Another important way of navigating the anti-racism paradoxes, as illustrated throughout this book, is pursuing opportunities to change the background conditions that are producing the paradoxes in order to reduce or even eliminate these tensions. For example, the polarization produced by the paradox of racial salience can be tempered by reducing the experiential segregation producing that polarization. This can be achieved by changing the physical or program design of an organization or community so that people in different racial positions interact regularly and share experiences that matter to them. That is what happened in the collaboration between Fisk, a historically Black university, and Vanderbilt, a predominantly white institution, when they created their joint and equal partnership aimed at full participation in the STEM fields. It happened in Judge Fein's trial court when people from different departments and in different roles were brought together to interact over an extended period around issues of race and to try experiments in their workplaces that would put into practice what they were learning. And that kind of spatial redesign at the community level, promoted by national policy, is what Richard Rothstein and Leah Rothstein are pushing for in *Just Action*.

When power is repurposed to advance full participation, the paradox of racialized power becomes easier to navigate. Moving from "power over" to "power with"—by deciding whose knowledge counts and how people make decisions—enables those involved in change work to figure out how best to use the power they each have. Instead of grappling with whether to step up or step back, the question becomes, "What do we, individually and together, have to contribute to this process, as we move toward shared goals?" This reframing helps all the participants figure out how to navigate the power they retain and offers ways to learn whether and when you might be exercising power to reinforce the status quo.

The places where I have seen this best enacted are institutions that have been set up by people of color and that have embodied the values of full participation from their inception. Morehouse College, Spelman College, and other Historically Black Colleges and Universities (HBCUs), initially created out of necessity to serve Black people barred from white educational institutions, have embodied social justice principles and practices of full participation from their inception. These values, "birthed during the height of racial terror and civic indifference," as Otis Moss III proclaimed in his 2022 Founder's Day speech to Morehouse College students, are the underpinnings of a culture that treats every person in the institution as worthy, enables them to realize their full potential, and expects them to give back to their community. As he continued in his passionate speech, he proclaimed the values, the process, and the mindset built into Morehouse's history and fabric:

> This is the house audacity built. This is the house ingenuity built. This is the house spiritual brilliance and ethical resolve built. . . . This is the space where you get to be one among many instead of being just one of the few. . . . In this house, your academic excellence will not be challenged as affirmative action, nor will your love of Black history and culture be banned because they say it's critical race theory. . . . In this house, brilliance will be expected. Leadership is the norm. Service is the standard. Activism is our brand, grinding is our ethic, and having a side hustle is typical and having swag is just what we do.[16]

Predominantly white institutions have much to learn about full participation from these institutions. These values and practices are embedded in their way of working, decision making, and assessment. Fisk brought those values to the collaboration with Vanderbilt, which enabled that predominantly white institution to achieve a level of full participation they could never have reached on their own. Institutions set up and led by people of color may be the best drivers of change toward full participation. Predominantly white institutions also have resources that they could, and I believe should, share with institutions led by people of color. By making research opportunities and resources available to Fisk faculty and students, Vanderbilt began to make higher education more equitable. Predominantly white institutions might have their greatest impact when they shift power and resources to nonwhite institutions or create partnerships with institutions set up to support the needs and interests of people of color. If this kind of power and resource sharing were pursued on a broader scale, transformative change that moves toward full participation seems possible.

The institutions and values that have managed to create this synthesis and that can model how to navigate these paradoxes deserve to be at the forefront of our national imagination. Without this, we may continue to replicate the errors of history. These vibrant fractals—imagining and enacting these ideals—can inspire ways to advance full participation, enabling predominantly white institutions to rescript the racial narrative. Just as the Fisk-Vanderbilt partnership is proof of the mutual benefit that flows from these collaborations, building genuine partnerships between predominantly white institutions and those set up by communities of color allows us to learn with and from each other, making each partner both resource rich and resourceful.

The story of the Mall of America offers a cautionary tale in this regard. As we saw in that example, when private business prioritizes profits, diversity efforts may well be short-lived. Indeed, months after the killing of George Floyd set off a racial reckoning, a host of companies escalated cuts of DEI professionals, according to a survey of more than six hundred companies from a data firm.[17] However, there are businesses that have begun taking the long-term well-being of the entire community into account. That has happened in Newark, where a group of nineteen anchors—all of the higher education institutions, hospitals, corporations, arts, and major cultural organizations in the city—have joined forces to encourage buying and hiring locally, as part of a recognition that supporting people of color—the majority there and soon to be across the nation—serves everyone's well-being.[18]

In his book titled *Cooperation: A Political, Economic, and Social Theory*, critical theorist and legal advocate Bernard Harcourt catalogs a growing number of economic enterprises in the United States and around the world that are partnering with communities, workers, and activists to transform the political economy of sectors and regions. One such project, called "Cooperation Jackson [Mississippi]," has as its mission "to transform Jackson's economy and social order by building a vibrant local social and solidarity economy anchored by worker and community owned enterprises that are grounded in sustainable practices of production, distribution, consumption, and recycling/reuse."[19] Part of a long tradition going back to the Reconstruction era in the "Black Belt counties," this "microspace of justice" has set its sights on constructing what it calls a "cooperative incubator," as well as a "cooperative school and training center, a network of local cooperatives, and a cooperative credit union for banking."[20]

Harcourt also documents more ambitious efforts to create what people call a solidarity economy. "A solidarity economy is grounded in notions of democratic decision making, inclusion, cooperation, mutual aid, social justice, equity, and diversity." Harcourt locates the prospects for cooperation in "our newfound interdependence" stemming from global warming, requiring "coordinated action by everyone on planet Earth to avoid imminent catastrophe." He observes hopefully that "cooperation is pervasive in contemporary economy and society, often hidden in plain sight and unacknowledged."[21] The examples Harcourt provides show that, spurred by impending global catastrophes, a zero-sum approach to both racism and the economy that has polarized communities and precluded cooperation can give way to a both/and approach, where people work together across racial lines for the well-being of all people.

What Might Be exhorts us to stay engaged over the long haul in navigating the paradoxes of anti-racism and gives us the tools to do this both as individuals and in our institutions. If we care about these values, what choice do we have other than to relentlessly pursue this work? We can't predict whether our efforts will be successful, but if we don't undertake them, failure is guaranteed. As we keep striving to make "what might be" a reality, we transform our lives and have the greatest hope of guiding our institutions toward full participation.

ACKNOWLEDGMENTS

THIS BOOK IS the result of decades of conversation and collaboration with students, colleagues, and change agents. I have benefited immeasurably from the commitment evident in their efforts, the insights they have shared in the process, and the relationships that made these collaborations work. Even after her untimely death in 2022, Lani Guinier continues to be an active collaborator, in both my radical imagination of our continuing dialogue and her extensive written work. I am deeply grateful to all who generously gave their time during my years of research, sharing their stories and efforts in extensive interviews and group sessions, sending relevant materials, and coauthoring work. Whether their stories appear in the book by name, pseudonym, as composites, or not at all, every one of them has contributed so generously and thoughtfully to the development of this book.

Nancy Cantor and Earl Lewis have been visionaries in curating this series, as well as stalwart supporters, sounding boards, and editors for this book. I am so grateful for the insight and inspiration they provided throughout the process of conceiving and writing the book. I marvel at their individual and shared capacity to use ideas as drivers of institutional transformation.

The commentators on the book—Anurima Bhargava, Freeman Hrabowski, and Goodwin Liu—have each inspired me by their unwavering pursuit of full participation. I am so thankful for their thoughtful commentaries. I also want to thank Sania Anwar, Liz Emens, Eunice Hong, Gillian Lester, Martha Minow, Reginald Oh, Colleen Shanahan, Kendall Thomas, and the outside reviewers who have served as thought partners and readers of the manuscript. I have also had the benefit of insightful and thorough research and editing by Clio Nudel Radomeysler, Jazly Liziano, Blair MacDonald, Melanni Minucci, Sabriya Pate, Felicitas Reyes, Stuti Shah, and Reakash Walters for which I am so appreciative. The Advisory Board members for the Our Compelling Interests series have offered helpful suggestions throughout the process.

Tamia Romo has also been a constant source of administrative, editorial, and personal support.

Doreen Tinajero has been the glue cementing together these moving parts and getting us to the finish line. I am also grateful to my wonderful copyeditor Jenn Backer, Eric Crahan, and the entire Princeton University Press team for their invaluable contributions to the editorial process.

This book would not have been possible without Shoshana Alexander, officially the developmental editor but really the midwife who helped me give birth to this book. Her unwavering support, clear-eyed interventions, and insistent questions enabled me to tell the stories that I really wanted to tell, to focus on the transportable points that were most important to the reader, and to discover a style that transcended my training and could reach across the divides I hoped to bridge through the book.

Lee Wexler, my spouse and partner in life, has supported me at every step of the way, from doing the work that gave rise to the stories told here through every phase of the writing process. I am so thankful to have a life partner who lives the values that animate so much of my work.

Commentary on Susan Sturm's
What Might Be

By Freeman Hrabowski

ANYONE READING Susan Sturm's book will be drawn in by her level of honesty as she addresses one of America's greatest challenges: racism. She describes her work with leaders from a variety of predominantly white institutions as they confront the "paradoxes of anti-racism," the contradictions in which the efforts to challenge and change inequitable arrangements of race and power also require enlisting people, practices, and categories that reinforce those racialized arrangements. What she finds over and over again is that, even with good intentions and considerable effort, racism still exists. We have much work to do.

As a child of the civil rights movement, I have spent my life struggling and grappling with the issues Sturm discusses. In April 2024, I accepted the National Academy of Sciences' Public Welfare Medal on behalf of my colleagues and students at the University of Maryland, Baltimore County (UMBC). The award recognized our work "transforming U.S. science education and increasing cultural diversity within the science workforce," and my acceptance remarks focused on this work as well as my own experiences. Sturm looks out across society and asks, how can we achieve full participation? I have spent much of my life looking at representation in science and asking how we reach that same goal.

The award presentation occurred in Washington, D.C., and I started my speech noting we were just four miles from the Washington National Cathedral, a spot where Dr. Martin Luther King Jr. preached his final Sunday sermon just days before his assassination in April 1968. In that sermon, King para-phrased theologian Theodore Parker: "We shall overcome because the arc of the moral universe is long but it bends towards justice."[1] Two decades later, historian Arthur M. Schlesinger Jr. observed that the "genius of America lies in its capacity to forge a single nation from peoples remarkably diverse in ra-cial, religious, and ethnic origins."[2]

These inspiring quotes remind us of who and what we want to be: a nation that is both one and just. And yet we know that a society does not automati-cally move toward wholeness and justice. Rather, it is our actions that bend the arc of history in this direction. This is especially true when thinking about the idea of inclusive excellence, whether in law, science, or society at large.

The power of Sturm's work in promoting inclusion and excellence begins with her framing of the central issues as a series of apparent paradoxes. As with all paradoxes, these are statements that have energy. They convey tension. Contemplating them can cause discomfort as we confront the limitations im-posed by language and our own understanding. Yet the statements also hint at the movement that is possible if we acknowledge these points of tension and work to move beyond them.

It is clear throughout Sturm's book that she has reflected deeply on her own experiences, both as a professor of law and as an expert working with people across sectors and professions. She provides a variety of stories focused on institutions and the challenges leaders encounter as they seek to strengthen diversity in their organizations. Among these is her account of a white trial judge who tries to address race in his court and yet manages instead to provoke backlash from white colleagues and skepticism from people of color. She goes on to describe the naivete of a white playwright who proposes strategies for addressing racism in his production, as well as the frustration of an academic administrator who convenes minority students and faculty to work with them on solutions and then is surprised by their reactions.

The essential question Sturm has been asking for some time is how to attain full participation of people of color in educational and legal institutions, in-cluding at Columbia Law School, in judicial clerkships and positions on the law review. What she and others doing this work across sectors have discov-ered, and what we see throughout the country in a variety of fields, is a series of failed attempts to reduce, if not eliminate, racial disparities and to advance diversity. This isn't simply about "hearing" students or addressing their con-cerns. More important, the goal is for them to excel academically and then to be able to contribute fully to their professions. Sturm observes correctly that universities and other institutions have studied these issues, developed diversity statements, held training sessions, and established offices of diversity, equity, and inclusion, with personnel focused on promoting the work.

And yet, we continue to face challenges. In my experience, simply creating a DEI office, or hiring a chief diversity officer, will have little impact if these steps do not reflect the commitment of the senior leadership team. Often there are questions about authority and the level of the DEI work; another critical question centers on what the focus of that work should be. On some campuses, a major challenge is the academic performance of students and gaps in graduation rates. On other campuses, the central concern is more about the general climate and how students feel about the college experience. Related questions focus on representation in the student body and across the faculty and staff. Often, we find far greater representation among staff members than on the faculty, which points to the persistent challenge of diversifying the professoriate.

Sturm recognizes that even those of us who are champions of this work have much to learn if we are to be effective. The necessary changes involve transformation of individuals as well as institutions. The work is not easy. Sturm recognizes the need for whites "to lean into their power to make needed change while simultaneously stepping back from exercising power in order to make space for people of color to lead." Effective initiatives must clearly identify race as a factor, and yet they must also talk about challenges that all groups share. And leaders must direct this work while understanding that the success of their efforts will ineluctably result in fundamental changes in their institutions.

Across these paradoxes, and across institutions of all kinds, the work is fundamentally about changing culture. That may sound easy enough, but the truth is that changing culture is a complex and often daunting challenge for leaders. Years ago, as part of a panel talking to an auditorium filled with college presidents, I commented that "changing the culture of an institution is hard as hell," and the audience erupted with laughter and applause.[3] The comment resonated with these campus leaders because they recognized the complexity of even discussing potential changes. Efforts to change culture frequently meet with reluctance or outright resistance. And even when initiatives are underway, progress can be halting and uneven, opening the door to second-guessing.

For many years as I've discussed these issues with audiences across the country, I've referenced a metaphor introduced by Eric Weiner, who suggested that "culture is the sea we swim in, so pervasive, so all-consuming, that we fail to notice it until we step out of it."[4] In other words, if your culture, values, goals, and actions do not align, your chances for success are dim. How do we change our culture and innovate? This is the question Sturm is asking. As I have shown in my own work,[5] culture change begins by looking in the mirror and being honest with oneself. It continues with tough conversations about problems, goals, resources, and actions.

Language is an important part of this. We must recognize that groups and organizations and individuals are all in different places and may be receptive to different messages. Specific words may be received differently depending on the time, the place, the audience, and other factors. The important thing is finding the points of connection, the commonalities, and building from there.

In this work, we may use a variety of methods, including those many of us are now calling "anti-racism strategies." Yet we should not assume that people will just accept what we mean, even when it is explained. At times, we may work with people who don't fully understand the concept of "anti-racism" or who may react to it in unexpected ways. Since retiring from UMBC in 2022 after thirty years as president, I've continued working with two- and four-year institutions across the country. After five decades in higher education, I'm still surprised at how much we all have in common, and yet how different we are as Americans depending on level of education, religion, race, region, and even zip code. Recognizing that some people in certain audiences will react negatively to "anti-racism" and other terms, my approach is often to talk about the substance of the work itself. Discussing Sturm's book, I may talk about examples, including those that illustrate for leaders how people resist change, reach different conclusions about the same situation, or resist taking ownership of problems involving discrimination.

Equally important are the strategies Sturm offers to effect change. She discusses how to revise existing narratives or teach people how to handle complexity. Starting with small initiatives can lead to increasingly major change over time, and building a cadre of people who become change agents can be important in navigating difficult situations. (This notion is one we have long embraced at UMBC; many of our graduates and faculty members have become change agents, not just on our campus but across the country.) She is on point alluding to Carol Dweck's work on the importance of developing a growth mindset rather than having a fixed mindset. All of us involved in this work must maintain a level of humility, knowing that there's more to learn, and we must be willing to consider new ideas. One such idea that I've used on campuses focuses on inclusion when thinking about the declining number of white males in higher education. As we talk to the public about DEI initiatives, we can be clear about ways this work can be helpful to the larger group.

Experiencing Change

During my time as UMBC's president, the culture of the university changed, as did our society. Progress itself presents an interesting paradox in that we are continually reminded as we move forward of how much further we still have to go and that the struggle will continue. That has been true during the course of my five decades working in higher education and, indeed, throughout my lifetime.

I was reminded of this when I was invited to deliver the first Martin Luther King Jr. Commemorative Lecture at Harvard University in 2022. (Before that, of course, individual schools at Harvard held MLK Day programs, but the event was the first time the entire university honored Dr. King in this way.) For me, remembering the significance of Dr. King and those involved in the civil rights movement provided an opportunity to reflect on the past in order to understand our current challenges—from the future of democracy to racial injustice and inequalities across society.

When we commemorate Dr. King, we remind ourselves of the bitter, divisive period of the late 1950s and early 1960s. The challenges of that time had an impact on all of us living during that period. In my church, my school, and my home, we were always discussing critical issues such as poverty and racism. Having Dr. King and others like him as role models served to inspire generations of African Americans and others. They conveyed the importance of speaking truth to power. They urged the nation to dismantle segregation and address social justice. This activism led Congress to enact, and President Lyndon Johnson to sign, critical legislation for civil rights, voting rights, housing, and education (elementary, secondary, and higher education). This success inspired similar efforts to secure the rights of women, Black people, other people of color, LGBTQ Americans, and Americans with disabilities.

For me, one of the powerful aspects of speaking that day at Harvard came from appreciating that the university's connection to Dr. King went back seventy years. As a student at Boston University in the early 1950s, Dr. King took courses in philosophy at Harvard, studying Plato and Alfred North Whitehead. In his days as a civil rights activist, he gave lectures at Harvard over several years in the late 1950s and early 1960s. In October 1962, sixty years before my own speech, King, then thirty-three, gave a lecture at Harvard Law

School in which he stated clearly that integration would only be realized through struggle.

While speaking at Harvard, I felt a personal connection to King's 1962 lecture because he came to my hometown, Birmingham, Alabama, in the spring of 1963, and I was inspired to join the Children's March. King himself led several protests in my city and was arrested, following which he wrote his celebrated *Letter from Birmingham Jail*. After his release, he and others called on the children to march. I was in church one weekday evening when I heard him say that if the children marched they could have an impact on the future, that our action was needed and would matter. Inspired, at age twelve I joined the Children's March on its third day, the day after Commissioner Bull Connor started using snarling dogs and firehoses on the children. My group and I marched through the streets to the City Hall, only to encounter Connor himself, who spat in my face. I was arrested and spent five terrifying nights in jail.

It was during this time that Dr. King came to the jail along with our parents, many of whom were weeping openly. He assured us, saying that what we were doing would change the lives of children not yet born. We knew his words were profound even though we did not fully understand them. In time, though, they would mean for me a career in education as a way of seeking the truth, of problem-solving to change lives, and of working for diversity in higher education, with a special emphasis on inclusion in science and engineering.

The rest of 1963 was tumultuous. By the summer, the elected officials and business leaders of the city of Birmingham agreed to integrate shops and schools. In August, Dr. King led the March on Washington and gave his "I Have a Dream" speech. In September, however, KKK members bombed the 16th Street Baptist Church, killing my friends—four little girls now immortalized in the Spike Lee documentary. It took decades before prosecutor Doug Jones, a future U.S. senator, was able to bring the murderers to justice.

In his 1962 speech at Harvard Law School, King said, "The law can't make a man love me, but it can keep him from lynching me." The effects of laws are more complicated than that, however. In spite of existing laws, in recent years we have seen increasing violence, including recurring police brutality, senseless shootings, and political violence and insurrection. We must speak out about what is not acceptable, and violence and discrimination against people based on race, ethnicity, religion, gender, disability, sexual orientation, gender identity, or income are always unacceptable. Our colleges and universities have a responsibility to society in the search for truth and solutions. Through research, policy development, and, perhaps most important, the preparation of our students for leadership our universities can shape our culture, our policies, and our future.

Legal decisions and legislation from *Brown v. Board of Education* to the Civil Rights Act, the Higher Education Act, and the Pell Amendments of 1972 made a difference, leading to increased access to higher education and greater college attainment. In 1965, just 10 percent of Americans over age twenty-five had earned a bachelor's degree. Today, that number is 38 percent. For whites, the figures were 11 percent in 1965 and 42 percent today; for Blacks, 4 percent and 28 percent. College attainment today is 61 percent for Asians, 20 percent for Hispanics, and lower for Native Americans. Significantly, most Blacks who earned bachelor's degrees in the early 1960s did so at an HBCU. Today, HBCUs enroll 9 percent of Black college students but still produce about 20 percent of Black college graduates and 25 percent of those in STEM.[6]

Legislation such as the act establishing the Pell Grant (1972) actually helped people of all backgrounds. A white, male CEO who served as chair of a local school board in Georgia made this point at a meeting of the Georgia Association of School Boards I attended. His father had died, and his mother was doing her best as a sharecropper. She saw that Black kids were going to college and determined that her son would, too, despite their financial challenges. The Pell Grant and other assistance made college a reality for him—and this changed his life.

Despite this progress, the work of the civil rights movement is not finished. In his recent book, David Kirp called our six-year bachelor's degree completion rate of 60 percent "the college dropout scandal."[7] But if it is a "scandal" when just 60 percent complete, what do we call it when just 42 percent of African Americans complete?

Bachelor's degree completion is important. We continue to hear the narrative that people are questioning the value of higher education, yet people who are college educated, regardless of political party, generally send their children to college. While college is not for everyone—there are other postsecondary options for those who want them—there is value in an associate's or bachelor's degree.

Diversity and Inclusion in Higher Education

The problem of educational disparities is especially acute in STEM. Peter Henderson and I recently wrote about doctoral education in *Issues in Science and Technology*, returning to a topic we examined together while working on the National Academy of Sciences' 2011 report, *Expanding Underrepresented Minority Participation: America's Science and Technology Talent at the Crossroads.*

> While African Americans make up 13% of the US population, Blacks who were US citizens or permanent residents in 2011 when the *Crossroads* report was published earned just 2.2% of all new PhDs awarded by US universities in the natural sciences and engineering. That figure increased—if you can call it that—to 2.3% in 2018. Similarly, while Hispanics comprise 18% of the US population, those who were US citizens or permanent residents earned 2.9% of all new PhDs awarded by US universities in the natural sciences and engineering in 2011, a figure that increased to 3.7% in 2018.[8]

We have also seen little progress in the social and behavioral sciences. Black PhDs in these fields increased from 6.2 percent in 2011 to 7.0 percent in 2018; for Hispanics, from 6.0 to 7.9 percent during that period.[9]

In February 2020, the National Academy of Sciences celebrated the seventy-fifth anniversary of Vannevar Bush's *Science: The Endless Frontier.* I was a speaker—one of just two Blacks on the agenda—at the convocation, and as I looked out at the audience, I saw very few people of color. This is troubling for many reasons. First, our scientific enterprise should look like America, for equity and participatory purposes. Underrepresented minorities have a right to be "in the room where it happens." Second, a strong case has been made that most intellectual enterprises benefit from diversity. When people bring different information, perspectives, and lived experiences to a situation, the conversations are richer and the potential for success and innovation increases. Third, when people do not see themselves as part of an enterprise, they are less likely to trust it—and that goes for any institution, including science. When people—who are voters—do not trust science, that undermines both the enterprise and the ability to disseminate critical new ideas (e.g., about climate change) and products (e.g., vaccines) among the population.

My research over the past forty years has focused on closing the achievement gap, broadening participation, and increasing diversity at every level of higher education across disciplines, with a special emphasis on the natural sciences and engineering. I have always been inspired by Fisk University and Harvard alumnus W.E.B. Du Bois and his notion of the "Talented Tenth," which encouraged focusing on those Blacks who were prepared to excel in professional fields as a way to enrich the Black community and provide role models for others. We are comfortable talking about talented basketball and football players. I asked, why can't we also be comfortable talking about talented humanists, scientists, and engineers?

When UMBC was founded in 1963, it was the first university in Maryland to open its doors at a time when students of all racial backgrounds could enroll. We pushed this experiment further when, twenty-five years later, we established the Meyerhoff Scholars program. My colleagues and I were concerned about the poor performance of Blacks in STEM and developed a program to address this with support from philanthropist Bob Meyerhoff (a graduate of MIT). Bob was concerned about finding ways to help Black men excel in something besides sports, and I was concerned about finding ways to help Black people succeed in STEM, so we married these ideas to see what we could accomplish. Bob Meyerhoff, now age ninety-nine, and I still have conversations about the challenges Black people face and about the challenges Meyerhoff Scholars and alumni face. He is a great example of a caring philanthropist who gives more than money.

What will surprise some is that we received considerable opposition from a number of colleagues when we started the program. Some thought it was unfair to have a special program for Black students. This opposition was not based on ideology but instead came from people who believed in being fair to all students—they simply had not considered the benefits of such a program or the possibility that what we learned from working with this group could be helpful to all our students. As an African American president, I faced an additional hurdle in having to show that I could be fair to all students even while focusing on particular groups and challenges.

While the Meyerhoff program started off with a focus on Black students, over time we broadened it to include students of all races interested in increasing diversity in STEM areas. (We made this change in 1995 after the Supreme Court let stand a ruling that the Benjamin Banneker scholarship program at the University of Maryland, College Park could not be open only to Black students.) Lessons from the program helped us develop a number of innovative projects, including the Chemistry Discovery Center, which transformed introductory chemistry by adding a new element to the course focused on working in groups and collaborating to solve problems. We later funded innovation grants that supported the development of everything from a "gym" for tutoring in math to redesigned courses in the arts, humanities, and social sciences. Across the campus, we placed much greater emphasis on group work and on finding ways to build community among students. Ultimately, by working to understand the challenges facing a particular race, we learned lessons that were helpful to all. The essential point is what Sturm describes as "forging linked fate."

In a broader sense, the civil rights movement also taught us valuable lessons about the process of change. These include the importance of identifying specific goals, placing those goals in the larger American narrative, using a comprehensive range of tactics, attracting resources, and organizing. Changing attitudes and culture is critical and involves tough conversations about the nature of the problem, the possible solutions, and the responsibility for taking action.[10] The initial goal of the Meyerhoff program was to diversify the pool of underrepresented minority undergraduates who could go on to earn PhDs in the natural sciences and engineering.[11] The program placed this goal in the American narrative—science and engineering are critical to the future of the United States and that enterprise can only be optimized through a robust and diverse workforce. The program includes a range of tools to provide participants with academic, social, financial, and professional support.

Understanding the Present

Our experience with the Meyerhoff program revealed the critical importance of specificity. To bring about change, we need to know where we are starting as well as where we are going. Often, this means disaggregating data so we can examine how different groups are performing in a variety of settings and circumstances.

For the Meyerhoff program, one critical outcome is the number of students who complete PhDs in the natural sciences and engineering. Over the years, my colleagues and I have had to work closely with the National Science Foundation (NSF) and others to track—by race and ethnicity—the baccalaureate origin institutions of students who complete PhDs in these disciplines. According to the most recent NSF data, UMBC is the number one baccalaureate institution for African American undergraduates who go on to earn PhDs in the natural sciences and engineering. In addition, according to the Association of American Medical Colleges, UMBC is the number one baccalaureate institution for African American undergraduates who go on to earn MD-PhDs.[12]

Even when data that track various outcomes by race are available, asking for these data can make people uncomfortable. My colleagues and I found this to be the case in 2020 as the Covid pandemic shut down much of the country and we, along with others, sought information about ways the disease might have various impacts for different groups. We described our efforts in an article for the *Proceedings of the National Academy of Sciences.*

> Although its high level of contagion means that everyone is vulnerable to the virus, the pandemic has also shined a bright light on intractable inequalities in our society. Several months ago, we, along with others, advocated for release of COVID-19 case data by race, arguing that we could not understand the impact of the virus unless we could see how it affected communities differently. When data were finally made available, the disparities were clear. Elderly and low-income Americans, African Americans, Native Americans, and Hispanics are infected by and dying from the virus in disproportionate numbers. Ibram Kendi has shown that the African American community has been particularly hard hit because of structural racism, economic inequalities, and health disparities. To paraphrase others, these differences provided the kindling and police brutality the match for the widespread fire of racial protest that has called for broad policy changes to address structural racism in America.[13]

Our focus on specificity also helped broaden the scope of our work. In particular, we recognized we cannot make progress at the doctorate level without progress at the preK–12 and undergraduate levels.

We all have seen the decline in math test scores around the country since the beginning of the pandemic. We must focus on sustaining and improving preK–12 education. One example of those who have been willing to ask good questions is Betsy Sherman and her late husband, George. The Shermans asked, "What would it take to produce qualified science and mathematics teachers for challenging schools?" George was an engineer and Betsy was at one time the only white teacher at an elementary school in Virginia. She believes that any person of any race or ethnicity can teach any student of any race or ethnicity. What it takes is a passion for teaching, experience in the classroom, and education in science. With the generous support of the Shermans, we established the Sherman STEM Teacher Scholars Program at UMBC.

This is the kind of innovative work we need in preK–12 education. The Shermans, in partnership with Northrop Grumman, have also supported our successful work with Lakeland Elementary in Baltimore City. Before the pandemic, Lakeland had substantial increases in student math test scores.

We must also continue to focus on the undergraduate level, which prepares students for graduate and professional study. When we take our eyes off the ball, our progress can melt away. For example, Hispanic bachelor's degree recipients in science and engineering have increased over a decade to 17 percent. Meanwhile, the rate for Black degree recipients in those fields has remained flat at about 9 percent, and only 5 percent in physics. This is not progress.[14]

We thought of the Meyerhoff Scholars program as an experiment. Our research question was: "Is it possible for a Predominantly White Institution to produce African American graduates so well qualified and so excited about science or engineering that they would go on to earn PhDs?" We wanted to base this program on evidence of what worked. When we looked at NSF's baccalaureate origins data for new PhDs, however, we found that there were no research universities that were producing even five African American undergraduates who went on to earn science or engineering doctorates.

My TED Talk focuses on the Meyerhoff program, its components, and its accomplishments.[15] Here, let me note four components that have been critical. The first is instilling high expectations in program participants. Beginning with the application process, we encourage students to aspire to a doctorate in the natural sciences or engineering and a research career. The second is building community. Students enter as a cohort, they experience a summer bridge program together before their first year, and they study together in groups. This community provides a sense of belonging that is critical for both persistence and learning. The third component is direct involvement in research. At UMBC we say, "It takes researchers to produce researchers." Faculty involvement in this work is critical and has been the backbone of the program and its success. By participating in research, students gain knowledge, build skills and agency, and strengthen their identities as scientists. The fourth component is assessment. We built evaluation into the Meyerhoff program from its inception, both to provide real-time data for improving the program and to collect comparative data that would demonstrate the program's success.

In *The Empowered University*, my colleagues and I wrote:

It was a moment that gave us goose bumps. In the summer of 2002, the American Society for Biochemistry and Molecular Biology (ASBMB) reported that something unexpected and special was happening at UMBC. In a study of 1998/99 data, ASBMB ranked the leading producers of chemistry and biochemistry degrees. UMBC was among them. It also ranked universities on the number of those degrees awarded to minorities. We were second. It also ranked universities on the award of these degrees to African Americans. UMBC was first.... Out of sixty-six undergraduate chemistry and biochemistry degrees, UMBC had awarded twenty-one, well ahead of any other institution.[16]

Once we had established the Meyerhoff Scholars Program as a national model, we worked with university and philanthropic partners to replicate and/or adapt it at other research universities. I would like to acknowledge the leadership of the Howard Hughes Medical Institute (HHMI)—particularly Erin O'Shea and Leslie Vosshall—for their support of our work at UMBC and for HHMI's investments in replicating the Meyerhoff program at UNC Chapel Hill and Penn State. Recently, HHMI committed up to $500 million to establish programs "similar to Meyerhoff" at another twenty-four research universities, as well as $1.5 billion to fund the Freeman Hrabowski Scholars Program for early career faculty poised to become leaders in research while creating diverse, inclusive lab environments. I was honored that the vision for these young scholars is for them to become change agents.

In addition, the Chan Zuckerberg Initiative has invested in replication of the Meyerhoff program at UC Berkeley and UC San Diego, as has the Karsh Family Foundation at Howard University and the Simons Foundation at SUNY Stony Brook. We were also very fortunate that the Sloan Foundation provided funding to UMBC to create a Meyerhoff Scholars Program track for students who intend to earn a PhD in economics. Federal government agencies, including NSF and the National Institutes of Health (NIH), are playing a critical role through programs that increase diverse participation in the STEM fields, such as INCLUDES, AGEP, BUILD, ADVANCE, and FIRST.[17] This support needs to be deepened. And institutions must step up to the plate and do the work. In the months since the Supreme Court issued its ruling on affirmative action, I have used the example of the Meyerhoff program to show that institutions committed to providing African Americans and other students of color with support can find ways of continuing to do so.

I cannot overstate the importance of the idea that it takes researchers to produce researchers. The National Academies recently released a report titled "Advancing Antiracism, Diversity, Equity, and Inclusion in STEMM Organizations." This report makes a critical point: "Gatekeepers possess power and can determine who is and who is not included in STEMM fields." They considered a gatekeeper to be "any individual who possesses power in a given STEMM context or situation, where power includes the control over valued outcomes and resources."[18] Most of the powerful gatekeepers in academic science—the most prestigious faculty—are white males. The report goes on to argue that for a variety of reasons—implicit bias and the benefits of the status quo among them—these "gatekeepers are unlikely to be change agents." The ineluctable question is whether university leaders and faculty are sufficiently committed to broadening participation in STEM such that they will examine their views, become allies in the work, and pull underrepresented students into the sciences.

At UMBC, for example, Mike Summers, a professor of biochemistry, HHMI investigator, and National Academy of Sciences (NAS) member, is a superb example of a change agent. A leader of efforts to replicate the Meyerhoff program on other campuses, he has also mentored numerous minority and women students in his lab, where they study how HIV-1 and other retroviruses assemble in infected cells. Some of these students have been undergraduate students in the Meyerhoff program and others graduate students in the Graduate Meyerhoff Program that Mike runs. Many of these students have become faculty at research universities and other institutions nationwide.

What is remarkable about Mike is that when he is invited to give a lecture at another university, he gives two. The first is about his scientific research; the second is about how to develop a program that supports underrepresented minorities in the natural sciences and engineering. His commitment is an example for others.

As Peter Henderson and I wrote in a recent article in *Issues in Science and Technology*, institutions can replicate and adapt practices that have been proven to work at other colleges and universities. We suggested that financial resources should flow to institutions that most successfully contribute to greater diversity—regardless of institutional type.[19]

We can also make a difference as individuals. Without the connections they need to advance, many talented minority students who have earned doctorates leave bench science even as colleges and universities say they have difficulty finding them. We need faculty to be both mentors and champions of students of color as they make the transition to faculty careers. We can actively recruit applicants of color for faculty positions and, once they are hired, we can treat and support them as colleagues, collaborating with them on grants, research, and papers; reading and citing their work; and inviting them to give talks.

One excellent example of a champion is Dr. Barney Graham, who served as deputy director of the NIH's Vaccine Research Center and who mentored UMBC alumna Kizzmekia Corbett. Dr. Corbett is a perfect example of what it means when we work intentionally to draw on all of our talent to unlock discoveries that benefit everyone. She is a young African American woman from a rural town in North Carolina. During high school she attended a summer program at UNC sponsored by Project SEED of the American Chemical Society. She continued after high school to UMBC, where she was a Meyerhoff Scholar, and she then earned a PhD at Chapel Hill before taking a postdoc at the NIH. In 2020, with Dr. Graham, she co-led the coronavirus vaccine development team at the National Institute of Allergy and Infectious Diseases (NIAID). She is now on the faculty at Harvard's T. H. Chan School of Public Health.

In 2021, Dr. Anthony Fauci, then director of NIAID, said of Corbett, "Her work will have a substantial impact on ending the worst respiratory disease pandemic in more than 100 years."[20] The New York Times wrote, "Kizzmekia Corbett helped lead a team of scientists contributing to one of the most stunning achievements in the history of immunizations: a highly effective, easily manufactured vaccine against COVID-19."[21]

In 2023, the William Fulbright Prize for International Understanding was awarded to Fauci and Corbett, "whose leadership and scientific discoveries have been critical to the abatement of the COVID-19 pandemic." With Barney Graham, she was Time magazine's Hero of the Year. She also received the 2021 Benjamin Franklin NextGen Award.

Let us remind ourselves that success requires each of us to encourage our institutions to build a broader talent pool.[22]

Several years ago, Sandy Williams, then dean of the Duke University Medical School, had serious conversations with Duke faculty about identifying and investing in a more diverse candidate pool. By becoming a champion for diversity and inclusion, Williams created a culture that supported the transition of minority students into the professoriate. A stunning outcome of his leadership is that four of UMBC's African American alumni are now on the faculty at Duke Medical School. Among them is Damon Tweedy, who holds both medical and law degrees and is the author of the bestselling book Black Man in a White Coat. Another is Kafui Dzirasa, who went on from UMBC to earn his MD-PhD at Duke and has recently become a tenured full professor there in psychiatry and neurobiology with an endowed chair. Kaf has won the Young Investigator Award of the Society for Neuroscience and the 2022 Benjamin Franklin NextGen Award. He was also recently elected to the National Academy of Medicine and is an HHMI investigator. He is a change agent on many levels. In addition to his research and teaching and work as a mentor, he writes regularly on issues of race, equality, and social justice in scientific research and in society.

Kaf, Damon, Kizzmekia, and so many others give me hope, both that we have made progress and that we can make much more. In science, and across professions and areas of human activity, we must believe in the power of reason. Susan Sturm understands that important point, and she inspires readers to bring another level of honesty to the challenges we face, to take a thoughtful approach in moving forward. Yes, we must look in the mirror, and we must look at each other with a new level of understanding, as well as with a sense of wonder, and even awe, at what people can accomplish if we believe in them, and we empower them.

That was my point in April when I spoke at the National Academy of Sciences. I concluded by talking about Kaf and his accomplishments, and then I asked him to stand. Next, I asked this very distinguished group of scientists—predominantly men, and predominantly white—to look into the face of this young Black man. They immediately gave him a standing ovation.

"This," I said, "is science, and medicine, reimagined."

And this is the vision Susan Sturm, through *What Might Be*, inspires us to pursue.

Commentary: Toward Inclusive Pedagogy

Goodwin Liu

THERE IS MUCH TO admire in Professor Susan Sturm's book *What Might Be: Confronting Racism to Transform Our Institutions*. At a time when our society is struggling with polarization, it is uplifting to read an account of how change-makers have worked across divides to build more inclusive and just institutions. Central to the book's methodology is a narrative approach: personal narratives from Professor Sturm's own experiences, as well as narratives of how others have engaged in the hard work of listening, learning, and sharing power. Through these narratives, Professor Sturm elucidates nuances and apparent contradictions—paradoxes—involved in addressing historical and structural inequality. No grand theory or silver-bullet solution can tell us the right thing to do in every situation. But we can learn from examples and adapt lessons from experience as we work toward a more hopeful future.

Like Professor Sturm, I have a lifelong passion for this topic. As a child of immigrants, I became aware of racism and cultural difference long before I had the vocabulary to name those concepts. As a law professor, much of my scholarship focused on racial inequality in education. As a judge, I have written many opinions on racial discrimination in jury selection, searches and arrests, and other areas where the justice system is vulnerable to bias. For years, I have been an avid student of research on implicit bias and recently coedited a volume of *Daedalus* on this topic in collaboration with the National Academy of Sciences.

I have also sought to advance diversity in the legal profession. This work includes ongoing research on the progress and challenges experienced by

Asian Americans lawyers. It also includes a recent coauthored study on law clerk selection and diversity based on individual interviews with fifty judges of the federal courts of appeals. The study explores how judges think about diversity when hiring clerks and reveals how some judges have succeeded in achieving diversity while others have not. Narratives are a powerful feature of this work, elucidating the intentionality and courage required to change the status quo.

Here I offer a set of insights about diversity and inclusion that I have gleaned from my own practice. I would like to share reflections from twenty years of law teaching on controversial subjects, with a focus on inclusive pedagogy. In keeping with the texture of Professor Sturm's book, the perspectives I will share are grounded in experience. They are very human and personal. That is because the process of teaching and learning is nothing like pouring water into empty vessels. It is interactive, dynamic, and recursive. It requires repeated engagement with people, not just perspectives. On difficult issues, few if any students are persuaded of one view or another by the sheer force of reason abstracted from our own priors or the priors we know or assume others to have. To hear and be heard and to embrace the contradictions involved in navigating race or other lines of difference require humility, vulnerability, and awareness of the subjectivity inherent in any human interaction.

Teaching Constitutional Law

Almost every year since I became a professor in 2003, I have taught a class on constitutional law. From a scan of daily headlines, we see that constitutional law is at the heart of many divisive issues: free speech, gun rights, affirmative action, church and state, the death penalty, police authority, privacy, gender equality, and more. How does one teach these subjects effectively? How does one teach these subjects when they elicit predictable cleavages along lines of race, gender, socioeconomic background, immigration status, or other dimensions of identity? And how does one teach these subjects during a time of ideological polarization and heightened sensitivity to certain words, concepts, or events?

I don't have complete answers to these questions, but I would like to share some general principles and practical ideas that guide my approach. These observations arise primarily from a course I have been teaching at Harvard Law School for the past nine years called Contemporary Issues in Constitutional Law. It is an advanced course for students who have taken basic constitutional law and wish to delve more deeply into specific topics to examine interpretive methodology, judicial behavior, and constitutional theory. The course has a distinctive format: it runs for two weeks during the middle of fall semester, with three hours of class each day, four days a week. This immersive format—"con law boot camp," as one student called it—began as a logistical accommodation to enable me, a judge from California, to teach a two-unit course on the East Coast in a compact time frame. But it has become my preferred format for teaching. The concentrated time that students spend together enables a level of continuity and depth that is hard to achieve in a class that meets only once or twice a week.

For each of the eight three-hour class periods, the class tackles one big topic: LGBTQ rights, religious freedom, campaign finance, voting rights, immigration, or affirmative action, among others. For each topic, I assign one or two recent Supreme Court cases and sometimes an article or commentary. Class time is spent almost entirely on discussion, not lecture. For several years, the class was limited to twenty-five students; in recent years, I have expanded it to over forty students.

The syllabus changes each year to incorporate recent cases. But the underlying pedagogical aims are the same. I want students to learn how to think critically without regard to ideology or orthodoxy, how to consider differing views even when they hold strong views themselves, and how to avoid unwarranted assumptions about individual Justices, fellow students, or the instructor. Difficult issues can be polarizing, but they are also full of nuance. For any issue, often a key question is whether there are any middle paths, partial answers, or resolutions short of winner-take-all. Although it is important for students to learn how to defend their views with careful reasoning, my hope is that they also learn how to move past trying to "win" the argument in order to consider what effective leadership means in a diverse democracy.

Principles Informing Pedagogy

How can we foster the hard conversations, active listening, and trust and vulnerability required for these deeper layers of learning? I have tried to be mindful of three principles. The first is *humanization*. In any relationship, including among student peers, an important precondition of honest conversation is the ability to see one other as three-dimensional individuals. I suspect it is familiar to anyone who has served on a board or similar deliberative body (including an appellate court) that social time in between doing business helps build personal bonds that facilitate discussion of serious issues. Learning about people's backgrounds, interests, and idiosyncrasies has a number of positive effects on group dynamics: It surfaces points of connection that people weren't aware of. It awakens curiosity in other people's perspectives. It directs our attention to the nuances of individuals rather than caricatures of groups. It builds trust, facilitates humor, and enables people to listen charitably, assuming good faith instead of ulterior motives. In the classroom, as in other settings, humanizing ourselves promotes empathy—and empathy is vital to hearing one another, especially when we disagree.

Second, I bring to the classroom an *awareness of hierarchies*, along with intentionality toward counteracting their potential effects on group dynamics. Students come to law school with different levels of social capital and economic or educational privilege. I am aware that men generally raise their hands more quickly than women and speak more frequently and confidently, whether warranted or not. I am aware that liberals greatly outnumber conservatives in the student bodies (and faculties) of elite law schools and that conservative viewpoints are not what elite universities are known for. I am aware that minority status on any dimension—whether it is race, disability, ideology, religious adherence, sexual orientation, or geographic origin—can cause students to feel vulnerable or cautious about expressing their views. I am also aware of the inherent hierarchy between my students and me, and the sensitivities that arise when students disagree with me or look to me to validate or invalidate comments made in class. All of these dynamics comprise the backdrop against which classroom learning occurs.

Third, in addition to the hierarchy just mentioned, I am conscious of other facets of my *positionality* in relation to my students and the material discussed in class. When I first started teaching twenty years ago, I was not much older than my students; today, we are one generation apart. I grew up before the advent of social media and before large attitudinal shifts on issues like climate change and gay rights. While I am wary of casual generalizations (e.g., Millennials, Gen Z, etc.), I am aware of differences in generational perspectives and try to use those differences for the benefit of learning. I am also aware of my identity as a judge and a scholar, which enables me to straddle internal and external points of view when discussing judicial opinions. Further, as an Asian American, I am familiar with the duality of being minoritized in some contexts while not counting as a (disadvantaged) minority in others. Acknowledging this in subtle yet candid ways resonates with the experiences of many students, whatever their background, and helps move discussion beyond simple binaries.

In addition, I am aware that students may perceive me as generally liberal, whether accurate or not, and may filter what I say through that preconception. Given such perceptions as well as the predominance of liberal-leaning students, I am especially intentional about questioning liberal orthodoxy, opening space for contrary views, and dislodging students' fear of "saying the wrong thing" in class. Every year, my course evaluations include comments along the lines of "I wish we could hear more of Justice Liu's views on the issues." But I generally try to keep my views to a minimum. My priority in the classroom is to elicit the best arguments on all sides and to frame opposing views in the most charitable way possible. I want my students to learn the habits of good lawyers and understand that many issues are more difficult and less one-sided than they might think.

Putting Principles into Practice

Over the years, I have experimented with a variety of techniques to foster inclusivity, trust, and candor in the classroom. In describing these strategies, I do not offer them as a one-size-fits-all approach for every type of class. Teaching is contextual and situational; like all forms of human interaction, it cannot be reduced to a how-to manual. Nevertheless, my hope is that sharing concrete ideas can help colleagues reflect on pedagogical challenges and gain new ideas for their teaching repertoire.

1. *Reconnaissance.* First impressions matter a lot in teaching, and preparing for the first day of class typically involves a long checklist: updating the syllabus, making readings accessible, writing teaching notes, creating a course website, and more. Equally important, I have found, are efforts to learn what I can about my students so that there are as few surprises as possible on Day One.

During the week before the first class, I ask students to fill out a simple Google form that asks for their name; email; year in law school; undergraduate school, major, and year of graduation; any graduate school, discipline, and year of degree; where they grew up; favorite constitutional law topics; activities in law school; interests or hobbies outside of school; and pronouns. This provides me with a "diversity dashboard" covering several dimensions, including geographic diversity, diversity by age and experience, and ideological diversity, as revealed by affiliations such as the Federalist Society or American Constitution Society. I also take note of students who have served in the military as well as international students. And knowing students' pronouns in advance is helpful.

In addition, the availability of students' photos (on the Canvas website) enables me to glean an initial sense of the gender and racial diversity in the class. The law school also has a practice of notifying me of any student with a disability requiring an accommodation. All of this information enables me to learn as much as possible about my students and to jump-start my thinking about how to build rapport among them and between them and me.

2. *Seating and architecture.* The physical layout of the classroom is important. I prefer a U-shaped or semicircular configuration that enables each student to make eye contact with every other student and minimizes the distance among students and between each student and me. I also prefer a room that is not oversized; if the room is too big, I designate the back rows off-limits and require students to fill the nearest rows, subject to any spacing requirements for public health. Although I use a lectern to hold readings and teaching notes, I regularly come out from behind the lectern and walk into the inner space of the classroom. Removing the physical barrier between my students and me connotes transparency and lessens hierarchy; it signals that what I say is open for examination and that I am not hiding behind my authority, symbolized by the lectern.

My aim is to make the physical aspects of the classroom most conducive to engagement, proximity, and intimacy. Architecture matters. A classroom arranged in rows with students facing forward toward the instructor behind a lectern has a different feel than a classroom arranged in a semicircle with students facing each other and the instructor facilitating discussion from the middle.

In addition, I require students to sit in a different seat each day. This counteracts the natural tendency for people to sit with friends or like-minded peers and prevents clustering by race, gender, or other characteristics. Also, as discussed below, I often ask students to interact with their neighbors during class, and the diversity of students' face-to-face communication with one another increases when they have different neighbors every class. Further, students literally gain a new perspective by sitting in a different seat and seeing different faces as a result of the daily shuffling.

Mixing up the students each day means I cannot rely on a seating chart to learn faces and names. But this has not been a problem in a forty-person class, with students using name placards. Moving students out of their comfort zones includes moving students spatially, thereby facilitating interactions that might otherwise not occur. Personal interactions are essential to building trust, and changing the seating arrangement each day increases the variety of such interactions.

3. *Introductions*. During the Covid-19 pandemic, I taught two full courses on Zoom. One concern was how to enable students to get to know one another in the online format. To this end, I created a Google slide presentation and asked each student to make a slide about himself or herself with a few photos and brief captions. I invited students to include photos of their families, friends, pets, travels, hobbies, and significant events. For each day of class, I asked a handful of students to take a minute to introduce themselves with their slides using the "share screen" function on Zoom.

To my delight and the evident enjoyment of the class, students made colorful slides with photos of their graduations, family weddings, Thanksgiving dinners, holiday gatherings, best friends, cherished pets, previous jobs, travel adventures, theater productions, athletic events, and favorite foods they cooked or baked. Although this idea began as a way to facilitate connection during the pandemic, I have since incorporated it into my in-person teaching. Through these visual introductions, students often learn they have much in common. They discover fellow pet-lovers; they have traveled to the same places; they enjoy cooking the same foods; they root for the same sports teams; they share many of the same hobbies. The slides also make students aware of some differences—most conspicuously in the images of their families and in the racial composition of their friends. These introductions enable students to see each other three-dimensionally and provide them with points of personal connection separate from what is discussed in class.

4. *Order of topics on the syllabus*. As noted, the two-week course is an upper-level elective that covers many hot-button topics in constitutional law. Students invariably bring tremendous insights to class discussion, and the optimal dynamic is when the students are learning from each other, not from me. Creating that dynamic is a gradual process whereby the students become increasingly familiar with one another and, day by day, strengthen their collective capacity to tackle tough topics together.

I try to scaffold this process by being attentive to the order of topics on the syllabus. I reserve topics like immigration or affirmative action, which many students see as implicating the legitimacy of their very presence in the classroom, for the later part of the course, after I've had several days to observe classroom dynamics and to facilitate rapport among the students. I usually begin the course with cases on same-sex marriage and LGBTQ rights because I have found that students of whatever background (at places like Harvard) generally have similar personal views on these topics. The legal issues can be difficult: Is *Obergefell* persuasive in its reliance on substantive due process?

Does *Bostock* indulge an untenable form of textualism? Is there room for compromise in resolving disputes like *303 Creative*? Students are typically able to approach these questions without suspicion that classmates who raise doubts about the legal underpinnings of liberal outcomes are somehow biased or intolerant. *Citizens United* is also a helpful case for building rapport. It involves a topic—campaign finance reform—that is not deeply personal for most students, and with careful study, they quickly realize it presents many complexities beyond the simplistic question of "whether money is speech" or "whether corporations are people."

In sum, by starting with topics where students find it easier to distinguish sound reasoning from desired outcomes, and by building their collective capacity to consider divergent views, I seek to lay a foundation for constructive engagement with more difficult topics as the course progresses.

5. *Polling.* Easy-to-use polling applications (e.g., Poll Everywhere) can be helpful in fostering classroom rapport. For example, when I introduce *Bostock*, I begin by having students do an online poll that asks whether they agree or disagree on a five-point scale (1 = total agreement, 5 = total disagreement) with various statements made by the Justices, such as:

- Justice Gorsuch (majority opinion): "It is impossible to discriminate against a person for being homosexual or transgender without discriminating against that individual based on sex."
- Justice Alito (dissent): "The Court updates Title VII to reflect what it regards as 2020 values."
- Justice Kavanaugh (dissent): "A literalist approach to interpreting phrases disrespects ordinary meaning and deprives the citizenry of fair notice of what the law is."

The polling application tracks responses in real time, and I share the results with the class on a projector screen. This exercise serves three purposes: First, it provides an accessible starting point for students to engage with the material. The anonymous, real-time format enables students to express tentative views without being put on the spot. Second, the poll enables me to see a quick mapping of the viewpoints in the classroom. It shows which perspectives are in the minority and suggests which themes or arguments may warrant greater attention in class. Third, the poll gives the students a clear visual of the diversity of viewpoints in the class. Students who hold a minority view may realize they are not alone and may be more willing to speak up knowing they are not alone. Students who hold a majority view are made aware that not everyone shares their view, and they may tread more cautiously or avoid making unwarranted assumptions during class discussion. Providing students with an anonymous mapping of the perspectives in the class can elicit discussion that is more candid, open-minded, and exploratory as opposed to argumentative.

6. *Priming.* Among any group of students, it is inevitable that some are more comfortable speaking in class than others. Unsurprisingly, I have found that those who feel most confident about speaking are disproportionately men or students with more social or cultural capital (e.g., perhaps one or both of their parents are lawyers). They are not the only students with insightful contributions, but they are often the quickest to volunteer.

A useful approach to mitigating this disparity is priming. By priming, I mean giving students an opportunity to discuss a topic or question in an interaction that is more informal and less intimidating than speaking to the entire class. It is as simple as posing a question to the class and then, instead of seeing which hands go up, saying, "Please discuss the question with your neighbor for ninety seconds." During that time, the classroom is filled with conversation, with students sharing their views in groups of two or three. These low-stakes interactions give students a chance to try out their answers to the question, and they often discover, despite initial hesitations, that they have something useful to say.

After a priming exercise, when I engage the class as a whole, I typically see more students and a wider range of students raise their hands. Giving students non-freighted opportunities to practice speaking and rehearse their ideas is another way of scaffolding classroom dynamics, and I have found that after a student has spoken once in class, the student is more apt to speak again. This leveling effect contributes to a norm that every student, not just the confident few, can hold space in the classroom and offer valuable insights. (This priming technique can also be applied in online teaching using the "breakout rooms" feature on Zoom.)

7. *Role-playing.* When students discuss a sensitive topic, or when I want students to carefully consider viewpoints they find objectionable, it can help to stand at a critical distance and depersonalize the arguments at hand. For example, if I were to ask my students whether the Harvard affirmative action plan was unlawful, few would say yes, and those with doubts may be unlikely to speak up. A different approach is to ask, "If you were the petitioner's lawyer in the Harvard affirmative action case, what are the best arguments you would make?" Another approach for teaching a challenging case is to divide the class spatially into three groups, with one group playing lawyers for the petitioner,

one group playing lawyers for the respondent, and one group playing Justices of the Supreme Court. The students spend a few minutes conferring and then engage in a mock oral argument, with each group of "lawyers" collectively arguing their side as the "Justices" pepper them with questions.

Role-playing engages students in perspective-taking that may not accord with their own views. This is useful because, as many lawyers would attest, when one is tasked with defending a position, one often comes to see merit in the position—or at least one comes to see the most charitable version of the position even if one does not ultimately agree with it. It may not be possible to fully bridge certain divides, but it is possible to cultivate empathy, to lessen polarization, and to counter the tendency to demonize people with views contrary to one's own.

This is especially important in the training of lawyers. An effective lawyer must be able to see the best arguments on all sides of an issue. And because lawyers owe a duty of loyalty to their clients, they must play a role that requires them to step outside of themselves and zealously advocate for their clients' positions. This is true even for lawyers who choose to work for causes or organizations aligned with their personal beliefs. Whether my students become nonprofit leaders, government officials, or public interest lawyers, they will encounter situations where they must defend or carry out policies they don't necessarily agree with. Moreover, every lawyer by oath is "an officer of the court" and, whatever one's personal views, has a professional duty to promote respect for the legal system and uphold the rule of law.

8. *Restate, validate, do not evaluate (right away).* When students speak in class, it is a natural reflex for the instructor to respond to what each student says. Many students expect this and seek confirmation as to whether comments made in class are right or wrong. Over the years, I have resisted this reflex and instead try to do three things when students speak in class. First, I briefly restate students' comments (e.g., "What I hear you saying is . . .") and sometimes distill or refine them to enhance their persuasiveness or smooth out rough edges. Second, I validate the comment (e.g., "Our poll showed some of the class likely agrees with you" or "I suspect Justice [X] would have a similar view"), with the important qualification that validation does not convey my endorsement or agreement. Third, I refrain from evaluating the comment, at least not immediately. Instead, I will direct the flow of conversation back to the class (e.g., "Does anyone have a different view?" or "What do you make of the argument that . . . ?").

The imagery this conjures for me is that I avoid playing "tennis" (hitting the ball back and forth) with my students and instead engage them in playing "soccer" or "basketball" (continually passing the ball, keeping it in motion) among themselves. My role is to steer the discussion to keep it within bounds of the topic at hand and to bring into focus the most difficult issues. On occasion, I will intervene to rephrase or redirect a comment that is inartfully stated or may trigger sensitive reactions, though I try to do so with humor or grace to avoid embarrassing any student. We have all said things that don't sound quite right, and I take care to convey that the classroom is a place for sounding out ideas, not for playing "gotcha."

This way of proceeding furthers two objectives. First, when students see that my typical response to their comments is not to judge but to validate and restate the comments in the best possible light, they may feel less hesitant to speak up. Good discussion does not require students to have fully formed ideas or to speak in full paragraphs. I want my students, especially those who feel less entitled to speak in class, to know that exploration and conjecture are not only encouraged but essential to learning.

Second, the "horizontal" trajectory of discussion from student to student helps decenter the "verticality" of the teacher-student hierarchy. My aim is to open a space and model the skills that enable students to learn from one another, as they will do as colleagues in a workplace, as peers in a profession, and as citizens in a democracy. The most difficult issues we face as a society are complicated, and looking to judges or experts to declare answers "right" or "wrong" can only take us so far. Pluralism, contestation, and dialogue are the lifeblood of democracy, and it is especially imperative to model this in the education of lawyers.

Anti-racism Paradoxes

In this commentary, I have not said much about anti-racism, and readers may wonder how these reflections on pedagogy are relevant to addressing the racial inequalities and implicit biases evident throughout our institutions. Although issues of race have been central to my work on the bench and as a scholar, I have described my approach in the classroom through the broader framing of an inclusive pedagogy.

This is not because race figures less prominently in the classroom, and especially not in a class on constitutional law, a subject permeated with the ideologies and contradictions of our nation's racial history. Rather, it is because I have found that issues of race can be engaged more effectively when students are adept at navigating other lines of difference. Active listening—whether across socioeconomic, ideological, religious, or racial divides—depends on the same foundation of trust, presumption of good faith, and ability to see the shared humanity and vulnerability of others. I do not mean to minimize why race is distinctive as a social category and marker of disadvantage; the original Constitution by its terms accommodated slavery, and formal abolition came only after the deadliest war in American history. But students of every race have other identities as well, and spotlighting race alone may result in missed opportunities to explore intersections between race and other categories and to enable each student to feel part of a majority at times and part of a minority at others.

What I strive to cultivate is a classroom that is not predictably polarized on a single axis but rather composed of shifting majorities and minorities from issue to issue. Such complexity fosters empathy and counters the tendency to make assumptions about individuals based on a single group characteristic. In my experience, race becomes less sensitive, easier to discuss, and more often discussed when it is buffered by other categories of difference that align students across race and when the habits of mind required for collective deliberation on difficult issues are strengthened through varied encounters. Hence, I suggest another racial paradox: Decentering race by situating it within a broader approach to inclusive pedagogy may well facilitate more constructive engagement with racial issues in the classroom.

My focus here has been on the affective dimensions of teaching and learning, and some readers may find this emphasis a bit warm and fuzzy. But my aim is not to make my students into best friends or to have them join hands and sing Kumbaya. In order to tackle the hardest issues, it matters not only what is discussed but how it is discussed. I want my students to learn that their most strongly held beliefs and their most brilliant arguments will not make a difference unless they have an audience that is open to hearing what they have to say. The prerequisites for listening and learning from one another—the preconditions of reasoned discourse—are the same in the classroom as they are in our diverse democracy. Although many conflicts in our society are deeply etched and cannot be fully reconciled, it is my hope and belief that the level of polarization can be reduced and the excesses on all sides can be avoided. These are worthy goals for any classroom pedagogy, especially in the training of lawyers.

Commentary: Institutional and Cultural Levers of Racial Transformation: Learnings

Anurima Bhargava

BY WAY OF INTRODUCTION, I was Susan Sturm's student in law school, where she laid the foundation for understanding how we can institute and sustain institutional change. Not only does this commentary reflect my reading of *What Might Be*, I was fortunate enough to have an extensive discussion with Sturm about the book—one that I've excerpted and integrated here.

Sturm's work is emerging at a time when efforts to center and promote diversity, equity, and inclusion and embed anti-racism are retreating and under attack. Central prongs of those attacks include—often without any example or evidence—that Diversity, Equity, and Inclusion and anti-racism efforts don't work, the efforts increase racial "shaming" and division, and the time for such work has passed. I've been a "DEI practitioner" for many years, first as a lawyer litigating cases on diversity in schools and institutions of higher education, and more recently as an advisor and consultant, conducting racial equity assessments and making recommendations about how to build and sustain safe and supportive environments in workplaces and schools. A central question—perhaps *the* central question in this time—is one that Sturm endeavors to address in the book: What do we actually do to make change, and how do we do that in a way that is focused on institutions and culture?

She draws upon decades of research of closely examining institutions and their leaders. She includes both personal experience and her own involvement in efforts that are—consistent with her lifetime of work—focused on institutional and cultural transformation. She provides insights and interventions that extend over and across time—literally going back decades—and consequently extend beyond the shifting climate regarding DEI. Indeed, this book was conceived before George Floyd's murder and the intense focus and performance of DEI and is emerging, as noted, in a time of abandoning and backlash to those efforts.

One of the first questions I asked Sturm about the book was whether there was a problem she was trying to address and to fix, and if so, what that problem was. I was channeling my sense that so many of the critiques of diversity and equity work are not aimed at fixing the continuing problems of systemic and institutional racism and inequality; rather, many such critiques proceed by presuming those problems no longer exist or by placing blame as part of efforts to divide and conquer communities. At the same time, much of the DEI academic literature is aimed at demonstrating the benefits and importance of diversity and equity efforts. Sturm's response illuminates the central question(s) driving the book and the broader set of challenges and gaps it seeks to address.

> I wouldn't say there was a problem I was trying to fix because I didn't think it was fixable. But I would say there was a gap or a space that needed more attention than it had gotten: How do people who are willing to change an institution that is problematic in the way it addresses issues of race, gender, and power do that work over the long haul, in the face of pushback and setbacks? What does the institutional change work look like? It often takes strategies like protest, litigation, or shaming to get it going, but for change to be sustainable, something has to change inside an institution at some point. And that has to be done in a way that is incremental and radical at the same time. And there wasn't very much that really explored the process by which that happened and how that process related to people's values.
>
> And then there was also this gap between the academic literature and the real-world stories and the applications that people could actually use. The academics were speaking in jargon and the practitioners who were telling stories or doing things that are more in a "how to" mindset were not necessarily providing everyday people with access to the scholarly literature. So much of the academic literature was divided up by discipline, and so much of the diversity literature was focused on things like training or implicit bias without necessarily connecting to institutional change. I had this

sense that I was in a position of bridging worlds, bridging discourses, bridging different kinds of knowledge so that perhaps people who wanted to make change would be able to do that informed by some of the strongest ideas for dealing with the challenges.

I have a similar goal in this commentary—to illuminate and provide richness to these questions of what is needed to bring about and operationalize institutional and cultural change, and how you sustain and embed that work—by delving into what I both learned from and grappled with in the book in a way that people can actually digest and use. I also hope to provide a window into the very fun and fascinating discussion we had about the book: it began with some of the challenges posed by and the critiques of the DEI work, touched upon the process of change and both the leadership and movements that had and could drive change, and then turned to the learnings about what actually worked, and is important, to bring about institutional and cultural change.

The Problem(s) with DEI

Before we delve into the discussion of the change process and what actually works, I want to first turn to our conversation about the problems with DEI and anti-racism work and the way in which that work has been approached and implemented over the past few years. Since 2019, I've engaged in racial equity assessments of many institutions, including foundations, public media, corporations, schools, and arts and media organizations. The most fulfilling part of that work is the listening and discovering—learning about people's experiences; their desire for connection and spaces to build connection; and the wounds and hurts that linger and shape so much of whether and how open, vulnerable, and safe people feel.

The Pressures Shaping DEI Work

As Sturm also reflects, DEI and anti-racism work faces many challenges in its framing and implementation. In 2020, a significant portion of the DEI work, in response to the murder of George Floyd in particular, was performative. Along with well-publicized commitments, institutions had a checklist for DEI work, performed the checklist, and then moved on. Institutional efforts often included setting up DEI task forces, hiring a DEI coordinator, and a focus on outreach and recruitment. Yet too much of that work did not address the institutional and cultural barriers, nor did it have the runway or patience that transformational change requires. Indeed, some efforts were dismantled within three years, while they were still in the process of being "tried on" and put into place—and long before they could settle in and be routinized and felt.

And then there are the shifting internal and external pressures. The internal pressures have been particularly acute in recent years, including for the people of color who came in on a groundswell of resources and commitments to lead institutions in the wake of George Floyd's murder and during Covid. They didn't get much time and space to get to work; some faced calls for their resignation within a day of starting the position; others were expected to right ships within a year of joining the organization and in the wake of Covid. My sense of institutional and cultural change work right now is that if it doesn't happen really fast, we don't have the patience for it—patience in the sense that people have a chance to breathe and get out of a defensive posture and out of crisis mode. As Sturm notes, change cannot take place in such conditions:

> Someone who comes into a position of leadership, whatever their race, where there's an expectation that you're going to transform the whole institution in a short period of time is doomed to fail because that's not how change happens. And in a time when there's so much polarization and people of different races are so often living in segregated worlds, people will read everything that's happening in very different ways unless there are very deliberate efforts to communicate in the varying ways in which people who are differently situated in terms of their race and occupational position will hear.

Sturm also routinely notes that people engaged in anti-racism and DEI work are often operating from a defensive posture and feel the pressure and attacks from all sides, which leads to silence and avoidance. The avoidance leads to the work being dropped—quietly and without fanfare—particularly when the external pressures to do the work are waning amid the continuing reality that, for the most part, there is no legal requirement that institutions engage in anti-racism or DEI work. We are witnessing very aggressive and widespread efforts to instill a reverse fear—that engagement in DEI and anti-racism efforts will be publicly called out and/or legally challenged. Indeed, Sturm's identification of how smaller places of change within an organization can be a source of internal pressure supporting DEI and anti-racism efforts is of increasing import.

The Definition and Practice of DEI

A related concern is that the definition and practice of DEI have become narrow, reductive, and defensive. Diversity is often viewed solely as token representation and measured by the numbers. Equity often plays into the American understanding that an issue only arises if someone who is in the same position as you is treated differently, no matter where you started, what obstacles you faced, or whether and how far you're able to move forward in a sustained manner. And at its worst, equity by that definition might mean that people are being treated the same—but all are being treated badly.

In our conversation, Sturm shared my dissatisfaction with diversity, equity, and inclusion, in language and in purpose, opting instead for the (admittedly imperfect) term "full participation." She also spoke about the anti-racism framing of the book:

> You talked about the problems of equity, which I share. Diversity is a fact. It doesn't actually tell you anything. And inclusion is problematic: even though my earlier work uses the phrase "architecture of inclusion," that term suggests recruiting people to something that's already existing rather than having the opportunity to refashion something so that everyone can fully participate. I've used the language of "full participation" as a kind of standard, but that language has also been problematic because it can read as a race-neutral term because it doesn't explicitly name racism. I mean it to be non–race neutral: what does it take for people of different races and backgrounds and cultures and genders to be able to fully realize their potential, to be able to fully shape their own participation, to be able to have a voice in what's decided, to be treated with dignity, to be supported in the ways that one needs to be supported in order to thrive in a particular organization or space.
>
> Along with full participation, I'm also using "anti-racism" in this book as the umbrella term for the paradoxes built into efforts to confront racism. I get criticized for using "anti-racism" because it's not really an affirmative concept. It's the opposite of a negative. And it's gotten politicized so much in the current environment. But I think it's very important to name race and racism in particular because as a taboo issue in the United States, race has to be raised explicitly for it to be addressed. So, I still don't have the language, the succinct word that I can use that I think adequately captures the value that I mean by "full participation." And certainly diversity, equity, and inclusion efforts don't necessarily promote full participation.

Like Sturm, many of us "DEI practitioners" have struggled with the language, as well as the connotations of the language we use to describe the work and ourselves. In my case, a primary descriptive shift has been from DEI to dignity, justice, and belonging work to account for the depth and breadth of the work in this time. I feel that dignity and justice account for our inherent worth and are expansive enough; they haven't been pegged in a narrow and defensive way . . . yet.

On a related note, I do think we can get too caught up in the language; as we try to bring in new concepts and descriptors, who and what we are talking about can get confused quickly. So there's a tension, and I found it to be one of the struggles I had with the book, which is that it introduced—at least to me—a lot of new language to frame and process the work of racial salience and institutional change, from "stretch collaboration" and "solidarity dividend" to "scripted stuckness" and "paradoxical possibility." I found myself stopping to try to grasp what these various phrases meant and getting a bit lost in that process. I understand and recognize that we need a shared vocabulary, and much of this kind of work has not been succinctly described and titled. I think there's still some work to be done to bring this into a better balance and to use language that can be a strong bridge between the academic and the useful.

Moving from the "What" to the "How"

The effort to build safe and supportive workplaces, schools, and communities, where people feel a sense of dignity, justice, and belonging, is among the most difficult, if not the most difficult, work I've been a part of. There are few easy answers or magic bullets and, as Sturm acknowledges, there is no fixed set of items that we know should put on those DEI checklists, particularly given the fact that each institution and space is different and faces quite specific challenges. Sturm spends a lot of time providing the language of frameworks and schema to help us understand what may work. But she readily acknowledges that "this book is not claiming, 'do this and this will work.' It's really more in the spirit of 'what do we learn from the efforts and the strategies that others have used when we have some perspective on what happened in the course of those narratives,' in each of the settings."

Both of us have been focused then on what we can learn from the efforts that have been made. In particular, have there been institutions that have opened themselves up to change and when they have settled back in have really centered the DEI work? When have we seen the instances when DEI has become far more than a checklist and more of a daily embedded practice?

The Study of Change

So much of the work on diversity has focused on why having diverse spaces is important, even necessary. At this point, I am beyond frustrated with that question, given that we have decades of research, experience, and testimony about the social, human, and economic benefits of diversity (we don't ask people to demonstrate the effectiveness of workplaces, boards, and classrooms that are homogeneous by race, ethnicity, gender, or class). Thankfully, Sturm does not spend significant time on that question and instead focuses, using specific examples, on case studies of how change happens and actually works.

There are two aspects to how change actually works. First, change is psychological and sociological and institutional and cultural. Much of the discipline-bound diversity research doesn't address how change happens because to study change requires examining many interacting variables; you can't run a double-blind study testing only one. Second, the kind of research that does document change is either action research or studies looking across disciplines and over time. You need to be in some way engaged in the change work to understand it, but sufficiently rigorous in thinking about it, that you're not just expressing your own wishes.

I was willing to make myself one of the case studies, understanding that I know things about myself that I can't know about anyone else, that I can share things about myself, including my failures, that I wouldn't ask anyone else to share. But I can see patterns in myself that I can then detect in other people. So I use myself not as a memoir but as an illustration of the kinds of struggles that I've experienced trying to make these kinds of changes. By buttressing narrative with empirical observations of what actually happened, I can step back and say, yes, that has produced some impact that really shifted the narrative or shifted the culture or shifted the number of people who could fully participate.

Power and Change in Legacy Institutions

It struck me that much of Sturm's focus in her study of change in this book is on legacy institutions, which in large part or even by definition have been predominantly white. I wanted to understand whether her focus suggested that those are the spaces where such institutional and cultural change needed to occur, where such change could occur, or more broadly a suggestion that more racially diverse institutions had different, or even lesser, challenges. I had the same questions about the organizational catalysts who are profiled in the book, many, though certainly not all, of whom have been white leaders. We explored both of those suppositions in our discussion, which I found to be some of the most enriching and clarifying parts of our time together. Sturm certainly recognizes the need to engage with and highlight legacy institutions, and the levers that provoke change within those institutions, but her reasoning was much broader than that.

> The institutions that I am struggling with most are institutions that have existed for decades and decades and were created at a time in which white men were really the only ones who were part of a decision-making process. And they might have involved women or people who were nonwhite, but those people were not in positions to dictate what mattered to the institution or how people were going to interact. These institutions are also set up with a particular understanding of power, notably with respect to the relationship between the people who were in positions to make decisions and everybody else: "power over." Most operate with a clear hierarchy. Decisions are based on the perspective of the people who run the institutions and involve little in the form of perspective taking of those affected by those decisions, let alone power sharing with them, whether that be students or people using a court system. There's a zero-sum understanding of power and very little accountability beyond the people who run the institution. Also, for a very long period of time there was an assumption about the unequivocal goodness of the institution, an institutional narrative that didn't face up to the ways in which, from the very beginning, these institutions were exclusionary and acting in ways that were actually in tension with their declared mission.
>
> I think all of the predominantly white institutions that I have occupied or worked within have had some kind of periodic, externally provoked reckoning. And they have all opened up their power structure in some way to varying degrees, but not to the point where you would say there was full participation in the shaping of the culture or the shaping of the narrative or the accountability or who benefits from the institution. So these are all institutions that are now in a place of either transition or contradiction in terms of the way they operate.

Sturm's own experience also impacted her focus and scope of inquiry.

> Most of case studies involve predominantly white institutions because those are the institutions that I know most about. Those are the institutions

that I've spent my entire career in. Those are the institutions about which I feel I can speak with legitimacy. But there are also examples that come from institutions that are not predominantly white, which have developed strategies that are among the most effective in supporting full participation. Institutions set up and led by people of color (such as historically Black colleges and universities) may be the best drivers of change toward full participation. Predominantly white institutions might have their greatest impact when they shift power and resources to nonwhite institutions or create partnerships with institutions set up to support the needs and interests of people of color.

Setting a Different Table

When I talk about DEI work, and the change we are seeking, I often use the following analogy. Diversity is a seat at the table. Inclusion is you're sitting at the table and get to choose what you order off the menu. Belonging is you are actually choosing the menu itself. But then there are those who have decided that they are just going to set their own table so that they don't necessarily have to adapt to the norms and standards that have already been set.

So if belonging is actually having agency at the table, what does it mean to have the agency to set a different table altogether? And what are the challenges and possibilities for setting a different table when you're talking about predominantly white legacy institutions whose very purpose is to continue that legacy? Sturm immediately began to describe the University of Maryland, Baltimore County (UMBC).

UMBC was interestingly not an elite white institution but a predominantly white institution when Freeman Hrabowski, who is Black, took the helm. And he very powerfully created ways to have different kinds of participation and different kinds of values happening simultaneously in the early stages. So he created the space that was really setting the table initially for Black boys, then Black boys and girls, and then Black and Brown kids, and then everybody. But he started by setting that table so that Black students could succeed in the sciences and providing them with a full range of supports. At the same time, he was really trying to build up the overall positive experience of people of a larger institution that had a hunger for improving itself, because no one was satisfied with the institution as it currently was. And then over time, those two things got brought together and the things that were learned from the experience of the table that was set by and for Black people melded with a set of values that are much more overarching and were then reflected in the culture that became a driver of broader change within the larger institution. I haven't looked at the institution now. But I would predict that while they have not been fully merged, the values of the institution, because it was led by someone with those values for twenty-five years, really became embedded in the culture of the institution.

Sturm then turned to Rutgers University, Newark, which was also a predominantly white institution that "underwent a decades-long process of change, first by getting more people of color in positions both as students and as faculty and eventually as administrators, and then becoming much more connected to the City of Newark and then changing, at least in some spaces, what was valued by the institution, which is a major thing. It was really about contributing to social impact in various ways, and is still a work in progress that has experienced some setbacks, but now the school is more of a Hispanic- and Black-serving institution."

Leadership Matters

Much of our discussion—particularly given that the book shares the histories and experiences of select individuals, such as Freeman Hrabowski and Judge Fein—focused on the lessons learned from many decades of transformational change work about who could make that change, from what role and vantage point within an institution one could (best) make change, where that change process could be well seeded and anchored, and what the salience is (if any) of the race of the organizational catalyst.

Formal vs. Informal Leadership: Finding Our Place in the Work

There are different roles you can play in institutional leadership. Part of our problem is that when we think about change, we often look to the people who are in those formal positions of authority. And part of what Sturm is suggesting is that there may be some real limitations to relying on them to do transformational work. And yet that doesn't mean they don't do the work. They just might have to do it in a different kind of way.

In my experience, one of the things that's essential for those in leadership positions is to create, in a nondefensive way, real spaces for a different kind of engagement involving people of color—and to recognize the value and the need for such spaces, even if those in leadership positions are not necessarily engaged in those positions themselves. Those spaces are necessary for movement to happen.

> If we rely on one leader at the top of a hierarchy to solve these problems, whatever their race, we will end up with limitations built into the existing power structure. When you are in a position of formal power, you often have to play a role in the institution in ways that will limit you. White leaders at the top of institutions who have made change happen have changed the way power is exercised so that more people can exercise power in ways that have real influence in the organization. They invest in the growth and development and leadership of people of color in ways that equip them to become institutional leaders, not only informally but also formally. And so you have to simultaneously be making changing from the top down and building up the leadership of the people who are pushing you from the outside or from the bottom up. And then you have to find ways to step out and create the space for new leadership to come in when the conditions have permitted a person of color to take the helm.
>
> I have found ways to share power and still feel really valued and significant. I say this with some hesitation because white people have centered having their needs met for quite some time. But people are human. And if they don't have their needs met, they're not going to last in the project. But there are ways to have their needs met without holding onto power over others. A big part of my value is using the power that I have to create a space for others to be able to really lead and then to support them in that leadership. That is very personally rewarding to me. We need to create space for new leadership to develop and lead, who have more of a connection to the concerns of the people who are coming up. So I think there is a role for white leadership, but it requires redefining what leadership means so that we're talking about distributed leadership and not top-down leadership.

Sturm also spoke about her own practice and understanding of formal leadership and the roles she has decided to take on.

> I have to take responsibility for the way in which people are experiencing themselves not only in my classroom but in the spaces that I have the power to influence. And I will take action to push and support and shift the culture

there in every way that I can. And I will also seize opportunities to influence the policies and practices of the institution.

What I haven't done is put myself in a formal position of top-down leadership in a predominantly white institution because I have observed that, unless the institution has brought you in with a mandate to make change, you actually have very limited opportunities to do transformational work in that position. Watching what happens to people who are really interested in transformation who assume formal leadership positions, such as becoming a dean, I saw that they ended up having to compromise and limit what they were able to do. If they refused to compromise, they typically ended up being pushed out of their position. If you undertake culture change without that mandate, your efforts will probably make it difficult for you to maintain your position in the face of resistance from people in positions of power within the institution.

I think people at the top need to understand that what they should be doing is creating an environment that enables and supports people at every level of the organization to have these kinds of experiences where they are pushing for and enabling full participation and transformation to happen.

THE EXERCISE OF LEADERSHIP

Sturm defines leadership not in terms of people's formal position of authority but rather in terms of someone's ability to mobilize collective action that moves toward full participation:

> I am focused on people who do the important work of building the capacity for this type of more thorough culture change to take place in any kind of institution, predominantly white institutions in particular. These are people who exercise leadership, not only in terms of running the organization but in the sense of being able to influence the environment that they're in either individually or collectively. When people come into positions at the top of organizations, if there is that expectation that they're going to fix things in a really short period of time, they will not have the space to do what Freeman did, which was to seed these different kinds of experiments that would enable people to build that kind of culture over time in spaces where they could fail, where they could learn, where they could speak across their divides. If he hadn't had that time and space, he wouldn't have succeeded.

I have a very firm conviction based on my research and my experience that successful community-engaged, full-participation initiatives start locally and then get linked to be able to build the constituency to sustain those efforts and empower the organizational catalysts who will be able to build the capacity to do this hard work, and who will be able to both push and support the leadership at the top. That has to happen in order for culture change to be real. And if I look at the way change has happened at other times in history, when the conditions overall seemed really to make it impossible, it was by undertaking change work outside of the space of visibility and seizing the opportunities when they arise to expand and embed those efforts by someone in a more visible and public position.

Beyond the building out of transformational change within an organization is the process by which such change begins. I think Sturm rightly notes that the change process starts with self-reflection, of understanding that you are coming into a space—whether it be your workplace, school, or community—with the intent to engage with others and serve as an organizational catalyst for any necessary change to occur.

Sturm identifies two important points of change in the process: (1) individuals who are self-reflective and in a position where emotionally, socially, and in terms of their own power they can be organizational catalysts; and (2) microspaces for justice, spaces where engagement is happening, and then those spaces start to transform some of the institutional structures.

AB: How do your own experiences with self-reflection and engagement play into your sense of how to change institutions like the University of Pennsylvania and Columbia Law School? And how did you think about your own journey and which spaces you talk about and which ones you didn't?

SS: I still struggle with this question to this very day about my own use of power in my own institution. And I would say the ways that I affirmatively have exercised my power have been, first of all, I have power over what happens in my own classroom, scholarship, and activism. And so I've really reshaped the way I exercise power, in the classroom, in the way I do my research, and in the center that I run, where I'm now sharing power with people who are leading these projects, who are not faculty members and who have firsthand experience with the criminal legal system. They are the directors of these projects. And similarly with students, there's a lot of power sharing in the way I do the work. . . . I use my power to equip other communities and leaders to be able to have impact and lend my own resources and support to that work where I thought it could be more transformational.

So I have navigated in a way that I think is consistent with the way I write, which is to create these kinds of third spaces and to support people who were in formal leadership positions in institutions where there was more of a prospect of their being transformational in their formal roles. My own sense was that I could have more impact in a way that was incremental but transformative by not being in formal positions of power.

I also asked Sturm how we think about the question of proximity. An essential problem of our time is that we aren't fixing the things that are most proximate to us. The mantra of "be proximate" is to be proximate to something external, but not necessarily to understand how we must do this work in proximity to the people who are literally sitting right next to us. Part of the premise of so much of my consulting and advisory work is for us to see transformational change in the world; we need to fix what's happening inside institutions, where too many are feeling stuck.

Racial Salience of Leadership

One of the questions that Sturm and I have long discussed and struggled with in our work is whether or not you can have the kind of institutional change that she has featured at UMBC without a leader of color. It feels particularly relevant in these days when we are seeing leaders of color come into legacy institutions and be immediately attacked such that they don't even have a space to pursue transformative work. So what are the possibilities for transformative change with a white leader? Could you have the kind of transformational change UMBC has experienced, at a predominantly white institution, when it is led by someone white? Are there examples?

One of the reasons I'm reluctant to say that this type of transformational change requires a Black or other nonwhite leader full stop is that I think there is ground that can be laid by a white person who's in a leadership position, who uses that position to create the space for leadership for people of color that didn't exist before in positions that are high enough up in the organization that they are then in a position to take up leadership going forward. Freeman Hrabowski came in as a provost at UMBC and then was promoted to the president position. I think there was some value in having had that opportunity. He was brought in by a white president and a white board. I see in my own situation, I am in a position to lead a center and support students of color, particularly because there aren't very many people of color on the faculty. I can then create an environment in which someone, either another faculty member or a person of color who has skills that I don't have, like a person who's directly affected by incarceration, could become the director of the center. That transition won't happen if I don't use my position as a white person to create space for a person of color to come in to the institution and lead.

And so I think one has to ask: how do you get an organization to the place where the kind of change that's really needed that requires leadership by people of color will take place? Freeman took the UMBC presidency because of what he could bring to the role and what he could promote. He had strategies for supporting students of color in a way that was really transformational. He came into the position with the opportunity to really do cultural change work. And he was committed to the institution over the long run, and stayed for a very long period of time, enabling him to shepherd change over decades. I don't think you have to be someone with Freeman's brilliant, charismatic leadership skills to be able to make that kind of change. But I don't think you could just say a person of color needs to be a leadership position, or conversely, that a white person in a leadership position can't set the institution up to be able to do this by investing in the leadership of people of all different races and setting up the institution to be able to welcome that person or at least create the conditions under which that person can succeed.

The Necessary Components of Transformational Change

AB: What are the necessary components for transformation? Does it require understanding oneself to be linked with others like this idea of linked fate? Does it require that you have common experiences and challenges and purpose and goals? Does it require collective work? And lastly, does it require accountability and accountability to whom? Are all the elements of transformation necessary, from the very beginning of awareness to some kind of accountability framework?

ss: I would say all of these things are necessary for an institution to transform in a way that's sustainable, that's going to move toward full participation as a matter of culture and practice. Each chapter of the book has an element necessary for institutional transformation to happen, because I don't think you're going to be able to sustain ongoing institutional transformation in a legacy institution if there's not some understanding of linked fate. Period. The work has to happen in lots of different spaces that are connected to each other. All of that requires collective work. And the kind of change that needs to happen is not going to happen only top down. It requires a level of mobilization provided by organizational catalysts. And accountability involves repurposing power. If you don't have shifts in power that are connected to various forms of accountability, that are not only to people in formal positions of power but to the people directly affected by these changes, by people who are engaged in doing the work and the people who are the ostensible beneficiaries of the work of the institution, then changes enabling full participation are not going to be sustained. So the trick is, when you have that moment of transformation, make the changes in the power structure so that you're sharing power with people who are much more directly linked to these interests over the long run. If you don't make the changes in the power structure, when the pushback comes, there's nothing to hold this transformational ethos in place.

AB: There's a way in which formal thinking about change often speaks to linear change, yet change hardly ever happens in that kind of way. Change doesn't happen in pieces or by completing checklists; have there been examples where there has been space for more tailored, fluid processes to take place?

ss: I have come to really believe that changing the power structure of the organization at every level such that the kind of proximity that we were talking about is built into some aspect of regular day-to-day work is necessary for this to get sustained over the long run. Otherwise the exclusionary values of a larger culture are going to resurface under conditions of crisis. That kind of change in power structure is difficult to accomplish. I think it can happen initially on a more localized level. I see it happening in my own work in the law school where there are now people who are directly impacted by incarceration who are an integral part of my work, and they're now starting to work with other people who are bringing them in as coequals. And as these practices spread, they're creating a constituency for this approach. If enough support develops, then there will be pressure to continue these practices and, eventually, for community leaders to become full members of the institution, in a position to make decisions. This will require organizational catalysts who are pushing for this at every step because it's not yet built into the value structure of the organization.

Is Empathy a Necessary Starting Point?

I asked Sturm whether she thought that empathy practice had to be part of any effort to reduce racism and increase full participation.

I think empathy practice is complicated because I have learned the hard way that under conditions of polarization and unequal power, it can really back-fire. If you start talking about feelings and needs when you do not care enough to take the risk of exposing your own vulnerability, empathy prac-tice can actually amplify concerns only for people just like you and increase resentment or marginalization of people who are different from you. But it's possible to build enough trust by interacting over a longer period of time so that you might actually come to care about people's well-being, even if you don't like them or trust them. And then you can use empathy practice at that point, which can help carry you over in situations where you have a lot of conflict.

Measuring Transformation

AB: I think the other challenge that we've had in this space is how do we gauge and measure the work of anti-racism?

SS: One measure is whether the organization has people from different backgrounds at every level and particularly in positions of power. And when the power gets redefined, does it get redefined so that it continues to include people in those varied positions. You can look at numbers and say people are in leadership positions of different racial backgrounds, as well as at decision-making practices showing that they have genuine power and can influence what happens and what matters. And when people struggle or fail, they're not simply kicked out, they're given support and the opportunity to grow and learn. When you achieve full participation, there's a quality of interaction that people can and do describe. What does it feel like to go to work? What happens when I struggle? How do I get support? Who am I connected to in the organization? What does the organization actually value? What are the things that matter? What happens when things go wrong: when people fail or the organization or the community fails?

Sturm describes the qualities of microspaces of justice as setting a possible standard by which to measure transformation. I asked her to describe those qualities.

Spaces where one can say: "I fully participate, I shape priorities, I thrive, I am respected, and I'm contributing to the thriving of others." So then we can use that as a way to actually assess what's happening in the larger institution. What is it like when that's not the case? What happens then? Because we know it can't be the case in the larger world we live in. It cannot be the case all the time. How far is the institution from what it feels like to fully participate? What is the experience of different stakeholders of this institution in relation to these sets of measures or values? So we can use the gap between what's happening in the microspace of justice and what's happening in the overall institution as a measure of improvement.

Who gets to exercise power and how in the organization is another really important measure. And then you add all that up and maybe that's something that leads you toward being able to reshape the narrative. How do we know if the narrative is reshaped? How are people experiencing themselves in the space? This leads you to be able to differentiate between incremental change that's preserving the status quo and transforming it. And it leads you to be able to pursue a space of full participation.

Narrative Shift

AB: Much of the book is anchored in narrative—we have descriptions of individuals, their histories, their experiences, what they're bringing to a space, how they might have been perceived or understood in that space, what they catalyze for people in a particular space. Yet we don't necessarily get the mapping of those spaces themselves. What does it look like to have a cross-racial space that is really engaged in transformation? How would you describe the spaces that are important for transformation? What do those feel like?

SS: When we talk about changing the racial narrative, it's a really deep cultural shift where people of different races and backgrounds and genders who have shaped the space can thrive. Their well-being matters in the space, whatever their position in the organization. And there's experimentation on an ongoing basis—small changes that connect to bigger things. To me, that's a really critical feature of the space. There's the ability to sit with and hold the contradictions that are built into the structure of the space. It can't just be an individual thing. It has to be something that the space itself supports and enables—the continual regeneration of change agents, these kinds of organizational catalysts operating not individually but in communities. That can't happen only in an individual context. That has to happen collectively. You have to change both the structure and how interactions happen in a group so that no one person or racial group can dictate to the entirety, and where everyone has a form of mutual accountability that's built into the space. And the only places I really experience that are in spaces that have been created more recently, or with those kinds of values in mind, such as the Broadway Advocacy Coalition or BATTLE, a class that was designed right from the beginning to have equal power in the way every level of the organization is set up. I intend the book not only as a story about individuals who are making change; it is about individuals who understand themselves as part of a group or part of a collective or part of a larger system striving for change.

Sustainability

AB: How does transformation get sustained? My sense is that understanding where transformation arises from relates to when transformation stops. Was it a particular moment? How do we keep it from ending, particularly when the space and the incentives go away?

SS: Change is unlikely to last if it has depended on a single leader and that leader leaves; if it was a moment in time and the pressure ends but it hasn't yet gotten built into the culture and value structure of the organization, the way people get rewarded; if it hasn't manifested in who's in the organization, the values they bring to the organization, so that people come into the organization with those values in mind. At the institutional level, if the work is in the early stages, then the change is very difficult to sustain if there's no external pressure to continue those kinds of changes. That's when retrenchment might occur. I think it's really difficult to sustain change only at the policy level, without also changing culture. This is why building these subcultures is so important to sustaining change. These spaces can carry people over during those pendulum swings of backsliding so that when the world shifts again toward encouraging change, you're not going all the way back to the beginning, because you have developed a set of organizational catalysts and some subcommunities that continue to build pressure inside and outside the organization for that type of change to happen. You may have rolled back halfway or a quarter of the way down, but you're not starting all the way at the bottom of the hill; you've rolled the boulder two-thirds up the hill already. And you have a group of people who are in a position to push the boulder up the hill and who are set up and care enough to push the boulder up the hill, whether they're inside or outside the organization.

This is why the zooming in and zooming out are really important. The pendulum swings can be really, really discouraging. You've built so much. You can see you're on the cusp of a real institutional change. Then the environment changes. The Supreme Court comes down with a case that shifts the legal incentives. There's economic or political backlash that can undermine the momentum. And then you start slipping down the hill. And I think that's very discouraging and makes it really important to have communities of practice where relationships and values matter.

For me, and I know I'm not alone in this, this is the kind of work that gives my life meaning. There's no way I'm not going to do this work. Hundreds of people that I've worked with over the years are that way too. Are they in the majority in their institution? No, they're not, at least in most the institutions. But if you have a community of people for whom life's meaning is being able to be with people who care about these values, to work on things like this, to watch the change happen, then you can sustain yourself in your community during those downtimes, even when the entire institution is not in a place where you're going to be moving toward institutional transformation. And this is where movement building becomes really important because the movement might sustain people to do work inside their institutions or with a particular institution, even when the institution has become opposed to that kind of work.

Closing Thoughts

Sturm talks about fractals—these mini spaces for change that can then infuse the larger institution. I also think it is extraordinarily important that we intentionally build institution-wide spaces that allow for a different type of learning about one another and more open, vulnerable engagement. I am continuously surprised, as an advisor and consultant, how much people are willing to share with a relative stranger things they had not had the opportunity or the willingness to share previously. Having intentional shared spaces—where people can be vulnerable, make mistakes, ask questions, both practice and feel empathy and compassion—is, in my view, very important for the kind of institutional and cultural change that Sturm describes. It creates a pathway of understanding that is too often lacking: that others may be experiencing pain and exclusion, even if they may also exhibit power and privilege; that each of us holds— and can carry—more than one intersection.

And it is important that those spaces are actively sustained and cultivated not just in response to and during a crisis but as long-term, shared collective work about understanding the ways in which we are linked. Diversity cannot be sustained or supported without a parallel effort to create space for people to engage with one another—and to hear, understand, and learn from one another.

I worry a lot about the ways in which we're trying to change predominantly white institutions. We formalized institutionalized responsibility for diversity, resulting in language and roles that do not really allow the kind of open, challenging, vulnerable spaces that are necessary. Indeed, in a formal structure, you get defensiveness and avoidance fast. Avoidance leads you into the very de facto institutionalized structures that we need to actually transform, because we don't acknowledge and engage with the things that are present and salient and important and try to understand them differently. Or allow them to have a dynamism and a fluidity that are part of humans, and humanity. Humanity is messy.

To me, saying you don't want to actually engage with race means you don't actually want to engage with humanity. Which makes this current moment—where there are widespread efforts to erase race entirely—an even more dangerous one. Part of what we have to get much better at is breaking through the silences in a way that allows people to make mistakes, ask questions, and learn on multiple sides. We're doing the very thing that we want people not to do, which is to suggest that people who are in leadership, particularly white people, should know better. But those in leadership don't know a lot of things. Many don't have a clue. And so part of what we have to allow for is, just because you're a leader doesn't mean you know everything or that you know best. We shouldn't do the very thing that we're saying we don't want to have happen, which is that we ascribe a certain power but also a certain goodness to leadership. And when they fail us, we're angry about that. Yet they don't know how to engage to begin with. This is the thing I love in some ways about someone like Ta-Nehisi Coates, who will often respond to questions with: "I don't know. I don't know the answer. I wrote a book. I'm a writer. I don't know how to figure this stuff out." We don't have enough of that.

The white leaders that I've found to be transformational in large institutions are comfortable saying, "I have no idea about that." A leader who has incredible institutional and historical power and privilege is acknowledging that they're in a very open learning process. It facilitates everyone else's ability to acknowledge that we have a lot of learning to do about each other, where race is not the only part of that.

Without that we're in trouble. And I think suggesting that we don't talk about race in the terms that we might view ourselves or view each other is erasure, as well as a shutting down of the open, vulnerable, and messy engagements that bring about transformational change.

NOTES

Author's Note

1. Susan Sturm, "Second Generation Employment Discrimination: A Structural Approach," *Columbia Law Review* 101, no. 3 (2001): 458–568.

2. Susan Sturm, "The Architecture of Inclusion: Advancing Workplace Equity in Higher Education," *Harvard Journal of Law and Gender* 29, no. 2 (2006): 249–334.

3. Lani Guinier and Gerald Torres, *The Miner's Canary: Enlisting Race, Resisting Power, Transforming Democracy* (Cambridge, MA: Harvard University Press, 2002), 292.

4. Clint Smith, *How the Word Is Passed: A Reckoning with the History of Slavery across America* (New York: Little, Brown, 2021), 271.

5. Richard Rothstein and Leah Rothstein, *Just Action: How to Challenge Segregation Enacted under the Color of Law* (New York: Liveright Publishing, 2023), 9.

6. Paula M. L. Moya and Hazel Rose Marcus, "Doing Race: An Introduction," in *Doing Race: 21 Essays for the 21st Century*, ed. Hazel Rose Marcus and Paula M. L. Moya (New York: W. W. Norton, 2010), 1–93.

7. Stuart Hall, "Race, the Floating Signifier: What More Is There to Say about 'Race'?" in *Selected Writings on Race and Difference*, ed. Paul Gilroy and Ruth Wilson Gilmore (Durham: Duke University Press, 2021), 361–62.

8. John Lewis (@repjohnlewis), #goodtrouble, Twitter, June 27, 2018, https://x.com /repjohnlewis/status/1011991303599607808?lang=en.

Introduction

1. Khalil Gibran Muhammad, "No Racial Barrier Left to Break (Except All of Them)," *New York Times*, January 14, 2017.

2. Jeannie Suk Gersen, "Education after Affirmative Action," *New Yorker*, November 7, 2022.

3. Patricia Gurin, "Group Interactions in Building a Connected Society," in *Our Compelling Interests: The Value of Diversity for Democracy and a Prosperous Society*, ed. Earl Lewis and Nancy Cantor (Princeton: Princeton University Press, 2016), 170–81.

4. Patricia Gurin, Jeffrey S. Lehman, and Earl Lewis, *Defending Diversity: Affirmative Action at the University of Michigan* (Ann Arbor: University of Michigan Press, 2004).

5. Gary Orfield, *The Walls around Opportunity: The Failure of Colorblind Policy for Higher Education* (Princeton: Princeton University Press, 2022).

6. Anthony Carnevale and Nicole Smith, "The Economic Value of Diversity," in *Our Compelling Interests: The Value of Diversity for Democracy and a Prosperous Society*, ed. Earl Lewis and Nancy Cantor (Princeton: Princeton University Press, 2016), 106–57.

7. William Frey, *A Diversity Explosion: How New Racial Demographics Are Remaking America* (Washington, DC: Brookings Institution Press, 2015).

8. Eduardo Porter, *American Poison: How Racial Hostility Destroyed Our Promise* (New York: Alfred A. Knopf, 2020).

9. Anthony P. Carnevale, Zachary Mabel, and Kathryn Peltier Campbell, "Race Conscious Affirmative Action: What's Next" (Washington, DC: Georgetown University Center on Education and the Workforce, 2023), 33, https://cew.georgetown.edu/cew-reports/diversity-without-race/#summary.

10. Richard Rothstein and Leah Rothstein, *Just Action: How to Challenge Segregation Enacted under the Color of Law* (New York: Liveright Publishing, 2023).

11. Elise C. Boddie, "The Future of Affirmative Action," *Harvard Law Review Forum* 130, no. 1 (2016): 49.

12. John Inazu, "Hope without a Common Good," in *Out of Many Faiths: Religious Diversity and the American Promise*, by Eboo Patel (Princeton: Princeton University Press, 2018), 133–50.

13. Richard Rothstein, *The Color of Law: A Forgotten History of How Our Government Segregated America* (New York: Liveright Publishing, 2017).

14. Vandeen Campbell, *Segregated Schooling in New Jersey: The Distribution of Opportunities to Learn by Race, Ethnicity, and Class* (Newark, NJ: Joseph C. Cornwall Center for Metropolitan Studies, Rutgers University-Newark, 2023).

15. Patricia Gurin, Biren (Ratnesh) A. Nagda, and Ximena Zúñiga, *Dialogue across Difference: Practice, Theory, and Research on Intergroup Dialogue* (New York: Russell Sage Foundation, 2013).

16. See "1968 Kerner Commission Report," https://belonging.berkeley.edu/1968-kerner-commission-report.

17. Orfield, *The Walls around Opportunity*, 143–88.

18. Earl Lewis and Nancy Cantor, eds., *Our Compelling Interests: The Value of Diversity for Democracy and a Prosperous Society* (Princeton: Princeton University Press, 2016), 6.

19. Katherine W. Phillips, "What Is the Real Value of Diversity in Organizations? Questioning Our Assumptions," in *The Diversity Bonus: How Great Teams Pay Off in the Knowledge Economy*, by Scott E. Page (Princeton: Princeton University Press, 2017), 223–45.

20. Scott E. Page, *The Diversity Bonus: How Great Teams Pay Off in the Knowledge Economy* (Princeton: Princeton University Press, 2017).

21. See, for example, the description of Guinier's push to fight on in Elie Mystal's obituary essay: "Lani Guinier Taught Me Almost Everything I Know about Voting Rights," *The Nation*, January 12, 2022.

Chapter One: The Paradoxes of Anti-Racism

1. I met Jeanine Tesori through my son Ben, who is also a composer and was working for Jeanine at that time. After receiving Britton's email, Jeanine asked Ben to reach out to me, knowing that I directed the Center for Institutional and Social Change at Columbia and was involved in a lot of social justice work. Ben followed up with an email to me, asking, "Do you

have any ideas? At Columbia or otherwise? Perhaps there is also a more lasting relationship that can be formed here, rather than just a space . . . The Broadway community is actively searching for ways to impact change in the wake of last week." Ben Wexler, email message to author, July 12, 2016. That email launched BAC's partnership with the Center and Columbia Law School.

2. "Three Special Tony Awards Announced," June 22, 2021, https://www.tonyawards.com/news/three-special-tony-awards-announced/.

3. Patricia J. Williams, *Seeing a Color-Blind Future: The Paradox of Race* (New York: Noonday Press, 1997), 12.

4. Two excellent anthologies gather the most influential writings of the critical race theory movement: Kimberlé Crenshaw, Neil Gotanda, Gary Peller, and Kendall Thomas, eds., *Critical Race Theory: The Key Writings That Formed the Movement* (New York: New Press, 1996), and Richard Delgado and Jean Stefancic, eds., *Critical Race Theory: The Cutting Edge*, 3rd ed. (Philadelphia: Temple University Press, 2013).

5. Cornel West, *Race Matters*, 25th Anniversary ed. (Boston: Beacon Press, 2017), 4.

6. Deepak Bhargava and Stephanie Luce, *Practical Radicals: Seven Strategies to Change the World* (New York: New Press, 2023), 33–34.

7. Lani Guinier and Gerald Torres, *The Miner's Canary: Enlisting Race, Resisting Power, Transforming Democracy* (Cambridge, MA: Harvard University Press, 2002), 259.

8. Susan Sturm, "The Architecture of Inclusion: Advancing Workplace Equity in Higher Education," *Harvard Journal of Law and Gender* 29, no. 2 (2006): 249–334; Susan Sturm, Tim Eatman, John Saltmarsh, and Adam Bush, "Full Participation: Building the Architecture for Diversity and Community Engagement in Higher Education," September 2011, https://iagathering.org/mainsite/wp-content/uploads/fullparticipation.pdf.

9. Robert M. Cover, "Foreword: Nomos and Narrative," *Harvard Law Review* 97, no. 1 (1983): 4, 10.

10. Kenwyn K. Smith and David N. Berg, *Paradoxes of Group Life: Understanding Conflict, Paralysis, and Movement in Group Dynamics* (San Francisco: Jossey-Bass, 1997), 15.

11. Adam Kahane, *Collaborating with the Enemy: How to Work with People You Don't Agree with or Like or Trust* (Oakland, CA: Berrett-Koehler Publishers, 2017), 53.

12. Bernard Williams and W. F. Atkinson, "Ethical Consistency," *Proceedings of the Aristotelian Society, Supplementary Volumes* 39 (1965): 103, 104.

13. For a comprehensive introduction to the growing literature on organizational paradox, see *The Oxford Handbook of Organizational Paradox*, ed. Wendy K. Smith, Marianne W. Lewis, Paula Jarzabkowski, and Ann Langley (Oxford: Oxford University Press, 2017).

14. Mario L. Barnes, "Racial Paradox in a Law and Society Odyssey," *Law & Society Review* 44, no. 3/4 (September/December 2010): 469–86.

15. Civil rights scholar and activist john powell uses the term "targeted universalism" to convey the necessity and possibility of adopting opposite and interdependent ways of "racing to justice." john a. powell, *Racing to Justice: Transforming Our Conceptions of Self and Other to Build an Inclusive Society* (Bloomington: Indiana University Press, 2012), 3.

16. Michelle Rhone-Collins, "Navigating Race and New Leadership in a Time of Upheaval," *Stanford Social Innovation Review*, September 16, 2020, https://ssir.org/articles/entry/navigating_race_and_new_leadership_in_a_time_of_upheaval#.

17. Marshall Ganz, "Leading Change: Leadership, Organization, and Social Movements," in *Handbook of Leadership Theory and Practice*, ed. Nitin Nohria and Rakesh Khurana (Boston: Harvard Business Press, 2010), 518.

18. Gary Orfield, *The Walls around Opportunity: The Failure of Colorblind Policy for Higher Education* (Princeton: Princeton University Press, 2022), 131.

19. Michelle M. Duguid and Melissa C. Thomas-Hunt, "Condoning Stereotyping? How Awareness of Stereotyping Prevalence Impacts Expression of Stereotypes," *Journal of Applied Psychology* 100, no. 2 (2015): 343–59, https//doi.org/10.1037/a0037908.

20. Valerie Purdie-Vaughns and Gregory M. Walton, "Is Multiculturalism Bad for African Americans? Redefining Inclusion through the Lens of Identity Safety," in *Moving beyond Prejudice Reduction: Pathways to Positive Intergroup Relations*, ed. Linda R. Tropp and Robyn K. Mallett (American Psychological Association, 2011), 159–77, https://doi.org/10.1037/12319-008.

21. Cheryl Kaiser, Brenda Major, Inez Jurcevic, Tessa Dover, Laura Brady, and Jenessar R. Shapiro, "Presumed Fair: Ironic Effects of Organizational Diversity Structures," *Journal of Personality and Social Psychology* 104, no. 3 (2013): 504–19.

22. Sara Ahmed, *Complaint!* (Durham: Duke University Press, 2021), 3.

23. Purdie-Vaughns and Walton, "Is Multiculturalism Bad for African Americans?" 168.

24. Stuart Hall, "Race, the Floating Signifier: What More Is There to Say about 'Race'?" in *Selected Writings on Race and Difference*, ed. Paul Gilroy and Ruth Wilson Gilmore (Durham: Duke University Press, 2021), 359.

25. Kimberlé Crenshaw, "Mapping the Margins: Intersectionality, Identity Politics, and Violence against Women of Color," *Stanford Law Review* 43, no. 6 (July 1991): 1252, https://doi.org/10.2307/1229039.

26. Audre Lorde, "Age, Race, Class, and Sex: Women Redefining Difference," in *Sister Outsider: Essays and Speeches* (Berkeley: Crossing Press, 2007), 116.

27. Students for Fair Admissions, Inc. v. President and Fellows of Harvard College, 600 U.S. 181 (2023).

28. CRT Forward, a project at UCLA's Critical Race Studies Program, provides a comprehensive database of anti–critical race theory measures across all levels of government and varying types of official action. The map can be accessed at https://crtforward.law.ucla.edu/map.

29. Joseph Fishkin, *Bottlenecks: A New Theory of Equal Opportunity* (New York: Oxford University Press, 2014), 13.

30. Robin J. Ely and Alexandra C. Feldberg, "Organizational Remedies for Discrimination," in *The Oxford Handbook of Workplace Discrimination*, ed. Adrienne J. Colella and Eden B. King (Oxford: Oxford University Press, 2016), 387–408.

31. Parents Involved in Community Schools v. Seattle School District, 551 U.S. 701 (2007).

32. Emilio J. Castilla, "Gender, Race, and Meritocracy in Organizational Careers," *American Journal of Sociology* 113 (2008): 1479–1526.

33. Evan P. Apfelbaum, Michael I. Norton, and Samuel R. Sommers, "Racial Color Blindness: Emergence, Practice, and Implications," *Current Directions in Psychological Science* 21, no. 3 (2012): 205–9, https://doi.org/10.1177/0963721411434980.

34. Valerie Purdie-Vaughns, Claude M. Steele, Paul G. Davies, Ruth Ditlmann, and Jennifer Randall Crosby, "Social Identity Contingencies: How Diversity Cues Signal Threat or Safety

for African Americans in Mainstream Institutions," *Journal of Personality and Social Psychology* 94, no. 4 (2008): 615–30, https://doi.org/10.1037/0022-3514.94.4.615.

35. Lorde, "Age, Race, Class, and Sex," 116.

36. Audre Lorde, "The Master's Tools Will Never Dismantle the Master's House," in *Sister Outsider: Essays and Speeches* (Berkeley: Crossing Press, 2007), 110–14.

37. Michael Omi and Howard Winant, *Racial Formation in the United States*, 3rd ed. (New York: Routledge, 2014).

38. Frederick Douglass, "The New President," *Douglass' Monthly* (March 1861): 419, quoted in Dorothy E. Roberts, "Foreword: Abolition Constitutionalism," *Harvard Law Review* 133, no. 1 (2019): 61.

39. Martin Luther King Jr., *Letter from Birmingham Jail* (London: Penguin Books, 2018), 14.

40. Richard Rothstein and Leah Rothstein, *Just Action: How to Challenge Segregation Enacted under the Color of Law* (New York: Liveright Publishing, 2023).

41. Lauren B. Edelman, "Legal Ambiguity and Symbolic Structures: Organizational Mediation of Civil Rights Law," *American Journal of Sociology* 97, no. 6 (May 1992): 1535.

42. E.g., Dara Kerr, "2 Black TikTok Workers Claim Discrimination: Both Were Fired after Complaining to HR," NPR, September 21, 2023, https://www.npr.org/2023/09/21/1200727549/2-black-tiktok-workers-claim-discrimination.

43. Castilla, "Gender, Race, and Meritocracy in Organizational Careers"; Frank Dobbin and Alexandra Kalev, *Getting to Diversity: What Works and What Doesn't* (Cambridge, MA: Harvard University Press, 2022).

44. Anthony P. Carnevale and Jeff Strohl, "Separate & Unequal: How Higher Education Reinforces the Intergenerational Reproduction of White Racial Privilege," Georgetown Public Policy Institute, July 2013, https://cew.georgetown.edu/wp-content/uploads/SeparateUnequal.FR_.pdf, 7; Orfield, *The Walls around Opportunity*.

45. Patricia Gándara recounts the decision of the regents of the University of California to discontinue use of standardized tests and to rely instead on "thirteen other factors, including things like overcoming challenges, having developed special talents, and receiving achievements and awards, to distinguish among similarly strong students." Patricia Gándara, "Higher Admissions, a California Perspective," commentary in Nicholas Lemann, *Higher Admissions: The Rise, Decline, and Return of Standardized Testing* (Princeton: Princeton University Press, 2024), 110–11.

46. Kimberlé Williams Crenshaw, "Race, Reform, and Retrenchment: Transformation and Legitimation in Antidiscrimination Law," *Harvard Law Review* 101, no. 7 (May 1988): 1384–87, https://doi.org/10.2307/1341398.

47. Warren Hoffman, *The Great White Way: Race and the Broadway Musical*, 2nd ed. (New Brunswick, NJ: Rutgers University Press, 2020), 4, 201–2, muse.jhu.edu/book/28850.

48. Asian American Performers Action Coalition (AAPAC), Pun Bandhu, and Julienne Hanzelka Kim, "The Visibility Report: Racial Representation on NYC Stages" (2021), p. 8, http://www.aapacnyc.org/2018-2019.html.

49. Victor Ray, "A Theory of Racialized Organizations," *American Sociological Review* 84, no. 1 (2019): 26–53.

50. Eduardo Bonilla-Silva, "The Structure of Racism in Color-Blind, 'Post-Racial' America," *American Behavioral Scientist* 59, no. 11 (2015): 1360, https://doi.org/10.1177/0002764215586826.

51. Kiara Alfonseca and Max Zahn, "How Corporate America Is Slashing DEI Workers amid Backlash to Diversity Programs," ABC News, July 7, 2023, https://abcnews.go.com/US /corporate-america-slashing-dei-workers-amid-backlash-diversity/story?id=100477952.

52. Susan Sturm, "Second Generation Employment Discrimination: A Structural Approach," *Columbia Law Review* 101, no. 3 (2001): 458, 459–60.

Chapter Two: Stuck in Groundhog Day

1. Kim Crenshaw calls this cycle "reform and retrenchment" and documents its recurrence throughout U.S. history. Kimberlé Williams Crenshaw, "Race, Reform, and Retrenchment: Transformation and Legitimation in Antidiscrimination Law," *Harvard Law Review* 101, no. 7 (May 1988): 1384–87, https://doi.org/10.2307/1341398.

2. In our initial conversation, the court administrator asked questions about how my scholarship related to action research I had done with organizations, including the Harvard Business School, *Yale Law Journal*, the National Institutes of Health, Imagining America, and Hostos College.

3. Charles Jeh Johnson, "Report from the Special Adviser on Equal Justice in the New York State Courts" (State of New York Unified Court System, 2020), 3, 27, https://www.nycourts.gov /whatsnew/pdf/SpecialAdviserEqualJusticeReport.pdf.

4. Mahzarin Banaji and Anthony Greenwald, the architects of the implicit attribution test revealing unconscious biases, call these unconscious biases "mindbugs—ingrained habits of thought that lead to errors in how we perceive, remember, reason, and make decisions." Mahzarin R. Banaji and Anthony G. Greenwald, *Blindspot: Hidden Biases of Good People* (New York: Random House Publishing Group, 2013), 4.

5. Perception Institute, "Implicit Bias," 2019, https://perception.org/research/implicit-bias /. For an accessible overview of implicit bias by the researchers who coined the phrase and created the implicit attribution test to detect its operation, see Banaji and Greenwald, *Blindspot*.

6. Russell K. Robinson, "Perceptual Segregation," *Columbia Law Review* 108, no. 5 (2008): 1093–1180; Evan P. Apfelbaum, Michael I. Norton, and Samuel R. Sommers, "Racial Color Blindness: Emergence, Practice, and Implications," *Current Directions in Psychological Science* 21, no. 3 (2012): 205–9, https://doi.org/10.1177/0963721411434980; Katherine Schaeffer and Khadijah Edwards, "Black Americans Differ from Other U.S. Adults over Whether Individual or Structural Racism Is a Bigger Problem," Pew Research Center, November 15, 2022, https:// www.pewresearch.org/short-reads/2022/11/15/black-americans-differ-from-other-u-s-adults -over-whether-individual-or-structural-racism-is-a-bigger-problem/.

7. Robinson, "Perceptual Segregation," 1127, 1137.

8. Samuel R. Sommers and Michael I. Norton, "Lay Theories about White Racists: What Constitutes Racism (and What Doesn't)," *Group Processes & Intergroup Relations* 9, no. 1 (January 2006): 117–38, https://doi.org/10.1177/1368430206059881; Eduardo Bonilla-Silva, *Racism without Racists: Color-Blind Racism and the Persistence of Racial Inequality in America* (Lanham, MD: Rowman & Littlefield, 2022), ProQuest Ebook Central, 1, 4, 37.

9. Crenshaw, "Race, Reform, and Retrenchment," 1341; Franklin D. Gilliam Jr., "The Architecture of a New Racial Discourse," FrameWorks, June 14, 2006, https://www.frameworksinstitute .org/publication/the-architecture-of-a-new-racial-discourse/.

10. Logan Cornett and Natalie Anne Knowlton, "Public Perspectives on Trust & Confidence in the Courts," Institute for the Advancement of the American Legal System, June 2020, https://iaals.du.edu/sites/default/files/documents/publications/public_perspectives_on_trust_and_confidence_in_the_courts.pdf; Cary Wu, Rima Wilkes, and David C. Wilson, "Race & Political Trust: Justice as a Unifying Influence on Political Trust," *Daedalus* 151, no. 4 (2022): 177–99, https://doi.org/10.1162/daed_a_01950.

11. Rachel Minkin, "Diversity, Equity and Inclusion in the Workplace," Pew Research Center, May 17, 2023, https://www.pewresearch.org/social-trends/2023/05/17/diversity-equity-and-inclusion-in-the-workplace/.

12. Carrie Blazina and Kiana Cox, "Black and White Americans Are Far Apart in Their Views of Reparations for Slavery," Pew Research Center, November 28, 2022, https://www.pewresearch.org/short-reads/2022/11/28/black-and-white-americans-are-far-apart-in-their-views-of-reparations-for-slavery/.

13. Charles Tilly, *Durable Inequality* (Berkeley: University of California Press, 1998).

14. Gary Orfield, *The Walls around Opportunity: The Failure of Colorblind Policy for Higher Education* (Princeton: Princeton University Press, 2022), 69–70.

15. In "Less Separate, Still Unequal: Diversity and Equality in 'Post–Civil Rights' America" (in *Our Compelling Interests: The Value of Diversity for Democracy and a Prosperous Society*, ed. Earl Lewis and Nancy Cantor [Princeton: Princeton University Press, 2017]), Tom Sugrue summarizes these demographic trends and realities, concluding that the United States is now at a critical juncture, "a period where new demographic realities have destabilized old racial categories, when the ideal of diversity and inclusion clashes with xenophobia and exclusion, and when many minorities still suffer constricted opportunities as a result of deeply entrenched historical patterns" (40).

16. Richard Rothstein and Leah Rothstein, *Just Action: How to Challenge Segregation Enacted under the Color of Law* (New York: Liveright Publishing, 2023), 2.

17. Richard Rothstein, *The Color of Law: A Forgotten History of How Our Government Segregated America* (New York: Liveright Publishing, 2017).

18. Rothstein and Rothstein, *Just Action*, 8.

19. Gary Orfield, Erica Frankenberg, Jongyeon Ee, and Jennifer B. Ayscue, "Harming Our Common Future: America's Segregated Schools 65 Years after *Brown*," Civil Rights Project, May 10, 2019, 22, https://www.civilrightsproject.ucla.edu/research/k-12-education/integration-and-diversity/harming-our-common-future-americas-segregated-schools-65-years-after-brown/Brown-65-050919v4-final.pdf.

20. Orfield, *The Walls around Opportunity*, 70.

21. Brennan Center for Justice, "State Supreme Court Diversity," May 2023, https://www.brennancenter.org/our-work/research-reports/state-supreme-court-diversity-may-2023-update.

22. Rothstein and Rothstein, *Just Action*, 15.

23. Kenji Yoshino, *Covering: The Hidden Assault on Our Civil Rights* (New York: Random House, 2007), ix.

24. Percival Everett's extraordinary novel retelling *Huckleberry Finn* from Jim's point of view vividly explains how enslaved children were instructed to use dialect and displays of ignorance

so white people wouldn't feel threatened by their knowledge and the power it afforded. Percival Everett, *James* (New York: Doubleday, 2024), 21.

25. Robinson, "Perceptual Segregation," 1124–25.

26. The Crafting Democratic Futures Initiative, housed at the University of Michigan's Center for Social Solutions, has assembled resources and syllabi that "delve into the foundations of reparations, illuminate its challenges, and offer insights for those looking to champion reparations work in their own communities," which can be accessed at https://craftingdemocraticfutures.org/resources/.

27. Sarah Schwartz, "Map: Where Critical Race Theory Is under Attack," *Education Week*, June 11, 2021, http://www.edweek.org/leadership/map-where-critical-race-theory-is-under-attack/2021/06; CRT Forward Tracking Project, https://crtforward.law.ucla.edu/map.

28. Susan T. Fiske and Shelley E. Taylor, *Social Cognition: From Brains to Culture*, 4th ed. (London: Sage, 2021); William H. Sewell, "A Theory of Structure: Duality, Agency, and Transformation," *American Journal of Sociology* 98, no. 1 (1992): 8, http://www.jstor.org/stable/2781191.

29. Barbara Flagg, "'Was Blind, but Now I See': White Race Consciousness and the Requirement of Discriminatory Intent," *Michigan Law Review* 91, no. 5 (1993): 957, https://doi.org/10.2307/1289678.

30. Patricia J. Williams, *Seeing a Color-Blind Future: The Paradox of Race* (New York: Noonday Press, 1997), 28.

31. In *Doing Race*, Hazel Marcus and Paula Moya summarize these recurring beliefs affecting how people understand and experience race. Paula M. L. Moya and Hazel Rose Marcus, "Doing Race: An Introduction," in *Doing Race: 21 Essays for the 21st Century*, ed. Hazel Rose Marcus and Paula M. L. Moya (New York: W. W. Norton, 2010), 1–93.

32. Judge Fein's adherence to a script dictated by the formalities of the adversarial process illustrates a more general pattern documented by researchers. Judges "exercised process control and wielded legal jargon in ways that maintained legal and procedural complexity in their courtrooms." Anna E. Carpenter, Colleen F. Shanahan, Jessica K. Steinberg, and Alyx Mark, "Judges in Lawyerless Courts," *Georgetown Law Journal* 110 (2022): 539.

33. Robinson, "Perceptual Segregation," 1097.

34. Cecilia L. Ridgeway, "Why Status Matters for Inequality," *American Sociological Review* 79, no. 1 (2014): 1–10.

35. Research shows that these views have been internalized by people of all races. FrameWorks Institute, "Framing Public Issues," https://www.frameworksinstitute.org/wp-content/uploads/2020/07/FramingPublicIssuesfinal.pdf; Gilliam, "The Architecture of a New Racial Discourse."

36. Mary Douglas, *How Institutions Think* (Syracuse: Syracuse University Press, 1986), 8.

37. Isabel Wilkerson, *Caste: The Origins of Our Discontents* (New York: Random House, 2020), 97.

38. W.E.B. Du Bois, *The Souls of Black Folk* (New York: Dover, 1994), 2.

39. Rachel D. Godsil and Brianna Goodale, "Telling Our Own Story: The Role of Narrative in Racial Healing," June 2013, https://perception.org/wp-content/uploads/2014/11/Telling-Our-Own-Story.pdf.

40. Alan Jenkins, "Shifting the Narrative: What It Takes to Reframe the Debate for Social Justice in the US," Othering & Belonging Institute, April 18, 2018, https://belonging.berkeley.edu/shifting-narrative.

41. Douglas, *How Institutions Think*, 8.

42. John T. Jost and Mahzarin Banaji, "The Role of Stereotyping in System-Justification and the Production of False Consciousness," *British Journal of Social Psychology* 33, no. 1 (1994): 2, https://doi.org/10.1111/j.2044-8309.1994.tb01008.x.

43. Matthew Tokson, "Judicial Resistance and Legal Change," *University of Chicago Law Review* 82, no. 2 (2015): 901, 916–23.

44. Applying the concept of opportunity hoarding first introduced by Charles Tilly, Elizabeth Anderson writes: "U.S. whites have long hoarded opportunities, by establishing school systems that provide no, or an inferior, education to Blacks, Latinos, and Native Americans." Elizabeth S. Anderson, *The Imperative of Integration* (Princeton: Princeton University Press, 2010), 8. She also explains how legitimizing narratives (i.e., racial ideology) sustain opportunity hoarding and its outcomes.

45. Michael I. Norton and Samuel R. Sommers, "Whites See Racism as a Zero-Sum Game That They Are Now Losing," *Perspectives on Psychological Science* 6, no. 2 (2011): 215–18.

46. Heather McGhee, *The Sum of Us: What Racism Costs Everyone and How We Can Prosper Together* (New York: One World, 2021), 16.

47. Derrick A. Bell Jr., "*Brown v. Board of Education* and the Interest Convergence Dilemma," *Harvard Law Review* 93, no. 3 (1980): 522, https://doi.org/10.2307/1340546.

48. McGhee, *The Sum of Us*, 134–35.

49. john a. powell, *Racing to Justice: Transforming Our Conceptions of Self and Other to Build an Inclusive Society* (Bloomington: Indiana University Press, 2012), 93.

50. Most law reviews are edited and produced by law students chosen for the editorial board by a highly competitive selection process by the outgoing board. See Michael I. Swygert and Jon W. Bruce, "The Historical Origins, Founding, and Early Development of Student-Edited Law Reviews," *Hastings Law Journal* 36 (1985): 739–91.

51. This tension emerged as a significant barrier to the *Yale Law Journal*'s efforts to increase full participation by people of color as editors and authors, as documented in a study I conducted in 2015, the results of which were published by the *Yale Law Journal*. Susan Sturm and Kinga Makovi, "Full Participation in the *Yale Law Journal*," *Yale Law Journal* (2015): 1–133, https://www.yalelawjournal.org/files/FullParticipationintheYaleLawJournal_otc6qdnr.pdf.

52. Ira Katznelson, *When Affirmative Action Was White: An Untold History of Racial Inequality in Twentieth-Century America* (New York: W. W. Norton, 2005), 114, 131–32.

53. Daria Roithmayr, *Reproducing Racism: How Everyday Choices Lock in White Advantage* (New York: New York University Press, 2014), 116.

54. Lani Guinier, *The Tyranny of the Meritocracy: Democratizing Higher Education in America* (Boston: Beacon Press, 2015), 27–42.

55. Roithmayr, *Reproducing Racism*, 116.

56. Bryan Stevenson, "We Need to Talk about an Injustice," TED Talk, March 2012, 23:21, https://www.ted.com/talks/bryan_stevenson_we_need_to_talk_about_an_injustice.

57. John J. Heldrich Center for Workforce Development, Rutgers University, "A Workplace Divided: How Americans View Discrimination and Race on the Job," January 17, 2002, https://www.heldrich.rutgers.edu/work/workplace-divided-how-americans-view-discrimination-and-race-job; Flagg, "'Was Blind, but Now I See'"; powell, *Racing to Justice*; Matthew Clair and Alix S. Winter, "How Judges Think about Racial Disparities: Situational Decision-Making in

the Criminal Justice System," *Criminology* 54, no. 2 (2016): 343, https://doi.org/10.1111/1745 -9125.12106.

58. Clair and Winter, "How Judges Think about Racial Disparities," 345.

59. Carpenter et al., "Judges in Lawyerless Courts," 509.

60. Robert M. Cover, *Justice Accused: Antislavery and the Judicial Process* (New Haven: Yale University Press, 1975).

61. Donald A. Schön, *The Reflective Practitioner: How Professionals Think in Action* (New York: Basic Books, 1983), 43.

62. Deepak Bhargava and Stephanie Luce, *Practical Radicals: Seven Strategies to Change the World* (New York: New Press, 2023), 38.

Chapter Three: The Promise of Paradoxical Possibility

1. Brené Brown, *Dare to Lead: Brave Work, Tough Conversations, Whole Hearts* (New York: Random House, 2018).

2. Peggy McIntosh, "White Privilege: Unpacking the Invisible Knapsack," *Peace and Freedom Magazine* (July/August 1989): 10, https://www.nationalseedproject.org/key-seed-texts/white -privilege-unpacking-the-invisible-knapsack.

3. Nancy Gertner, a Harvard Law professor who previously served as a judge for seventeen years, has written about the ways that judges can become drivers of anti-racism and systems change, notwithstanding the constraints imposed by their role. Nancy Gertner, "Reimagining Judging," in *Parsimony and Other Radical Ideas about Justice*, ed. Jeremy Travis and Bruce Western (New York: New Press, 2023), 268–81.

4. Carol Dweck, *Mindset: The New Psychology of Success* (New York: Random House, 2006).

5. Barry Johnson, *Polarity Management: Identifying and Managing Unsolvable Problems* (Amherst, MA: HRD Press, 1992), 23.

6. Johnson, *Polarity Management*, 85–86.

7. Kenwyn K. Smith and David N. Berg, *Paradoxes of Group Life: Understanding Conflict, Paralysis, and Movement in Group Dynamics* (San Francisco: Jossey-Bass, 1987), 3.

8. W.E.B. Du Bois, *The Souls of Black Folk* (New York: Dover, 1994), 2.

9. Mari J. Matsuda, "When the First Quail Calls: Multiple Consciousness as Jurisprudential Method," *Women's Rights Law Reporter* 11, no. 1 (1989): 7, 8.

10. Martha Minow, *Making All the Difference* (Ithaca: Cornell University Press, 2016), 25.

11. Paolo Freire, *Pedagogy of the Oppressed* (1970; New York: Continuum, 2011), 90.

12. Melanie Tervalon and Jann Murray-García, "Cultural Humility versus Cultural Competence: A Critical Distinction in Defining Physician Training Outcomes in Multicultural Education," *Journal of Health Care for the Poor and Underserved* 9, no. 2 (1998): 123, https://doi.org/10 .1353/hpu.2010.0233.

13. Amy C. Edmondson, *The Fearless Organization: Creating Psychological Safety in the Workplace for Learning, Innovation, and Growth* (Hoboken, NJ: Wiley, 2018), 167–69.

14. Mikko Annala, Juha Leppänen, Silva Mertsola, and Charles F. Sabel, "Humble Government: How to Realize Ambitious Reforms Prudently" (report, Helsinki, 2020), 3, https:// tietokayttoon.fi/documents/1927382/2158283/Humble+Government.pdf.

15. Susan Sturm, "The Architecture of Inclusion: Advancing Workplace Equity in Higher Education," *Harvard Journal of Law and Gender* 29, no. 2 (2006): 257.

16. Martin Luther King Jr., *Letter from Birmingham Jail* (London: Penguin Books, 2018), 5, 6.

17. Susan Sturm and Kinga Makovi, "Full Participation in the *Yale Law Journal*," *Yale Law Journal* (2015): 1–133, https://www.yalelawjournal.org/files/FullParticipationintheYaleLawJournal_e929dpx1.pdf.

18. Chuck Sabel and Bill Simon have documented the role that litigation can play in destabilizing stuck bureaucracies and launching an ongoing process of experimentation and reflection. Charles F. Sabel and William H. Simon, "Destabilization Rights: How Public Law Litigation Succeeds," *Harvard Law Review* 117, no. 4 (2004): 1016, https://doi.org/10.2307/4093364.

19. For examples of court systems that have undertaken systemic approaches to addressing racism, see Columbia Justice Lab, "Shifting Roles, Responsibilities, and Resources to Communities," in *Taking on Transformation* (forthcoming), https://www.takingontransformation.org/topics/community-support-for-youth; Jane M. Spinak, *The End of Family Court: How Abolishing the Court Brings Justice to Children and Families* (New York: New York University Press, 2023), 285–88.

20. Robert Cover, "Foreword: Nomos and Narrative," *Harvard Law Review* 97, no. 1 (1983): 4.

21. adrienne maree brown, *Emergent Strategy: Shaping Change, Changing Worlds* (Chico, CA: AK Press, 2017), 24, 58.

22. Michael C. Dorf and Charles F. Sabel, "A Constitution of Democratic Experimentalism," *Columbia Law Review* 98, no. 2 (1998): 267, https://doi.org/10.2307/1123411.

23. Adam Kahane, *Collaborating with the Enemy: How to Work with People You Don't Agree with or Like or Trust* (Oakland, CA: Berrett-Koehler Publishers, 2017), 76.

24. Patricia J. Williams, *Seeing a Color-Blind Future: The Paradox of Race* (New York: Noonday Press, 1997), 15.

25. I first began using the term "personal board of directors" during my collaboration with Lani Guinier, as an important part of our strategy for building multiracial learning communities. Tasha Eurich coined the phrase "loving critics" to describe people who would be willing to give honest feedback that will help people cultivate both internal and external self-awareness. Tasha Eurich, "What Self-Awareness Really Is (and How to Cultivate It)," *Harvard Business Review*, January 4, 2018.

26. Rachel Hynson, "Creating Connections Consortium, Summary Report, 2013–2023," May 2023, https://bpb-us-e2.wpmucdn.com/sites.middlebury.edu/dist/2/2727/files/2023/10/C3-Summary-Report-For-general-distribution.pdf.

Chapter Four: Forging Linked Fate

1. August Wilson, "The Ground on Which I Stand," *Callaloo* 20, no. 3 (1997): 495, http://www.jstor.org/stable/3299355.

2. Wilson, "The Ground on Which I Stand," 503.

3. Michael Dawson, *Behind the Mule: Race and Class in African-American Politics* (Princeton: Princeton University Press, 1995), 77.

4. Deepak Bhargava and Stephanie Luce, *Practical Radicals: Seven Strategies to Change the World* (New York: New Press, 2023).

5. Bhargava and Luce, *Practical Radicals*, 25.

6. Ruth Wilson Gilmore, interview by Chenjerai Kumanyika, *Intercepted* (podcast), *The Intercept*, June 10, 2020, https://theintercept.com/2020/06/10/ruth-wilson-gilmore-makes-the-case-for-abolition/.

7. Heather McGhee, *The Sum of Us: What Racism Costs Everyone and How We Can Prosper Together* (New York: One World, 2021), 19, 21.

8. The account that follows draws from numerous interviews and articles in which Jeanine Tesori describes her history, her pathway into music, her interest in race, and her activism, as well as a series of articles, blog posts, and public discussions where Jeanine, Tazewell Thompson (the lyricist), and company members recount their experiences in creating and performing *Blue*.

9. Raymond Knapp and Holley Replogle-Wong, "A Conversation with Jeanine Tesori," *Studies in Musical Theatre* 17, no. 1 (2023): 39, https://doi.org/10.1386/smt_00114_7.

10. Victoria Myers, "An Interview with Jeanine Tesori," *The Interval*, March 18, 2015, https://www.theintervalny.com/interviews/2015/03/an-interview-with-jeanine-tesori/.

11. Jeanine Tesori and Tazewell Thompson, "The Libretto I Wrote for *Blue* Was My Personal Letter to the World," interview by Jasmijn van Wijnen, *Nationale Opera and Ballet*, March 21, 2022, https://www.operaballet.nl/en/articles/libretto-i-wrote-blue-was-my-personal-letter-world.

12. Rob Weinert-Kendt, "Jeanine Tesori Feels the Pull of Opera," *American Theatre* (July 9, 2019), https://www.americantheatre.org/2019/07/09/jeanine-tesori-feels-the-pull-of-opera/. This article is actually the transcript of an interview with Jeanine Tesori, conducted by the listed author.

13. "The Making of WNO's *Blue*: The Documentary," https://www.kennedy-center.org/video/digital-stage/opera/2022/blue-documentary/ (transcript on file with author).

14. Weinert-Kendt, "Jeanine Tesori Feels the Pull of Opera."

15. Tazewell Thompson, "My Journey to Writing an Opera about Police Violence," *Seattle Opera* (blog), May 11, 2021, http://seattleopera.blogspot.com/; Tazewell Thompson, "My Journey to Writing an Opera about Police Violence," *New York Times*, June 17, 2020, https://www.nytimes.com/2020/06/17/arts/music/blue-opera-police-violence.html.

16. Transcript, "*Blue*: The Documentary: Go Behind the Scenes of the Making of *Blue*," the Kennedy Center, March 25, 2022, https://youtu.be/UqYXIOCDbfU?feature=shared; Weinert-Kendt, "Jeanine Tesori Feels the Pull of Opera."

17. "The Making of WNO's *Blue*."

18. Tesori and Thompson, "The Libretto I Wrote for *Blue* Was My Personal Letter to the World."

19. Thompson, "My Journey to Writing an Opera about Police Violence" (*New York Times*); "A Conversation with Jeanine Tesori," *Seattle Opera* (blog), January 7, 2022, https://www.seattleoperablog.com/search?q=tesori.

20. Frank J. Oteri, "Jeanine Tesori: Holding Center Stage," NewMusic USA, December 1, 2018, https://newmusicusa.org/nmbx/jeanine-tesori-holding-center-stage/.

21. Yale Educational Travel and Yale Alumni College Q&A, Jeanine Tesori, https://alumni.yale.edu/news/yale-educational-travel-yale-alumni-college-qa-jeanine-tesori-lecturer-yales-shen-curriculum; Naomi Andre, "Staging Justice in a Three Dimensional Humanity," program, Jeanine Tesori & Tazewell Thompson, *Blue*, Washington National Opera, p. 21.

22. Frances E. Kendall, *Understanding White Privilege: Creating Pathways to Authentic Relationships across Race* (New York: Routledge, 2013), 22–23.

23. National Advisory Commission on Civil Disorders United States, "Kerner Commission Report on the Causes, Events, and Aftermaths of the Civil Disorders of 1967" (report, Washington, DC, 1967), 1.

24. BAC's three-part Broadway for Black Lives Matter Forum attracted over fifteen thousand participants and contributed to the decision to award BAC a first-ever organizational Tony for its providing "an unparalleled platform for marginalized members of our theater community and tools to help us all do better as we strive for equity." Julia Jacobs, "Tony Awards Announce First Three Recipients," *New York Times*, June 22, 2021. The Zoom recording is available at https://www.tonyawards.com/news/three-special-tony-awards-announced/.

25. "We See You, White American Theater," open letter, n.d., https://www.weseeyouwat.com/statement.

26. Beverly Daniel Tatum, "The Development of White Identity," in *Why Are All the Black Kids Sitting Together in the Cafeteria? And Other Conversations about Race* (1997; New York: Basic Books, 2017), 82. Tatum draws on the work of Janet Helms: *Black and White Racial Identity: Theory, Research, and Practice* (Westport, CT: Praeger, 1990).

27. James Baldwin, "The White Man's Guilt," in *Collected Essays*, ed. Toni Morrison (New York: Penguin Random House, 1998), 722.

28. Derrick A. Bell Jr., "*Brown v. Board of Education* and the Interest-Convergence Dilemma," *Harvard Law Review* 93, no. 3 (1980): 523, https://doi.org/10.2307/1340546.

29. Derrick Bell, *Faces at the Bottom of the Well: The Permanence of Racism* (New York: Basic Books, 2018), 8.

30. Robin Ely and David Thomas, "Getting Serious about Diversity: Enough Already with the Business Case," *Harvard Business Review*, November–December 2020, https://hbr.org/2020/11/getting-serious-about-diversity-enough-already-with-the-business-case.

31. Robin DiAngelo, *White Fragility: Why It's So Hard for White People to Talk about Racism* (Boston: Beacon Press, 2018).

32. Charles F. Sabel, "Studied Trust: Building New Forms of Cooperation in a Volatile Economy," *Human Relations* 46, no. 9 (1993): 1134, https://doi.org/10.1177/001872679304600907.

33. Adam Kahane, *Collaborating with the Enemy: How to Work with People You Don't Agree with or Like or Trust* (Oakland, CA: Berrett-Koehler Publishers, 2017), 9–10.

34. Audre Lorde, "Learning from the 60s," in *Sister Outsider: Essays and Speeches* (New York: Crossing Press, 1984), 134–35.

35. Martha Minow, *Making All the Difference* (Ithaca: Cornell University Press, 2016), 25.

36. Valerie Purdie-Vaughns, Claude M. Steele, Paul G. Davies, Ruth Ditlmann, and Jennifer Randall Crosby, "Social Identity Contingencies: How Diversity Cues Signal Threat or Safety for African Americans in Mainstream Institutions," *Journal of Personality and Social Psychology* 94, no. 4 (2008): 615–30, https://doi.org/10.1037/0022-3514.94.4.615.

37. Martin Luther King Jr., *Letter from Birmingham Jail* (London: Penguin Books, 2018), 3.

38. Sabel, "Studied Trust," 1136–37.

39. Paolo Freire, *Pedagogy of the Oppressed* (1970; New York: Continuum, 2011), 128.

40. Roger V. Gould, *Insurgent Identities: Class, Community, and Protest in Paris from 1848 to the Commune* (Chicago: University of Chicago Press, 1995).

41. Freeman A. Hrabowski III, *Holding Fast to Dreams: Empowering Youth from the Civil Rights Crusade to STEM Achievement* (Boston: Beacon Press, 2016), 85.

42. Lani Guinier and Gerald Torres, *The Miner's Canary: Enlisting Race, Resisting Power, Transforming Democracy* (Cambridge, MA: Harvard University Press, 2002), 11.

43. Transcript, Ford Foundation, Transformative Leadership Working Group Meeting, December 13, 2010 (in author's possession).

44. Bill LaCourse, interview by the author, April 28, 2014, UMBC, pp. 18–19 (transcript in author's possession).

45. LaCourse, interview, 9, 29.

46. Freeman Hrabowski, Philip J. Rous, and Peter H. Henderson, *The Empowered University: Shared Leadership, Culture Change, and Academic Success* (Baltimore: Johns Hopkins University Press, 2019), 81, 152–54.

47. McGhee, *The Sum of Us*, 19–20.

48. Matt Kizer, "The Ten out of Twelve: It's a Lie," *Scenic & Lighting Design*, August 16, 2021, https://scenicandlighting.com/article/the-ten-out-of-twelve-its-a-lie/.

49. Kizer, "The Ten out of Twelve: It's a Lie."

50. Researchers have documented the increase in long hours in both high-end and low-end jobs. Sylvia Ann Hewlett and Carolyn Buck Luce, "Extreme Jobs: The Dangerous Allure of the 70-Hour Workweek," *Harvard Business Review* (December 2006): 1–12.

51. For example, the Center for Worklife Law (https://worklifelaw.org/projects/) "works toward a future where no one is forced to choose between providing care for their loved ones and keeping the paying job they need to survive."

52. Rachel Spencer Hewitt, "Introduction" (speech, Public Theater, New York, December 6, 2019).

53. Jerald Raymond Pierce, "Time for a Change: What If We Cut the Long Hours?" *American Theatre*, August 8, 2020, https://www.americantheatre.org/2020/08/20/time-for-a-change-what-if-we-cut-the-long-hours/; Kizer, "The Ten out of Twelve: It's a Lie"; "No More 10 out of 12s," *In 1: The Podcast*, November 11, 2021, https://in1podcast.com/106-no-more-10-out-of-12s/; "No More 10s out of 12s," panel discussion, USITT, January 27, 2021, https://www.youtube.com/watch?v=vxgu-oVM-z8.

54. PAAL Statement of Commitment to Racial Justice + Call to Action provides: "The fight for caregiver support shouldn't just 'include' intersectional realities of race and gender: the fight for caregiver support must center the intersectional realities of race and gender." https://www.paaltheatre.com/anti-racism.

55. Kahane, *Collaborating with the Enemy*, 35, 44.

56. Kahane, *Collaborating with the Enemy*, 44.

57. Executive Order 203, New York State Police Reform and Reinvention Collaborative, June 12, 2020, https://www.governor.ny.gov/sites/default/files/atoms/files/EO_203.pdf.

58. "Reimagining Public Safety: Findings from Qualitative Data and Community Input" (draft report), presented by Drs. Belisa González and Sean Eversley Bradwell, https://drive.google.com/drive/u/0/folders/1NTZ6j6WRze75m5fTuf-wC4BgC-1ddJnO.

59. "Implementing the City of Ithaca's New Public Safety Agency: Suggestions from the City of Ithaca's Reimagining Public Safety Working Group," February 23, 2022, https://www.cityofithaca.org/DocumentCenter/View/13725/WG_IthacaReport_Final.

60. Jimmy Jordan, "Almost Three Years since Ithaca's Police Reform Efforts Began, Plans Start to Move Forward," *Ithaca Voice*, April 7, 2023.

61. Tanner Harding, "'Reimagining' Process Prompts Questions about Ethics, Legalities and Misconceptions," *Ithaca Times Daily*, April 12, 2022, https://www.ithaca.com/news/ithaca /reimagining-process-prompts-questions-about-ethics-legalities-and-misconceptions/article _848de84c-badd-11ec-8af5-e74a630977f7.html.

62. Jimmy Jordan, "CJC Sets Sights on Mental Health Co-response, More Reforms in 2023 Workplan," *Ithaca Voice*, January 4, 2023, https://ithacavoice.org/2023/01/cjc-sets-sights-on -mental-health-co-response-more-reforms-in-2023-workplan/; Judy Lucas, "Community Jus- tice Center Launches Public Safety, Criminal Justice System Data Dashboard," *Ithaca Voice*, April 16, 2024, https://ithacavoice.org/2024/04/community-justice-center-launches-public -safety-criminal-justice-system-data-dashboard/.

63. Matt Steeker, "Department of Community Safety: What You Need to Know about New Ithaca Public Safety Plans," *Ithaca Journal*, March 3, 2022, https://www.ithacajournal.com/story /news/local/2022/03/03/ithaca-department-community-safety-plans-unveiled/9341367002/; Jessica Wickham, "Officials Talk Public Safety Reform after City's Report," *Tompkins Weekly*, March 16, 2022.

64. Transcript, "Community Members and Law Enforcement on Community Healing," June 2023, https://www.youtube.com/watch?v=bfdz-Zdwpak&list=PL0FoCrvXrxA3I8XAKp ddWQSqhcMUPKAUc&index=2.

Chapter Five: Building Bridges, Weaving Dreams

1. Robert Cover, "Foreword: Nomos and Narrative," *Harvard Law Review* 97, no. 1 (1983): 4, 10.

2. Patricia Gurin, Biren (Ratnesh) A. Nagda, and Ximena Zúñiga, *Dialogue across Difference: Practice, Theory, and Research on Intergroup Dialogue* (New York: Russell Sage Foundation, 2013).

3. Gurin, Nagda, and Zúñiga, *Dialogue across Difference*, 28–29, 55.

4. Students for Fair Admissions, Inc. v. President and Fellows of Harvard College, 600 U.S. 181 (2023).

5. Pew Research Center, "On Views of Race and Inequality, Blacks and Whites Are Worlds Apart," June 27, 2016, https://www.pewresearch.org/social-trends/2016/06/27/on-views-of -race-and-inequality-blacks-and-whites-are-worlds-apart/. Social psychologists have provided more nuance to understanding cross-racial differences in communication. Black individuals interested in influencing white people to be more concerned about racial justice often combine messages conveying warmth and acceptance of the other person with messages about racial injustice. See Ruth K. Ditlmann, John F. Dovidio, Valerie Purdie-Vaughns, John F. Dovidio, and Michael J. Naft, "The Implicit Power Motive in Intergroup Dialogues about the History of Slav- ery," *Journal of Personality and Social Psychology* 112, no. 1 (2017): 116–35, https://doi.org/10.1037 /pspp0000118.

6. Valerie Purdie-Vaughns and Gregory M. Walton, "Is Multiculturalism Bad for African Americans? Redefining Inclusion through the Lens of Identity Safety," in *Moving beyond Preju- dice Reduction: Pathways to Positive Intergroup Relations*, ed. Linda R. Tropp and Robyn K. Mal- lett (American Psychological Association, 2011), 162, https://doi.org/10.1037/12319-008.

7. Douglas Stone, Bruce Patton, and Sheila Heen, *Difficult Conversations: How to Discuss What Matters Most* (New York: Penguin, 2010).

8. Carol Dweck, *Mindset: The New Psychology of Success* (New York: Random House, 2006), 6–7.

9. Lani Guinier, "From Racial Liberalism to Racial Literacy: *Brown v. Board of Education* and the Interest-Divergence Dilemma," *Journal of American History* 91, no. 1 (2004): 92–118, https://doi.org/10.2307/3659616.

10. Rhonda V. Magee, *The Inner Work of Racial Justice: Healing Ourselves and Transforming Our Communities through Mindfulness* (New York: TarcherPerigee, 2019), 35.

11. Howard C. Stevenson, *Promoting Racial Literacy in Schools: Differences That Make a Difference* (New York: Teachers College Press, 2014), 16–17.

12. Adam D. Galinsky, Gillian Ku, and Cynthia S. Wang, "Perspective-Taking and Self-Other Overlap: Fostering Social Bonds and Facilitating Social Coordination," *Group Processes & Intergroup Relations* 8, no. 2 (2005): 110, https://doi.org/10.1177/1368430205051060.

13. Gurin, Nagda, and Zúñiga, *Dialogue across Difference*, 82–83, 152–53; Gillian Ku, Cynthia S. Wang, and Adam D. Galinsky, "The Promise and Perversity of Perspective-Taking in Organizations," *Research in Organizational Behavior* 35 (2015): 79–102, https://doi.org/10.1016/j.riob.2015.07.003.

14. Lani Guinier and Gerald Torres, *The Miner's Canary: Enlisting Race, Resisting Power, Transforming Democracy* (Cambridge, MA: Harvard University Press, 2002), 292–93.

15. Danielle Allen, "Toward a Connected Society," in *Our Compelling Interests: The Value of Diversity for Democracy and a Prosperous Society*, ed. Earl Lewis and Nancy Cantor (Princeton: Princeton University Press, 2016), 71, 87–88, 90–91.

16. Lani Guinier, *Lift Every Voice: Turning a Civil Rights Setback into a New Vision of Social Justice* (New York: Simon & Schuster, 2003), 67.

17. Guinier, *Lift Every Voice*, 64–67.

18. Guinier, *Lift Every Voice*, 57, 58–61.

19. Brené Brown has documented how willingness to be vulnerable builds trust and creates the conditions under which people are more willing to engage with difference, take risks, and pursue change. Brené Brown, *Dare to Lead: Brave Work, Tough Conversations, Whole Hearts* (New York: Random House, 2018), 10–11.

20. Richard Rothstein and Leah Rothstein, *Just Action: How to Challenge Segregation Enacted under the Color of Law* (New York: Liveright Publishing, 2023), 17–20.

21. Angel Idowu, "Folded Map Project Highlights Chicago Segregation, Gentrification," WTTW, February 11, 2020, https://news.wttw.com/2020/02/11/folded-map-project-highlights-chicago-segregation-gentrification.

22. Palmigiano v. Garrahy, 443 F. Supp. 956, 984 (D.R.I. 1977).

23. My first foray into research and my first publication was my law journal note, still relevant today, providing an overview and critique of the role of special masters in prison litigation, based on a five-state study. See Susan Sturm, "'Mastering' Intervention in Prisons," *Yale Law Journal* 88, no. 5 (1979): 1062–91.

24. Alec Karakatsanis, *Usual Cruelty: The Complicity of Lawyers in the Criminal Injustice System* (New York: New Press, 2019).

25. On July 7, 2022, the Academy of Court-Appointed Masters approved a resolution to change its name to the Academy of Court-Appointed Neutrals (https://www .courtappointedneutrals.org/). Only after George Floyd's murder did the engineering field halt use of the "master-slave" terminology, introduced in 1904 as an analogy for a technical description of a control relationship between two devices: https://en.m.wikipedia.org/wiki /Master%E2%80%93slave_(technology).

26. Bryan Stevenson, "We Need to Talk about an Injustice," TED Talk, March 2012, 23:21, https://www.ted.com/talks/bryan_stevenson_we_need_to_talk_about_an_injustice.

27. Lani and I wrote an article describing the impact of the law school culture on students' connection to their values and purpose. Susan Sturm and Lani Guinier, "The Law School Matrix: Reforming Legal Education in a Culture of Competition and Conformity," *Vanderbilt Law Review* 60, no. 2 (2007): 515–53.

28. See Susan Sturm and Vivian Nixon, "Home-Grown Social Capital: How Higher Education for Formerly Incarcerated Women Facilitates Family and Community Transformation" (Aspen Ascend Institute, 2018), https://ascend.aspeninstitute.org/wp-content/uploads/2017 /10/2015093020Social20Capital_Sturm_Nixon_2.pdf; Susan P. Sturm and Haran Tae, "Leading with Conviction: The Transformative Role of Formerly Incarcerated Leaders in Reducing Mass Incarceration" (Center for Institutional and Social Change, 2017), https://scholarship.law .columbia.edu/faculty_scholarship/2033.

29. Jonathan Lippman, "A More Just New York City: Independent Commission on New York City Criminal Justice and Incarceration Reform" (New York, 2017), https://static1 .squarespace.com/static/5b6de4731aef1de914f43628/t/5b96c6f81ae6cf5e9c5f186d /1536607993842/Lippman%2BCommission%2BReport%2BFINAL%2BSingles.pdf. Following the Lippman Commission Report's publication and the mobilization of Campaign to Close Rikers, led by people and families directly affected by Rikers' inhumane conditions, then mayor DiBlasio released a road map for the closure of the prison. For a timeline on the plan to close Rikers, see Kimberly Gonzalez, Sara Dorn, and Sahalie Johnson, "A Timeline on the Closure of Rikers Island," *City & State New York*, March 6, 2024, https://www.cityandstateny.com/politics /2024/03/timeline-closure-rikers-island/376662/.

30. In 1994, Congress removed Pell Grant eligibility for incarcerated people. For over two decades, incarcerated people who wanted a college education had to pay for classes with personal funds or gain access to classes through privately funded programs. In December 2020, Congress reinstated Pell Grant eligibility for students incarcerated in federal or state penal institutions and students who are subject to involuntary commitments. Pell Grants for Prison Education Programs, 87 Fed. Reg. 65426 (October 28, 2022) (to be codified as 34 C.F.R. § 600, 668, 690), https://perma .cc/VGX2-MUMX. For a discussion of the impact of higher education on people who are currently incarcerated and those formerly incarcerated, see Nixon and Sturm, "Home-Grown Social Capital"; Niloufer Taber, Lina Cook, Chris Mai, and Jennifer Hill, "The Impacts of College-in-Prison Participation on Safety and Employment in New York State: An Analysis of College Students Funded by the Criminal Justice Investment Initiative," Vera Institute of Justice, November 2023, https:// www.vera.org/downloads/publications/Impacts-of-College-in-Prison-in-NYS-Report.pdf.

31. Alejo Dao'ud Rodriguez, "Sing Sing Sits Up the River," in *The Outlaw Bible of American Poetry*, ed. Alan Kaufman (New York: Thunder's Mouth Press, 1999), 621.

32. Alejo wrote a law review article about the problems with parole, drawing on both personal experience and research on the constitutional law issues relating to parole. See Alejo Rodriguez, "The Obscure Legacy of Mass Incarceration: Parole Board Abuses of People Serving Parole Eligible Life Sentences," *City University of New York Law Review* 22, no. 2 (2019): 33–59.

33. Eddie Ellis, "Open Letter to Our Friends on the Question of Language," *Parole Preparation & Appeal Resources* (2020), https://ir.lawnet.fordham.edu/pp/5.

34. Information about BATTLE and Paralegal Pathways Initiative can be found on the website of the Center for Institutional and Social Change: https://change-center.law.columbia.edu/.

35. For a fuller description of NSF ADVANCE and its approach to institutional transformation, see Susan Sturm, "The Architecture of Inclusion: Advancing Workplace Equity in Higher Education," *Harvard Journal of Law and Gender* 29, no. 2 (2006): 249–334.

36. Abigail J. Stewart, "Choosing Both: Finding a Path as an Academic Feminist," in *Reflections from Pioneering Women in Psychology*, ed. Jamila Bookwala and Nicky J. Newton (Cambridge: Cambridge University Press, 2022), 305, 312, 313.

37. These quotes involving STRIDE come from transcripts of interviews conducted as part of the research leading to "The Architecture of Inclusion." Names are omitted to preserve confidentiality.

38. Abby has integrated the social science that underlies her work in ADVANCE into a book, written in collaboration with Virginia Valian, another organizational catalyst. Abigail J. Stewart and Virginia Valian, *An Inclusive Academy: Achieving Diversity and Excellence* (Cambridge, MA: MIT Press, 2018).

39. Lauren Love, "U-M ADVANCE Works to Improve Faculty Diversity through Hiring," *University Record*, September 15, 2021, https://record.umich.edu/articles/u-m-advance-works-to-improve-faculty-diversity-through-hiring/.

Chapter Six: Repurposing Power

1. Kimberly Hayes Taylor, "Urban Teens Strut Stuff in Megahangout," *Star Tribune*, June 30, 1994; Kimberly Hayes Taylor, "For Teens, Mall Is a Place They Can Count On," *Star Tribune*, June 30, 1994.

2. Sheila McMillen, "Mall of America: Darden Case No. UVA-BC-0129," 2001, https://dx.doi.org/10.2139/ssrn.907738.

3. "Mall Officials Call Shooting an Isolated Incident," *Star Ledger*, February 8, 1993.

4. The story and quotes come from a series of newspaper articles and reports written about the Mall of America during the period from 1992 through 1997, as well as author interviews with Mall of America personnel and staff, conducted in 1997.

5. Randy Furst, "What Price Will Teens Pay?" *Star Ledger*, January 24, 1996, B3.

6. "Blacks Call Escort Policy Racist; Official Says It's about Behavior," *Star Ledger*, June 21, 1996.

7. Steven Lukes, *Power: A Radical View* (1974; New York: Palgrave Macmillan, 2005). In an essay written in 1924, Follett coined the terms "power-over" and "power-with," differentiating between coercive, top-down power and reciprocal, co-active participatory power, and advocated for noncoercive power sharing using "power-with." Mary P. Follett, *Dynamic Administration: The Collected Papers of Mary Parker Follett*, ed. E. M. Fox and L. Urwick (London: Pitman Publishing, 1940).

8. John Gaventa subsequently created an online resource summarizing types of power and offering tools for people involved in social change. See "Powercube: Understanding Power for Social Change," September 6, 2009, https://www.powercube.net/an-introduction-to-power -analysis/.

9. Kimberly Hayes Taylor, "Mighty Moms Make Mark at Megamall," *Star Tribune*, April 27, 1996.

10. Deepak Bhargava and Stephanie Luce provide a helpful overview of the forms that power can take, which include ideological power, political power, economic power, military and police power, solidarity power, and disruptive power. Each of these forms could be exercised as power over, power with, and power to. Deepak Bhargava and Stephanie Luce, *Practical Radicals: Seven Strategies to Change the World* (New York: New Press, 2023), 46–55.

11. Editorial, "Teens and the Megamall," *Star Tribune*, August 23, 1996.

12. Lani Guinier and Gerald Torres, *The Miner's Canary: Enlisting Race, Resisting Power, Transforming Democracy* (Cambridge, MA: Harvard University Press, 2002), 15.

13. Lukes, *Power*, 56–57.

14. John Gaventa, "Finding the Spaces for Change: A Power Analysis," *Institute of Developmental Studies Bulletin* 37, no. 6 (2006): 23–33.

15. Marc Galanter, "Why the 'Haves' Come Out Ahead: Speculations on the Limits of Legal Change," *Law and Society Review* 9, no. 1 (1974): 95–160.

16. Cecilia L. Ridgeway, "Why Status Matters for Inequality," *American Sociological Review* 79, no. 1 (2013): 2–3.

17. Ibram X. Kendi, *How to Be an Antiracist* (New York: One World, 2019), 40–41.

18. Ian Shearn, "The Forging of Ras Baraka: How He Was Made for This Fight," NJ Spotlight News, August 31, 2020, https://www.njspotlightnews.org/2020/08/newark-mayor-ras-baraka -poet-amiri-cops-arrests-protests-street-activist/.

19. Governor's Select Commission on Civil Disorder, State of New Jersey, "Report for Action," February 1968, https://www.ojp.gov/pdffiles1/Digitization/69748NCJRS.pdf.

20. Clement Alexander Price, "Newark Remembers the Summer of 1967, So Should We All," *The Positive Community* (July/August 2007): 20–21.

21. Eric Kiefer, "Watch Newark Mayor's State of the City Speech: 'Belief in Ourselves,'" *Patch*, March 16, 2022, https://patch.com/new-jersey/newarknj/watch-newark-mayor-s-state -city-speech-belief-ourselves, https://www.facebook.com/watch/?ref=embed_video&v =354941466527239.

22. Shearn, "The Forging of Ras Baraka."

23. Marc Bussanich, "Newark Swears in Ras Baraka as Mayor," *Labor Press*, July 2, 2014, https://www.laborpress.org/newark-swears-in-ras-baraka-as-mayor/; Kate Zernike, "Defying Expectations, Mayor Ras Baraka Is Praised in All Corners of Newark," *New York Times*, August 30, 2015.

24. Marquise Francis, "Newark Was One of the Deadliest Cities in the U.S. Now It Wants to Set an Example on Public Safety Reform," Yahoo! News, June 25, 2022, https://www.yahoo .com/news/newark-was-one-of-the-deadliest-cities-in-america-now-it-wants-to-be-a-blueprint -for-public-safety-reform-163320757.html.

25. United States Department of Justice, Civil Rights Division, "Investigation of the Newark Police Department," United States Attorney's Office District of New Jersey, July 22, 2014,

https://www.justice.gov/sites/default/files/crt/legacy/2014/07/22/newark_findings_7-22
-14.pdf.

26. Shearn, "The Forging of Ras Baraka."

27. There is a growing literature documenting the need to democratize professionalism generally and in the field of criminal justice in particular. See Albert W. Dzur, *Democratic Professionalism: Citizen Participation and the Construction of Professional Ethics, Identity, and Practice* (University Park: Penn State University Press, 2008); Donald A. Schön, *The Reflective Practitioner: How Professionals Think in Action* (New York: Basic Books, 1983); Benjamin Levin, "Criminal Justice Expertise," *Fordham Law Review* 90, no. 6 (2022): 2777–2840; Bernard Harcourt, "The Systems Fallacy: A Genealogy and Critique of Public Policy and Cost-Benefit Analysis," *Journal of Legal Studies* 47 (2018): 419.

28. Monica Bell, "Safety, Friendship, and Dreams," *Harvard Civil Rights-Civil Liberties Law Review* 54 (2019): 703, 710.

29. Susan Sturm and Haran Tae, "Leading with Conviction: The Transformative Role of Formerly Incarcerated Leaders in Reducing Mass Incarceration" (Center for Institutional and Social Change, 2017), https://scholarship.law.columbia.edu/faculty_scholarship/2033, 16.

30. Bell, "Safety, Friendship, and Dreams," 712.

31. Robert J. Chaskin, Prudence Brown, Sudhir Venkatesh, and Avid Vidal, *Building Community Capacity* (New York: Walter de Gruyter, 2001), 14.

32. Jorja Leap, Mark Leap, Karrah Lompa, and Whitney Gouche, *Evaluation of the Newark Community Street Team* (February 2024), https://www.newarkcommunitystreetteam.org/wp-content/uploads/2024/03/NCST-Innovations-CBCR-Evaluation_FINAL.pdf.

33. Aquil Basheer and Christina Hoag, *Peace in the Hood: Working with Gang Members to End the Violence* (Nashville: Turner Publishing Company, 2014).

34. Leap et al., *Newark Community Street Team*, 54.

35. Basheer and Hoag, *Peace in the Hood*, 100.

36. Leap et al., *Newark Community Street Team*, 35,

37. Cantor is the co-chair of the Anchor Institutions Task Force, "a think tank and movement-building organization working to deepen and extend the democratic engagement of anchor institutions in their neighborhoods, cities, and regions." Anchor Institutions Task Force, https://www.margainc.com/initiatives/aitf.

38. Levin, "Criminal Justice Expertise," 2780.

39. Harry Boyte, *Civic Agency and the Cult of the Expert* (Dayton: Kettering Foundation, 2009).

40. See Nancy Cantor, "Transforming the Academy: The Urgency of Recommitting Higher Education to the Public Good," *Liberal Education* 106, no. 1/2 (2020); Nancy Cantor, "The Urgency of Recommitting Higher Education to the Public Good in 2020 and Beyond" (keynote address presented upon receiving the 10th Annual Ernest Boyer Award at the Annual Meeting of the Association of American Colleges and Universities, January 23, 2020).

41. For a discussion of how different conceptions of expertise operate in shaping the criminal justice policy debate, see Levin, "Criminal Justice Expertise."

42. This account of the Newark Public Safety Collaborative is based on publications and media reports, publicly available recordings of meetings, and interviews with the project leadership. Alejandro Gimenez-Santana, Joel M. Caplan, and Leslie W. Kennedy, "Data-informed

Community Engagement: The Newark Public Safety Collaborative," in *The Globalization of Evidence-Based Policing: Innovations in Bridging the Research-Practice Divide*, ed. Eric L. Piza and Brandon C. Welsh (London: Routledge, 2022), 191–205; Andres Rengifo and Lorena Avila, "The Future of Public Safety: Exploring the Power & Possibility of Newark's Reimagined Public Safety Ecosystem," n.d., https://newarksafety.org/wp-content/uploads/2023/02/TheFuture OfPublicSafety.pdf; Tom Jackman, "Data and Analytics Enable Community Groups to Become Partners in Public Safety," *Washington Post*, December 14, 2021.

43. Mayor Ras J. Baraka, State of the City Address Part II: "Newark. And Proud of It," https://www.youtube.com/watch?v=pa0vKAUi2o0.

44. Susan Sturm, "The Architecture of Inclusion: Advancing Workplace Equity in Higher Education," *Harvard Journal of Law and Gender* 29, no. 2 (2006): 249–334.

45. Newark Opportunity Youth Network, "Reimagining Public Safety in Newark," n.d., https://static1.squarespace.com/static/5f31746071617a7025df2436/t/6179f85ea21f9d0b787 2975a/1635383393517/NOYN_Report_10-27.pdf.

46. Cara Buckley and Daniel Victor, "What Did Frances McDormand Mean by an 'Inclusion Rider' at the Oscars?" *New York Times*, March 5, 2018, https://www.nytimes.com/2018/03/05 /movies/inclusion-rider-frances-mcdormand-oscars.html#:~:text=%E2%80%9CI%20 have%20two%20words%20to,standing%20had%20stories%20to%20tell.

47. This narrative draws from an interview with Andrea Levere, conducted by the author over Zoom on October 22, 2023.

48. Andrea Levere, "Making the Case for Enterprise Capital: One Nonprofit's Path to Financial Sustainability and Increased Impact," Bridgespan Group, January 13, 2022, https://www .bridgespan.org/insights/making-the-case-for-enterprise-capital.

49. Jennifer Gordon, *Suburban Sweatshops: The Fight for Immigrant Rights* (Cambridge, MA: Harvard University Press, 2005).

50. For a fuller description of the Fisk-Vanderbilt Master's-to-Ph.D. program, see Keivan G. Stassun, Susan P. Sturm, Kelly Holley-Bockelmann, Arnold Burger, David J. Ernst, and Donna Webb, "The Fisk-Vanderbilt Master's-to-Ph.D. Bridge Program: Recognizing, Enlisting, and Cultivating Unrealized or Unrecognized Potential in Underrepresented Minority Students," *American Journal of Physics* 79, no. 4 (2011): 374–79, https://doi.org/10.1119/1.3546069; Keivan G. Stassun, Arnold Burger, and Sheila Edwards Lange, "The Fisk-Vanderbilt Masters-to-PhD Program: A Model for Broadening Participation of Underrepresented Groups in the Physical Sciences through Effective Partnerships with Minority-Serving Institutions," *Journal of Geoscience Education* 58, no. 3 (2010): 135–44.

51. Nancy Cantor, Peter Englot, and Marilyn Higgins, "Making the Work of Anchor Institutions Stick: Building Coalitions and Collective Expertise," *Journal of Higher Education Outreach and Engagement* 17, no. 3 (2013): 17, 27.

52. Baraka, State of the City Address Part II: "Newark. And Proud of It."

Chapter Seven: Anti-Racism over the Long Haul

1. For a detailed and moving account of Jonathan Conyers's journey and transformative leadership, see Jonathan Conyers, *I Wasn't Supposed to Be Here: Finding My Voice, Finding My People, Finding My Way* (New York: Legacy Lit, 2023).

2. Rachel López, "Participatory Law Scholarship," *Columbia Law Review* 123, no. 6 (2023): 1795–1854.

3. Eesha Pendharker, "The Evolution of the Anti-CRT Movement: A Timeline," *Education Week*, December 13, 2022.

4. Martin Luther King Jr., *Letter from Birmingham Jail* (London: Penguin Books, 2018), 14.

5. Lani Guinier, *Lift Every Voice: Turning a Civil Rights Setback into a New Vision of Social Justice* (New York: Simon & Schuster, 2003), 58.

6. Activists Deepak Bhargava and Stephanie Luce underscore this insight in *Practical Radicals: Seven Strategies to Change the World* (New York: New Press, 2023).

7. Building Moving Project, Social Change Ecosystem Map, https://buildingmovement.org/our-work/movement-building/social-change-ecosystem-map; Erica Ariel Fox, Big Four Profile Survey, https://www.ericaarielfox.com/resources/big-four-profile/.

8. Lani Guinier, "From Racial Liberalism to Racial Literacy: *Brown v. Board of Education* and the Interest-Divergence Dilemma," *Journal of American History* 91, no. 1 (2004): 93, https://doi.org/10.2307/3659616.

9. Justice Sotomayor's dissent, 600 U.S. at 316, 318–19, criticizes the Court's majority for cementing "a superficial rule of colorblindness as a constitutional principle in an endemically segregated society where race has always mattered and continues to matter. The Court subverts the constitutional guarantee of equal protection by further entrenching racial inequality in education, the very foundation of our democratic government and pluralistic society." Justice Jackson's dissent, 600 U.S. at 407–8, expounds upon "the universal benefits of considering race in this context" and concludes that "the best that can be said of the majority's perspective is that it proceeds (ostrich-like) from the hope that preventing consideration of race will end racism. But if that is its motivation, the majority proceeds in vain. If the colleges of this country are required to ignore a thing that matters, it will not just go away. It will take longer for racism to leave us. And, ultimately, ignoring race just makes it matter more."

10. Lani Guinier, "Foreword: Demosprudence through Dissent," *Harvard Law Review* 122, no. 4 (2007): 4, 12.

11. Tina Rosenberg, *Join the Club: How Peer Pressure Can Transform the World* (New York: W. W. Norton, 2011), 123, quoted in Lani Guinier, *The Tyranny of the Meritocracy: Democratizing Higher Education in America* (Boston: Beacon Press, 2015), 92.

12. Nayantara Sen and Terry Keleher, *Creating Cultures and Practices for Racial Equity* (tool kit, Race Forward's Racial Equity in the Arts Innovation Lab, 2021), https://www.raceforward.org/system/files/Creating%20Cultures%20and%20Practices%20For%20Racial%20Equity_7.pdf.

13. Anthony S. Bryk, Louis M. Gomez, Alicia Grunow, and Paul G. LaMahieu, *Learning to Improve: How America's Schools Can Get Better at Getting Better* (Cambridge, MA: Harvard University Press, 2015).

14. Remarks of Assistant Attorney General Amy L. Solomon at the Giffords Center for Violence Intervention Community Violence Intervention Conference, Los Angeles, CA, June 27, 2023, https://www.ojp.gov/files/archives/speeches/2023/remarks-assistant-attorney-general-amy-l-solomon-giffords-center-violence-intervention.

15. Transcript of panel, "Intergenerational Movement Lawyering": "With All Deliberate Speed: The Past, Present, and Future of Racial Equity in Higher Education," April 4, 2024, https://www.youtube.com/watch?v=UfDFRbq_VQ0.

16. Reverend Dr. Otis Moss III, "In This 'House,'" Founder's Day Address, February 17, 2022, Morehouse College, https://www.youtube.com/watch?v=m5zlNL7Ltkc.

17. Reyhan Ayas, Paulina Tilly, and Devan Rawlings, "Cutting Costs at the Expense of Diversity," Revelio Labs, February 7, 2023, https://www.reveliolabs.com/news/social/cutting-costs-at-the-expense-of-diversity/; Kiara Alfonseca and Max Zahn, "How Corporate America Is Slashing DEI Workers amid Backlash to Diversity Programs," ABC News, July 7, 2023, https://abcnews.go.com/US/corporate-america-slashing-dei-workers-amid-backlash-diversity/story?id=100477952.

18. Marga Inc., and Newark Anchor Collaborative, "Promoting Racial Equity and Equitable Growth," May 2022, https://static1.squarespace.com/static/639cd715b33192583d618677/t/63fce2f8dc9af9027bde4eff/1677517563428/Newark-Anchor-Collaborative-Case-Study.pdf.

19. Bernard E. Harcourt, *Cooperation: A Political, Economic, and Social Theory* (New York: Columbia University Press, 2024), 60.

20. Harcourt, *Cooperation*, 62.

21. Harcourt, *Cooperation*, 9, 62, 141.

Commentary on Susan Sturm's *What Might Be*

1. From https://www.si.edu/spotlight/mlk?page=4&iframe=true. Note: many parts of this commentary are based on my acceptance remarks at the National Academy of Sciences annual meeting on April 30, 2023, and on a second speech, this one delivered at Harvard University on October 12, 2022.

2. Arthur M. Schlesinger Jr., *The Disuniting of America: Reflections on a Multicultural Society* (New York: W. W. Norton, 1992), 142, quoted in Jon Meacham, *The Soul of America: The Battle for Our Better Angels* (New York: Random House, 2018), 6.

3. Freeman A. Hrabowski, Philip J. Rous, and Peter H. Henderson, *The Empowered University: Shared Leadership, Culture Change, and Academic Success* (Baltimore: Johns Hopkins University Press, 2019), 35.

4. Eric Weiner, *The Geography of Bliss: One Grump's Search for the Happiest Places in the World* (New York: Hachette, 2008), 3.

5. Hrabowski, Rous, and Henderson, *The Empowered University*; Freeman A. Hrabowski, *The Resilient University: How Purpose and Inclusion Drive Student Success* (Baltimore: Johns Hopkins University Press, 2024).

6. See Hrabowski, Rous, and Henderson, *The Empowered University*.

7. David Kirp, *The College Dropout Scandal* (New York: Oxford University Press, 2019).

8. Freeman A. Hrabowski III and Peter H. Henderson, "Nothing Succeeds Like Success," *Issues in Science and Technology* (July 29, 2021), https://issues.org/nothing-succeeds-like-success-underrepresented-minorities-stem/.

9. Hrabowski and Henderson, "Nothing Succeeds Like Success."

10. My coauthors and I develop this idea in *The Empowered University*.

11. Initially, our stated goal was to increase the number of PhDs, assuming that would lead to a diverse faculty. In hindsight, we should have explicitly stated the goal of increasing diversity in the faculty.

12. Hrabowski and Henderson, "Nothing Succeeds Like Success."

13. Freeman Hrabowski, J. Tracy, and Peter Henderson, "Opinion: At a Crossroads: Reimagining Science, Engineering, and Medicine—and Its Practitioners," *Proceedings of the National Academy of Sciences* 117, no. 31 (2020): 18137, https://doi.org/10.1073/pnas.2013588117.

14. "Report: Science and Engineering Degrees Earned," National Science Foundation, https://ncses.nsf.gov/pubs/nsf23315/report/science-and-engineering-degrees-earned.

15. Freeman Hrabowski, "4 Pillars of College Success in Science," TED Talk, February 2013, https://www.ted.com/talks/freeman_hrabowski_4_pillars_of_college_success_in_science.

16. Hrabowski, Rous, and Henderson, *The Empowered University*, 111.

17. NSF INCLUDES (Inclusion across the Nation of Communities of Learners of Underrepresented Discoverers in Engineering and Science) transforms education and career pathways to help broaden participation in science and engineering. AGEP (Alliances for Graduate Education and the Professoriate) "supports alliances among institutions of higher education to design and implement strategies that increase the number of historically underrepresented STEM faculty and promote systemic change." NSF's "Build and Broaden" focuses on increasing participation in the social, behavioral, and economic sciences through support for research and training at minority-serving institutions. NSF ADVANCE supports system change projects to increase gender equity and inclusion for STEM faculty. NIH's FIRST program (Faculty Institutional Recruitment for Sustainable Transformation) aims to enhance and maintain cultures of inclusive excellence in the biomedical research community.

18. "Advancing Antiracism, Diversity, Equity, and Inclusion in STEMM Organizations," National Academies, 2023, https://nap.nationalacademies.org/catalog/26803/advancing-antiracism-diversity-equity-and-inclusion-in-stemm-organizations-beyond.

19. Hrabowski and Henderson, "Nothing Succeeds Like Success."

20. Anthony Fauci, "Kizzmekia Corbett," *Time*, February 17, 2021, https://time.com/collection/time100-next-2021/5937718/kizzmekia-corbett/.

21. "Kizzmekia Corbett Unlocked the Science of the Covid Vaccine," *New York Times*, February 9, 2023, https://www.nytimes.com/2023/02/09/science/covid-vaccine-kizzmekia-corbett.html.

22. Hrabowski, Tracy, and Henderson, "At a Crossroads."

BIBLIOGRAPHY

Adelstein, Janna, and Alicia Bannon. "State Supreme Court Diversity—April 2021 Update." Brennan Center for Justice, April 20, 2021. https://www.brennancenter.org/our-work /research-reports/state-supreme-court-diversity-april-2021-update.

Ahmed, Sara. *Complaint!* Durham: Duke University Press, 2021.

Alfonseca, Kiara, and Max Zahn. "How Corporate America Is Slashing DEI Workers amid Backlash to Diversity Programs." ABC News, July 7, 2023. https://abcnews.go.com/US/corporate -america-slashing-dei-workers-amid-backlash-diversity/story?id=100477952.

Allen, Danielle. "Toward a Connected Society." In *Our Compelling Interests: The Value of Diversity for Democracy and a Prosperous Society*, ed. Earl Lewis and Nancy Cantor, 71–105. Princeton: Princeton University Press, 2016.

"Anchor Institutions Task Force (AITF)." Marga Inc. https://www.margainc.com/initiatives/ aitf.

Annala, Mikko, Juha Leppänen, Silva Mertsola, and Charles Sabel. "Humble Government: How to Realize Ambitious Reforms Prudently." Helsinki, 2020. https://tietokayttoon.fi /documents/1927382/2158283/Humble+Government.pdf/.

Apfelbaum, Evan P., Michael I. Norton, and Samuel R. Sommers. "Racial Color Blindness: Emergence, Practice, and Implications." *Current Directions in Psychological Science* 21, no. 3 (2012): 205–9. https://doi.org/10.1177/0963721411434980.

Armstrong, Megan, Eathyn Edwards, and Duwain Pinder. "Corporate Commitments to Racial Justice: An Update." McKinsey Institute for Black Mobility, February 21, 2023. https://www .mckinsey.com/bem/our-insights/corporate-commitments-to-racial-justice-an-update.

Asian American Performers Action Coalition (AAPAC), Pun Bandhu, and Julienne Hanzelka Kim. "The Visibility Report: Racial Representation on NYC Stages." 2021. http://www .aapacnyc.org/2018-2019.html.

Bahr, Sarah. "White Actors and Directors Still Dominate Broadway Stages, Report Finds." *New York Times*, October 1, 2020. https://www.nytimes.com/2020/10/01/theater/new-york -theater-diversity-report.html.

Baldwin, James. *Collected Essays*. Ed. Toni Morrison. New York: Penguin Random House, 1998.

Banaji, Mahzarin R., and Anthony G. Greenwald. *Blindspot: Hidden Biases of Good People*. New York: Random House Publishing Group, 2013.

Barnes, Mario L. "Racial Paradox in a Law and Society Odyssey." *Law & Society Review* 44, no. 3/4 (September/December 2010): 469–86. https://doi.org/10.1111/j.1540-5893.2010 .00411.x.

Basheer, Aquil, and Christina Hoag. *Peace in the Hood: Working with Gang Members to End the Violence*. Nashville: Turner Publishing Company, 2014.

Bell, Derrick A. "*Brown v. Board of Education* and the Interest Convergence Dilemma." *Harvard Law Review* 93, no. 3 (1980): 518–33. https://doi.org/10.2307/1340546.

———. *Faces at the Bottom of the Well: The Permanence of Racism*. New York: Basic Books, 1992.

Bell, Monica. "Safety, Friendship, and Dreams." *Harvard Civil Rights-Civil Liberties Law Review* 54 (2019): 703–39.

Bhargava, Deepak, and Stephanie Luce. *Practical Radicals: Seven Strategies to Change the World*. New York: New Press, 2023.

Blazina, Carrie, and Kiana Cox. "Black and White Americans Are Far Apart in Their Views of Reparations for Slavery." Pew Research Center, November 28, 2022. https://www.pewresearch.org/short-reads/2022/11/28/black-and-white-americans-are-far-apart-in-their-views-of-reparations-for-slavery/.

"*Blue*: The Documentary: Go Behind the Scenes of the Making of *Blue*." The Kennedy Center, March 25, 2022. https://youtu.be/UqYXIOCDbfU?feature=shared.

Bonilla-Silva, Eduardo. *Racism without Racists: Color-Blind Racism and the Persistence of Racial Inequality in America*. Lanham, MD: Rowman & Littlefield, 2022.

———. "The Structure of Racism in Color-Blind, 'Post-Racial' America." *American Behavioral Scientist* 59, no. 11 (2015): 1358–76. https://doi.org/10.1177/0002764215586826.

Boyte, Harry. *Civic Agency and the Cult of the Expert*. Dayton: Kettering Foundation, 2009.

brown, adrienne maree. *Emergent Strategy: Shaping Change, Changing Worlds*. Chico, CA: AK Press, 2017.

Brown, Brené. *Dare to Lead: Brave Work, Tough Conversations, Whole Hearts*. New York: Random House, 2018.

Bryk, Anthony S., Louis M. Gomez, Alicia Grunow, and Paul G. LeMahieu. *Learning to Improve: How America's Schools Can Get Better at Getting Better*. Cambridge, MA: Harvard Education Press, 2015.

Buckley, Cara, and Daniel Victor. "What Did Frances McDormand Mean by an 'Inclusion Rider' at the Oscars?" *New York Times*, March 5, 2018. https://www.nytimes.com/2018/03/05/movies/inclusion-rider-frances-mcdormand-oscars.html#:~:text=%E2%80%9CI%20have%20two%20words%20to,standing%20had%20stories%20to%20tell.

Bussanich, Marc. "Newark Swears in Ras Baraka as Mayor." *Labor Press*, July 2, 2014. https://www.laborpress.org/newark-swears-in-ras-baraka-as-mayor.

Cantor, Nancy. "Transforming the Academy: The Urgency of Recommitting Higher Education to the Public Good." *Liberal Education* 106, no. 1/2 (2020).

Cantor, Nancy, Peter Englot, and Marilyn Higgins, "Making the Work of Anchor Institutions Stick: Building Coalitions and Collective Expertise." *Journal of Higher Education Outreach and Engagement* 17, no. 3 (2013): 17–46.

Carnevale, Anthony P., and Jeff Strohl. "Separate & Unequal: How Higher Education Reinforces the Intergenerational Reproduction of White Racial Privilege." Georgetown Public Policy Institute, July 2013. https://cew.georgetown.edu/wp-content/uploads/SeparateUnequal.FR_.pdf.

Carpenter, Anna E., Colleen F. Shanahan, Jessica K. Steinberg, and Alyx Mark. "Judges in Lawyerless Courts." *Georgetown Law Journal* 110 (2022): 509–67.

Castilla, Emilio J. "Gender, Race, and Meritocracy in Organizational Careers." *American Journal of Sociology* 113 (2008): 1479–1526.

Chaskin, Robert J., Prudence Brown, Sudhir Venkatesh, and Avid Vidal. *Building Community Capacity.* New York: Walter de Gruyter, 2001.

Clair, Matthew, and Alix S. Winter. "How Judges Think about Racial Disparities: Situational Decision-Making in the Criminal Justice System." *Criminology* 54, no. 2 (2016): 332–59. https://doi.org/10.1111/1745-9125.12106.

Columbia Justice Lab. "Shifting Roles, Responsibilities, and Resources to Communities." In *Taking on Transformation.* Forthcoming. https://www.takingontransformation.org/topics /community-support-for-youth.

Conyers, Jonathan. *I Wasn't Supposed to Be Here: Finding My Voice, Finding My People, Finding My Way.* New York: Legacy Lit, 2023.

Cornett, Logan, and Natalie Anne Knowlton. "Public Perspectives on Trust & Confidence in the Courts." Institute for the Advancement of the American Legal System, June 2020. https://iaals.du.edu/sites/default/files/documents/publications/public_perspectives_on _trust_and_confidence_in_the_courts.pdf.

Cover, Robert M. "Foreword: Nomos and Narrative." *Harvard Law Review* 97, no. 1 (1983): 4–68.

Crafting Democratic Futures. "Reparations Syllabi." https://craftingdemocraticfutures.org /reparations-syllabi/.

Crenshaw, Kimberlé. "Mapping the Margins: Intersectionality, Identity Politics, and Violence against Women of Color." *Stanford Law Review* 43, no. 6 (July 1991): 1241–99. https://doi .org/10.2307/1229039.

Crenshaw, Kimberlé Williams. "Race, Reform, and Retrenchment: Transformation and Legiti- mation in Antidiscrimination Law." *Harvard Law Review* 101, no. 7 (May 1988): 1384–87. https://doi.org/10.2307/1341398.

Crenshaw, Kimberlé, Neil Gotanda, Gary Peller, and Kendall Thomas, eds. *Critical Race Theory: The Key Writings That Formed the Movement.* New York: New Press, 1996.

"CRT Forward Tracking Project." https://crtforward.law.ucla.edu/map.

Dawson, Michael C. *Behind the Mule: Race and Class in African-American Politics.* Princeton: Princeton University Press, 1995.

Delgado, Richard, and Jean Stefancic. *Critical Race Theory: The Cutting Edge.* Philadelphia: Temple University Press, 2013.

Diamond, John B., and Amanda E. Lewis. "Opportunity Hoarding and the Maintenance of 'White' Educational Space." *American Behavioral Scientist* 66, no. 11 (May 18, 2022): 1470–89. https://doi.org/10.1177/00027642211066048.

DiAngelo, Robin. *White Fragility: Why It's So Hard for White People to Talk about Racism.* Bos- ton: Beacon Press, 2018.

Ditlmann, Ruth K., Valerie Purdie-Vaughns, John F. Dovidio, and Michael J. Naft. "The Implicit Power Motive in Intergroup Dialogues about the History of Slavery." *Journal of Personality and Social Psychology* 112, no. 1 (2017): 116–35. https://doi.org/10.1037/pspp0000118.

Dorf, Michael C., and Charles F. Sabel. "A Constitution of Democratic Experimentalism." *Co- lumbia Law Review* 98, no. 2 (1998): 267–473. https://doi.org/10.2307/1123411.

Douglas, Mary. *How Institutions Think.* Syracuse: Syracuse University Press, 1986.

Douglass, Frederick. "The New President." *Douglass' Monthly* (March 1861): 419.

Du Bois, W.E.B. *The Souls of Black Folk*. New York: Dover, 1994.

Duguid, Michelle M., and Melissa C. Thomas-Hunt. "Condoning Stereotyping? How Awareness of Stereotyping Prevalence Impacts Expression of Stereotypes." *Journal of Applied Psychology* 100, no. 2 (2015): 343–59. https://doi.org/10.1037/a0037908.

Dweck, Carol S. *Mindset: The New Psychology of Success*. New York: Random House, 2006.

Dzur, Albert W. *Democratic Professionalism: Citizen Participation and the Construction of Professional Ethics, Identity, and Practice*. University Park: Penn State University Press, 2008.

Edelman, Lauren B. "Legal Ambiguity and Symbolic Structures: Organizational Mediation of Civil Rights Law." *American Journal of Sociology* 97, no. 6 (May 1992): 1531–76. https://doi.org/10.1086/229939.

Edmondson, Amy C. *The Fearless Organization: Creating Psychological Safety in the Workplace for Learning, Innovation, and Growth*. Hoboken, NJ: Wiley, 2018.

Ellis, Eddie. "An Open Letter to Our Friends on the Question of Language." *Parole Preparation & Appeal Resources* (2020). https://ir.lawnet.fordham.edu/pp/5.

Ely, Robin J., and Alexandra C. Feldberg. "Organizational Remedies for Discrimination." In *The Oxford Handbook of Workplace Discrimination*, ed. Adrienne J. Colella and Eden B. King, 387–408. New York: Oxford University Press, 2016.

Ely, Robin, and David Thomas. "Getting Serious about Diversity: Enough Already with the Business Case." *Harvard Business Review*, November–December 2020. https://hbr.org/2020/11/getting-serious-about-diversity-enough-already-with-the-business-case.

Eurich, Tasha. "What Self-Awareness Really Is (and How to Cultivate It)." *Harvard Business Review*, January 4, 2018.

Fishkin, Joseph. *Bottlenecks: A New Theory of Equal Opportunity*. New York: Oxford University Press, 2014.

Fiske, Susan T., and Shelley E. Taylor. *Social Cognition: From Brains to Culture*. 4th ed. London: Sage, 2021.

Flagg, Barbara J. "'Was Blind, but Now I See': White Race Consciousness and the Requirement of Discriminatory Intent." *Michigan Law Review* 91, no. 5 (1993): 953–1017. https://doi.org/10.2307/1289678.

Follett, Mary Parker. *Dynamic Administration: The Collected Papers of Mary Parker Follett*, ed. E. M. Fox and L. Urwick. London: Pitman Publishing, 1940.

Francis, Marquise. "Newark Was One of the Deadliest Cities in the U.S. Now It Wants to Set an Example on Public Safety Reform." *Yahoo! News*, June 25, 2022. https://www.yahoo.com/news/newark-was-one-of-the-deadliest-cities-in-america-now-it-wants-to-be-a-blueprint-for-public-safety-reform-163320757.html.

Freire, Paulo. *Pedagogy of the Oppressed*. 1970. New York: Continuum, 2011.

Galanter, Marc. "Why the 'Haves' Come Out Ahead: Speculations on the Limits of Legal Change." *Law and Society Review* 9, no. 1 (1974): 95–160.

Galinsky, Adam D., Gillian Ku, and Cynthia S. Wang. "Perspective-Taking and Self-Other Overlap: Fostering Social Bonds and Facilitating Social Coordination." *Group Processes & Intergroup Relations* 8, no. 2 (2005): 109–24. https://doi.org/10.1177/1368430205051060.

Ganz, Marshall. "Leading Change: Leadership, Organization, and Social Movements." In *Handbook of Leadership Theory and Practice*, ed. Nitin Nohria and Rakesh Khurana. Boston: Harvard Business Press, 2010.

Gaventa, John. "Finding the Spaces for Change: A Power Analysis." *Institute of Developmental Studies Bulletin* 37, no. 6 (2006): 23–33.

———. "Powercube: Understanding Power for Social Change." September 6, 2009. https://www.powercube.net/an-introduction-to-power-analysis/.

Gertner, Nancy. "Reimagining Judging." In *Parsimony and Other Radical Ideas about Justice*, ed. Jeremy Travis and Bruce Western. New York: New Press, 2023.

Gilliam, Franklin D., Jr. "The Architecture of a New Racial Discourse." FrameWorks, June 14, 2006. https://www.frameworksinstitute.org/publication/the-architecture-of-a-new-racial-discourse.

Gilmore, Ruth Wilson. Interview by Chenjerai Kumanyika. *Intercepted* (podcast), *The Intercept*, June 10, 2020. https://theintercept.com/2020/06/10/ruth-wilson-gilmore-makes-the-case-for-abolition/.

Godsil, Rachel, and Brianna Goodale. "Telling Our Own Story: The Role of Narrative in Racial Healing." June 2013. https://perception.org/wp-content/uploads/2014/11/Telling-Our-Own-Story.pdf.

Gonzalez, Kimberly, Sara Dorn, and Sahalie Donaldson. "A Timeline on the Closure of Rikers Island." *City & State New York*, March 6, 2024. https://www.cityandstateny.com/politics/2024/03/timeline-closure-rikers-island/376662/.

Gordon, Jennifer. *Suburban Sweatshops: The Fight for Immigrant Rights*. Cambridge, MA: Harvard University Press, 2005.

Gould, Roger V. *Insurgent Identities: Class, Community, and Protest in Paris from 1848 to the Commune*. Chicago: University of Chicago Press, 1995.

Governor's Select Commission on Civil Disorder, State of New Jersey. "Report for Action." February 1968. https://www.ojp.gov/pdffiles1/Digitization/69748NCJRS.pdf.

Guinier, Lani. "From Racial Liberalism to Racial Literacy: *Brown v. Board of Education* and the Interest-Divergence Dilemma." *Journal of American History* 91, no. 1 (2004): 92–118. https://doi.org/10.2307/3659616.

———. *Lift Every Voice: Turning a Civil Rights Setback into a New Vision of Social Justice*. New York: Simon & Schuster, 2003.

———. *The Tyranny of the Meritocracy: Democratizing Higher Education in America*. Boston: Beacon Press, 2015.

Guinier, Lani, and Gerald Torres. *The Miner's Canary: Enlisting Race, Resisting Power, Transforming Democracy*. Cambridge, MA: Harvard University Press, 2002.

Gurin, Patricia, Biren (Ratnesh) A. Nagda, and Ximena Zúñiga. *Dialogue across Difference: Practice, Theory, and Research on Intergroup Dialogue*. New York: Russell Sage Foundation, 2013.

Harcourt, Bernard. "The Systems Fallacy: A Genealogy and Critique of Public Policy and Cost-Benefit Analysis." *Journal of Legal Studies* 47 (2018): 419–47.

Helms, Janet E. *Black and White Racial Identity: Theory, Research, and Practice*. Westport, CT: Praeger, 1990.

Hewlett, Sylvia Ann, and Carolyn Buck Luce. "Extreme Jobs: The Dangerous Allure of the 70-Hour Workweek." *Harvard Business Review* (December 2006): 1–12.

Hoffman, Warren. *The Great White Way: Race and the Broadway Musical*. 2nd ed. New Brunswick, NJ: Rutgers University Press, 2020.

Hrabowski, Freeman A. *Holding Fast to Dreams: Empowering Youth from the Civil Rights Crusade to STEM Achievement.* Boston: Beacon Press, 2016.

Hrabowski, Freeman, Philip J. Rous, and Peter H. Henderson. *The Empowered University: Shared Leadership, Culture Change, and Academic Success.* Baltimore: Johns Hopkins University Press, 2019.

Hynson, Rachel. "Creating Connections Consortium, Summary Report, 2013–2023." May 2023. https://bpb-us-e2.wpmucdn.com/sites.middlebury.edu/dist/2/2727/files/2023/10/C3-Summary-Report-For-general-distribution.pdf.

Idowu, Angel. "Folded Map Project Highlights Chicago Segregation, Gentrification." WTTW, February 11, 2020. https://news.wttw.com/2020/02/11/folded-map-project-highlights-chicago-segregation-gentrification.

Iyer, Deepa. "Social Change Ecosystem Map." 2017. https://buildingmovement.org/our-work/movement-building/social-change-ecosystem-map.

Jackman, Tom. "Data and Analytics Enable Community Groups to Become Partners in Public Safety." *Washington Post,* December 14, 2021.

Jenkins, Alan. "Shifting the Narrative: What It Takes to Reframe the Debate for Social Justice in the US." Othering & Belonging Institute, April 18, 2018. https://belonging.berkeley.edu/shifting-narrative.

John J. Heldrich Center for Workforce Development, Rutgers University. "A Workplace Divided: How Americans View Discrimination and Race on the Job." January 17, 2002. https://www.heldrich.rutgers.edu/work/workplace-divided-how-americans-view-discrimination-and-race-job.

Johnson, Barry. *Polarity Management: Identifying and Managing Unsolvable Problems.* Amherst, MA: HRD Press, 1992.

Johnson, Charles Jeh. "Report from the Special Adviser on Equal Justice in the New York State Courts." State of New York Unified Court System, 2020. https://www.nycourts.gov/whatsnew/pdf/SpecialAdviserEqualJusticeReport.pdf.

Jost, John T., and Mahzarin R. Banaji. "The Role of Stereotyping in System-Justification and the Production of False Consciousness." *British Journal of Social Psychology* 33, no. 1 (1994): 1–27. https://doi.org/10.1111/j.2044-8309.1994.tb01008.x.

Kahane, Adam. *Collaborating with the Enemy: How to Work with People You Don't Agree with or Like or Trust.* Oakland, CA: Berrett-Koehler Publishers, 2017.

Karakatsanis, Alec. *Usual Cruelty: The Complicity of Lawyers in the Criminal Injustice System.* New York: New Press, 2019.

Katznelson, Ira. *When Affirmative Action Was White: An Untold History of Racial Inequality in Twentieth-Century America.* New York: W. W. Norton, 2005.

Kendall, Frances E. *Understanding White Privilege: Creating Pathways to Authentic Relationships across Race.* New York: Routledge, 2013.

Kendi, Ibram X. *How to Be an Antiracist.* New York: One World, 2019.

Kerr, Dara. "2 Black TikTok Workers Claim Discrimination: Both Were Fired after Complaining to HR." NPR, September 21, 2023. https://www.npr.org/2023/09/21/1200727549/2-black-tiktok-workers-claim-discrimination.

Kiefer, Eric. "Watch Newark Mayor's State of the City Speech: 'Belief in Ourselves.'" *Patch,* March 16, 2022. https://patch.com/new-jersey/newarknj/watch-newark-mayor-s-state-city

-speech-belief-ourselves; https://www.facebook.com/watch/?ref=embed_video&v
=354941466527239.

King, Martin Luther, Jr. *Letter from Birmingham Jail*. London: Penguin Books, 2018.

Kizer, Matt. "The Ten out of Twelve: It's a Lie." *Scenic & Lighting Design*, August 16, 2016. https://
scenicandlighting.com/article/the-ten-out-of-twelve-its-a-lie/.

Knapp, Raymond, and Holley Replogle-Wong. "A Conversation with Jeanine Tesori." *Studies in
Musical Theatre* 17, no. 1 (2023): 35–53. https://doi.org/10.1386/smt_00114_7.

Ku, Gillian, Cynthia S. Wang, and Adam D. Galinsky. "The Promise and Perversity of
Perspective-Taking in Organizations." *Research in Organizational Behavior* 35 (2015): 79–102.
https://doi.org/10.1016/j.riob.2015.07.003.

Leap, Jorja, Mark Leap, Karrah Lompa, and Whitney Gouche. *Evaluation of the Newark Community Street Team* (February 2024). https://www.newarkcommunitystreetteam.org/wp
-content/uploads/2024/03/NCST-Innovations-CBCR-Evaluation_FINAL.pdf.

Levin, Benjamin. "Criminal Justice Expertise." *Fordham Law Review* 90, no. 6 (2022): 2777–2840.

Lippman, Jonathan. "A More Just New York City: Independent Commission on New York City
Criminal Justice and Incarceration Reform." New York, 2017. https://static1.squarespace
.com/static/5b6de4731aef1de914f43628/t/5b96c6f81ae6cf5e9c5f186d/1536607993842
/Lippman%2BCommission%2BReport%2BFINAL%2BSingles.pdf.

López, Rachel. "Participatory Law Scholarship." *Columbia Law Review* 123, no. 6 (2023):
1795–1854.

Lorde, Audre. "Age, Race, Class, and Sex: Women Redefining Difference." In *Sister Outsider:
Essays and Speeches*, 114–23. New York: Crossing Press, 1984.

———. "Learning from the 60s." In *Sister Outsider: Essays and Speeches*, 134–44. New York:
Crossing Press, 1984.

———. "The Master's Tools Will Never Dismantle the Master's House." In *Sister Outsider: Essays and Speeches*, 110–14. New York: Crossing Press, 1984.

Lukes, Steven. *Power: A Radical View*. 1974. New York: Palgrave Macmillan, 2005.

Magee, Rhonda V. *The Inner Work of Racial Justice: Healing Ourselves and Transforming Our
Communities through Mindfulness*. New York: TarcherPerigree, 2019.

Marga Inc., and Newark Anchor Collaborative. "Promoting Racial Equity and Equitable
Growth." May 2022. https://static1.squarespace.com/static/639cd715b33192583d618677
/t/63fce2f8dc9af9027bde4eff/1677517563428/Newark-Anchor-Collaborative-Case
-Study.pdf.

Matsuda, Mari J. "When the First Quail Calls: Multiple Consciousness as Jurisprudential
Method." *Women's Rights Law Reporter* 11, no. 1 (1989): 7–10.

McGhee, Heather C. *The Sum of Us: What Racism Costs Everyone and How We Can Prosper
Together*. New York: One World, 2021.

McIntosh, Peggy. "White Privilege: Unpacking the Invisible Knapsack." *Peace and Freedom
Magazine* (July/August 1989): 10–12. https://www.nationalseedproject.org/key-seed-texts
/white-privilege-unpacking-the-invisible-knapsack.

Minkin, Rachel. "Diversity, Equity and Inclusion in the Workplace." Pew Research Center,
May 17, 2023. https://www.pewresearch.org/social-trends/2023/05/17/diversity-equity
-and-inclusion-in-the-workplace/.

Minow, Martha. *Making All the Difference*. Ithaca: Cornell University Press, 2016.

Myers, Victoria. "An Interview with Jeanine Tesori." *The Interval*, March 18, 2015. https://www
.theintervalny.com/interviews/2015/03/an-interview-with-jeanine-tesori/.

National Advisory Commission on Civil Disorders United States. "Kerner Commission Report
on the Causes, Events, and Aftermaths of the Civil Disorders of 1967." Washington, DC,
1967.

Newark Opportunity Youth Network. "Reimagining Public Safety in Newark." N.d. https://
static1.squarespace.com/static/5f31746071617a7025df2436/t/6179f85ea21f9d0b7872975a
/1635383393517/NOYN_Report_10-27.pdf.

Omi, Michael, and Howard Winant. *Racial Formation in the United States*. 3rd ed. New York:
Routledge, 2014.

Orfield, Gary. *The Walls around Opportunity: The Failure of Colorblind Policy for Higher Education*. Princeton: Princeton University Press, 2022.

Orfield, Gary, Erica Frankenberg, Jongyeon Ee, and Jennifer B. Ayscue. "Harming Our Common
Future: America's Segregated Schools 65 Years after *Brown*." Civil Rights Project, May 10, 2019.
https://www.civilrightsproject.ucla.edu/research/k-12-education/integration-and-diversity
/harming-our-common-future-americas-segregated-schools-65-years-after-brown.

Oteri, Frank J. "Jeanine Tesori: Holding Center Stage." NewMusic USA, December 1, 2018.
https://newmusicusa.org/nmbx/jeanine-tesori-holding-center-stage/.

Pendharkar, Eesha. "The Evolution of the Anti-CRT Movement: A Timeline." *Education Week*,
December 13, 2023.

Perception Institute. "Implicit Bias." 2019. https://perception.org/research/implicit-bias/.

Pew Research Center. "On Views of Race and Inequality, Blacks and Whites Are Worlds Apart."
June 27, 2016. https://www.pewresearch.org/social-trends/2016/06/27/on-views-of-race
-and-inequality-blacks-and-whites-are-worlds-apart/.

Piza, Eric L., and Brandon C. Welsh. *The Globalization of Evidence-Based Policing: Innovations
in Bridging the Research-Practice Divide*. London: Routledge, 2022.

powell, john a. *Racing to Justice: Transforming Our Conceptions of Self and Other to Build an Inclusive Society*. Bloomington: Indiana University Press, 2012.

Price, Clement Alexander. "Newark Remembers the Summer of 1967, So Should We All." *The
Positive Community* (July/August 2007): 20–21.

Purdie-Vaughns, Valerie, Claude M. Steele, Paul G. Davies, Ruth Ditlmann, and Jennifer Randall
Crosby. "Social Identity Contingencies: How Diversity Cues Signal Threat or Safety for
African Americans in Mainstream Institutions." *Journal of Personality and Social Psychology*
94, no. 4 (2008): 615–30. https://doi.org/10.1037/0022-3514.94.4.615.

Purdie-Vaughns, Valerie, and Gregory M. Walton. "Is Multiculturalism Bad for African Americans? Redefining Inclusion through the Lens of Identity Safety." In *Moving beyond Prejudice
Reduction: Pathways to Positive Intergroup Relations*, ed. Linda R. Tropp and Robyn K. Mallett, 159–77. American Psychological Association, 2011. https://doi.org/10.1037/12319-008.

Rengifo, Andres, and Lorena Avila. "The Future of Public Safety: Exploring the Power & Possibility of Newark's Reimagined Public Safety Ecosystem." N.d. https://Newarksafety.org
/Wp-Content/Uploads/2023/02/TheFutureOfPublicSafety.pdf.

Rhone-Collins, Michelle. "Navigating Race and New Leadership in a Time of Upheaval." *Stanford Social Innovation Review*, September 16, 2020. https://ssir.org/articles/entry/navigating
_race_and_new_leadership_in_a_time_of_upheaval#.

Ridgeway, Cecilia L. "Why Status Matters for Inequality." *American Sociological Review* 79, no. 1 (2014): 1–10.

Robinson, Russell K. "Perceptual Segregation." *Columbia Law Review* 108, no. 5 (2008): 1093–1180.

Rodriguez, Alejo. "The Obscure Legacy of Mass Incarceration: Parole Board Abuses of People Serving Parole Eligible Life Sentences." *City University of New York Law Review* 22, no. 2 (2019): 33–59.

Rodriguez, Alejo Dao'ud. "Sing Sing Sits Up the River." In *The Outlaw Bible of American Poetry*, ed. Alan Kaufman. New York: Thunder's Mouth Press, 1999.

Roithmayr, Daria. *Reproducing Racism: How Everyday Choices Lock in White Advantage.* New York: New York University Press, 2014.

Rosenberg, Tina. *Join the Club: How Peer Pressure Can Transform the World.* New York: W. W. Norton, 2011.

Rothstein, Richard. *The Color of Law: A Forgotten History of How Our Government Segregated America.* New York: Liveright Publishing, 2017.

Rothstein, Richard, and Leah Rothstein. *Just Action: How to Challenge Segregation Enacted under the Color of Law.* New York: Liveright Publishing, 2023.

Sabel, Charles F. "Studied Trust: Building New Forms of Cooperation in a Volatile Economy." *Human Relations* 46, no. 9 (1993): 1133–70. https://doi.org/10.1177/001872679304600907.

Sabel, Charles F., and William H. Simon. "Destabilization Rights: How Public Law Litigation Succeeds." *Harvard Law Review* 117, no. 4 (2004): 1015–1101. https://doi.org/10.2307/4093364.

Schaeffer, Katherine, and Khadijah Edwards. "Black Americans Differ from Other U.S. Adults over Whether Individual or Structural Racism Is a Bigger Problem." Pew Research Center, November 15, 2022. https://www.pewresearch.org/short-reads/2022/11/15/black-americans-differ-from-other-u-s-adults-over-whether-individual-or-structural-racism-is-a-bigger-problem/.

Schön, Donald A. *The Reflective Practitioner: How Professionals Think in Action.* New York: Basic Books, 1983.

Sen, Nayantara, and Terry Keleher. *Creating Cultures and Practices for Racial Equity.* Tool kit, Race Forward's Racial Equity in the Arts Innovation Lab, 2021. https://www.raceforward.org/system/files/Creating%20Cultures%20and%20Practices%20For%20Racial%20Equity_7.pdf.

Sewell, William H. "A Theory of Structure: Duality, Agency, and Transformation." *American Journal of Sociology* 98, no. 1 (1992): 1–29. http://www.jstor.org/stable/2781191.

Shearn, Ian. "The Forging of Ras Baraka: How He Was Made for This Fight." NJ Spotlight News, August 31, 2020. https://www.njspotlightnews.org/2020/08/newark-mayor-ras-baraka-poet-amiri-cops-arrests-protests-street-activist/.

Smith, Clint. *How the Word Is Passed: A Reckoning with the History of Slavery across America.* New York: Little, Brown, 2021.

Smith, Kenwyn K., and David N. Berg. *Paradoxes of Group Life: Understanding Conflict, Paralysis, and Movement in Group Life.* San Francisco: Jossey-Bass, 1987.

Smith, Wendy K., Marianne W. Lewis, Paula Jarzabkowski, and Ann Langley, eds. *The Oxford Handbook of Organizational Paradox.* Oxford: Oxford University Press, 2017.

Sommers, Samuel R., and Michael I. Norton. "Lay Theories about White Racists: What Constitutes Racism (and What Doesn't)." *Group Processes & Intergroup Relations* 9, no. 1 (January 2006): 117–38. https://doi.org/10.1177/1368430206059881.

Spencer Hewitt, Rachel. "Introduction." Speech. Public Theater, New York, December 6, 2019.

Spinak, Jane M. *The End of Family Court: How Abolishing the Court Brings Justice to Children and Families.* New York: New York University Press, 2023.

Stassun, Keivan G., Susan P. Sturm, Kelly Holley-Bockelmann, Arnold Burger, David J. Ernst, and Donna Webb. "The Fisk-Vanderbilt Master's-to-Ph.D. Bridge Program: Recognizing, Enlisting, and Cultivating Unrealized or Unrecognized Potential in Underrepresented Minority Students." *American Journal of Physics* 79, no. 4 (2011): 374–79. https://doi.org/10.1119/1.3546069.

Stevenson, Bryan. "We Need to Talk about an Injustice." TED Talk, March 2012. https://www.ted.com/talks/bryan_stevenson_we_need_to_talk_about_an_injustice.

Stevenson, Howard C. *Promoting Racial Literacy in Schools: Differences That Make a Difference.* New York: Teachers College Press, 2014.

Stewart, Abigail J. "Choosing Both: Finding a Path as an Academic Feminist." In *Reflections from Pioneering Women in Psychology,* ed. Jamila Bookwala and Nicky J. Newton, 305–17. Cambridge: Cambridge University Press, 2022.

Stewart, Abigail J., and Virginia Valian. *An Inclusive Academy: Achieving Diversity and Excellence.* Cambridge, MA: MIT Press, 2018.

Stone, Douglas, Bruce Patton, and Sheila Heen. *Difficult Conversations: How to Discuss What Matters Most.* New York: Penguin, 2010.

Sturm, Susan. "The Architecture of Inclusion: Advancing Workplace Equity in Higher Education." *Harvard Journal of Law and Gender* 29, no. 2 (2006): 247–334.

———. "'Mastering' Intervention in Prisons." *Yale Law Journal* 88, no. 5 (1979): 1062–91.

———. "Second Generation Employment Discrimination: A Structural Approach." *Columbia Law Review* 101, no. 3 (2001): 458–568.

Sturm, Susan, Tim Eatman, John Saltmarsh, and Adam Bush. "Full Participation: Building the Architecture for Diversity and Community Engagement in Higher Education." September 2011. https://iagathering.org/mainsite/wp-content/uploads/fullparticipation.pdf.

Sturm, Susan, and Lani Guinier. "The Law School Matrix: Reforming Legal Education in a Culture of Competition and Conformity." *Vanderbilt Law Review* 60, no. 2 (2007): 515–53.

Sturm, Susan, and Kinga Makovi. "Full Participation in the *Yale Law Journal.*" *Yale Law Journal* (2015): 1–133. https://www.yalelawjournal.org/files/FullParticipationintheYaleLawJournal_otc6qdnr.pdf.

Sturm, Susan, and Vivian Nixon. "Home-Grown Social Capital: How Higher Education for Formerly Incarcerated Women Facilitates Family and Community Transformation." Aspen Ascend Institute, 2018. https://ascend.aspeninstitute.org/wp-content/uploads/2017/10/2015093020Social20Capital_Sturm_Nixon_2.pdf.

Sturm, Susan P., and Haran Tae. "Leading with Conviction: The Transformative Role of Formerly Incarcerated Leaders in Reducing Mass Incarceration." Center for Institutional and Social Change, 2017. https://scholarship.law.columbia.edu/faculty_scholarship/2033.

Sugrue, Tom. "Less Separate, Still Unequal: Diversity and Equality in 'Post–Civil Rights' America." In *Our Compelling Interests: The Value of Diversity for Democracy and a Prosperous Society*, ed. Earl Lewis and Nancy Cantor, 39–70. Princeton: Princeton University Press, 2017.

Taber, Niloufer, Lina Cook, Chris Mai, and Jennifer Hill. "The Impacts of College-in-Prison Participation on Safety and Employment in New York State: An Analysis of College Students Funded by the Criminal Justice Investment Initiative." Vera Institute of Justice, November 2023. https://www.vera.org/downloads/publications/Impacts-of-College-in-Prison-in-NYS-Report.pdf.

Tatum, Beverly Daniel. "The Development of White Identity." In *Why Are All the Black Kids Sitting Together in the Cafeteria? And Other Conversations about the Development of Racial Identity*. New York: Basic Books, 1997.

Taylor, Kimberly Hayes. "For Teens, Mall Is a Place They Can Count On." *Star Tribune*, June 30, 1994.

———. "Urban Teens Strut Stuff in Megahangout." *Star Tribune*, June 30, 1994.

Tervalon, Melanie, and Jann Murray-García. "Cultural Humility versus Cultural Competence: A Critical Distinction in Defining Physician Training Outcomes in Multicultural Education." *Journal of Health Care for the Poor and Underserved* 9, no. 2 (1998): 117–25. https://doi.org/10.1353/hpu.2010.0233.

Tesori, Jeanine, and Tazewell Thompson. "The Libretto I Wrote for *Blue* Was My Personal Letter to the World." Interview by Jasmijn van Wijnen. *Nationale Opera & Ballet*, March 21, 2021. https://www.operaballet.nl/en/articles/libretto-i-wrote-blue-was-my-personal-letter-world.

Thompson, Tazewell. "My Journey to Writing an Opera about Police Violence." *Seattle Opera* (blog), May 11, 2021. https://www.seattleoperablog.com/2021/05/my-journey-to-writing-opera-about.html.

———. "My Journey to Writing an Opera about Police Violence." *New York Times*, June 17, 2020. https://www.nytimes.com/2020/06/17/arts/music/blue-opera-police-violence.html.

Tilly, Charles. *Durable Inequality*. Berkeley: University of California Press, 1998.

Tokson, Matthew. "Judicial Resistance and Legal Change." *University of Chicago Law Review* 82, no. 2 (2015): 901–73.

United States Department of Justice, Civil Rights Division. "Investigation of the Newark Police Department." United States Attorney's Office District of New Jersey, July 22, 2014. https://www.justice.gov/sites/default/files/crt/legacy/2014/07/22/newark_findings_7-22-14.pdf.

"We See You, White American Theater." Open Letter, n.d. https://www.weseeyouwat.com/statement.

Weinert-Kendt, Robert. "Jeanine Tesori Feels the Pull of Opera." *American Theater*, July 9, 2019. https://www.americantheatre.org/2019/07/09/jeanine-tesori-feels-the-pull-of-opera/.

West, Cornel. *Race Matters*. 25th Anniversary ed. Boston: Beacon Press, 2017.

Williams, Bernard, and W. F. Atkinson. "Ethical Consistency." *Proceedings of the Aristotelian Society, Supplementary Volumes* 39 (1965): 103–38.

Williams, Patricia J. *Seeing a Color-Blind Future*. New York: Farrar, Straus and Giroux, 2016.

———. *Seeing a Color-Blind Future: The Paradox of Race*. New York: Noonday Press, 1997.

Wilson, August. "The Ground on Which I Stand." *Callaloo* 20, no. 3 (1997): 493–503. http://www.jstor.org/stable/3299355.

Wu, Cary, Rima Wilkes, and David C. Wilson. "Race & Political Trust: Justice as a Unifying Influence on Political Trust." *Daedalus* 151, no. 4 (2022): 177–99. https://doi.org/10.1162/daed_a_01950.

Yoshino, Kenji. *Covering: The Hidden Assault on Our Civil Rights.* New York: Random House, 2007.

Zernike, Kate. "Defying Expectations, Mayor Ras Baraka Is Praised in All Corners of Newark." *New York Times*, August 30, 2015.

INDEX

A Broader Way (arts empowerment program for young women), 81

Adult Correctional Institute (ACI), 133–34; Breed's effort at enlisting cooperation with incarcerated people, 134; incarceration/inhuman treatment of Black and Brown people, 133–34

ADVANCE project/initiative (University of Michigan), 144, 217

affirmative action: contradictory approaches to, 1; effectiveness of, 1; fear of divisive backlash from, 4; Katznelson's book on, 55; reparative justice approaches to, 1; student class multiracial collaboration at University of Pennsylvania Law School, 120–25; Supreme Court's ruling on, 26, 34, 120; universities' commitment to maintaining, 32; University of Michigan lawsuits, 2

African Americans: comparative perceptions of incarceration rates, 51; Covid-19 death rate comparison, 215; Dawson and linked fate across class and politics, 82; M. Bell's observation on ghettoized treatment of, 164–65; Tesori and Tazewell, podcast discussion, 88. *See also* Black people

Afriye, Obi, 197

agenda-setting power, 160–61, 168

Allen, Danielle, 125

Alternatives to Violence Project: 140

American Poison? How Racial Hostility Destroyed Our Promise (Porter), 3

Anchor Institutions Task Force, 195

anti-racism: contradictions of, xii, xiii, 1, 10; definition (of author), 237; federal courts' stance against efforts, 31; finding common ground in, 6–7; impact of George Floyd's murder, 23; impact of racial salience on, 26; institutions working to advance goals of, x, 4; learning from contradictions, failures, messiness, 64; paradoxes of, 8–35 (*see also* anti-racism paradoxes); questioning of/learning how to do, 2–3; questions asked in conversations, 36; reasons for failures in white organizations, 115; reparation movement successes, 46; role of repurposing of power in, 158; role of white institutions, 30; small steps toward big changes, 73–75; use of race-neutral strategies, 27–28; warnings against using the term, 22; Williams on creative experimentation with, 74

anti-racism paradoxes, 8–35; benefits of embracing, 15; Bhargava and, 237–38; examples of, 17–18; Hrabowski commenting on, 205–7, 209; impact of experiential segregation (*see also* experiential segregation), 40; impact of language, xiii; impact of role rigidity, 40 (*see also* role rigidity); impact of scripted stuckness, 40 (*see also* scripted stuckness); impact of status quo bias (*see also* status quo bias), 40; impact on personal, scholarly stories, 2; of the legal system, 31;

OUR COMPELLING INTERESTS

Steering Committee

Anthony Appiah, Professor of Philosophy and Law, New York University

Saleem Badat, Research Professor in History, University of the Free State

Armando I. Bengochea, Senior Program Officer and Director of the
   Mellon Mays Undergraduate Fellowship Program, The Andrew W. Mellon
   Foundation

Nancy Cantor, Co-chair, President, Hunter College

Rosario Ceballo, Dean of the College of Literature, Science, and the Arts,
   University of Michigan

Tabbye Chavous, Vice Provost for Equity & Inclusion and Chief Diversity
   Officer at the University of Michigan and Professor of Education and
   Psychology

Sumi Cho, Director of Strategic Initiatives, African American Policy Forum

Angela Dillard, Vice Provost for Undergraduate Education, and
   Richard A. Meisler Collegiate Professor of Afroamerican and African
   Studies and History in the College of Literature, Science, and the Arts,
   University of Michigan

Stephanie A. Fryberg, Professor of Psychology, Northwestern University

Patricia Y. Gurin, Nancy Cantor Distinguished University Professor Emerita of
   Psychology and Women's Studies, University of Michigan

Makeba Morgan Hill, Founder and CEO, Dr. Makeba & Friends, LLC

Earl Lewis, Thomas C. Holt Distinguished University Professor of History,
   Afroamerican and African Studies and Public Policy, and Director,
   Center for Social Solutions

Gary Orfield, Distinguished Research Professor of Education, Law, Political
   Science and Urban Planning and Co-director, Civil Rights Project /
   Proyecto Derechos Civiles, University of California at Los Angeles

Scott E. Page, John Seely Brown Distinguished University Professor of
   Complexity, Social Science, and Management, Williamson Family
   Professor of Business Administration, Professor of Management and

Organizations, Political Science, Complex Systems, and Economics, University of Michigan

Eboo Patel, Founder and President, Interfaith America

George J. Sanchez, Professor of American Studies and Ethnicity, and History, University of Southern California

Claude M. Steele, I. James Quillen Endowed Dean, Emeritus at the Stanford University Graduate School of Education, and Lucie Stern Professor in the Social Sciences, Emeritus, Stanford University

Susan P. Sturm, George M. Jaffin Professor of Law and Social Responsibility, Director of the Center for Institutional and Social Change, Columbia University Law School

Thomas J. Sugrue, Julius Silver Professor of Social and Cultural Analysis and History, Director of the NYU Cities Collaborative, New York University

Beverly Daniel Tatum, President Emerita, Spelman College

Doreen N. Tinajero, Project Senior Manager, Center for Social Solutions, University of Michigan

Sarah E. Turner, University Professor of Economics and Education, Souder Family Professor, University of Virginia

Michele S. Warman, Experienced Practitioner in Residence, Columbia Law School

Laura Washington, President & Chief Executive Officer, Community Foundations of the Hudson Valley

Alford Young Jr., University Diversity and Social Transformation Professor, Edgar G. Epps Collegiate Professor of Sociology, Arthur F. Thurnau Professor of Sociology, Afroamerican and African Studies, and Public Policy, Associate Director, Center for Social Solutions, Faculty Director, Anti-Racism Collaborative, National Center for Institutional Diversity, University of Michigan